Anonymous

The Chapel Hymnal

Anonymous

The Chapel Hymnal

ISBN/EAN: 9783744780780

Printed in Europe, USA, Canada, Australia, Japan

Cover: Foto ©Lupo / pixelio.de

More available books at **www.hansebooks.com**

The Chapel Hymnal ✠

Philadelphia
The Presbyterian Board of Publication
and Sabbath-School Work
1898

This Hymnal has been compiled by a Committee of The Presbyterian Board of Publication and Sabbath-School Work, consisting of:—

   The Hon. ROBERT N. WILLSON, *Chairman.*
   The Rev. ELIJAH R. CRAVEN, D. D., LL.D.
   FRANKLIN L. SHEPPARD, Esq.
   The Rev. LOUIS F. BENSON, D. D.

   The Rev. LOUIS F. BENSON, D. D., *Editor.*

PREFACE

THIS book is the second in a series of three hymnals intended to cover the needs of the Church through the whole range of its public worship. The first, The Hymnal, was prepared as a complete manual of praise, covering especially the Sunday services, but including also every side of church worship and work; the second, The Chapel Hymnal, is prepared for those who prefer a smaller book for use in prayer meetings, young people's societies, and other social services; and the last of the series is to cover the services of the Sabbath-school.

The Chapel Hymnal consists principally of those hymns in The Hymnal which are best adapted for use in devotional meetings and of such tunes as can be used to good advantage on such occasions; and ordinarily the association of hymn and tune has been retained. In addition there have been included in this book some standard hymns and tunes reserved for this use when The Hymnal was prepared, together with some fresh selections of a popular character and a number of the more desirable "Gospel Hymns."

The pages of the book are so arranged as to provide a choice of tunes in the case of a large number of the hymns.

It is the usage of many of our churches to sing the Amen at the close of each hymn, and the proper chords are provided for any who may wish to use them.

In the choice of material for this book the Committee has had the advantage of the counsel and coöperation of the Rev. George M. Boynton, D. D., and M. C. Hazard, Ph. D., who have represented the Congregational Sunday-School and Publishing Society, to the end that the book may be adapted for introduction and use in the churches of both denominations.

Preface

The Committee would acknowledge the favor of those who freely granted the use of copyright hymns and tunes; especially of Messrs. Houghton, Mifflin & Co., for the hymns of Dr. Holmes and Mr. Whittier; the Rev. Robert Lowry, D. D., for No. 255; and Messrs. E. P. Dutton & Co. and Mr. Lewis H. Redner, for No. 76.

April 20, 1898.

NOTE

As far as possible the hymns are printed as their authors wrote them. When any changes have been adopted, the fact has invariably been noted beneath the hymn. The dates set to the tunes are the dates of first publication. The dates set to the hymns are the earliest dates obtainable, ordinarily that of their composition, in some cases necessarily that of their first publication. Where two dates are given, they indicate that of the original form of the hymn and that of the author's revised text used in this book. The abbreviation "publ." indicates that the date of writing is unknown, and that the date of publication is posthumous. The letter *c.* (*circa*) before a date is used where exact certainty is unobtainable. Where dates, either of hymns or tunes, are altogether wanting, the dates of the author's or composer's birth and death are given in brackets, *e. g.* (1816–1893), or where living, that of his birth only, *e. g.* (1838–), or the date of death when that alone is known, *e. g.* (–1850).

CONTENTS

	PAGE		PAGE
Preface	v	The Lord's Prayer	xvii
Index of First Lines	ix	The Commandments	xvii
Alphabetical Index of Tunes	xii	The Apostles' Creed	xvii
Metrical Index of Tunes	xiv		

The Hymns

I. TIMES OF WORSHIP

	HYMNS		HYMNS
Morning	1–3	At the Opening of Service	22–28
Evening	4–16	At the Close of Service	29–32
The Lord's Day	17–21		

II. THE FATHER, THE SON, AND THE HOLY GHOST

The Holy Trinity	33–34	The Life, Ministry, and Example	79–88
		The Passion and Crucifixion	89–98
God the Father Almighty		The Resurrection	99–104
His Majesty and Fatherhood	35–55	The Ascension	105
		The Second Coming and Judgment	106–110
Jesus Christ our Lord			
Praise to Christ Exalted	56–68		
The Advent	69–70	The Holy Ghost	
The Nativity	71–77	Invocation and Praise	111–121
The Epiphany	78	Inspiration of the Holy Scriptures	122–127

III. THE CHURCH

The Church	128–132	The Ministry	144
Baptism	133–134	Consecration and Service	145–171
Confession of Faith	135–138	Charities and Missions	172–192
The Lord's Supper	139–143	The Communion of Saints	193–200

Contents

IV. HYMNS OF SALVATION

	Hymns		Hymns
The Grace of God in Christ	201–205	Trust	258–285
Invitation	206–221	Love, and Communion with Christ	286–314
Acceptance			
Repentance and Confession of Sin	222–230	Prayer	315–327
Faith in Christ	231–241		
Conflict with Sin	242–257	Aspiration	328–341

V. THE LIFE EVERLASTING

Death . . . . 342–346 | The Life Everlasting 347–358

VI. OCCASIONAL HYMNS

The Opening and Closing of the Year	359–361	National	366–368
		Temperance	369
Harvest and Thanksgiving	362–364	Farewell Service	370
Anniversary	365		

DOXOLOGIES

Index of First Lines

	HYMN
A CHARGE to keep I have	251
Abide with me; fast falls the eventide	9
According to Thy gracious word	139
Alas! and did my Saviour bleed	98
All hail the power of Jesus' Name	57
All praise to Thee, Eternal Lord	72
All praise to Thee, my God, this night	6
Am I a soldier of the cross	247
And is the time approaching	184
Angel voices, ever singing	55
Another six days' work is done	19
Approach, my soul, the mercy-seat	244
Art thou weary, art thou languid	215
As the sun doth daily rise	2
As with gladness men of old	78
Asleep in Jesus! blessed sleep	343
Awake, and sing the song	65
Awake, my soul, and with the sun	1
Awake, my soul, in joyful lays	311
Awake, my soul, stretch every nerve	242
BEGIN, my tongue, some heavenly theme	44
Behold, a Stranger's at the door	209
Behold, the Master passeth by	88
Behold the throne of grace	318
Beneath the cross of Jesus	97
Beyond the starry skies	103
Blessed are the sons of God	196
Blessed Saviour, Thee I love	308
Blest be the tie that binds	195
Blow ye the trumpet, blow	176
Break Thou the bread of life	125
Breast the wave, Christian	252
By cool Siloam's shady rill	133
CALL them in! the poor, the wretched	179
Cast thy burden on the Lord	282
Children of the heavenly King	194
Christ, above all glory seated	68
Christ for the world we sing	172
Christ, of all my hopes the Ground	313
Christ the Lord is risen again	99
Christ the Lord is risen to-day	100
Christian, seek not yet repose	246
Come, dearest Lord, descend and dwell	114
Come, gracious Spirit, heavenly Dove	112
Come, Holy Spirit, come	111
Come, Holy Spirit, heavenly Dove	120
Come, let us join our cheerful songs	58
Come, let us join our friends above	197
Come, Lord, and tarry not	110
Come, my soul, thy suit prepare	320
Come, said Jesus' sacred voice	217

	HYMN
Come, sound His praise abroad	48
Come, Thou Almighty King	26
Come, Thou Fount of every blessing	314
Come, Thou long-expected Jesus	69
Come to the Saviour now	212
Come, we that love the Lord	50
Come, ye disconsolate, where'er ye languish	219
Come, ye thankful people, come	363
Crown Him with many crowns	56
DAILY, daily sing the praises	358
Day by day the manna fell	283
Day is dying in the west	11
Days and moments quickly flying	360
Dear Lord and Father of mankind	334
Dear Lord and Master mine	151
Depth of mercy! can there be	226
Did Christ o'er sinners weep	79
FAR from my heavenly home	335
Father, again in Jesus' Name we meet	28
Father, hear Thy children's call	227
Father of all, from land and sea	193
Father of Love, our Guide and Friend	263
Father, whate'er of earthly bliss	285
Fight the good fight with all thy might	248
Fling out the banner! let it float	183
For all the saints who from their labors rest	200
Forth in Thy Name, O Lord, I go	340
From all that dwell below the skies	49
From every stormy wind that blows	317
From Greenland's icy mountains	185
GENTLY, Lord, O gently lead us	254
Give me the wings of faith to rise	198
Glorious things of thee are spoken	131
Glory to Thee, my God, this night	
See All praise to Thee, my God	6
Go, labor on: spend, and be spent	159
Go to dark Gethsemane	91
God be with you till we meet again	370
God bless our native land	366
God calling yet! shall I not hear	208
God is Love; His mercy brightens	52
God is the Refuge of His saints	279
God moves in a mysterious way	35
God of mercy, God of grace	39
Golden harps are sounding	105
Grace! 'tis a charming sound	204
Gracious Spirit, Dove Divine	116
Gracious Spirit, Holy Ghost	119
Great God, we sing that mighty hand	361
Guide me, O Thou Great Jehovah	270

ix

Index of First Lines

	Hymn
HAIL to the Lord's Anointed	181
Hark! hark! my soul, angelic songs are	356
Hark! my soul, it is the Lord	216
Hark! ten thousand harps and voices	64
Hark, the glad sound! the Saviour comes	70
Hark! the herald angels sing	74
Hark! the voice of Jesus crying	148
Hark! the voice of love and mercy	94
Hark! what mean those holy voices	77
He leadeth me: O blessed thought	267
He that goeth forth with weeping	156
High in the heavens, Eternal God	38
Holy Father, hear my cry	225
Holy, Holy, Holy, Lord God Almighty	33
Holy Spirit, faithful Guide	113
Holy Spirit, Truth Divine	115
How beauteous are their feet	144
How firm a foundation, ye saints of the	271
How gentle God's commands	280
How precious is the book Divine	122
How shall I follow Him I serve	87
How sweet the Name of Jesus sounds	289
I AM coming to the cross	240
I am Thine, O Lord, I have heard Thy	305
I am trusting Thee, Lord Jesus	260
I do not ask, O Lord, that life may be	277
I gave my life for thee	
See Thy life was given for me	201
I hear Thy welcome voice	238
I heard the voice of Jesus say	235
I know no life divided	292
I lay my sins on Jesus	237
I love Thy kingdom, Lord	129
I love to steal awhile away	4
I love to tell the story	218
I need Thee every hour	255
I say to all men, far and near	101
I was a wandering sheep	230
I would not live alway	345
If Christ is mine, then all is mine	304
I'm but a stranger here	347
I'm not ashamed to own my Lord	138
Immortal Love, for ever full	286
In all things like Thy brethren, Thou	
See Lord, Thou in all things like wast	81
In heavenly love abiding	269
In the cross of Christ I glory	93
In the hour of trial	256
It came upon the midnight clear	75
It is not death to die	344
I've found a Friend; O such a Friend	296
JERUSALEM, my happy home	351
Jerusalem the golden	350
Jesus, and shall it ever be	135
Jesus calls us, o'er the tumult	154
Jesus, I love thy charming Name	290

	Hymn
Jesus, I my cross have taken	147
Jesus, Lover of my soul	234
Jesus, Master, whose I am	309
Jesus, merciful and mild	307
Jesus, my Saviour, look on me	257
Jesus, Saviour, pilot me	245
Jesus shall reign where'er the sun	191
Jesus, the very thought of Thee	291
Jesus, these eyes have never seen	297
Jesus, Thou art the sinner's Friend	298
Jesus, Thou Joy of loving hearts	142
Jesus, Thy Name I love	66
Jesus, where'er Thy people meet	23
Jesus, with Thy Church abide	128
Joy to the world!—the Lord is come	71
Just as I am, without one plea	236
LEAD, kindly Light, amid the encircling	274
Lead on, O King Eternal	163
Let children hear the mighty deeds	365
Let us with a gladsome mind	40
Lift up, lift up your voices now	102
Light of the lonely pilgrim's heart	107
Light of those whose dreary dwelling	108
Lo! on a narrow neck of land	
See O God, mine inmost soul convert	106
Look from the sphere of endless day	188
Lord, as to Thy dear cross we flee	82
Lord, dismiss us with Thy blessing	30
Lord, I believe; Thy power I own	241
Lord, I hear of showers of blessing	326
Lord, in the morning Thou shalt hear	3
Lord, lead the way the Saviour went	174
Lord of all being, throned afar	45
Lord, speak to me, that I may speak	160
Lord, Thou hast searched and seen me	46
Lord, Thou in all things like wast made	81
Lord, Thy word abideth	124
Lord, to Thee alone we turn	222
Lord, we come before Thee now	25
Lord, when we bend before Thy throne	22
Love Divine, all loves excelling	294
MAJESTIC sweetness sits enthroned	287
More love to Thee, O Christ	329
Much in danger, oft in woe	
See Oft in danger	155
Must Jesus bear the cross alone	168
My country, 'tis of thee	368
My days are gliding swiftly by	348
My dear Redeemer and my Lord	84
My faith looks up to Thee	233
My God and Father, while I stray	258
My God, and is Thy table spread	143
My God, how endless is Thy love	54
My God, is any hour so sweet	323
My God, my Father, while I stray	
See My God and Father	258

x

Index of First Lines

	Hymn
My God, permit me not to be	337
My Jesus, as Thou wilt	266
My soul, be on thy guard	253
My soul, repeat His praise	51
My spirit on Thy care	301
My times are in Thy hand	273
NEARER, my God, to Thee	328
No, no, it is not dying	346
No, not despairingly	228
Not all the blood of beasts	203
Not worthy, Lord, to gather up the crumbs	140
Now God be with us, for the night is closing	16
Now I resolve with all my heart	136
Now may He who from the dead	32
Now the day is over	12
O BROTHERS, lift your voices	150
O Christ, our true and only Light	192
O come, all ye faithful	73
O could I find, from day to day	339
O could I speak the matchless worth	62
O daughters blest of Galilee	180
O day of rest and gladness	20
O for a closer walk with God	330
O for a faith that will not shrink	333
O for a heart to praise my God	332
O for a thousand tongues to sing	59
O God, beneath Thy guiding hand	367
O God, mine inmost soul convert	106
O God of Bethel, by whose hand	265
O God of mercy, God of might	173
O God, the Rock of Ages	47
O God, we praise Thee, and confess	34
O happy band of pilgrims	165
O help us, Lord; each hour of need	243
O Holy Saviour, Friend unseen	302
O Jesus, I have promised	162
O Jesus, King most wonderful	288
O Jesus, Thou art standing	210
O Lamb of God, still keep me	293
O little town of Bethlehem	76
O Lord, Thy work revive	
See Revive thy work, O Lord	153
O Love Divine, that stooped to share	276
O Love that wilt not let me go	312
O Master, let me walk with Thee	86
O mean may seem this house of clay	83
O Mother dear, Jerusalem	355
O Paradise, O Paradise	349
O praise our God to-day	177
O sacred Head, now wounded	89
O Saviour, precious Saviour	60
O Son of man, Thyself hast proved	
See Lord, Thou in all things	81
O still in accents sweet and strong	170
O the bitter shame and sorrow	306
O Thou, before whose presence	369

	Hymn
O Thou that hear'st when sinners cry	229
O Thou, the contrite sinners' Friend	321
O Thou, to whose all-searching sight	336
O what, if we are Christ's	199
O where are kings and empires now	132
O where shall rest be found	352
O Word of God Incarnate	123
O'er the gloomy hills of darkness	186
Oft in danger, oft in woe	155
On our way rejoicing	166
One sweetly solemn thought	342
One there is, above all others	303
Onward, Christian soldiers	164
Our blest Redeemer, ere He breathed	118
Our God, our Help in ages past	36
PASS me not, O gentle Saviour	327
Peace, perfect peace, in this dark world	300
Praise, my soul, the King of heaven	364
Praise the Lord: ye heavens adore Him	53
Praise to God, immortal praise	362
Prayer is the soul's sincere desire	325
REJOICE, all ye believers	109
Revive Thy work, O Lord	153
Rise, my soul, and stretch thy wings	338
Rock of Ages, cleft for me	239
SAFELY through another week	17
Salvation! O the joyful sound	213
Saviour, again to Thy dear Name we raise	29
Saviour, blessed Saviour	61
Saviour, breathe an evening blessing	13
Saviour, more than life to me	310
Saviour, teach me, day by day	299
Saviour, Thy dying love	169
Saviour, when in dust to Thee	224
Saviour, who Thy flock art feeding	134
Shepherd of souls, refresh and bless	141
Since Jesus is my Friend	281
So let our lips and lives express	161
Softly and tenderly Jesus is calling	206
Softly now the light of day	7
Soldiers of Christ, arise	145
Soldiers of the cross, arise	175
Sometimes a light surprises	268
Songs of praise the angels sang	41
Souls of men, why will ye scatter	
See Was there ever kindest shepherd	205
Spirit Divine, attend our prayers	24
Spirit of God, descend upon my heart	117
Stand up, my soul; shake off thy fears	250
Stand up, stand up for Jesus	149
Still with Thee, O my God	31
Sun of my soul, Thou Saviour dear	5
Surrounded by unnumbered foes	249
Sweet hour of prayer	316
Sweet is Thy mercy, Lord	319

xi

Alphabetical Index of Tunes

	HYMN
Sweet the moments rich in blessing	95
TAKE me, O my Father, take me	231
Take my life, and let it be	152
Take up thy cross, the Saviour said	207
Tarry with me, O my Saviour	14
Tell me the old, old story	220
The Church's one Foundation	130
The day is past and over	10
The day of resurrection	104
The heavens declare Thy glory, Lord	127
The King of love my Shepherd is	259
The Lord my Shepherd is	272
The Lord's my Shepherd, I'll not want	264
The morning light is breaking	182
The sands of time are sinking	354
The shadows of the evening hours	8
The Son of God goes forth to war	167
The spacious firmament on high	37
The Spirit breathes upon the word	126
There is a fountain filled with blood	202
There is a green hill far away	96
There is a land of pure delight	353
There is a safe and secret place	278
There is an eye that never sleeps	324
There is an hour of peaceful rest	357
Thine for ever! God of love	137
This is the day the Lord hath made	21
This night, O Lord, we bless Thee	15
Thou art my Hiding-place, O Lord	275
Thou art the Way: to Thee alone	85
Thou didst leave Thy throne and Thy	232
Through all the changing scenes of life	42
Through good report and evil, Lord	158
Thy home is with the humble, Lord	121

	HYMN
Thy life was given for me	201
Thy way, not mine, O Lord	261
'Tis midnight; and on Olive's brow	92
To-day Thy mercy calls me	211
To morrow, Lord, is Thine	214
To Thee, O dear, dear Saviour	295
To Thy temple I repair	27
True-hearted, whole-hearted	157
WAIT, my soul, upon the Lord	284
Was there ever kindest shepherd	205
Watchman, tell us of the night	189
We are living, we are dwelling	190
We bless Thee for Thy peace, O God	341
We give Thee but Thine own	178
Weary of earth, and laden with my sin	223
Welcome, sweet day of rest	18
What a Friend we have in Jesus	315
What grace, O Lord, and beauty shone	80
When all Thy mercies, O my God	43
When cold our hearts, and far from Thee	322
When I can read my title clear	331
When I survey the wondrous cross	90
When morning gilds the skies	67
While Thee I seek, protecting Power	262
While with ceaseless course the sun	359
With Thee, my Lord, my God	
See Still with Thee, O my God	31
Work, for the night is coming	171
YE Christian heralds, go proclaim	187
Ye servants of God, your Master proclaim	63
Ye servants of the Lord	146
Yet there is room: the Lamb's bright hall	221

Alphabetical Index of Tunes

ADESTE FIDELES	73, 271
Ajalon	91
Albert	303
Alexandria	330
All Saints New	167
All Saints, *see* Wareham.	
Alma	219
Almsgiving	193
America	368
Amsterdam	338
Angel Choir	77
Angel Voices	55
Angel's Story	162
Antioch	71
Ariel	62
Arlington	21, 85
Aurelia	15, 130
Austrian Hymn	131
Autumn	254

Avon, *see* Martyrdom.	
Azmon	213
BALERMA	264
Beatitudo	262
Beatrice	326
Beethoven, *see* Germany.	
Belmont	243, 331
Benevento	359
Bentley	268
Bera	336
Bernard, *see* Belmont.	
Bethany	328
Bethany, *see* Crucifer.	
Blairgowrie	211
Blumenthal	224
Boylston	195
Bread of Life	125
Brocklesbury	108, 134

Brookfield	135
Brown	197
Bullinger	260
Byefield	325
CALL Them In	179
Canonbury	54, 72, 160, 340
Cantus	221
Carol	75
Chester	275
Christmas	242
Clolata	208
Colyton	166
Come, Ye Disconsolate, *see* Alma.	
Constance	296
Cooling	339
Coronation	57
Coventry	333

xii

Alphabetical Index of Tunes

Cowper	202
Creation	37
Crucifer	147, 205
Cutler, see All Saints New.	
DAILY, Daily	358
Dalehurst	22, 330
Dallas	27, 137
Dedham	58
Denfield, see Azmon.	
Dennis	31, 280
Devotion	201
Diademata	56
Dix	39, 78
Dominus Regit Me	259
Dorrnance	95
Dort	366
Downs	42
Dundee	34, 122
Durham, see Innocents.	
EAGLEY	107
Eckhardtsheim	304
Edina	61
Elizabethtown	322
Ellers	29
Ellesdie	148
Elliott, see Almsgiving.	
Elmhurst	173, 321
Erie	315
Ernan	19
Evan	138, 324
Evangel	220
Even Me	326
Evening Hymn	6
Evening Praise	11
Evening Prayer	13
Eventide	9
Every Day	310
Ewing	350
FABEN	53
Faith	286
Faithful Guide	113
Federal Street	84, 114
Ferguson	151
Fiat Lux	172
Flemming	302
Forgiveness	217
Frederick	345
GENEVA	43
Gerhardt	89
Germany	192, 361
Gethsemane, see Ajalon.	
God Be with You	370
Gorton	301
Gottschalk, see Mercy.	
Gower's Litany	227
Grace Church	188
Green Hill	82, 278
Greenland	109
Greenwood	281, 344

HAMBURG	90, 229
Hanford	158, 257
Harwell	64
He Leadeth Me	267
Heaven is My Home	347
Heber	290
Hebron	23
Hendon	313
Herbert	323
Hermas	105
Hermon	121
Hodnet	293
Hollingside	234
Holy Cross	101, 288, 351
Holy Guide	261
Holy Trinity	291
Horsley	96
Horton	320
Hursley	5
Hymn to Joy	231
I AM Thine	305
I Love to Tell the Story	218
Inasmuch	180
Innocents	2
Invitation	212
Italian Hymn, see Trinity.	
JACOB'S CHANT	342
Jesu, Magister Bone	292, 369
Jewett	266
Just as I Am	236
KEDRON	228
Kocher	165
LABAN	146, 251
Lambeth	24, 241
Lancashire	104, 150
Langran	223
Langton	110
Latter Day	190
Laudes Domini	67
Lebanon	230
Leighton	65
Lenox	176
Lisbon	18
Litany, Gower's	227
Litany, Woodward's	283
Longwood	28
Louvan	45
Love Divine	294
Loving-Kindness	311
Lowton	154
Lucerne	52
Lux Benigna	274
Lux Vespera	119
Lyons	63
Lyte	335
MAITLAND	168
Manoah	44
Margaret	232
Marlow	247

Martyn	234
Martyrdom	98, 244
Materna	355
Meditation	96
Mendebras	20
Mendelssohn	74
Mendon	250
Mercy	115, 282
Meribah	106
Messiah	307
Messiah, see Christmas.	
Miriam	237
Missionary Chant	187
Missionary Hymn	185
Monkland	40
Monsell, see St. Andrew.	
Morecambe	117, 140
Morning Hymn	1
Mozart	248
Munich	123
NAOMI	285
Narenza	103
Nearer to Thee	329
Need	255
Nettleton	314
Newland	272
Newton, see Sabbath.	
Nicaea	33
Nightfall, see Now God Be with Us.	
Northrepps	198, 341
Now God Be with Us	16
Nuremberg	41, 362
O PARADISE, see Paradise.	
Old Hundredth	49, Dox. 1
Oliphant	270
Olivet	233
Olmutz	203
Onward	252
Ortonville	126, 287
PARADISE	349
Park Street	191
Parting Hymn, see Ellers.	
Pass Me Not	327
Patmos	152
Pax Tecum	300
Penitence	256
Pilgrims	356
Pilot	245
Pleyel's Hymn	194
Portugese Hymn, see Adeste Fideles.	
QUEBEC	142, 207
RAMOTH	222
Rathbun	93
Redhead No. 45	175
Refuge	234
Refuge, see Blumenthal.	
Regent Square	364

Metrical Index of Tunes

Remsen 174	St. Thomas 50	Trusting 240
Repose 12	Sarum 200	
Rest 343	Savoy Chapel 295	UNIVERSITY COLLEGE 100, 155
Retreat 317	Sawley 297	Uxbridge 127
Rhodes 79	Saxby 86, 112	
Rockingham New 136	Schubert 47, 184	VESPERS 276
Rockingham Old 143	Schumann 178, 253	Vigil 177, 214
Rosefield 196	Seven Words 128	Vigilate 246
Rotterdam 20	Seymour 7, 226	Vox Dilecti 235
Rutherford 354	Shining Shore 348	
	Shirland 129	WAKEFIELD 346
SABBATH 17	Sicilian Mariners 30	Waltham 183
St. Agnes 120, 141	Siloam 80, 133	Ward 279
St. Anatolius 10	Silver Street 48, 204	Ware 38
St. Andrew 319	Softly and Tenderly . . . 206	Wareham 102, 161, 367
St. Anne 36, 132	Soldiers of Christ 145	Warwick 3
St. Bees 25, 216	Solitude 32, 299	Watchman 189
St. Christopher 97	Spanish Hymn 308	Wavertree 249
St. Cuthbert 118	Staincliffe 87	Webb 149, 181
St. Cyprian 124	State Street 318	Weber, *see* Seymour.
St. Edith 210	Stephanos 215	Welcome Voice 238
St. George 153	Stobel 66	Whittier 334
St. George's, Windsor . . 363	Stockwell 156	Wildersmouth 186
St. Gertrude 164	Stuttgart 68	Williams 159
St. Jude 306	Submission 277	Winterton 169
St. Leonard (Hiles) . . . 8	Sweet Hour of Prayer . . 316	Wirtemburg 99
St. Leonard (Smart) . . . 57		Woodland 357
St. Louis 76	TALLIS's Evening Hymn . 6	Woodstock 4
St. Margaret 312	Tennent 163	Woodward's Litany . . . 283
St. Marguerite 353	Thatcher 144	Woodworth 236
St. Mark 170	The Hymn to Joy 231	Woolwich 199
St. Martin's 365	The Old Hundredth 49, Dox. 1	Work-Song 171
St. Paul's College 352	The Seven Words 128	
St. Peter 289	Toplady 239	ZEPHYR 92, 209
St. Saviour 70	Trinity 26	Zion 94
St. Sylvester 14, 360	True-Hearted 157	Zoan 60

Metrical Index of Tunes

S. M.

	Silver Street 48, 204	Brown 197
Boylston 195	Soldiers of Christ 145	Byefield 325
Dennis 31, 280	State Street 318	Christmas 242
Ferguson 151	Thatcher 144	Cooling 339
Gorton 301	Vigil 177, 214	Coronation 57
Greenwood 281, 344	Welcome Voice (with Re-	Coventry 333
Laban 146, 251	frain) 238	Cowper 202
Langton 110	Woolwich 199	Dalehurst 22, 330
Leighton 65		Dedham 58
Lisbon 18	### S. M. D.	Downs 42
Lyte 335	Diademata 56	Dundee 34, 122
Narenza 103	Lebanon 230	Eagley 107
Newland 272		Eckhardtsheim 304
Olmutz 203	### C. M.	Elizabethtown 322
Rhodes 79	Alexandria 330	Evan 138, 324
St. Andrew 319	Antioch 71	Faith 286
St. George 153	Arlington 21, 85	Geneva 43
St. Paul's College 352	Azmon 213	Green Hill 82, 278
St. Thomas 50	Balerma 264	Heber 290
Schumann 178, 253	Beatitudo 262	Hermon 121
Shirland 129	Belmont 243, 331	Holy Cross . . . 101, 288, 351

Metrical Index of Tunes

Holy Trinity 291	Waltham 183	**7. 6. 7. 6.**
Horsley 96	Ward 279	Kocher 165
Lambeth 24, 241	Ware 38	
Maitland 168	Wareham . . . 102, 161, 367	**7. 6. 7. 6. 7. 6. 7. 5.**
Manoah 44	Wavertree 249	Rutherford 354
Marlow 247	Williams 159	
Martyrdom 98, 244	Woodworth 236	**7. 6. 7. 6. D.**
Meditation 96	Zephyr 92, 209	Angels' Story 162
Naomi 285		Aurelia 15, 130
Northrepps 198, 341	**L. M. D.**	Bentley 268
Ortonville 126, 287	He Leadeth Me 267	Blairgowrie 211
Remsen 174	Sweet Hour of Prayer . . 316	Ewing 350
St. Agnes 120, 141		Gerhardt 89
St. Anne 36, 132	**5. 5. 5. 5. 6. 5. 6. 5.**	Greenland 109
St. Leonard (Smart) . . . 57	Onward 252	Hodnet 293
St. Marguerite 353		Jesu, Magister Bone . 292, 369
St. Mark 170	**6. 4. 6. 4. with Refrain**	Lancashire . . . 104, 150
St. Martin's 365	Need 255	Mendebras 20
St. Peter 289		Miriam 237
St. Saviour 70	**6. 4. 6. 4. D.**	Missionary Hymn . . . 185
Sawley 297	Bread of Life 125	Munich 123
Siloam 80, 133		Rotterdam 20
Warwick 3	**6. 4. 6. 4. 6. 6. 4.**	St. Edith 210
Woodstock 4	Bethany 328	Savoy Chapel 295
	Kedron 228	Schubert 47, 184
C. M. D.	Nearer to Thee 329	Tennent 163
All Saints New 167		Webb 149, 181
Carol 75	**6. 4. 6. 4. 6. 6. 6. 4.**	Zoan 60
Chester 275	Heaven is My Home . . 347	
Materna 355	Winterton 169	**7. 6. 7. 6. D with Refrain**
St. Leonard (Hiles) . . . 8		Evangel 220
Vox Dilecti 235	**6. 5. 6. 5. D.**	I Love to Tell the Story . 218
	Colyton 166	
L. M.	Edina 61	**7. 6. 7. 7. 6.**
Bera 336	Repose 12	Wakefield 346
Brookfield 135	Penitence 256	
Canonbury . . 54, 72, 160, 340		**7. 6. 7. 6. 7. 7. 7. 6.**
Ciolata 208	**6. 5. 6. 5. 12 l.**	Amsterdam 338
Creation 37	Hermas 105	
Ernan 19	St. Gertrude 164	**7. 6. 7. 6. 8. 8.**
Federal Street . . . 84, 114		St. Anatolius 10
Germany 192, 361	**6. 6. 4. 6. 6. 6. 4.**	
Grace Church 188	America 368	**7. 6. 8. 6. 8. 6. 8. 6.**
Hamburg 90, 229	Dort 366	St. Christopher 97
Hebron 23	Fiat Lux 172	
Hursley 5	Olivet 233	**7. 7. 7. 3.**
Loving-Kindness . . . 311	Stobel 66	Vigilate 246
Louvan 45	Trinity 26	
Mendon 250		**7. 7. 7. 5.**
Missionary Chant . . . 187	**6. 6. 6. 6.**	Lux Vespera 119
Morning Hymn 1	Holy Guide 261	
Mozart 248	St. Cyprian 124	**7. 7. 7. 6.**
Old Hundredth . . 49, Dox. 1		Gower's Litany 227
Park Street 191	**6. 6. 6. 6. 6.**	The Seven Words . . . 128
Quebec 142, 207	Devotion 201	
Rest 343	Laudes Domini 67	**7. 7. 7. 7.**
Retreat 317		Dallas 27, 137
Rockingham New . . . 136	**6. 6. 6. 6. D.**	Forgiveness 217
Rockingham Old . . . 143	Invitation 212	Hendon 313
Saxby 86, 112	Jewett 266	Horton 320
Staincliffe 87		Innocents 2
Tallis's Evening Hymn . 6	**6. 6. 6. 6. 8. 8.**	Mercy 115, 282
Uxbridge 127	Lenox 176	Monkland 40
Vespers 276	**7. 6. 7. 5. D.**	Nuremberg 41, 362
	Work-Song 171	

Metrical Index of Tunes

Patmos 152
Pleyel's Hymn 194
Redhead No. 45 175
St. Bees 25, 216
Seymour 7, 226
Solitude 32, 299
Trusting (with Refrain) . 240
University College . . 100, 155
Wirtemburg (with Alleluia) 99
Woodward's Litany . . . 283

7. 7. 7. 7. 4. with Refrain
Evening Praise 11

7. 7. 7. 7. 7. 7.
Ajalon 91
Dix 39, 78
Pilot 245
Rosefield 196
Sabbath 17
Spanish Hymn 308
Toplady 239

7. 7. 7. 7. D.
Benevento 359
Blumenthal 224
Faithful Guide 113
Hollingside 234
Martyn 234
Mendelssohn 74
Messiah 307
Ramoth 222
Refuge 234
St. George's, Windsor . 363
Watchman 189

7. 9. 7. 9. with Refrain
Every Day 310

8. 5. 8. 3.
Bullinger 260
Stephanos 215

8. 5. 8. 5. with Refrain
Pass Me Not 327

8. 5. 8. 5. 8. 4. 3.
Angel Voices 55

8. 6. 8. 4.
St. Cuthbert 118

8. 6. 8. 6. 6. 6. 6. 6.
Paradise 349

8. 6. 8. 6. 7. 6. 8 6.
St. Louis 76

8. 6. 8. 6. 8. 8. 6.
Whittier 334

8. 6. 8. 8. 6.
Woodland 357

8. 7. 8. 7.
Angel Choir 77
Beatrice 326
Brocklesbury . . . 108, 134
Dominus Regit Me . . . 259
Dorrnance 95
Even Me (with Refrain) . 326
Evening Prayer 13
Lowton 154
Lucerne 52
Rathbun 93
St. Sylvester . . . 14, 360
Stockwell 156
Stuttgart 68

8. 7. 8. 7. 4. 7.
Oliphant 270
Regent Square 364
Sicilian Mariners . . . 30
Wildersmouth 186
Zion 94

8. 7. 8. 7. 7. 7.
Albert 303
Harwell (with Refrain) . 64

8. 7. 8. 7. D.
Austrian Hymn 131
Autumn 254
Call Them In (with Ref.) 179
Constance 296
Crucifer 147, 205
Daily, Daily 358
Erie 315
Ellesdie 148
Faben 53
Latter Day 190
Love Divine 294
Nettleton 314
Shining Shore 348
The Hymn to Joy 231

8. 7. 8. 7.
St. Jude 306

8. 8. 6. 8. 8. 6.
Ariel 62
Meribah 106

8. 8. 8.
Inasmuch 180

8. 8. 8. 4.
Almsgiving 193
Hanford 158, 257
Herbert 323

8. 8. 8. 6.
Elmhurst 173, 321
Flemming 302
Just as I am 236
Woodworth 236

8. 8. 8. 8. 6.
St. Margaret 312

8. 8. 8. 8. 8. 8.
Wavertree 249

9. 8. 8. 9. with Refrain
God Be with You 370

10. 4. 10. 4.
Submission 277

10. 4. 10. 4. 10. 10.
Lux Benigna 274

10. 7. 10. 7. with Refrain
I am Thine 305

10. 10.
Pax Tecum 300

10. 10. 10.
Cantus 221

10. 10. 10. 4.
Sarum 200

10. 10. 10. 10.
Ellers 29
Eventide 9
Langran 223
Longwood 28
Morecambe 117, 140

10. 10. 11. 11.
Lyons 63

11. 7. 11. 7. with Refrain
Softly and Tenderly . . 206

11. 10. 11. 10.
Alma 219
True-Hearted (with Ref.) 157

11. 10. 11. 10. 9. 11.
Pilgrims 356

11. 11. 11. 5.
Now God Be with Us . . 16

11. 11. 11. 11.
Adeste Fideles 271
Frederick 345

11. 12. 12. 10.
Nicæa 33

Irregular.
Adeste Fideles 73
Jacob's Chant 342
Margaret 232

The Lord's Prayer

OUR FATHER WHICH ART IN HEAVEN, HALLOWED BE THY NAME; THY KINGDOM COME; THY WILL BE DONE IN EARTH AS IT IS IN HEAVEN; GIVE US THIS DAY OUR DAILY BREAD; AND FORGIVE US OUR DEBTS, AS WE FORGIVE OUR DEBTORS; AND LEAD US NOT INTO TEMPTATION, BUT DELIVER US FROM EVIL; FOR THINE IS THE KINGDOM, AND THE POWER, AND THE GLORY, FOR EVER. AMEN.

The Ten Commandments

GOD spake all these words, saying, I am the LORD thy God, which have brought thee out of the land of Egypt, out of the house of bondage.

I. Thou shalt have no other gods before Me.

II. Thou shalt not make unto thee any graven image, or any likeness of any thing that is in heaven above, or that is in the earth beneath, or that is in the water under the earth: thou shalt not bow down thyself to them, nor serve them: for I the LORD thy God am a jealous God, visiting the iniquity of the fathers upon the children unto the third and fourth generation of them that hate Me; and showing mercy unto thousands of them that love Me, and keep My commandments.

III. Thou shalt not take the Name of the LORD thy God in vain; for the LORD will not hold him guiltless that taketh His Name in vain.

IV. Remember the Sabbath-day, to keep it holy. Six days shalt thou labor, and do all thy work: but the seventh day is the Sabbath of the LORD thy God; in it thou shalt not do any work, thou, nor thy son, nor thy daughter, thy man-servant, nor thy maid-servant, nor thy cattle, nor thy stranger that is within thy gates; for in six days the LORD made heaven and earth, the sea, and all that in them is, and rested the seventh day: wherefore the LORD blessed the Sabbath-day and hallowed it.

V. Honor thy father and thy mother: that thy days may be long upon the land which the LORD thy God giveth thee.

VI. Thou shalt not kill.

VII. Thou shalt not commit adultery.

VIII. Thou shalt not steal.

IX. Thou shalt not bear false witness against thy neighbor.

X. Thou shalt not covet thy neighbor's house, thou shalt not covet thy neighbor's wife, nor his man-servant, nor his maid-servant, nor his ox, nor his ass, nor any thing that is thy neighbor's.

HEAR also the words of our Lord Jesus, how He saith: Thou shalt love the Lord thy God with all thy heart, and with all thy soul, and with all thy mind. This is the first and great commandment. And the second is like unto it: Thou shalt love thy neighbor as thyself. On these two commandments hang all the law and the prophets.

The Apostles' Creed

I BELIEVE in GOD THE FATHER Almighty, Maker of heaven and earth:

And in JESUS CHRIST His only Son our Lord; who was conceived by the Holy Ghost; born of the Virgin Mary; suffered under Pontius Pilate; was crucified, dead, and buried; He descended into hell; * the third day He rose again from the dead; He ascended into heaven; and sitteth on the right hand of God the Father Almighty; from thence He shall come to judge the quick and the dead.

I believe in the HOLY GHOST; the holy Catholic Church; the Communion of Saints; the Forgiveness of sins; the Resurrection of the body; and the Life everlasting. Amen.

* *i. e.* Continued in the state of the dead and under the power of death until the third day.

Morning

1 MORNING HYMN L. M.   François H. Barthélémon, 1791

1 A-wake, my soul, and with the sun Thy dai-ly stage of du-ty run: Shake off dull sloth, and joy-ful rise To pay thy morn-ing sac-ri-fice. A-MEN.

2 Thy precious time misspent redeem;
Each present day thy last esteem;
Improve thy talent with due care;
For the great day thyself prepare.

3 By influence of the light Divine
Let thy own light to others shine;
Reflect all heaven's propitious rays
In ardent love and cheerful praise.

4 Wake and lift up thyself, my heart,
And with the angels bear thy part,
Who all night long, unwearied, sing
High praise to the Eternal King.

5 All praise to Thee, who safe hast kept,
And hast refreshed me whilst I slept:
Grant, Lord, when I from death shall wake,
I may of endless light partake.

6 Direct, control, suggest, this day,
All I design, or do, or say;
That all my powers, with all their might,
In Thy sole glory may unite.

                        Bishop Thomas Ken, 1695 (Text of 1709)

Morning

2 INNOCENTS 7. 7. 7. 7.   Old French Melody

1 As the sun doth dai - ly rise, Bright-ening all the morn-ing skies,
So to Thee with one ac - cord Lift we up our hearts, O Lord! A - MEN.

2 Day by day provide us food,
For from Thee come all things good :
Strength unto our souls afford
From Thy living Bread, O Lord!

3 Be our Guard in sin and strife ;
Be the Leader of our life ;
Lest like sheep we stray abroad,
Stay our wayward feet, O Lord!

4 Quickened by the Spirit's grace
All Thy holy will to trace,
While we daily search Thy word,
Wisdom true impart, O Lord!

5 When the sun withdraws his light,
When we seek our beds at night,
Thou, by sleepless hosts adored,
Hear the prayer of faith, O Lord!

6 Praise we, with the heavenly host,
Father, Son, and Holy Ghost ;
Thee would we with one accord
Praise and magnify, O Lord!

Anon. (Latin.) Tr. "O. B. C." Recast by Earl Nelson, 1864

3 (WARWICK) C. M.

1 LORD, in the morning Thou shalt hear
My voice ascending high ;
To Thee will I direct my prayer,
To Thee lift up mine eye :

2 Up to the hills, where Christ is gone
To plead for all His saints,
Presenting at His Father's throne
Our songs and our complaints.

3 Thou art a God before whose sight
The wicked shall not stand ;

Sinners shall ne'er be Thy delight,
Nor dwell at Thy right hand.

4 But to Thy house will I resort,
To taste Thy mercies there ;
I will frequent Thy holy court,
And worship in Thy fear.

5 O may Thy Spirit guide my feet
In ways of righteousness ;
Make every path of duty straight
And plain before my face.

Rev. Isaac Watts, 1719

Evening

4 WOODSTOCK C. M. — Deodatus Dutton, Jr., 1829

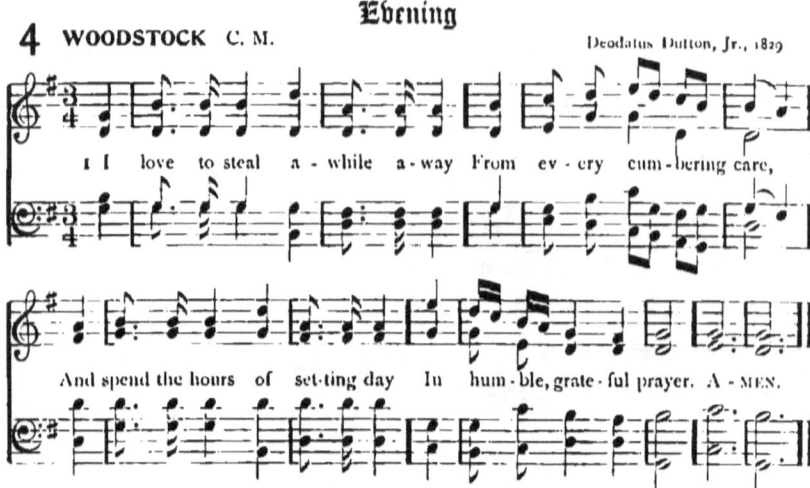

1 I love to steal a-while away From ev-ery cum-bering care, And spend the hours of set-ting day In hum-ble, grate-ful prayer. A-MEN.

2 I love in solitude to shed
　The penitential tear,
And all His promises to plead
　Where none but God can hear.

3 I love to think on mercies past,
　And future good implore,
And all my cares and sorrows cast
　On Him whom I adore.

4 I love by faith to take a view
　Of brighter scenes in heaven;
The prospect doth my strength renew
　While here by tempests driven.

5 Thus, when life's toilsome day is o'er,
　May its departing ray
Be calm as this impressive hour,
　And lead to endless day.

Phœbe H. Brown, 1818; alt. in Village Hymns, 1824

WARWICK C. M. — Samuel Stanley, 1800

1 Lord, in the morn-ing Thou shalt hear My voice as-cend-ing high; To Thee will I di-rect my prayer, To Thee lift up mine eye: A-MEN.

Evening

5 HURSLEY L. M.   Ascribed to Peter Ritter, 1792. Arr. by Wm. H. Monk, 1861

1 Sun of my soul, Thou Saviour dear, It is not night if Thou be near;
O may no earth-born cloud arise To hide Thee from Thy servant's eyes. A - MEN.

2 When the soft dews of kindly sleep
My wearied eyelids gently steep,
Be my last thought, how sweet to rest
For ever on my Saviour's breast.

3 Abide with me from morn till eve,
For without Thee I cannot live ;
Abide with me when night is nigh,
For without Thee I dare not die.

4 If some poor wandering child of Thine
Have spurned to-day the voice Divine,
Now, Lord, the gracious work begin ;
Let him no more lie down in sin.

5 Watch by the sick ; enrich the poor
With blessings from Thy boundless store;
Be every mourner's sleep to-night,
Like infants' slumbers, pure and light.

6 Come near and bless us when we wake,
Ere through the world our way we take,
Till in the ocean of Thy love
We lose ourselves in heaven above.

Rev. John Keble, 1820

6 (TALLIS'S EVENING HYMN) L. M.

1 ALL praise to Thee, my God, this night,
For all the blessings of the light ;
Keep me, O keep me, King of kings,
Beneath Thy own almighty wings.

2 Forgive me, Lord, for Thy dear Son,
The ill that I this day have done ;
That with the world, myself, and Thee,
I, ere I sleep, at peace may be.

3 O may my soul on Thee repose,
And with sweet sleep mine eyelids close ;
Sleep that may me more vigorous make
To serve my God when I awake.

4 When in the night I sleepless lie,
My soul with heavenly thoughts supply ;
Let no ill dreams disturb my rest,
No powers of darkness me molest.

5 O when shall I in endless day
For ever chase dark sleep away,
And hymns with the supernal choir
Incessant sing, and never tire !

Bishop Thomas Ken, 1693 (Text of 1709)

Evening

7 SEYMOUR 7. 7. 7. 7. Arr. from Carl M. von Weber, 1826

1 Softly now the light of day Fades upon my sight away; Free from care, from labor free, Lord, I would commune with Thee. A-MEN.

2 Thou, whose all-pervading eye
Naught escapes, without, within,
Pardon each infirmity,
Open fault, and secret sin.

3 Soon for me the light of day
Shall for ever pass away;

Then, from sin and sorrow free,
Take me, Lord, to dwell with Thee.

4 Thou who, sinless, yet hast known
All of man's infirmity;
Then, from Thine eternal throne,
Jesus, look with pitying eye.

Bishop George W. Doane, 1824

TALLIS'S EVENING HYMN L. M. Alt. from Thomas Tallis, 1560

1 All praise to Thee, my God, this night, For all the blessings of the light; Keep me, O keep me, King of kings, Beneath Thy own almighty wings. A-MEN.

Evening

8 ST. LEONARD (HILES) C. M. D. — Henry Hiles, 1868

1. The shadows of the evening hours
Fall from the darkening sky;
Upon the fragrance of the flowers
The dews of evening lie:
Before Thy throne, O Lord of heaven,
We kneel at close of day;
Look on Thy children from on high,
And hear us while we pray. A-MEN.

2 Slowly the rays of daylight fade;
So fade within our heart
The hopes in earthly love and joy
That one by one depart.
Slowly the bright stars, one by one,
Within the heavens shine;
Give us, O Lord, fresh hopes in heaven,
And trust in things Divine.

3 Let peace, O Lord, Thy peace, O God,
Upon our souls descend;
From midnight fears and perils, Thou
Our trembling hearts defend:
Give us a respite from our toil,
Calm and subdue our woes;
Through the long day we labor, Lord,
O give us now repose.

Adelaide Anne Procter, 1862: verse 3, l. 7, alt.

Evening

9 EVENTIDE 10. 10. 10. 10. William H. Monk, 1861

1 Abide with me: fast falls the eventide; The darkness deepens; Lord, with me abide: When other helpers fail, and comforts flee, Help of the helpless, O abide with me. A-MEN.

2 Swift to its close ebbs out life's little day;
Earth's joys grow dim, its glories pass away;
Change and decay in all around I see;
O Thou who changest not, abide with me.

3 I need Thy presence every passing hour;
What but Thy grace can foil the tempter's power?
Who like Thyself my guide and stay can be?
Through cloud and sunshine, O abide with me.

4 I fear no foe, with Thee at hand to bless:
Ills have no weight, and tears no bitterness.
Where is death's sting? where, grave, thy victory?
I triumph still, if Thou abide with me.

5 Hold Thou Thy cross before my closing eyes;
Shine through the gloom, and point me to the skies:
Heaven's morning breaks, and earth's vain shadows flee:
In life, in death, O Lord, abide with me.

Rev. Henry F. Lyte, 1847

Evening

10 ST. ANATOLIUS 7.6.7.6.8.8.   Arthur H. Brown, 1862

1. The day is past and o-ver: All thanks, O Lord, to Thee; I pray Thee that of-fence-less The hours of dark may be. O Je-sus, keep me in Thy sight, And save me thro' the com-ing night. A-MEN.

2 The joys of day are over:
   I lift my heart to Thee,
And call on Thee that sinless
   The hours of gloom may be.
O Jesus, make their darkness light,
And save me through the coming
   night.

3 The toils of day are over:
   I raise the hymn to Thee,
And ask that free from peril
   The hours of fear may be.
O Jesus, keep me in Thy sight,
And guard me through the coming
   night.

4 Lighten mine eyes, O Saviour,
   Or sleep in death shall I,
And he, my wakeful tempter,
   Triumphantly shall cry,
"He could not make their darkness
   light,
Nor guard them through the hours of
   night."

5 Be Thou my soul's Preserver,
   O God, for Thou dost know
How many are the perils
   Through which I have to go.
Lover of men, O hear my call,
And guard and save me from them all.

                    Cento from early Greek Service Bk.
                    Tr. Rev. John M. Neale, 1853, 1862

Evening

II EVENING PRAISE 7. 7. 7. 7. 4. with Refrain   William F. Sherwin, 1877

1 Day is dy-ing in the west; Heaven is touch-ing earth with rest; Wait and wor-ship while the night Sets her eve-ning lamps a-light Through all the sky.

REFRAIN.
Ho-ly, Ho-ly, Ho-ly, Lord God of Hosts! Heaven and earth are full of Thee; Heaven and earth are prais-ing Thee, O Lord Most High! A-MEN.

Copyright by J. H. Vincent

2 Lord of life, beneath the dome
Of the universe, Thy home,
Gather us who seek Thy face
To the fold of Thy embrace,
For Thou art nigh.—REF.

3 While the deepening shadows fall,
Heart of Love, enfolding all,
Through the glory and the grace
Of the stars that veil Thy face,
Our hearts ascend.—REF.

4 When for ever from our sight
Pass the stars, the day, the night,
Lord of angels, on our eyes
Let eternal morning rise,
And shadows end.—REF.

Mary Ann Lathbury, 1877

Evening

12 REPOSE 6.5.6.5. D.

1 Now the day is o-ver, Night is draw-ing nigh, Shadows of the even-ing
Steal a-cross the sky. Now the dark-ness gath-ers, Stars be-gin to peep;
Birds, and beasts, and flow-ers Soon will be a-sleep. A-MEN.

2 Je-sus, give the wear-y Calm and sweet re-pose; With Thy tenderest bless-ing
May mine eye-lids close. Grant to lit-tle chil-dren Visions bright of Thee;
Guard the sail-ors, toss-ing On the deep blue sea.

3 Comfort every sufferer
Watching late in pain;
Those who plan some evil
From their sin restrain.
Through the long night-watches
May Thine angels spread
Their white wings above me,
Watching round my bed.

4 When the morning wakens,
Then may I arise
Pure, and fresh, and sinless
In Thy holy eyes.
Glory to the Father,
Glory to the Son,
And to Thee, blest Spirit,
Whilst all ages run.

Rev. Sabine Baring-Gould, 1865

13 (EVENING PRAYER) 8.7.8.7.

1 SAVIOUR, breathe an evening bless-
Ere repose our spirits seal;   [ing,
Sin and want we come confessing:
Thou canst save, and Thou canst heal.

2 Though the night be dark and dreary,
Darkness cannot hide from Thee;
Thou art He who, never weary,
Watchest where Thy people be.

3 Though destruction walk around us,
Though the arrow past us fly,
Angel-guards from Thee surround us;
We are safe if Thou art nigh.

4 Should swift death this night o'ertake
And our couch become our tomb,[us,
May the morn in heaven awake us,
Clad in light and deathless bloom.

James Edmeston, 1820

Evening

14 ST. SYLVESTER 8. 7. 8. 7. Rev John B. Dykes, 1862

1 Tar-ry with me, O my Saviour, For the day is pass-ing by;
See! the shades of even-ing gath-er, And the night is draw-ing nigh. A-MEN.

2 Deeper, deeper grow the shadows,
  Paler now the glowing west,
  Swift the night of death advances;
  Shall it be the night of rest?

3 Let me hear Thy voice behind me,
  Calming all these wild alarms;
  Let me, underneath my weakness,
  Feel the everlasting arms.

4 Feeble, trembling, fainting, dying,
  Lord, I cast myself on Thee;
  Tarry with me through the darkness;
  While I sleep, still watch by me.

5 Tarry with me, O my Saviour,
  Lay my head upon Thy breast
  Till the morning; then awake me—
  Morning of eternal rest.

Caroline L. Smith, 1853; recast in Plymouth Coll., 1855, and Songs of the Church, 1862

EVENING PRAYER 8. 7. 8. 7. George C. Stebbins, 1878

1 Sav-iour, breathe an even-ing bless-ing, Ere re-pose our spir-its seal;
Sin and want we come con-fess-ing: Thou canst save, and Thou canst heal. A-MEN.

Copyright by George C. Stebbins

Evening

15 AURELIA 7.6.7.6.D. — Samuel S. Wesley, 1864

1. This night, O Lord, we bless Thee For Thy protecting care,
And, ere we rest, address Thee In lowly, fervent prayer:
From evil and temptation Defend us through the night,
And round our habitation Be Thou a wall of light. A-MEN.

2 On Thee our whole reliance
  From day to day we cast,
To Thee, with firm affiance,
  Would cleave from first to last;
To Thee, through Jesus' merit,
  For needful grace we come,
And trust that Thy good Spirit
  Will guide us safely home.

3 What may be on the morrow
  Our foresight cannot see;
But be it joy or sorrow,
  We know it comes from Thee.
And nothing can take from us,
  Where'er our steps may move,
The staff of Thy sure promise,
  The shield of Thy true love.

Rev. James D. Burns, 1856

Evening

16 NOW GOD BE WITH US 11. 11. 11. 5.   Sir Joseph Barnby, 1872

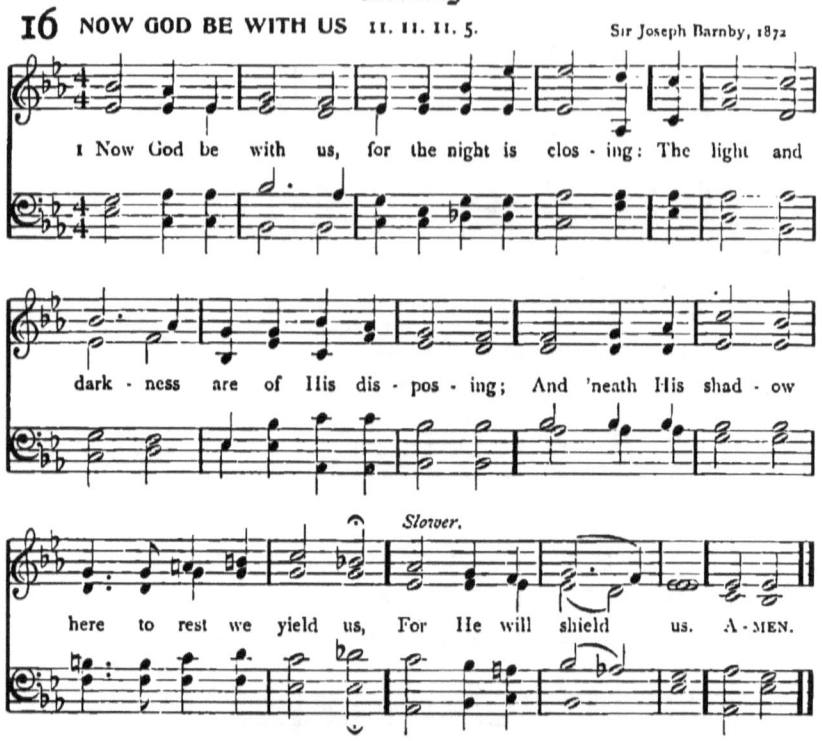

1 Now God be with us, for the night is closing: The light and darkness are of His disposing; And 'neath His shadow here to rest we yield us, For He will shield us. A-MEN.

2 Let evil thoughts and spirits flee before us;
  Till morning cometh, watch, O Master, o'er us;
  In soul and body Thou from harm defend us,
    Thine angels send us.

3 Let holy thoughts be ours when sleep o'ertakes us;
  Our earliest thoughts be Thine when morning wakes us;
  All day serve Thee, in all that we are doing
    Thy praise pursuing.

4 As Thy beloved, soothe the sick and weeping,
  And bid the prisoner lose his griefs in sleeping;
  Widows and orphans, we to Thee commend them,
    Do Thou befriend them.

5 We have no refuge, none on earth to aid us,
  Save Thee, O Father, who Thine own hast made us;
  But Thy dear presence will not leave them lonely,
    Who seek Thee only.

                    Rev. Petrus Herbert, 1566. Tr. Catherine Winkworth, 1863

The Lord's Day

17 SABBATH 7.7.7.7.7.7.   Lowell Mason, 1824

1. Safely through another week God has brought us on our way;
   Let us now a blessing seek, [*Omit*] . . . .
   Waiting in His courts to-day;
   Day of all the week the best, Emblem of eternal rest;
   Day of all the week the best; Emblem of eternal rest. A-MEN.

2. While we pray for pardoning grace,
   Through the dear Redeemer's Name,
   Show Thy reconciled face ;
   Take away our sin and shame ;
   From our worldly cares set free,
   May we rest this day in Thee.

3. Here we come Thy Name to praise,
   Let us feel Thy presence near ;
   May Thy glory meet our eyes,
   While we in Thy house appear :
   Here afford us, Lord, a taste
   Of our everlasting feast.

4. May Thy gospel's joyful sound
   Conquer sinners, comfort saints ;
   May the fruits of grace abound,
   Bring relief for all complaints :
   Thus may all our Sabbaths prove
   Till we join the Church above.

   Rev. John Newton, 1774 : alt.

18 (LISBON) S. M.

1. WELCOME, sweet day of rest,
   That saw the Lord arise :
   Welcome to this reviving breast,
   And these rejoicing eyes.

2. The King Himself comes near,
   And feasts His saints to-day ;
   Here we may sit, and see Him here,
   And love, and praise, and pray.

3. One day amidst the place
   Where my dear God hath been,
   Is sweeter than ten thousand days
   Of pleasurable sin.

4. My willing soul would stay
   In such a frame as this,
   And wait to hail the brighter day
   Of everlasting bliss.

   Rev. Isaac Watts, 1709 : verse 4, ll. 3, 4, alt.

The Lord's Day

19 ERNAN L. M.   Lowell Mason, 1850

1 Another six days' work is done, Another Sabbath is begun; Return, my soul, enjoy thy rest, Improve the day thy God hath blest. A-MEN.

2 Come, bless the Lord, whose love assigns
So sweet a rest to wearied minds,
Provides an antepast of heaven,
And gives this day the food of seven.

3 O that our thoughts and thanks may rise,
As grateful incense, to the skies;
And draw from heaven that sweet repose
Which none but he that feels it knows.

4 This heavenly calm within the breast
Is the dear pledge of glorious rest
Which for the Church of God remains,
The end of cares, the end of pains.

5 In holy duties let the day,
In holy pleasures, pass away:
How sweet a Sabbath thus to spend,
In hope of one that ne'er shall end.

Rev. Joseph Stennett, publ. 1732; alt. Ash and Evans Coll. 1769

LISBON S. M.   Daniel Read, 1785

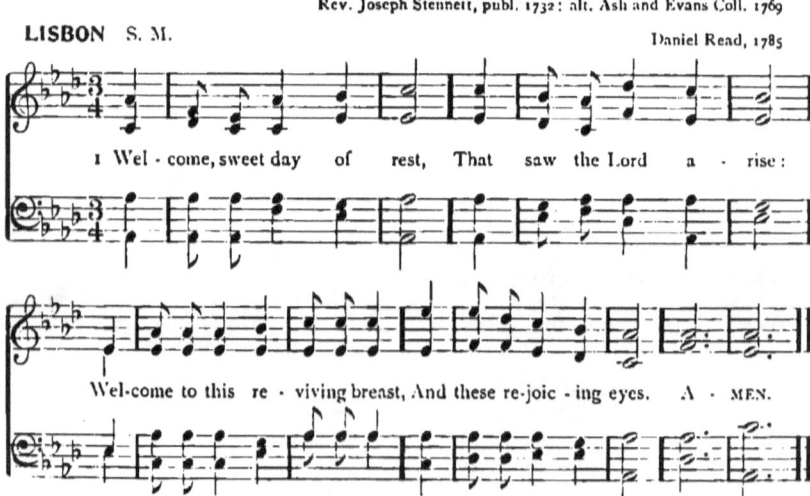

1 Welcome, sweet day of rest, That saw the Lord arise: Welcome to this reviving breast, And these rejoicing eyes. A-MEN.

The Lord's Day

20 ROTTERDAM 7. 6. 7. 6. D.   Berthold Tours, 1875

1. O day of rest and gladness,
O day of joy and light,
O balm of care and sadness,
Most beautiful, most bright;
On thee the high and low-ly,
Through ages joined in tune,
Sing Holy, Holy, Holy,
To the great God Triune. A-MEN.

2. On thee, at the creation,
The light first had its birth;
On thee, for our salvation,
Christ rose from depths of earth;
On thee our Lord, victorious,
The Spirit sent from heaven;
And thus on thee, most glorious,
A triple light was given.

3. To-day on weary nations
The heavenly manna falls:
To holy convocations
The silver trumpet calls,
Where gospel light is glowing
With pure and radiant beams,
And living water flowing
With soul-refreshing streams.

4. New graces ever gaining
From this our day of rest,
We reach the rest remaining
To spirits of the blest.
To Holy Ghost be praises,
To Father, and to Son;
The Church her voice upraises
To Thee, blest Three in One.

Bishop Christopher Wordsworth, 1862

The Lord's Day

21 ARLINGTON C. M. Arr. from Thomas A. Arne, 1762

1 This is the day the Lord hath made; He calls the hours His own;
Let heaven rejoice, let earth be glad, And praise surround the throne. A-MEN.

2 To-day He rose and left the dead,
And Satan's empire fell ;
To-day the saints His triumphs spread,
And all His wonders tell.

3 Hosanna to the anointed King,
To David's holy Son !
Help us, O Lord ; descend and bring
Salvation from the throne.

4 Blest be the Lord, who comes to men
With messages of grace ;
Who comes in God His Father's Name
To save our sinful race.

5 Hosanna in the highest strains
The Church on earth can raise !
The highest heavens in which He reigns
Shall give Him nobler praise.

Rev. Isaac Watts, 1719

MENDEBRAS 7. 6. 7. 6. D. German Melody ; arr. by Lowell Mason, 1839

1 O day of rest and gladness, O day of joy and light,
O balm of care and sadness, Most beautiful, most bright;
On thee the high and lowly, Through ages joined in tune, Sing Ho-ly, Ho-ly, Ho-ly, To the great God Triune. A-MEN.

At the Opening of Service

22 DALEHURST C. M.   Arthur Cottman, 1872

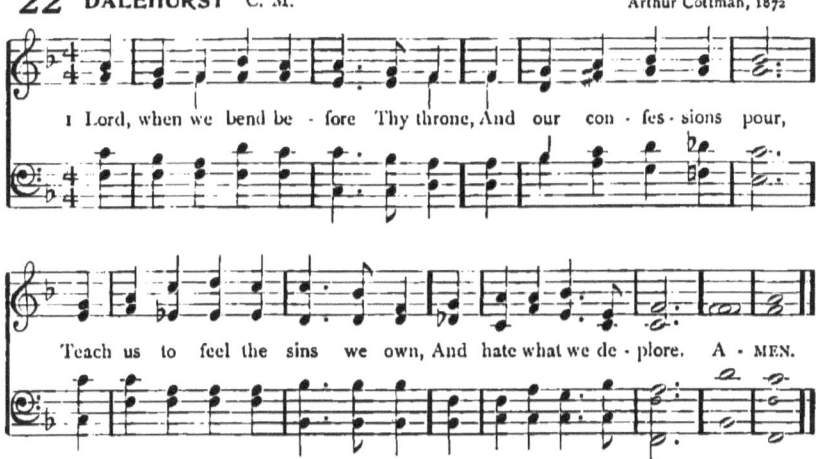

1 Lord, when we bend before Thy throne, And our confessions pour, Teach us to feel the sins we own, And hate what we deplore. A-MEN.

2 Our broken spirits pitying see,
And penitence impart;
Then let a kindling glance from Thee
Beam hope upon the heart.

3 When our responsive tongues essay
Their grateful hymns to raise,
Grant that our souls may join the lay,
And mount to Thee in praise.

4 When we disclose our wants in prayer,
May we our wills resign;
And not a thought our bosom share
Which is not wholly Thine.

5 Let faith each meek petition fill,
And waft it to the skies;
And teach our hearts 'tis goodness still
That grants it, or denies.

                         Rev. Joseph D. Carlyle, 1802

LAMBETH C. M.

1 Spirit Divine, attend our prayers, And make this house Thy home; Descend with all Thy gracious powers, O come, great Spirit, come. A-MEN.

At the Opening of Service

23 HEBRON L. M. *Lowell Mason, 1830*

1 Jesus, wher-e'er Thy people meet,
There they behold Thy mercy seat;
Wher-e'er they seek Thee, Thou art found,
And every place is hallowed ground : A-MEN.

2 For Thou, within no walls confined,
Inhabitest the humble mind ;
Such ever bring Thee where they come,
And going, take Thee to their home.

3 Dear Shepherd of Thy chosen few,
Thy former mercies here renew ;
Here to our waiting hearts proclaim
The sweetness of Thy saving Name.

4 Here may we prove the power of prayer
To strengthen faith, and sweeten care,
To teach our faint desires to rise,
And bring all heaven before our eyes.

5 Lord, we are few, but Thou art near ;
Nor short Thine arm, nor deaf Thine ear:
O rend the heavens, come quickly down,
And make a thousand hearts Thine own.

William Cowper, 1769

24 (LAMBETH) C. M.

1 SPIRIT Divine, attend our prayers,
And make this house Thy home ;
Descend with all Thy gracious powers,
O come, great Spirit, come.

2 Come as the light ; to us reveal
Our emptiness and woe ;
And lead us in those paths of life
Where all the righteous go.

3 Come as the fire ; and purge our hearts,
Like sacrificial flame :
Let our whole soul an offering be
To our Redeemer's Name.

4 Come as the dove ; and spread Thy wings,
The wings of peaceful love ;
And let Thy Church on earth become
Blest as Thy Church above.

5 Spirit Divine, attend our prayers ;
Make a lost world Thy home ;
Descend with all Thy gracious powers,
O come, great Spirit, come.

Rev. Andrew Reed, 1829

At the Opening of Service

25 ST. BEES 7. 7. 7. 7.   Rev. John B. Dykes, 1862

1 Lord, we come before Thee now;
At Thy feet we humbly bow;
O do not our suit disdain:
Shall we seek Thee, Lord, in vain? A-MEN.

2 Lord, on Thee our souls depend;
In compassion now descend;
Fill our hearts with Thy rich grace,
Tune our lips to sing Thy praise.

3 In Thine own appointed way,
Now we seek Thee, here we stay:
Lord, we know not how to go,
Till a blessing Thou bestow.

4 Send some message from Thy word,
That may joy and peace afford;
Let Thy Spirit now impart
Full salvation to each heart.

5 Comfort those who weep and mourn,
Let the time of joy return;
Heal the sick, the captive free,
Let us all rejoice in Thee.

Rev. William Hammond, 1745

DALLAS 7. 7. 7. 7.   Arr. from Maria L. Cherubini (1760-1842)

1 To Thy temple I repair;
Lord, I love to worship there,
When within the veil I meet
Christ before the mercy-seat. A-MEN.

At the Opening of Service

26 TRINITY 6.6.4.6.6.6.4.   Felice de Giardini, 1769

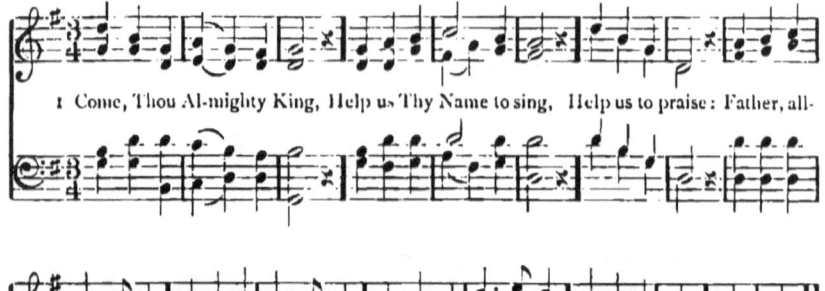

1 Come, Thou Almighty King, Help us Thy Name to sing, Help us to praise: Father, all-glorious, O'er all victorious, Come, and reign over us, Ancient of days. A - MEN.

2 Come, Thou Incarnate Word,
Gird on Thy mighty sword,
Our prayer attend:
Come, and Thy people bless,
And give Thy word success;
Spirit of holiness,
On us descend.

3 Come, Holy Comforter,
Thy sacred witness bear
In this glad hour:
Thou who almighty art,
Now rule in every heart,
And ne'er from us depart,
Spirit of power.

4 To the great One in Three
Eternal praises be
Hence evermore.
His sovereign majesty
May we in glory see,
And to eternity
Love and adore.

                                Anon. c. 1757

27 (DALLAS) 7.7.7.7.

1 TO Thy temple I repair;
Lord, I love to worship there,
When within the veil I meet
Christ before the mercy-seat.

2 While thy glorious praise is sung,
Touch my lips, unloose my tongue,
That my joyful soul may bless
Thee, the Lord my Righteousness.

3 While the prayers of saints ascend,
God of love, to mine attend;
Hear me, for Thy Spirit pleads;
Hear, for Jesus intercedes.

4 While I hearken to Thy law,
Fill my soul with humble awe,
Till Thy gospel bring to me
Life and immortality.

5 From Thy house when I return,
May my heart within me burn,
And at evening let me say,—
I have walked with God to-day.

                                James Montgomery, 1812

At the Opening of Service

28 LONGWOOD 10. 10. 10. 10.   Sir Joseph Barnby, 1872

1 Father, again in Jesus' Name we meet, And bow in penitence beneath Thy feet: Again to Thee our feeble voices raise, To sue for mercy, and to sing Thy praise. A-MEN.

    2 O we would bless Thee for Thy ceaseless care,
      And all Thy works from day to day declare:
      Is not our life with hourly mercies crowned?
      Does not Thine arm encircle us around?

    3 Alas, unworthy of Thy boundless love,
      Too oft with careless feet from Thee we rove;
      But now, encouraged by Thy voice, we come,
      Returning sinners to a Father's home.

    4 O by that Name in whom all fulness dwells,
      O by that love which every love excels,
      O by that blood so freely shed for sin,
      Open blest mercy's gate, and take us in.

        Lady Lucy E. G. Whitmore, 1824: verse 3, l. 2, verse 4, l. 4, alt.

At the Close of Service

29 ELLERS 10. 10. 10. 10.   Edward J. Hopkins, 1868

1 Sav-iour, a-gain to Thy dear Name we raise With one ac-cord our part-ing hymn of praise; We stand to bless Thee ere our wor-ship cease; Then, low-ly kneel-ing, wait Thy word of peace. A-MEN.

2 Grant us Thy peace upon our homeward way;
With Thee began, with Thee shall end the day:
Guard Thou the lips from sin, the hearts from shame,
That in this house have called upon Thy Name.

3 Grant us Thy peace, Lord, through the coming night;
Turn Thou for us its darkness into light;
From harm and danger keep Thy children free,
For dark and light are both alike to Thee.

4 Grant us Thy peace throughout our earthly life,
Our balm in sorrow, and our stay in strife;
Then, when Thy voice shall bid our conflict cease,
Call us, O Lord, to Thine eternal peace.

Rev. John Ellerton, 1866 (Text of 1868)

At the Close of Service

30 SICILIAN MARINERS 8.7.8.7.4.7. Sicilian Melody

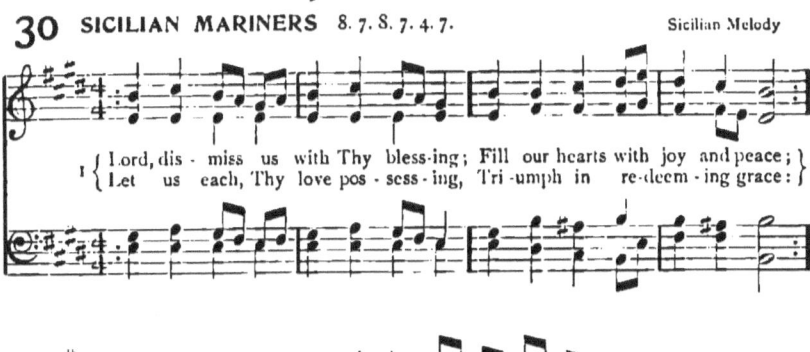

1. Lord, dismiss us with Thy blessing;
   Fill our hearts with joy and peace;
   Let us each, Thy love possessing,
   Triumph in redeeming grace:
   O refresh us, O refresh us,
   Travelling through this wilderness. A-MEN.

2 Thanks we give and adoration
  For Thy gospel's joyful sound:
  May the fruits of Thy salvation
  In our hearts and lives abound:
  Ever faithful
  To the truth may we be found;

3 So that when Thy love shall call us,
  Saviour, from the world away,
  Let no fear of death appal us,
  Glad Thy summons to obey:
  May we ever
  Reign with Thee in endless day.

Anon. 1773 (ascribed to Rev. John Fawcett);
verse 1, l. 6, alt.; verse 3, recast by Rev. G. Thring

31 (DENNIS) S. M.

1 STILL with Thee, O my God,
    I would desire to be,
  By day, by night; at home, abroad,
    I would be still with Thee.

2 With Thee when dawn comes in
    And calls me back to care,
  Each day returning to begin
    With Thee, my God, in prayer.

3 With Thee amid the crowd
    That throngs the busy mart,
  To hear Thy voice, where time's is loud,
    Speak softly to my heart.

4 With Thee when day is done,
    And evening calms the mind;
  The setting as the rising sun
    With Thee my heart would find.

5 With Thee, in Thee, by faith
    Abiding, I would be;
  By day, by night, in life, in death,
    I would be still with Thee.

Rev. James D. Burns, 1857

At the Close of Service

32 SOLITUDE 7. 7. 7. 7. — Lewis T. Downes, 1851

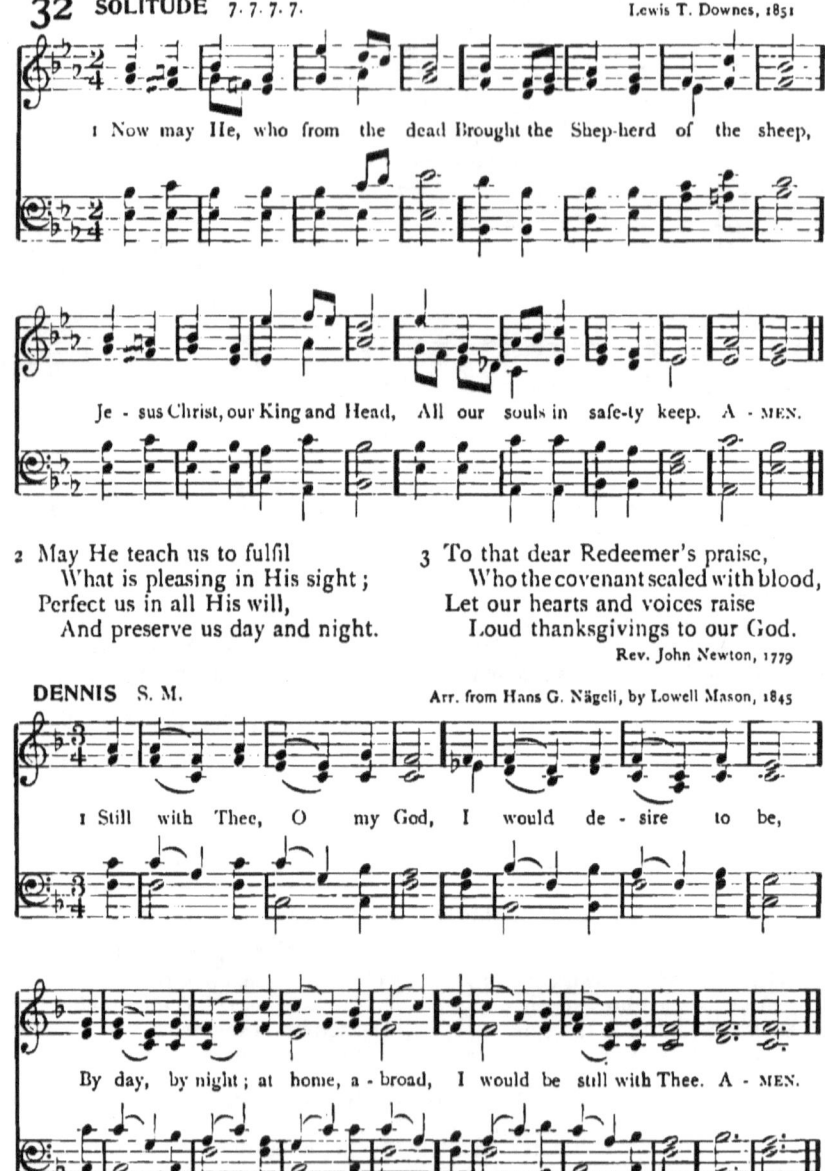

1 Now may He, who from the dead Brought the Shepherd of the sheep, Jesus Christ, our King and Head, All our souls in safety keep. A-MEN.

2 May He teach us to fulfil
　What is pleasing in His sight;
　Perfect us in all His will,
　And preserve us day and night.

3 To that dear Redeemer's praise,
　Who the covenant sealed with blood,
　Let our hearts and voices raise
　Loud thanksgivings to our God.
　　　　　　　Rev. John Newton, 1779

DENNIS S. M. — Arr. from Hans G. Nägeli, by Lowell Mason, 1845

1 Still with Thee, O my God, I would desire to be, By day, by night; at home, abroad, I would be still with Thee. A-MEN.

The Holy Trinity

33 NICÆA 11.12.12.10. Rev. John B. Dykes, 1861

1 Holy, Holy, Holy, Lord God Almighty! Early in the morning our song shall rise to Thee; Holy, Holy, Holy! Merciful and Mighty! God in Three Persons, blessed Trinity! A-MEN.

2 Holy, Holy, Holy! All the saints adore Thee,
Casting down their golden crowns around the glassy sea;
Cherubim and seraphim falling down before Thee,
 Who wert, and art, and evermore shalt be.

3 Holy, Holy, Holy! Though the darkness hide Thee,
Though the eye of sinful man Thy glory may not see,
Only Thou art holy; there is none beside Thee
 Perfect in power, in love, and purity.

4 Holy, Holy, Holy, Lord God Almighty!
All Thy works shall praise Thy Name, in earth and sky and sea;
Holy, Holy, Holy! Merciful and Mighty!
 God in Three Persons, blessed Trinity!

Bishop Reginald Heber, publ. 1827

The Holy Trinity

34 DUNDEE C. M. Arr. from Christopher Tye, 1553

1 O God, we praise Thee; and con-fess That Thou, the on-ly Lord
And Ev-er-last-ing Fa-ther, art By all the earth a-dored. A-MEN.

2 To Thee all angels cry aloud;
  To Thee the powers on high,
  Both cherubim and seraphim,
  Continually do cry :—

3 O Holy, Holy, Holy Lord,
  Whom heavenly hosts obey,
  The world is with the glory filled
  Of Thy majestic ray.

4 The apostles' glorious company,
  And prophets crowned with light,

With all the martyrs' noble host,
Thy constant praise recite.

5 The holy Church throughout the world,
  O Lord, confesses Thee,
  That Thou Eternal Father art,
  Of boundless majesty;

6 Thy honored, true, and only Son;
  And Holy Ghost, the Spring
  Of never-ceasing joy: O Christ,
  Of glory Thou art King.

Anon. (Latin, 5th Century.) Tr. Tate and Brady's Supplement, c. 1700

God the Father Almighty

35 (DUNDEE) C. M.

1 GOD moves in a mysterious way
   His wonders to perform;
  He plants His footsteps in the sea,
   And rides upon the storm.

2 Deep in unfathomable mines
   Of never-failing skill
  He treasures up His bright designs,
   And works His sovereign will.

3 Ye fearful saints, fresh courage take;
   The clouds ye so much dread

Are big with mercy, and shall break
 In blessings on your head.

4 Judge not the Lord by feeble sense,
   But trust Him for His grace;
  Behind a frowning providence
   He hides a smiling face.

5 Blind unbelief is sure to err,
   And scan His work in vain;
  God is His own Interpreter,
   And He will make it plain.

William Cowper, 1774

God the Father Almighty

36 ST. ANNE C. M. William Croft, 1708

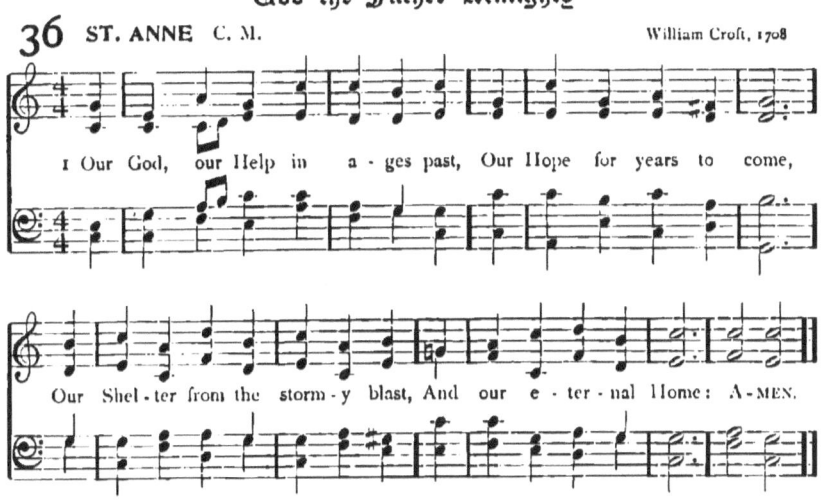

1 Our God, our Help in a-ges past, Our Hope for years to come, Our Shel-ter from the storm-y blast, And our e-ter-nal Home: A-MEN.

2 Before the hills in order stood,
Or earth received her frame,
From everlasting Thou art God,
To endless years the same.

3 A thousand ages in Thy sight
Are like an evening gone ;
Short as the watch that ends the night
Before the rising sun.

4 Time, like an ever-rolling stream,
Bears all its sons away ;
They fly forgotten, as a dream
Dies at the opening day.

5 Our God, our Help in ages past ;
Our Hope for years to come ;
Be Thou our Guard while troubles last,
And our eternal Home.

Rev. Isaac Watts, 1719

WARE L. M. George Kingsley, 1838

1 High in the heavens, E-ter-nal God, Thy good-ness in full glo-ry shines; Thy truth shall break through every cloud That veils and darkens Thy de-signs. A-MEN.

God the Father Almighty

37 CREATION L. M. *Arr. from Joseph Haydn, 1798*

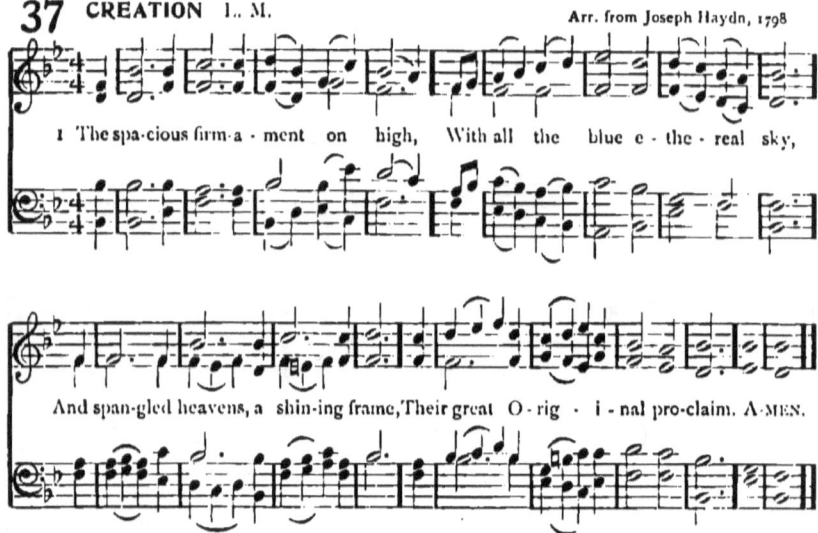

1 The spacious firmament on high,
With all the blue ethereal sky,
And spangled heavens, a shining frame,
Their great Original proclaim. AMEN.

2 The unwearied sun, from day to day,
Does his Creator's power display,
And publishes to every land
The work of an almighty hand.

3 Soon as the evening shades prevail,
The moon takes up the wondrous tale,
And nightly to the listening earth
Repeats the story of her birth;

4 Whilst all the stars that round her burn,
And all the planets in their turn,
Confirm the tidings as they roll,
And spread the truth from pole to pole.

5 What though in solemn silence all
Move round the dark terrestrial ball?
What though nor real voice nor sound
Amid their radiant orbs be found?

6 In reason's ear they all rejoice,
And utter forth a glorious voice;
For ever singing, as they shine,
"The hand that made us is Divine."

Joseph Addison, 1712

38 (WARE) L. M.

1 HIGH in the heavens, Eternal God,
Thy goodness in full glory shines;
Thy truth shall break through every cloud
That veils and darkens Thy designs.

2 For ever firm Thy justice stands,
As mountains their foundations keep;
Wise are the wonders of Thy hands;
Thy judgments are a mighty deep.

3 Thy providence is kind and large,
Both man and beast Thy bounty share;
The whole creation is Thy charge,
But saints are Thy peculiar care.

4 From the provisions of Thy house
We shall be fed with sweet repast;
There mercy like a river flows,
And brings salvation to our taste.

5 Life, like a fountain, rich and free,
Springs from the presence of my Lord;
And in Thy light our souls shall see
The glories promised in Thy word.

Rev. Isaac Watts, 1719

God the Father Almighty

39 DIX 7.7.7.7.7.7. Arr. from Conrad Kocher, 1838

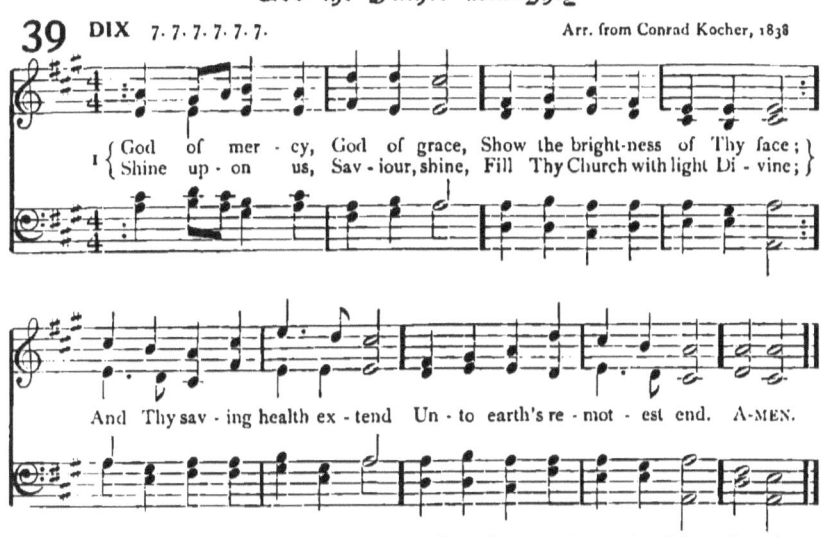

1 { God of mercy, God of grace, Show the brightness of Thy face;
    Shine upon us, Saviour, shine, Fill Thy Church with light Divine; }
And Thy saving health extend Unto earth's remotest end. A-MEN.

2 Let the people praise Thee, Lord;
Be by all that live adored:
Let the nations shout and sing,
Glory to their Saviour King;
At Thy feet their tributes pay,
And Thy holy will obey.

3 Let the people praise Thee, Lord;
Earth shall then her fruits afford;
God to man His blessing give,
Man to God devoted live;
All below, and all above,
One in joy, and light, and love.

Rev. Henry F. Lyte, 1834

NUREMBERG 7.7.7.7. Alt. from Johann R. Ahle, 1664

1 Songs of praise the angels sang, Heaven with alleluias rang,
When Jehovah's work begun, When He spake, and it was done. A-MEN.

God the Father Almighty

40 MONKLAND 7. 7. 7. 7.   Arr. by John B. Wilkes, 1861

1 Let us with a gladsome mind Praise the Lord, for He is kind:
For His mercies aye endure, Ever faithful, ever sure. A-MEN.

2 Let us blaze His Name abroad,
For of gods He is the God:
For His mercies aye endure,
Ever faithful, ever sure.

3 He, with all-commanding might,
Filled the new-made world with light:
For His mercies aye endure,
Ever faithful, ever sure.

4 All things living He doth feed ;
His full hand supplies their need :
For His mercies aye endure,
Ever faithful, ever sure.

5 He hath with a piteous eye
Looked upon our misery :
For His mercies aye endure,
Ever faithful, ever sure.

6 Let us therefore warble forth
His high majesty and worth :
For His mercies aye endure,
Ever faithful, ever sure.   John Milton, 1624 : alt.

41 (NUREMBERG) 7. 7. 7. 7.

1 SONGS of praise the angels sang,
Heaven with alleluias rang,
When Jehovah's work begun,
When He spake, and it was done.

2 Songs of praise awoke the morn,
When the Prince of Peace was born :
Songs of praise arose, when He
Captive led captivity.

3 Heaven and earth must pass away,
Songs of praise shall crown that day :
God will make new heavens, new earth,
Songs of praise shall hail their birth.

4 And can man alone be dumb,
Till that glorious kingdom come?
No : the Church delights to raise
Psalms, and hymns, and songs of praise.

5 Saints below, with heart and voice,
Still in songs of praise rejoice,
Learning here, by faith and love,
Songs of praise to sing above.   James Montgomery, 1819

God the Father Almighty

42 DOWNS C. M. — Lowell Mason, 1832

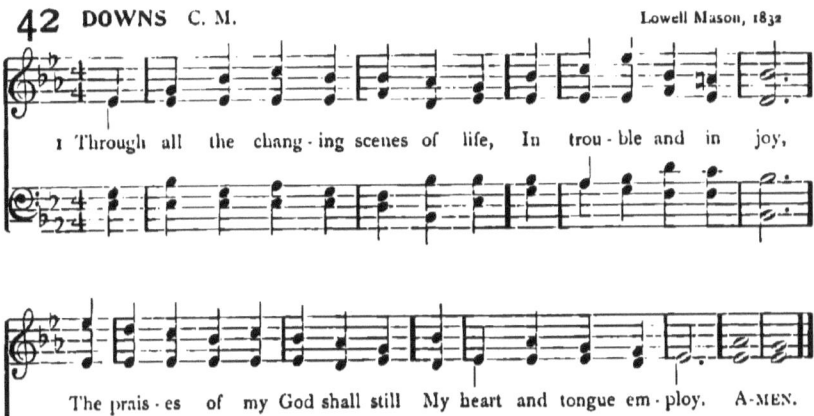

1 Through all the chang-ing scenes of life,
In trou-ble and in joy,
The prais-es of my God shall still
My heart and tongue em-ploy. A-MEN.

2 Of His deliverance I will boast,
Till all that are distressed
From my example comfort take,
And charm their griefs to rest.

3 O magnify the Lord with me,
With me exalt His Name;
When in distress to Him I called,
He to my rescue came.

4 The hosts of God encamp around
The dwellings of the just;
Deliverance He affords to all
Who on His succor trust.

5 O make but trial of His love;
Experience will decide,
How blest are they, and only they,
Who in His truth confide.

6 Fear Him, ye saints; and you will then
Have nothing else to fear:
Make you His service your delight,
He'll make your wants His care.

Tate and Brady's New Version, 1696, 1698

43 (GENEVA or DOWNS) C. M.

1 WHEN all Thy mercies, O my God,
My rising soul surveys,
Transported with the view, I'm lost
In wonder, love, and praise.

2 Unnumbered comforts to my soul
Thy tender care bestowed,
Before my infant heart conceived
From whom those comforts flowed.

3 When worn with sickness, oft hast Thou
With health renewed my face;
And, when in sins and sorrows sunk,
Revived my soul with grace.

4 Ten thousand thousand precious gifts
My daily thanks employ;
Nor is the least a cheerful heart
That tastes those gifts with joy.

5 Through every period of my life
Thy goodness I'll pursue;
And after death, in distant worlds,
The glorious theme renew.

6 Through all eternity to Thee
A joyful song I'll raise;
For O, eternity's too short
To utter all Thy praise.

Joseph Addison, 1712

God the Father Almighty

44 MANOAH C. M. — Arr. from Gioachino Rossini (1792-1868)

1 Begin, my tongue, some heavenly theme, And speak some boundless thing, The mighty works, or mightier Name, Of our Eternal King. A-MEN.

2 Tell of His wondrous faithfulness,
And sound His power abroad;
Sing the sweet promise of His grace,
And the performing God.

3 His very word of grace is strong
As that which built the skies;
The voice that rolls the stars along
Speaks all the promises.

4 O might I hear Thy heavenly tongue
But whisper, "Thou art Mine,"
Those gentle words should raise my song
To notes almost Divine.

Rev. Isaac Watts, 1707

GENEVA C. M. — John Cole, 1800

1 When all Thy mercies, O my God, My rising soul surveys, Transported with the view, I'm lost In wonder, love, and praise. A-MEN.

God the Father Almighty

45 LOUVAN L. M.   Virgil C. Taylor, 1847

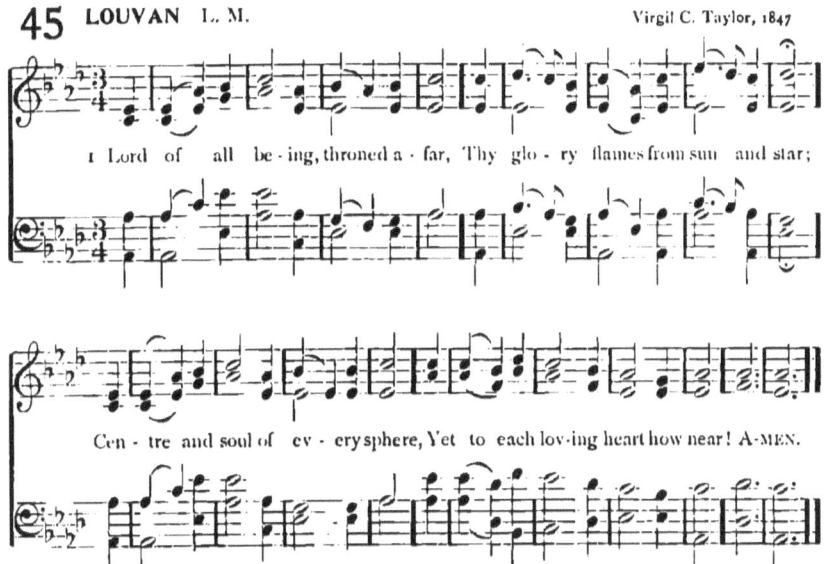

1 Lord of all being, throned afar, Thy glory flames from sun and star; Centre and soul of every sphere, Yet to each loving heart how near! A-MEN.

2 Sun of our life, Thy quickening ray
Sheds on our path the glow of day;
Star of our hope, Thy softened light
Cheers the long watches of the night.

3 Our midnight is Thy smile withdrawn;
Our noontide is Thy gracious dawn;
Our rainbow arch, Thy mercy's sign;
All, save the clouds of sin, are Thine.

4 Lord of all life, below, above,
Whose light is truth, whose warmth is love,
Before Thy ever-blazing throne
We ask no lustre of our own.

5 Grant us Thy truth to make us free,
And kindling hearts that burn for Thee;
Till all Thy living altars claim
One holy light, one heavenly flame.

Oliver Wendell Holmes, 1848

46 (LOUVAN) L. M.

1 LORD, Thou hast searched and seen me through;
Thine eye commands with piercing view
My rising and my resting hours,
My heart and flesh, with all their powers.

2 My thoughts, before they are my own,
Are to my God distinctly known;
He knows the words I mean to speak,
Ere from my opening lips they break.

3 Within Thy circling power I stand;
On every side I find Thy hand:
Awake, asleep, at home, abroad,
I am surrounded still with God.

4 Amazing knowledge, vast and great!
What large extent, what lofty height!
My soul, with all the powers I boast,
Is in the boundless prospect lost.

5 O may these thoughts possess my breast,
Where'er I rove, where'er I rest:
Nor let my weaker passions dare
Consent to sin, for God is there.

Rev. Isaac Watts, 1719

God the Father Almighty

47 SCHUBERT 7.6.7.6. D. Arr. from Schubert by Wm. W. Gilchrist, 1895

1 O God, the Rock of Ages, Who evermore hast been,
What time the tempest rages, Our dwelling-place serene:
Before Thy first creations, O Lord, the same as now,
To endless generations The Everlasting Thou! A-MEN.

Copyright, 1895, by The Trustees of The Presbyterian Board of Publication and Sabbath-School Work

2 Our years are like the shadows
  On sunny hills that lie,
Or grasses in the meadows
  That blossom but to die;
A sleep, a dream, a story
  By strangers quickly told,
An unremaining glory
  Of things that soon are old.

3 O Thou, who canst not slumber,
  Whose light grows never pale,
Teach us aright to number
  Our years before they fail;
On us Thy mercy lighten,
  On us Thy goodness rest,
And let Thy Spirit brighten
  The hearts Thyself hast blessed.

Bishop Edward H. Bickersteth, 1860

God the Father Almighty

48 SILVER STREET S. M. Isaac Smith, 1770

1 Come, sound His praise abroad, And hymns of glory sing: Jehovah is the sovereign God, The universal King. A-MEN.

2 He formed the deeps unknown,
He gave the seas their bound;
The watery worlds are all His own,
And all the solid ground.

3 Come, worship at His throne;
Come, bow before the Lord:

We are His works, and not our own;
He formed us by His Word.

4 To-day attend His voice,
Nor dare provoke His rod;
Come, like the people of His choice,
And own your gracious God.

Rev. Isaac Watts, 1719

49 OLD HUNDREDTH L. M. Genevan Psalter, 1551

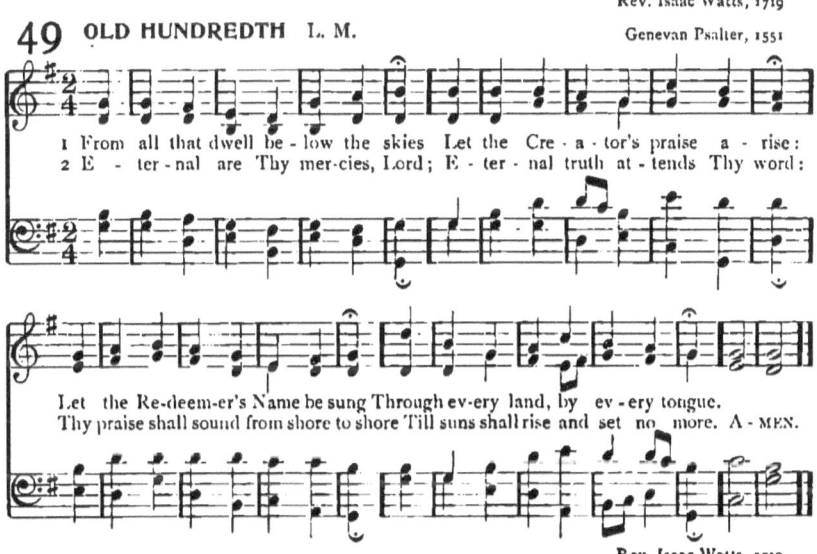

1 From all that dwell below the skies Let the Creator's praise arise:
2 Eternal are Thy mercies, Lord; Eternal truth attends Thy word:
Let the Redeemer's Name be sung Through ev-ery land, by ev-ery tongue.
Thy praise shall sound from shore to shore Till suns shall rise and set no more. A-MEN.

Rev. Isaac Watts, 1719

God the Father Almighty

50 ST. THOMAS S. M. — Aaron Williams, 1763

1 Come, we that love the Lord, And let our joys be known;
Join in a song with sweet ac-cord, And thus sur-round the throne. A-MEN.

2 Let those refuse to sing
That never knew our God;
But children of the heavenly King
May speak their joys abroad.

3 The men of grace have found
Glory begun below;
Celestial fruits on earthly ground
From faith and hope may grow.

4 The hill of Zion yields
A thousand sacred sweets,
Before we reach the heavenly fields,
Or walk the golden streets.

5 Then let our songs abound,
And every tear be dry;
We're marching through Emmanuel's ground
To fairer worlds on high.

Rev. Isaac Watts, 1707: verse 2, l. 3, alt.

51 (ST. THOMAS) S. M.

1 MY soul, repeat His praise
Whose mercies are so great,
Whose anger is so slow to rise,
So ready to abate.

2 High as the heavens are raised
Above the ground we tread,
So far the riches of His grace
Our highest thoughts exceed.

3 His power subdues our sins,
And His forgiving love,
Far as the east is from the west,
Doth all our guilt remove.

4 The pity of the Lord
To those that fear His Name
Is such as tender parents feel;
He knows our feeble frame.

5 Our days are as the grass,
Or like the morning flower;
If one sharp blast sweep o'er the field,
It withers in an hour.

6 But Thy compassions, Lord,
To endless years endure;
And children's children ever find
Thy words of promise sure.

Rev. Isaac Watts, 1719

God the Father Almighty

52 LUCERNE 8.7.8.7.   T. A. Willis, 1876

1 God is Love; His mercy brightens All the path in which we rove; Bliss He wakes, and woe He lightens: God is Wisdom, God is Love. A-MEN.

2 Chance and change are busy ever;
Man decays, and ages move;
But His mercy waneth never:
God is Wisdom, God is Love.

3 E'en the hour that darkest seemeth
Will His changeless goodness prove;
From the mist His brightness streameth:
God is Wisdom, God is Love.

4 He with earthly cares entwineth
Hope and comfort from above;
Everywhere His glory shineth:
God is Wisdom, God is Love.

Sir John Bowring, 1825

CANONBURY L. M.   Arr. from Robert Schumann, 1839

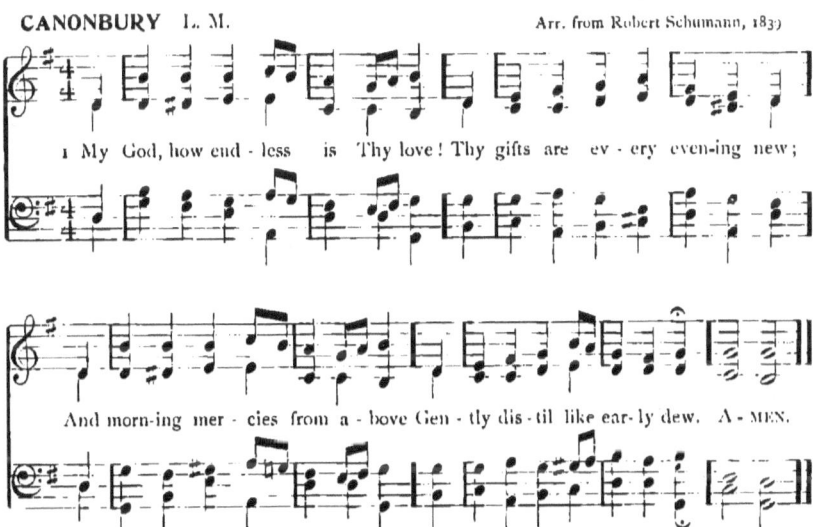

1 My God, how endless is Thy love! Thy gifts are every evening new; And morning mercies from above Gently distil like early dew. A-MEN.

God the Father Almighty

53 FABEN 8.7.8.7. D.　　　　　　　　　John H. Willcox, 1849

1 Praise the Lord: ye heavens adore Him; Praise Him, angels, in the height;
Sun and moon, rejoice before Him; Praise Him, all ye stars and light.
Praise the Lord, for He hath spoken; Worlds His mighty voice obeyed;
Laws which never shall be broken For their guidance hath He made.

2 Praise the Lord, for He is glorious; Never shall His promise fail:
God hath made His saints victorious; Sin and death shall not prevail.
Praise the God of our salvation; Hosts on high, His power proclaim;
Heaven and earth and all creation, Laud and magnify His Name. A-MEN.

Anon. c. 1801

54 (CANONBURY) L. M.

1 MY God, how endless is Thy love!
　Thy gifts are every evening new;
　And morning mercies from above
　Gently distil like early dew.

2 Thou spread'st the curtains of the night,
　Great Guardian of my sleeping hours;
　Thy sovereign word restores the light,
　And quickens all my drowsy powers.

3 I yield my powers to Thy command,
　To Thee I consecrate my days;
　Perpetual blessings from Thy hand
　Demand perpetual songs of praise.

Rev. Isaac Watts, 1709

God the Father Almighty

55 ANGEL VOICES 8. 5. 8. 5. 8. 4. 3. Sir Arthur Sullivan, 1872

1 Angel voices, ever singing Round Thy throne of light,
Angel harps, for ever ringing, Rest not day nor night;
Thousands only live to bless Thee, And confess Thee Lord of might. A-MEN.

2 Thou who art beyond the farthest
   Mortal eye can scan,
Can it be that Thou regardest
   Songs of sinful man?
Can we feel that Thou art near us,
   And wilt hear us?
     Yea, we can.

3 Yea, we know Thy love rejoices
   O'er each work of Thine;
Thou didst ears and hands and voices
   For Thy praise combine;
Craftsman's art and music's measure
   For Thy pleasure
     Didst design.

4 Here, great God, to-day we offer
   Of Thine own to Thee;
And for Thine acceptance proffer,
   All unworthily,
Hearts and minds, and hands and voices,
   In our choicest
     Melody.

5 Honor, glory, might, and merit,
   Thine shall ever be,
Father, Son, and Holy Spirit,
   Blessèd Trinity:
Of the best that Thou hast given
   Earth and heaven
     Render Thee.

Rev. Francis Pott, 1861

Praise to Christ Exalted

56 DIADEMATA S. M. D. *Sir George J. Elvey, 1868*

1 Crown Him with many crowns, The Lamb upon His throne;
Hark, how the heavenly anthem drowns All music but its own:
Awake, my soul, and sing Of Him who died for thee,
And hail Him as thy matchless King Through all eternity. A-MEN.

2 Crown Him the Lord of love: Behold His hands and side,
Rich wounds, yet visible above, In beauty glorified:
No angel in the sky Can fully bear that sight,
But downward bends his burning eye At mysteries so bright.

3 Crown Him the Lord of peace;
Whose power a sceptre sways
From pole to pole, that wars may cease,
Absorbed in prayer and praise:
His reign shall know no end;
And round His piercèd feet
Fair flowers of Paradise extend
Their fragrance ever sweet.

4 Crown Him the Lord of years,
The Potentate of time;
Creator of the rolling spheres,
Ineffably sublime:
All hail, Redeemer, hail!
For Thou hast died for me:
Thy praise shall never, never fail
Throughout eternity.

Matthew Bridges, 1851

Jesus Christ our Lord

57 CORONATION C. M. — Oliver Holden, 1793

1 All hail the power of Jesus' Name! Let angels prostrate fall; Bring forth the royal diadem, And crown Him Lord of all; Bring forth the royal diadem, And crown Him Lord of all. A-MEN.

2 Ye seed of Israel's chosen race,
Ye ransomed of the fall,
Hail Him who saves you by His grace,
And crown Him Lord of all.

3 Sinners, whose love can ne'er forget
The wormwood and the gall,
Go, spread your trophies at His feet,
And crown Him Lord of all.

4 Let every kindred, every tribe,
On this terrestrial ball,
To Him all majesty ascribe,
And crown Him Lord of all.

5 O that with yonder sacred throng
We at His feet may fall;
We'll join the everlasting song,
And crown Him Lord of all.

Rev. Edward Perronet, 1779-80
Verse 1, l. 4, alt., verse 4, recast, verse 5, added, Rev. John Rippon, 1787

ST. LEONARD (SMART) C. M. — Henry Smart, 1867

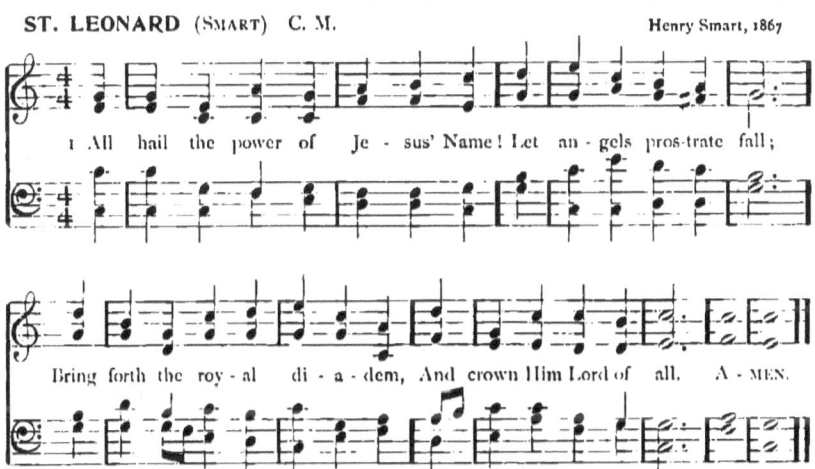

1 All hail the power of Jesus' Name! Let angels prostrate fall; Bring forth the royal diadem, And crown Him Lord of all. A-MEN.

Praise to Christ Exalted

58 DEDHAM C. M. 　　　　　　　William Gardiner, 1812

1 Come, let us join our cheerful songs
With angels round the throne;
Ten thousand thousand are their tongues,
But all their joys are one. A-MEN.

2 "Worthy the Lamb that died," they [cry,
"To be exalted thus:"
"Worthy the Lamb," our lips reply,
"For He was slain for us."

3 Jesus is worthy to receive
Honor and power Divine;
And blessings, more than we can give,
Be, Lord, for ever Thine.

4 Let all that dwell above the sky,
And air, and earth, and seas,
Conspire to lift Thy glories high,
And speak Thine endless praise.

5 The whole creation join in one,
To bless the sacred Name
Of Him that sits upon the throne,
And to adore the Lamb.

　　　　　　　　　　Rev. Isaac Watts, 1707

59 (DEDHAM or ST. LEONARD) C. M.

1 O FOR a thousand tongues to sing
My dear Redeemer's praise,
The glories of my God and King,
The triumphs of His grace.

2 My gracious Master and my God,
Assist me to proclaim,
To spread through all the earth abroad,
The honors of Thy Name.

3 Jesus, the Name that charms our fears,
That bids our sorrows cease;
'Tis music in the sinner's ears,
'Tis life, and health, and peace.

4 He breaks the power of reigning sin,
He sets the prisoner free:
His blood can make the foulest clean,
His blood availed for me.

5 He speaks, and, listening to His voice,
New life the dead receive;
The mournful, broken hearts rejoice;
The humble poor believe.

　　　　　　Rev. Charles Wesley, 1739: verse 4, l. 1, alt.

Jesus Christ our Lord

60 ZOAN 7. 6. 7. 6. D. Rev. William H. Havergal, 1845

1 O Saviour, precious Saviour, Whom yet unseen we love,
O Name of might and favor, All other names above;
We worship Thee, we bless Thee, To Thee alone we sing;
We praise Thee, and confess Thee Our holy Lord and King. A-MEN.

2 O Bringer of salvation,
Who wondrously hast wrought,
Thyself the revelation
Of love beyond our thought;
We worship Thee, we bless Thee,
To Thee alone we sing;
We praise Thee, and confess Thee
Our gracious Lord and King.

3 In Thee all fulness dwelleth,
All grace and power Divine:
The glory that excelleth,
O Son of God, is Thine;
We worship Thee, we bless Thee,
To Thee alone we sing;
We praise Thee, and confess Thee
Our glorious Lord and King.

Frances R. Havergal, 1870

Praise to Christ Exalted

61 EDINA 6. 5. 6. 5. D.   Sir Herbert S. Oakeley, 1868

1 Saviour, blessed Saviour, Listen while we sing; Hearts and voices raising Praises to our King: All we have we offer, All we hope to be, Body, soul, and spirit, All we yield to Thee. A-MEN.

2 Nearer, ever nearer,
   Christ, we draw to Thee,
Deep in adoration
   Bending low the knee:
Thou for our redemption
   Cam'st on earth to die;
Thou, that we might follow,
   Hast gone up on high.

3 Great and ever greater
   Are Thy mercies here;
True and everlasting
   Are the glories there,
Where no pain nor sorrow,
   Toil nor care is known,
Where the angel-legions
   Circle round Thy throne.

4 Brighter still and brighter
   Glows the western sun,
Shedding all its gladness
   O'er our work that's done:
Time will soon be over,
   Toil and sorrow past,
May we, blessèd Saviour,
   Find a rest at last.

5 Onward, ever onward,
   Journeying o'er the road
Worn by saints before us,
   Journeying on to God;
Leaving all behind us,
   May we hasten on,
Backward never looking
   Till the prize is won.

6 Higher, then, and higher,
   Bear the ransomed soul,
Earthly toils forgetting,
   Saviour, to its goal;
Where in joys unthought of
   Saints with angels sing,
Never weary, raising
   Praises to their King.

Rev. Godfrey Thring, 1862

Jesus Christ our Lord

62 ARIEL 8.8.6.8.8.6.   Arr. from Mozart, by Lowell Mason, 1836

1 O could I speak the matchless worth, O could I sound the glories forth Which in my Saviour shine, I'd soar, and touch the heavenly strings, And vie with Gabriel while he sings In notes almost Divine, In notes almost Divine. A-MEN.

2 I'd sing the precious blood He spilt,
My ransom from the dreadful guilt
Of sin, and wrath Divine:
I'd sing His glorious righteousness,
In which all-perfect, heavenly dress
My soul shall ever shine.

3 I'd sing the characters He bears,
And all the forms of love He wears,
Exalted on His throne:
In loftiest songs of sweetest praise,
I would to everlasting days
Make all His glories known.

4 Well, the delightful day will come
When my dear Lord will bring me home,
And I shall see His face;
Then with my Saviour, Brother, Friend,
A blest eternity I'll spend,
Triumphant in His grace.

Rev. Samuel Medley, 1789

Praise to Christ Exalted

63 LYONS 10. 10. 11. 11. Arr. from Michael Haydn (1737-1806)

1 Ye servants of God, your Master proclaim, And publish abroad His wonderful Name; The Name, all-victorious, of Jesus extol; His kingdom is glorious, and rules over all. A-MEN.

2 God ruleth on high, almighty to save;
And still He is nigh—His presence we have:
The great congregation His triumph shall sing,
Ascribing salvation to Jesus, our King.

3 Salvation to God, who sits on the throne!
Let all cry aloud, and honor the Son:
The praises of Jesus the angels proclaim,
Fall down on their faces and worship the Lamb.

4 Then let us adore, and give Him His right,
All glory and power, and wisdom and might,
All honor and blessing, with angels above,
And thanks never ceasing, and infinite love.

Rev. Charles Wesley, 1744: verse 3, line 3, alt

Jesus Christ our Lord

64 HARWELL. 8. 7. 8. 7. 7. 7. with Refrain   Lowell Mason, 1840

1. Hark! ten thousand harps and voices Sound the note of praise above;
Jesus reigns, and heaven rejoices; Jesus reigns, the God of love:
See, He sits on yonder throne; Jesus rules the world alone.

Refrain. Alleluia! Alleluia! Alleluia! Amen. A-MEN.

2 King of glory, reign for ever,
  Thine an everlasting crown;
Nothing from Thy love shall sever
  Those whom Thou hast made Thine own:
Happy objects of Thy grace,
Destined to behold Thy face.—REF.

3 Saviour, hasten Thine appearing;
  Bring, O bring the glorious day,
When, the awful summons hearing,
  Heaven and earth shall pass away:
Then, with golden harps, we'll sing,
" Glory, glory to our King!"—REF.

                                 Rev. Thomas Kelly, 1806

65 (LEIGHTON) S. M.

1 AWAKE, and sing the song
  Of Moses and the Lamb;
Wake every heart and every tongue
  To praise the Saviour's Name.

2 Sing of His dying love;
  Sing of His rising power;
Sing how He intercedes above
  For those whose sins He bore.

3 Sing on your heavenly way,
  Ye ransomed sinners, sing;
Sing on, rejoicing every day
  In Christ the Eternal King.

4 Soon shall ye hear Him say,
  "Ye blessèd children, come;"
Soon will He call you hence away,
  And take His wanderers home.

        William Hammond, 1745. alt. Rev. Geo. Whitefield, 1753, and Rev. Martin Madan, 1760

Jesus Christ our Lord

67 LAUDES DOMINI 6.6.6.6.6.6. — Sir Joseph Barnby, 1868

1. When morning gilds the skies,
My heart awaking cries
    May Jesus Christ be praised:
Alike at work and prayer
To Jesus I repair;
    May Jesus Christ be praised. A-MEN.

2. When sleep her balm denies,
My silent spirit sighs
    May Jesus Christ be praised:
When evil thoughts molest,
With this I shield my breast,
    May Jesus Christ be praised.

3. Does sadness fill my mind?
A solace here I find,
    May Jesus Christ be praised:
Or fades my earthly bliss?
My comfort still is this,
    May Jesus Christ be praised.

4. In heaven's eternal bliss
The loveliest strain is this,
    May Jesus Christ be praised:
The powers of darkness fear,
When this sweet chant they hear,
    May Jesus Christ be praised.

5. Let earth's wide circle round
In joyful notes resound,
    May Jesus Christ be praised:
Let air and sea and sky,
From depth to height, reply,
    May Jesus Christ be praised.

Anon. (German.) Tr. Rev. Edward Caswall, 1853, 1858

Praise to Christ Exalted

68 STUTTGART 8.7.8.7. Gotha Cantional, 1715

1 Christ, above all glory seated, King triumphant, strong to save,
Dying, Thou hast death defeated, Buried, Thou hast spoiled the grave. A-MEN.

2 Thou art gone where now is given
What no mortal might could gain,
On the eternal throne of heaven
In Thy Father's power to reign.

3 There Thy kingdoms all adore Thee,
Heaven above and earth below;
While the depths of hell before Thee
Trembling and amazèd bow.

4 We, O Lord, with hearts adoring,
Follow Thee beyond the sky:
Hear our prayers Thy grace imploring,
Lift our souls to Thee on high;

5 So when Thou again in glory
On the clouds of heaven shalt shine,
We Thy flock may stand before Thee,
Owned for evermore as Thine.

6 Hail! all hail! In Thee confiding,
Jesus, Thee shall all adore,
In Thy Father's might abiding
With one Spirit evermore.

Anon. (Latin, 6th or 7th cent.) Tr. Bishop James R. Woodford, 1852

The Advent

69 (STUTTGART) 8.7.8.7.

1 COME, Thou long-expected Jesus,
Born to set Thy people free;
From our fears and sins release us;
Let us find our rest in Thee.

2 Israel's Strength and Consolation,
Hope of all the earth Thou art;
Dear Desire of every nation,
Joy of every longing heart.

3 Born Thy people to deliver,
Born a child, and yet a King,
Born to reign in us for ever,
Now Thy gracious kingdom bring.

4 By Thine own eternal Spirit
Rule in all our hearts alone;
By Thine all-sufficient merit
Raise us to Thy glorious throne.

Rev. Charles Wesley, 1744

Jesus Christ Our Lord

70 ST. SAVIOUR C. M. Frederick G. Baker, 1876

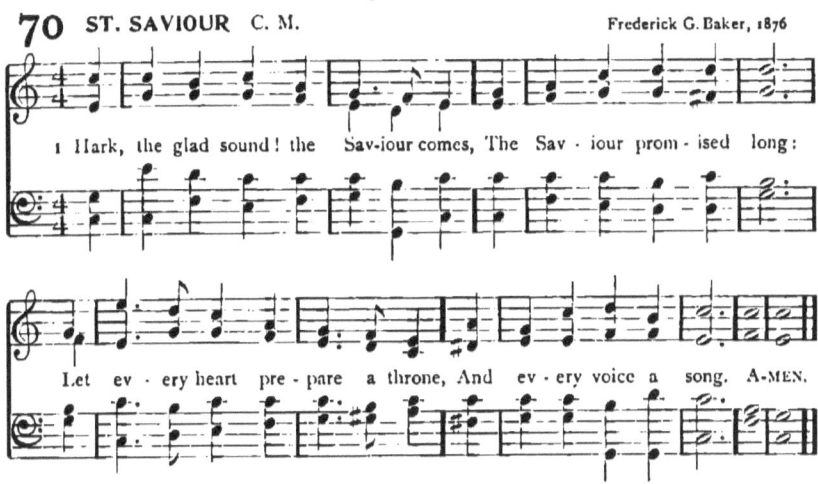

1 Hark, the glad sound! the Saviour comes, The Saviour promised long: Let every heart prepare a throne, And every voice a song. A-MEN.

2 On Him the Spirit, largely poured,
  Exerts its sacred fire;
  Wisdom and might, and zeal and love,
  His holy breast inspire.

3 He comes, the prisoners to release
  In Satan's bondage held;
  The gates of brass before Him burst,
  The iron fetters yield.

4 He comes, the broken heart to bind,
  The bleeding soul to cure;
  And with the treasures of His grace
  To enrich the humble poor.

5 Our glad hosannas, Prince of Peace,
  Thy welcome shall proclaim;
  And heaven's eternal arches ring
  With Thy belovèd Name.

Rev. Philip Doddridge, 1735

CANONBURY L. M. Arr. from Robert Schumann, 1839

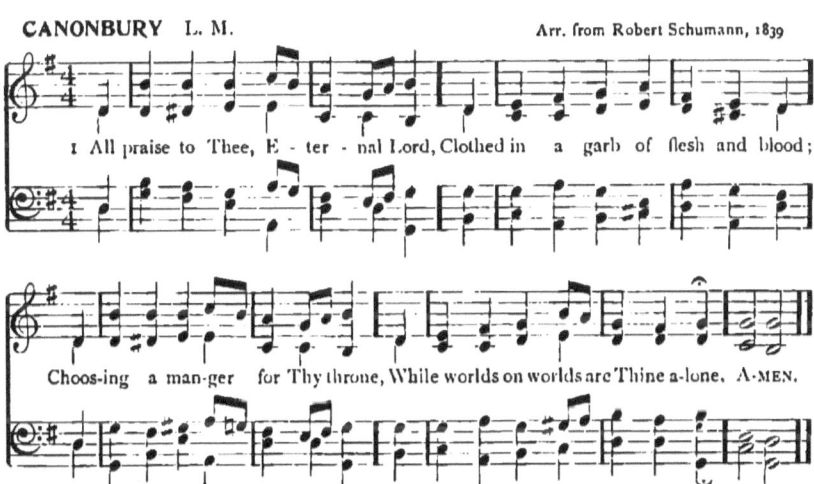

1 All praise to Thee, Eternal Lord, Clothed in a garb of flesh and blood; Choosing a manger for Thy throne, While worlds on worlds are Thine alone. A-MEN.

The Nativity

71 ANTIOCH C. M.
Arr. from George F. Handel, 1742

1 Joy to the world! the Lord is come: Let earth re-ceive her King; Let ev-ery heart pre-pare Him room, And heaven and na-ture sing, And heaven and na-ture sing, And heaven, and heaven and na-ture sing. A-MEN.

2 Joy to the earth! the Saviour reigns:
Let men their songs employ;
While fields and floods, rocks, hills,
and plains
Repeat the sounding joy.

3 No more let sins and sorrows grow,
Nor thorns infest the ground;
He comes to make His blessings flow
Far as the curse is found.

4 He rules the world with truth and grace,
And makes the nations prove
The glories of His righteousness,
And wonders of His love.

Rev. Isaac Watts, 1719

72 (CANONBURY) L. M.

1 ALL praise to Thee, Eternal Lord,
Clothed in a garb of flesh and blood;
Choosing a manger for Thy throne,
While worlds on worlds are Thine alone.

2 Once did the skies before Thee bow;
A Virgin's arms contain Thee now;
Angels who did in Thee rejoice
Now listen for Thine infant voice.

3 A little Child, Thou art our Guest,
That weary ones in Thee may rest;
Forlorn and lowly is Thy birth,
That we may rise to heaven from earth.

4 Thou comest in the darksome night
To make us children of the light,
To make us, in the realms Divine,
Like Thine own angels round Thee shine.

5 All this for us Thy love hath done;
By this to Thee our love is won:
For this we tune our cheerful lays,
And shout our thanks in ceaseless praise.

Martin Luther, 1524. Tr. Anon. Sabbath Hy. Bk. 1858

Jesus Christ our Lord

73 ADESTE FIDELES Irregular

1. O come, all ye faith - ful, Joy - ful and tri - um - phant,
2. God of . . . God, . . . Light . . of . . Light; . .
3. Sing, choirs of an - gels; Sing in ex - ult - a - tion,
4. Yea, Lord, we greet Thee, Born this hap - py morn - ing:

O come ye, O come ye to Beth - le - hem;
Lo, He ab - hors not the Vir - gin's womb:
Sing, all ye cit - i - zens of heaven a - bove;
Je - sus, to Thee . . . be glo - ry given;

Come and be - hold Him Born the King of an - gels; O come, let us a-dore Him,
Ver - y . . God, Be - got - ten, not cre - at - ed;
Glo - ry to God . . In . . the . high - est;
Word of the Fa - ther, Late in flesh ap-pear - ing;

O come, let us a-dore Him, O come, let us a - dore Him, Christ the Lord. A-MEN.

Anon. (Latin, 17th or 18th cent.) Tr. Rev. Frederick Oakeley, 1841; verse 1, ll. 1, 2, alt.

The Nativity

74 MENDELSSOHN 7.7.7.7. D.
Arr. from Mendelssohn, 1840
by William H. Cummings, 1850

1 Hark! the herald angels sing, "Glory to the new-born King; Peace on earth, and mercy mild, God and sinners reconciled!" Joyful, all ye nations, rise, Join the triumph of the skies; With the angelic host proclaim, "Christ is born in Bethlehem!" Hark! the herald angels sing, "Glory to the new-born King." A-MEN.

2 Christ, by highest heaven adored;
Christ, the Everlasting Lord!
Late in time behold Him come,
Offspring of the Virgin's womb:
Veiled in flesh the Godhead see;
Hail the Incarnate Deity,
Pleased as man with men to dwell,
Jesus, our Emmanuel.
　　Hark! the herald angels sing,
　　"Glory to the new-born King."

3 Hail, the heaven-born Prince of Peace!
Hail, the Sun of Righteousness!
Light and life to all He brings,
Risen with healing in His wings.
Mild He lays His glory by,
Born that man no more may die,
Born to raise the sons of earth,
Born to give them second birth.
　　Hark! the herald angels sing,
　　"Glory to the new-born King."

Rev. Charles Wesley, 1739; alt. G. Whitefield, 1753, M. Madan, 1760,
Suppl. to New Version, c. 1782, J. Kempthorne, 1810

Jesus Christ our Lord

75 CAROL C. M. D. Richard S. Willis, 1850

1. It came up-on the mid-night clear, That glo-rious song of old, From an-gels bend-ing near the earth To touch their harps of gold: "Peace on the earth, good will to men, From heaven's all-gra-cious King:" The world in sol-emn still-ness lay, To hear the an-gels sing. A-MEN.

2. Still through the clo-ven skies they come, With peace-ful wings un-furled, And still their heaven-ly mu-sic floats O'er all the wea-ry world: A-bove its sad and low-ly plains They bend on hov-ering wing, And ev-er o'er its Ba-bel-sounds The bless-ed an-gels sing.

3. And ye, beneath life's crushing load,
Whose forms are bending low,
Who toil along the climbing way
With painful steps and slow,—
Look now! for glad and golden hours
Come swiftly on the wing:
O rest beside the weary road,
And hear the angels sing.

4. For lo, the days are hastening on,
By prophet bards foretold,
When with the ever-circling years
Comes round the age of gold ;
When peace shall over all the earth
Its ancient splendors fling,
And the whole world give back the song
Which now the angels sing.

Rev. Edmund H. Sears, 1850

The Nativity

76 ST. LOUIS 8. 6. 8. 6. 7. 6. 8. 6.   Lewis H. Redner, 1868

1 O lit-tle town of Bethlehem, How still we see thee lie; Above thy deep and dream-less sleep The si-lent stars go by: Yet in thy dark streets shineth The ev-er-last-ing Light; The hopes and fears of all the years Are met in thee to-night. A-MEN.

2 For Christ is born of Mary;
  And gathered all above,
While mortals sleep, the angels keep
  Their watch of wondering love.
O morning stars, together
  Proclaim the holy birth;
And praises sing to God the King,
  And peace to men on earth.

3 How silently, how silently,
  The wondrous gift is given!
So God imparts to human hearts
  The blessings of His heaven.
No ear may hear His coming,
  But in this world of sin,
Where meek souls will receive Him still,
  The dear Christ enters in.

4 O holy Child of Bethlehem,
  Descend to us, we pray;
Cast out our sin, and enter in,
  Be born in us to-day.
We hear the Christmas angels
  The great glad tidings tell;
O come to us, abide with us,
  Our Lord Emmanuel.

                              Bishop Phillips Brooks, 1868

Jesus Christ our Lord

77 ANGEL CHOIR 8. 7. 8. 7. John H. Gower, 1895

1 Hark! what mean those ho-ly voi-ces, Sweet-ly warb-ling in the skies? Sure the an-gel-ic host re-joi-ces, Loud-est al-le-lu-ias rise. A-MEN.

Copyright, 1895, by The Trustees of The Presbyterian Board of Publication and Sabbath-School Work

2 Listen to the wondrous story,
   Which they chant in hymns of joy:
  " Glory in the highest, glory;
   Glory be to God Most High!

3 " Peace on earth, good-will from heaven,
   Reaching far as man is found;
   Souls redeemed, and sins forgiven;
   Loud our golden harps shall sound.

4 " Christ is born, the great Anointed;
   Heaven and earth His glory sing:
   Glad receive whom God appointed
   For your Prophet, Priest, and King.

5 " Hasten, mortals, to adore Him;
   Learn His Name, and taste His joy;
   Till in heaven you sing before Him,
   Glory be to God Most High!"

Rev. John Cawood, 1819

The Epiphany

78 (DIX) 7. 7. 7. 7. 7. 7.

1 AS with gladness men of old
  Did the guiding star behold;
  As with joy they hailed its light,
  Leading onward, beaming bright;
  So, most gracious God, may we
  Evermore be led to Thee.

2 As with joyful steps they sped
  To that lowly manger-bed,
  There to bend the knee before
  Him whom heaven and earth adore;
  So may we with willing feet
  Ever seek Thy mercy-seat.

3 As they offered gifts most rare
  At that manger rude and bare;
  So may we with holy joy,
  Pure, and free from sin's alloy,
  All our costliest treasures bring,
  Christ, to Thee, our heavenly King.

4 Holy Jesus, every day
  Keep us in the narrow way;
  And, when earthly things are past,
  Bring our ransomed souls at last
  Where they need no star to guide,
  Where no clouds Thy glory hide.

William C. Dix, 1861

The Life, Ministry, and Example

79 RHODES S. M.   C. Warwick Jordan, 1875

1 Did Christ o'er sinners weep, And shall our cheeks be dry? Let floods of penitential grief Burst forth from every eye. A-MEN.

2 The Son of God in tears
The wondering angels see:
Be thou astonished, O my soul;
He shed those tears for thee.

3 He wept that we might weep;
Each sin demands a tear;
In heaven alone no sin is found,
And there's no weeping there.
                      Rev. Benjamin Beddome, 1787

DIX 7. 7. 7. 7. 7. 7.   Arr. from Conrad Kocher, 1838

1 { As with gladness men of old Did the guiding star behold;
    As with joy they hailed its light, Leading onward, beaming bright; }
So, most gracious God, may we Evermore be led to Thee. A-MEN.

Jesus Christ our Lord

80 SILOAM C. M. *Isaac B. Woodbury, 1842*

1 What grace, O Lord, and beauty shone around Thy steps below;
What patient love was seen in all Thy life and death of woe. A-MEN.

2 For ever on Thy burdened heart
  A weight of sorrow hung;
  Yet no ungentle, murmuring word
  Escaped Thy silent tongue.

3 Thy foes might hate, despise, revile,
  Thy friends unfaithful prove;
  Unwearied in forgiveness still,
  Thy heart could only love.

4 O give us hearts to love like Thee
  Like Thee, O Lord, to grieve
  Far more for others' sins than all
  The wrongs that we receive.

5 One with Thyself, may every eye
  In us, Thy brethren, see
  That gentleness and grace that spring
  From union, Lord, with Thee.

Sir Edward Denny, Bart., 1839

81 (SILOAM) C. M.

1 LORD, Thou in all things like was't
    made
  To us, yet free from sin;
  Then how unlike to us, O Lord,
  Replies the voice within.

2 Our faith is weak; O Light of Light,
  Clear Thou our clouded view;
  That Son of Man, and Son of God,
  We give Thee honor due.

3 O Son of Man, Thyself hast proved
  Our trials and our tears;
  Life's thankless toil and scant repose,
  Death's agonies and fears.

4 O Son of God, in glory raised,
  Thou sittest on Thy throne:
  Thence, by Thy pleadings and Thy
    grace,
  Still succoring Thine own.

5 Brother and Saviour, Friend and Judge!
  To Thee, O Christ, be given
  To bind upon Thy crown the names
  Most blest in earth and heaven.

Joseph Anstice, 1836; verse 1, ll. 1, 3, alt.

The Life, Ministry, and Example

82 GREEN HILL C. M.   Albert L. Peace, 1885

1 Lord, as to Thy dear cross we flee, And plead to be for-given,
So let Thy life our pat-tern be, And form our souls for heaven. A-MEN.

2 Help us, through good report and ill,
    Our daily cross to bear ;
  Like Thee, to do our Father's will,
    Our brethren's griefs to share.

3 Let grace our selfishness expel,
    Our earthliness refine ;
  And kindness in our bosoms dwell,
    As free and true as Thine.

4 Should friends misjudge, or foes defame,
    Or brethren faithless prove,
  Then, like Thine own, be all our aim
    To conquer them by love.

5 Kept peaceful in the midst of strife,
    Forgiving and forgiven,
  O may we lead the pilgrim's life,
    And follow Thee to heaven.

Rev. John H. Gurney, 1838

83 (GREEN HILL) C. M.

1 O MEAN may seem this house of clay,
    Yet 'twas the Lord's abode ;
  Our feet may mourn this thorny way,
    Yet here Emmanuel trod.

2 This fleshly robe the Lord did wear,
    This watch the Lord did keep,
  These burdens sore the Lord did bear,
    These tears the Lord did weep.

3 Our very frailty brings us near
    Unto the Lord of heaven ;
  To every grief, to every tear,
    Such glory strange is given.

4 But not this fleshly robe alone
    Shall link us, Lord, to Thee ;
  Not only in the tear and groan
    Shall the dear kindred be.

5 We shall be reckoned for Thine own
    Because Thy heaven we share,
  Because we sing around Thy throne,
    And Thy bright raiment wear.

6 O mighty grace, our life to live,
    To make our earth Divine ;
  O mighty grace, Thy heaven to give,
    And lift our life to Thine.

Thomas H. Gill, 1850

Jesus Christ our Lord

84 FEDERAL STREET L. M. Henry K. Oliver, 1832

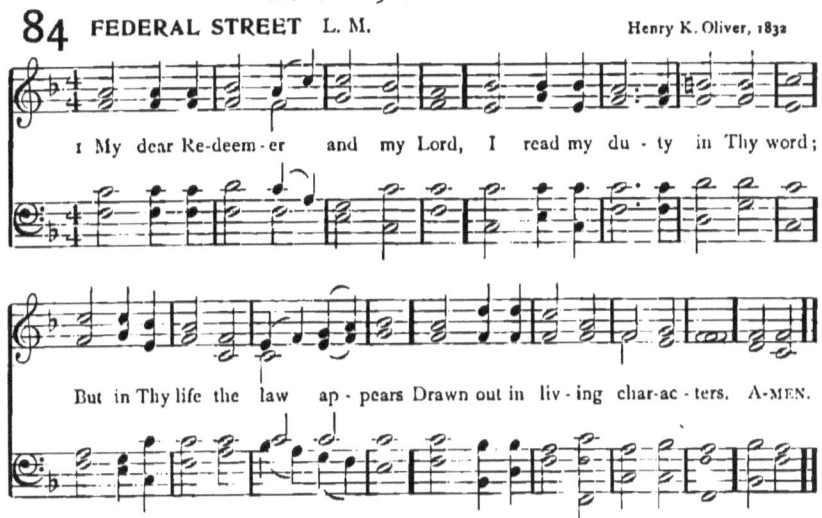

1 My dear Redeemer and my Lord, I read my duty in Thy word;
But in Thy life the law appears Drawn out in living characters. A-MEN.

2 Such was Thy truth, and such Thy zeal,
Such deference to Thy Father's will,
Such love, and meekness so Divine,
I would transcribe and make them mine.

3 Cold mountains and the midnight air
Witnessed the fervor of Thy prayer;
The desert Thy temptations knew,
Thy conflict and Thy victory too.

4 Be Thou my Pattern; make me bear
More of Thy gracious image here:
Then God the Judge shall own my name
Amongst the followers of the Lamb.

Rev. Isaac Watts, 1709

SAXBY L. M. Rev. Timothy R. Matthews (1826–)

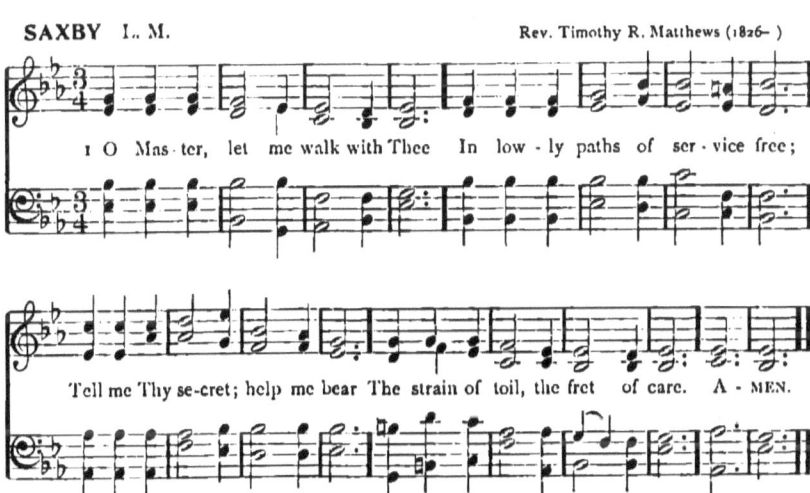

1 O Master, let me walk with Thee In lowly paths of service free;
Tell me Thy secret; help me bear The strain of toil, the fret of care. A-MEN.

The Life, Ministry, and Example

85 ARLINGTON C. M.
Arr. from Thomas A. Arne, 1762

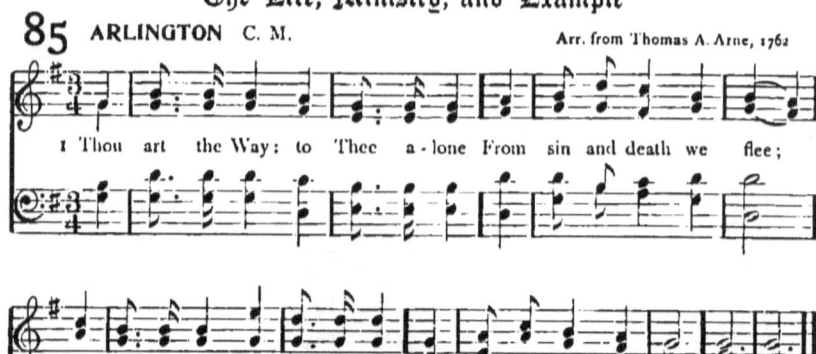

1 Thou art the Way: to Thee alone
From sin and death we flee;
And he who would the Father seek
Must seek Him, Lord, by Thee. A-MEN.

2 Thou art the Truth: Thy word alone
True wisdom can impart;
Thou only canst inform the mind,
And purify the heart.

3 Thou art the Life: the rending tomb
Proclaims Thy conquering arm,
And those who put their trust in Thee
Nor death nor hell shall harm.

4 Thou art the Way, the Truth, the Life:
Grant us that Way to know,
That Truth to keep, that Life to win,
Whose joys eternal flow.

Bishop George W. Doane, 1824

86 (SAXBY) L. M.

1 O MASTER, let me walk with Thee
In lowly paths of service free;
Tell me Thy secret; help me bear
The strain of toil, the fret of care.

2 Help me the slow of heart to move
By some clear winning word of love;
Teach me the wayward feet to stay,
And guide them in the homeward way.

3 Teach me Thy patience; still with Thee
In closer, dearer company,
In work that keeps faith sweet and strong,
In trust that triumphs over wrong;

4 In hope that sends a shining ray
Far down the future's broadening way;
In peace that only Thou canst give,
With Thee, O Master, let me live.

Rev. Washington Gladden, 1879

Jesus Christ our Lord

87 STAINCLIFFE L. M.   Robert W. Dixon, 1875

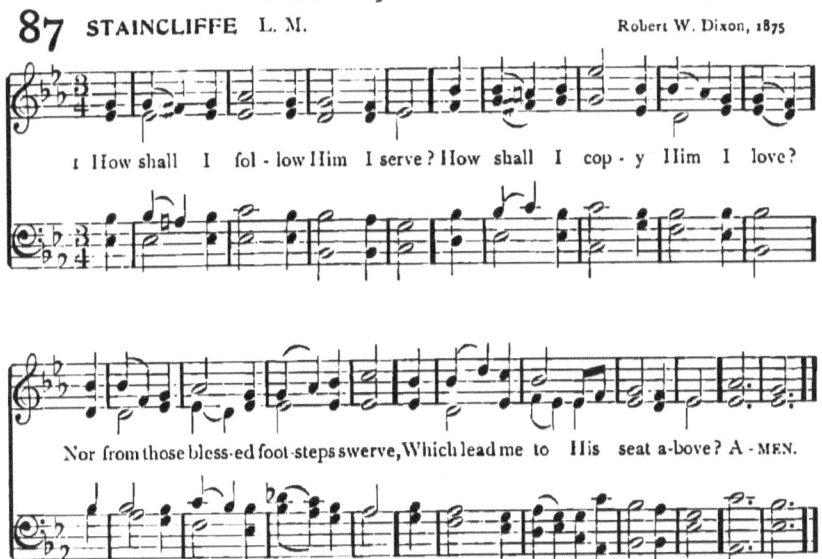

1 How shall I follow Him I serve? How shall I copy Him I love? Nor from those blessed foot-steps swerve, Which lead me to His seat above? A-MEN.

2 Privations, sorrows, bitter scorn,
The life of toil, the mean abode,
The faithless kiss, the crown of thorn,—
Are these the consecrated road?

3 'Twas thus He suffered, though a Son,
Foreknowing, choosing, feeling all,
Until the perfect work was done,
And drunk the bitter cup of gall.

4 Lord, should my path through suffering lie,
Forbid it I should e'er repine;
Still let me turn to Calvary,
Nor heed my griefs, remembering Thine.

                                Josiah Conder, 1824, 1836

88 (STAINCLIFFE) L. M.

1 BEHOLD, the Master passeth by!
O seest thou not His pleading eye?
With low sad voice He calleth thee,
"Leave this vain world, and follow Me."

2 O soul, bowed down with harrowing care,
Hast thou no thought for heaven to spare?
From earthly toils lift up thine eye;
Behold, the Master passeth by!

3 One heard Him calling long ago,
And straightway left all things below,
Counting his earthly gain as loss
For Jesus and His blessèd cross.

4 That "Follow Me" his faithful ear
Seemed every day afresh to hear:
Its echoes stirred his spirit still,
And fired his hope, and nerved his will.

5 God gently calls us every day;
Why should we then our bliss delay?
Thou, Lord, e'en now art calling me;
I will leave all, and follow Thee.

                  Bishop William W. How (verses 4, 5, alt. from Bishop Ken, publ. 1721) 1871

The Passion and Crucifixion

89 GERHARDT 7.6.7.6. D. Joseph P. Holbrook, 1862

1. O sa-cred Head, now wound-ed, With grief and shame weighed down;
2. O no-blest brow and dear-est, In oth er days the world

Now scorn-ful-ly sur-round-ed With thorns, Thine on-ly crown:
All feared when Thou ap-pear-edst; What shame on Thee is hurled!

O sa-cred Head, what glo-ry, What bliss till now was Thine!
How art Thou pale with an-guish, With sore a-buse and scorn;

Yet, though de-spised and go-ry, I joy to call Thee mine. A-MEN.
How does that vis-age lan-guish Which once was bright as morn!

3. What Thou, my Lord, hast suffered
Was all for sinners' gain :
Mine, mine was the transgression,
But Thine the deadly pain.
Lo, here I fall, my Saviour !
'Tis I deserve Thy place ;
Look on me with Thy favor,
Vouchsafe to me Thy grace.

4. What language shall I borrow
To thank Thee, dearest Friend,
For this Thy dying sorrow,
Thy pity without end ?
O make me Thine for ever ;
And should I fainting be,
Lord, let me never, never
Outlive my love to Thee.

Ascribed to Bernard of Clairvaux (1091–1153). Tr. Rev. Paul
Gerhardt, 1656. Tr. Rev. James W. Alexander, 1830

Jesus Christ our Lord

90 HAMBURG L. M.   Arr. from a Gregorian Chant, by Lowell Mason, 1824

1 When I sur-vey the won-drous cross On which the Prince of glo-ry died, My rich-est gain I count but loss, And pour contempt on all my pride. A-MEN.

2 Forbid it, Lord, that I should boast,
  Save in the death of Christ my God:
  All the vain things that charm me most,
  I sacrifice them to His blood.

3 See, from His head, His hands, His feet,
  Sorrow and love flow mingled down:

Did e'er such love and sorrow meet,
Or thorns compose so rich a crown?

4 Were the whole realm of nature mine,
  That were a present far too small;
  Love so amazing, so Divine,
  Demands my soul, my life, my all.
              Rev. Isaac Watts, 1707

ZEPHYR L. M.   William B. Bradbury, 1844

1 'Tis midnight; and on Ol-ive's brow The star is dimmed that late-ly shone: 'Tis midnight; in the gar-den, now, The suffering Saviour prays a-lone. A-MEN.

The Passion and Crucifixion

91 AJALON 7.7.7.7.7.7.   Richard Redhead, 1853

1 Go to dark Gethsemane,
  Ye that feel the tempter's power;
  Your Redeemer's conflict see;
  Watch with Him one bitter hour:
  Turn not from His griefs away;
  Learn of Jesus Christ to pray. A-MEN.

2 Follow to the judgment-hall;
  View the Lord of life arraigned.
  O the wormwood and the gall!
  O the pangs His soul sustained!
  Shun not suffering, shame, or loss;
  Learn of Him to bear the cross.

3 Calvary's mournful mountain climb;
  There, adoring at His feet,
  Mark that miracle of time,
  God's own sacrifice complete:
  "It is finished!"—hear the cry;
  Learn of Jesus Christ to die.

4 Early hasten to the tomb
  Where they laid His breathless clay:
  All is solitude and gloom;
  Who hath taken Him away?
  Christ is risen! He meets our eyes.
  Saviour, teach us so to rise.

James Montgomery, 1820 (text of 1853)

92 (ZEPHYR) L. M.

1 'TIS midnight; and on Olive's brow
  The star is dimmed that lately shone:
  'Tis midnight; in the garden, now,
  The suffering Saviour prays alone.

2 'Tis midnight; and, from all removed,
  Emmanuel wrestles lone with fears:
  E'en the disciple that He loved
  Heeds not his Master's grief and tears.

3 'Tis midnight; and, for others' guilt,
  The Man of Sorrows weeps in blood:
  Yet He that hath in anguish knelt
  Is not forsaken by His God.

4 'Tis midnight; from the heavenly plains
  Is borne the song that angels know:
  Unheard by mortals are the strains
  That sweetly soothe the Saviour's woe.

William B. Tappan, 1822

Jesus Christ our Lord

93 RATHBUN 8.7.8.7. — Ithamar Conkey, 1851

1 In the cross of Christ I glory, Tow-er-ing o'er the wrecks of time; All the light of sa-cred sto-ry Gath-ers round its head sub-lime. A-MEN.

2 When the woes of life o'ertake me,
  Hopes deceive, and fears annoy,
  Never shall the cross forsake me:
  Lo! it glows with peace and joy.

3 When the sun of bliss is beaming
  Light and love upon my way,
  From the cross the radiance streaming
  Adds more lustre to the day.

4 Bane and blessing, pain and pleasure,
  By the cross are sanctified;
  Peace is there that knows no measure,
  Joys that through all time abide.

5 In the cross of Christ I glory,
  Towering o'er the wrecks of time;
  All the light of sacred story
  Gathers round its head sublime.

Sir John Bowring, 1825

DORRNANCE 8.7.8.7. — Isaac B. Woodbury, 1848

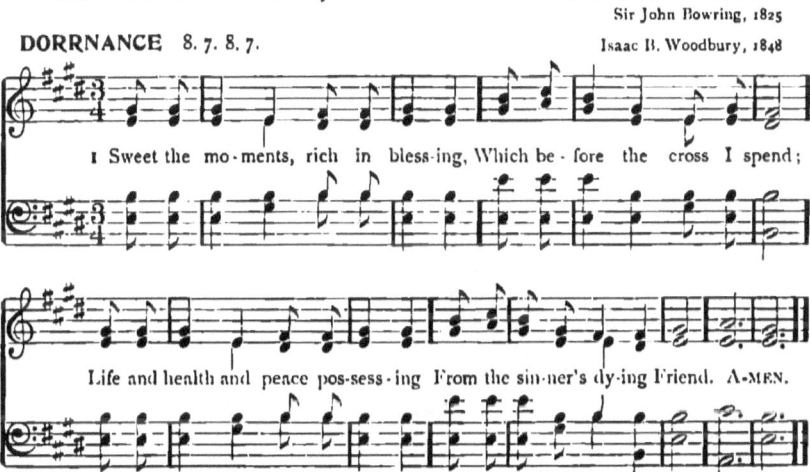

1 Sweet the mo-ments, rich in bless-ing, Which be-fore the cross I spend; Life and health and peace pos-sess-ing From the sin-ner's dy-ing Friend. A-MEN.

The Passion and Crucifixion

94 ZION S. 7. 8. 7. 4. 7. — Thomas Hastings, 1830

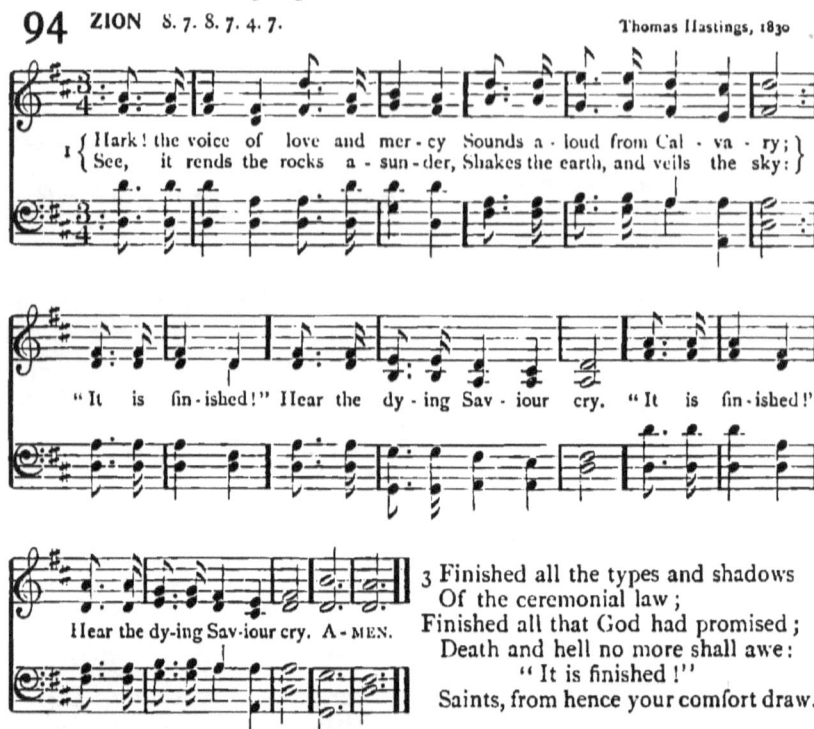

1 Hark! the voice of love and mercy Sounds aloud from Calvary;
See, it rends the rocks asunder, Shakes the earth, and veils the sky:
"It is finished!" Hear the dying Saviour cry. "It is finished!"
Hear the dying Saviour cry. A-MEN.

2 "It is finished!"—O what pleasure
Do these precious words afford;
Heavenly blessings, without measure,
Flow to us from Christ the Lord:
"It is finished!"
Saints, the dying words record.

3 Finished all the types and shadows
Of the ceremonial law;
Finished all that God had promised;
Death and hell no more shall awe:
"It is finished!"
Saints, from hence your comfort draw.

4 Tune your harps anew, ye seraphs,
Join to sing the pleasing theme;
All in earth, and all in heaven,
Join to praise Emmanuel's Name:
Alleluia!
Glory to the bleeding Lamb.

Rev. Jonathan Evans, 1784

95 (DORRNANCE) S. 7. 8. 7.

1 SWEET the moments, rich in blessing,
Which before the cross I spend;
Life and health and peace possessing
From the sinner's dying Friend.

2 Here I'll sit, for ever viewing
Mercy's streams in streams of blood;
Precious drops, my soul bedewing,
Plead and claim my peace with God.

3 Truly blessèd is this station,
Low before His cross to lie,
While I see Divine compassion
Pleading in His languid eye.

4 Love and grief my heart dividing,
With my tears His feet I'll bathe;
Constant still in faith abiding,
Life deriving from His death.

Rev. Walter Shirley, 1770 (based on Rev. James Allen, 1757): verse 3, l. 4, alt.

Jesus Christ our Lord

96 HORSLEY C. M. William Horsley, 1844

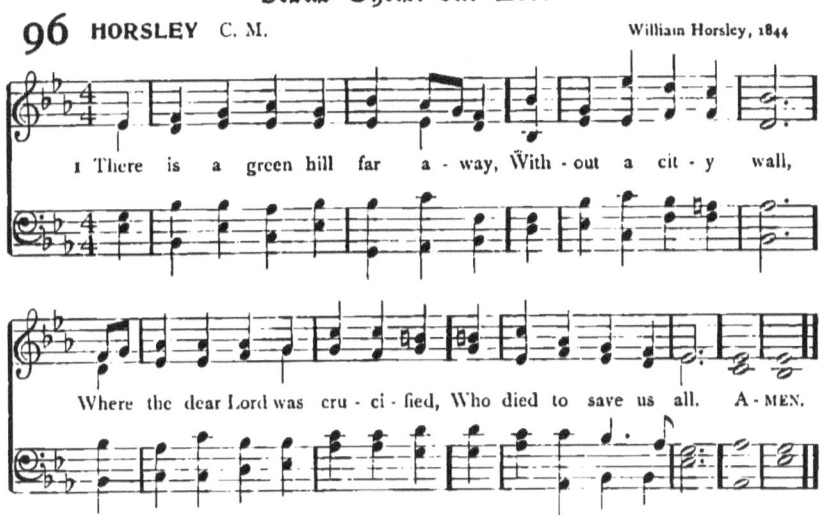

1 There is a green hill far a-way, With-out a cit-y wall, Where the dear Lord was cru-ci-fied, Who died to save us all. A-MEN.

2 We may not know, we cannot tell,
  What pains He had to bear;
  But we believe it was for us
  He hung and suffered there.

3 He died that we might be forgiven,
  He died to make us good,
  That we might go at last to heaven,
  Saved by His precious blood.

4 There was no other good enough
  To pay the price of sin;
  He only could unlock the gate
  Of heaven, and let us in.

5 O dearly, dearly has He loved,
  And we must love Him too,
  And trust in His redeeming blood,
  And try His works to do.

Cecil F. Alexander, 1848

MEDITATION C. M. John H. Gower, 1890

1 There is a green hill far a-way, With-out a cit-y wall, Where the dear Lord was cru-ci-fied, Who died to save us all. A-MEN.

Copyright by John H. Gower

The Passion and Crucifixion

97 ST. CHRISTOPHER 7.6.8.6.8.6.8.6. Frederick C. Maker, 1881

1 Beneath the cross of Jesus I fain would take my stand,
The shadow of a mighty Rock Within a weary land;
A home within the wilderness, A rest upon the way,
From the burning of the noon-tide heat, And the burden of the day. A-MEN.

2 Upon that cross of Jesus
  Mine eye at times can see
The very dying form of One
  Who suffered there for me:
And from my smitten heart with tears
  Two wonders I confess,—
The wonders of His glorious love
  And my own worthlessness.

3 I take, O cross, thy shadow
  For my abiding-place:
I ask no other sunshine than
  The sunshine of His face;
Content to let the world go by,
  To know no gain nor loss,
My sinful self my only shame,
  My glory all the cross.

        Elizabeth C. Clephane, publ. 1872

Jesus Christ our Lord

98 MARTYRDOM C. M. Hugh Wilson, c. 1825

1 Alas! and did my Saviour bleed, And did my Sovereign die! Would He devote that sacred head For such a worm as I! AMEN.

2 Was it for crimes that I had done
He groaned upon the tree!
Amazing pity! Grace unknown!
And love beyond degree!

3 Well might the sun in darkness hide,
And shut his glories in,
When He, the mighty Maker, died
For man the creature's sin.

4 Thus might I hide my blushing face
While His dear cross appears;
Dissolve my heart in thankfulness,
And melt my eyes to tears.

5 But drops of grief can ne'er repay
The debt of love I owe;
Here, Lord, I give myself away,
'Tis all that I can do.

Rev. Isaac Watts, 1707: verse 3, l. 3, alt.

The Resurrection

99 (WIRTEMBURG) 7. 7. 7. 7. with Alleluia

1 CHRIST the Lord is risen again;
Christ hath broken every chain:
Hark, angelic voices cry,
Singing evermore on high, Alleluia!

2 He who gave for us His life,
Who for us endured the strife,
Is our Paschal Lamb to-day;
We too sing for joy, and say, Alleluia!

3 He who bore all pain and loss
Comfortless upon the Cross,
Lives in glory now on high,
Pleads for us and hears our cry; Alleluia!

4 He who slumbered in the grave,
Is exalted now to save;
Now through Christendom it rings
That the Lamb is King of kings. Alleluia!

5 Now he bids us tell abroad
How the lost may be restored,
How the penitent forgiven, [luia!
How we too may enter heaven. Alle-

6 Thou our Paschal Lamb indeed,
Christ, to-day Thy people feed;
Take our sins and guilt away,
That we all may sing for aye, Alleluia!

Rev. Michael Weisse, 1531. Tr. Catherine Winkworth, 1858; verse 1, l. 3, alt.

The Resurrection

100 UNIVERSITY COLLEGE 7. 7. 7. 7. Henry J. Gauntlett, 1848

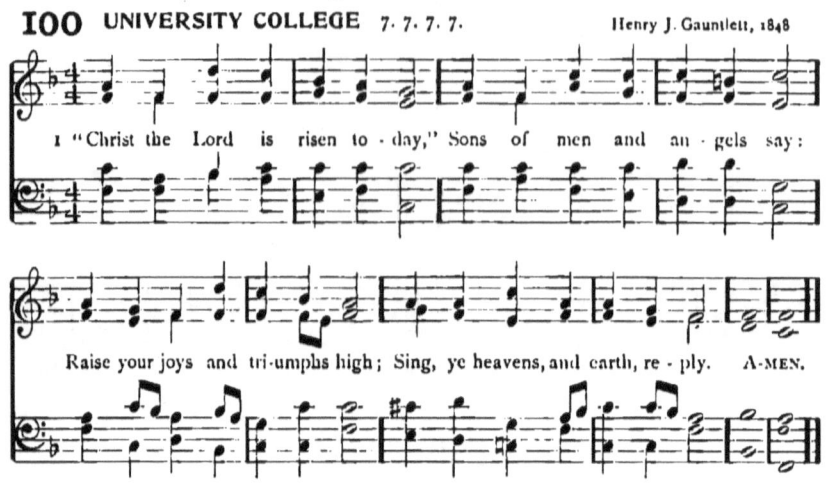

1 "Christ the Lord is risen to-day," Sons of men and an-gels say: Raise your joys and tri-umphs high; Sing, ye heavens, and earth, re-ply. A-MEN.

2 Vain the stone, the watch, the seal;
Christ has burst the gates of hell:
Death in vain forbids His rise;
Christ has opened Paradise.

3 Lives again our glorious King:
Where, O death, is now thy sting?
Once He died, our souls to save:
Where thy victory, O grave?

4 Soar we now where Christ has led,
Following our exalted Head:
Made like Him, like Him we rise;
Ours the cross, the grave, the skies.

5 Hail the Lord of earth and heaven!
Praise to Thee by both be given:
Thee we greet triumphant now:
Hail, the Resurrection Thou!

Rev. Charles Wesley, 1739; verse 3, l. 3, alt.

WIRTEMBURG 7. 7. 7. 7. with Alleluia Hundert Geistliche Arien, Dresden, 1694

1 Christ the Lord is risen a-gain; Christ hath broken ev-ery chain: Hark, an-gel-ic voi-ces cry, Sing-ing ev-er-more on high, Al-le-lu-ia! A-MEN.

Jesus Christ our Lord

101 HOLY CROSS C. M. Arr. by James C. Wade, 1865

1 I say to all men, far and near, That He is risen a-gain; That He is with us now and here, And ev-er shall re-main. A-MEN.

2 And what I say, let each this morn
  Go tell it to his friend,
  That soon in every place shall dawn
  His kingdom without end.

3 Now first to souls who thus awake
  Seems earth a fatherland;
  A new and endless life they take
  With rapture from His hand.

4 The fears of death and of the grave
  Are whelmed beneath the sea,
  And every heart, now light and brave,
  May face the things to be.

5 The way of darkness that He trod
  To heaven at last shall come,
  And he who hearkens to His word
  Shall reach His father's home.

G. F. P. von Hardenberg, 1802: tr. Catherine Winkworth, 1858

NARENZA S. M. Old German Chorale;
Arr. by Rev. Wm. H. Havergal, 1849

1 Be-yond the star-ry skies, Far as the e-ter-nal hills, There, in the bound-less world of light, Our great Re-deem-er dwells. A-MEN.

The Resurrection

102 WAREHAM L. M. — William Knapp, 1738

1 Lift up, lift up your voices now;
The whole wide world rejoices now:
The Lord hath triumphed gloriously,
The Lord shall reign victoriously. A-MEN.

2 In vain with stone the cave they barred;
In vain the watch kept ward and guard:
Majestic from the spoilèd tomb,
In pomp of triumph Christ is come.

3 He binds in chains the ancient foe;
A countless host He frees from woe,
And heaven's high portal open flies,
For Christ has risen, and man shall rise.

4 And all He did, and all He bare,
He gives us as our own to share;
And hope and joy and peace begin,
For Christ has won, and man shall win.

5 O Victor, aid us in the fight,
And lead through death to realms of light:
We safely pass where Thou hast trod,
In Thee we die to rise to God.

6 Thy flock, from sin and death set free,
Glad alleluias raise to Thee;
And ever with the heavenly host
Praise Father, Son, and Holy Ghost.

Cento, based on Rev. John M. Neale, 1854

103 (NARENZA) S. M.

1 BEYOND the starry skies,
Far as the eternal hills,
There, in the boundless world of light,
Our great Redeemer dwells.

2 Around Him angels fair,
In countless armies, shine;
And ever, in exalted lays,
They offer songs Divine.

3 "Hail, Prince of life!" they cry,
"Whose unexampled love
Moved Thee to quit these glorious realms
And royalties above."

4 And when He stooped to earth,
And suffered rude disdain,
They cast their honors at His feet,
And waited in His train.

5 They saw Him on the cross,
While darkness veiled the skies,
And when He burst the gates of death,
They saw the Conqueror rise.

6 They thronged His chariot-wheels,
And bore Him to His throne;
Then swept their golden harps, and sang,
"The glorious work is done."

Cento, based on Rev. James Fanch, 1776, and Rev. Daniel Turner, 1794

Jesus Christ our Lord

104 LANCASHIRE 7. 6. 7. 6. D. Henry Smart, 1836

1. The day of res-ur-rec-tion! Earth, tell it out a-broad;
The Pass-o-ver of glad-ness, The Pass-o-ver of God.
From death to life e-ter-nal, From this world to the sky,
Our Christ hath brought us o-ver, With hymns of vic-to-ry. A-MEN.

2 Our hearts be pure from evil,
   That we may see aright
The Lord in rays eternal
   Of resurrection-light;
And, listening to His accents,
   May hear, so calm and plain,
His own "All hail!" and hearing,
   May raise the victor-strain.

3 Now let the heavens be joyful
   Let earth her song begin;
Let the round world keep triumph,
   And all that is therein;
Invisible and visible,
   Their notes let all things blend,
For Christ the Lord hath risen,
   Our Joy that hath no end.

John of Damascus (8th cent.). Tr. Rev. John M. Neale, 1862: verse 1, l. 1, alt.

The Ascension

105 HERMAS 6.5.6.5. 121. *Frances R. Havergal, 1871*

1 Golden harps are sounding, Angel voices ring, Pearly gates are opened, Opened for the King: Christ, the King of Glory, Jesus, King of love, Is gone up in triumph To His throne above. *Refrain.* All His work is ended, Joyfully we sing; Jesus hath ascended: Glory to our King! A-MEN.

2 He who came to save us,
   He who bled and died,
 Now is crowned with glory
   At His Father's side.
 Never more to suffer,
   Never more to die,
 Jesus, King of Glory,
   Is gone up on high.—REF.

3 Praying for His children
   In that blessèd place,
 Calling them to glory,
   Sending them His grace;
 His bright home preparing,
   Faithful ones, for you;
 Jesus ever liveth,
   Ever loveth too.—REF.

Frances R. Havergal, 1871

Jesus Christ our Lord

106 MERIBAH 8.8.6.8.8.6. Lowell Mason, 1839

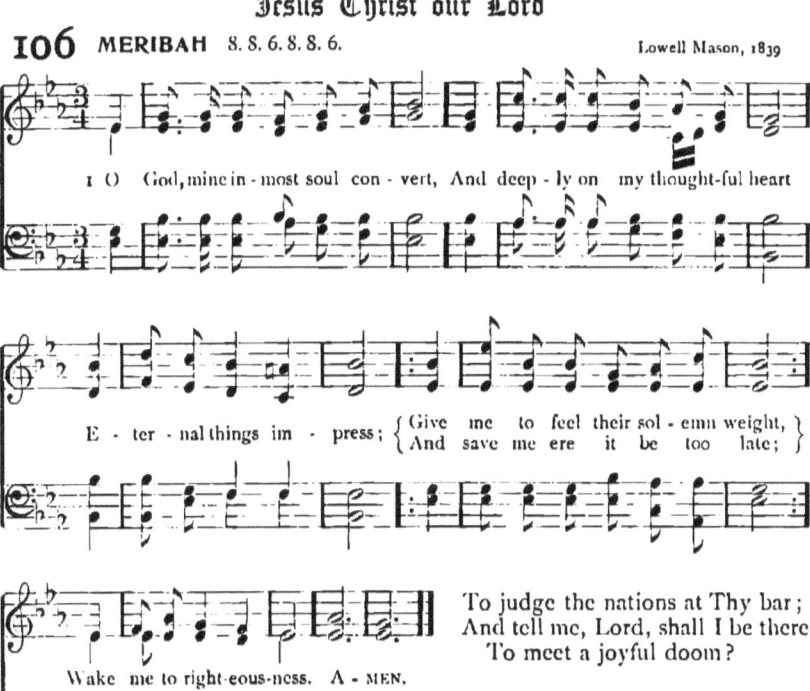

1 O God, mine inmost soul convert,
And deeply on my thoughtful heart
Eternal things impress;
Give me to feel their solemn weight,
And save me ere it be too late;
Wake me to righteousness. A-MEN.

2 Before me place in dread array
The pomp of that tremendous day,
When Thou with clouds shalt come
To judge the nations at Thy bar;
And tell me, Lord, shall I be there
To meet a joyful doom?

3 Then, Saviour, then my soul receive,
Transported from the vale, to live
And reign with Thee above,
Where faith is sweetly lost in sight,
And hope in full, supreme delight,
And everlasting love.

Rev. Charles Wesley, 1749: verse 1, ll. 5, 6, alt.

107 (EAGLEY) C. M.

1 LIGHT of the lonely pilgrim's heart,
Star of the coming day,
Arise, and with Thy morning beams
Chase all our griefs away.

2 Come, blessèd Lord, bid every shore
And answering island sing
The praises of Thy royal Name,
And own Thee as their King.

3 Lord, Lord, Thy fair creation groans,
The air, the earth, the sea,
In unison with all our hearts,
And calls aloud for Thee.

4 Come, then, with all Thy quickening power,
With one awakening smile,
And bid the serpent's trail no more
Thy beauteous realms defile.

5 Thine was the cross, with all its fruits
Of grace and peace Divine:
Be Thine the crown of glory now,
The palm of victory Thine.

Sir Edward Denny, Bart., 1842

The Second Coming and Judgment

108 BROCKLESBURY 8. 7. 8. 7.　　　Charlotte A. Barnard (1830–1869)

1 Light of those whose dreary dwelling Borders on the shades of death, Come, and by Thy love's revealing, Dissipate the clouds beneath. A-MEN.

2 Still we wait for Thine appearing;
　Life and joy Thy beams impart,
Chasing all our fears, and cheering
　Every poor benighted heart.

3 Come and manifest the favor
　God hath for our ransomed race;
Come, Thou glorious God and Saviour,
　Come and bring the gospel grace.

4 Save us in Thy great compassion,
　O Thou mild, pacific Prince;
Give the knowledge of salvation,
　Give the pardon of our sins.

5 By Thine all-restoring merit
　Every burdened soul release;
Every weary, wandering spirit
　Guide into Thy perfect peace.

Rev. Charles Wesley, 1744: verse 3, l. 3, alt.

EAGLEY C. M.　　　James Walch, 1860

1 Light of the lonely pilgrim's heart, Star of the coming day, Arise, and with Thy morning beams Chase all our griefs away. A-MEN.

Jesus Christ Our Lord

109 GREENLAND 7.6.7.6.D.   Arr. from Michael Haydn (1737-1806)

1 Rejoice, all ye believers, And let your lights appear;
The evening is advancing, And darker night is near:
The Bridegroom is arising, And soon He draweth nigh;
Up, pray, and watch, and wrestle: At midnight comes the cry. A-MEN.

2 See that your lamps are burning;
  Replenish them with oil;
And wait for your salvation,
  The end of earthly toil.
The watchers on the mountain
  Proclaim the Bridegroom near,
Go meet Him as He cometh,
  With alleluias clear.

3 Our Hope and Expectation,
  O Jesus, now appear;
Arise, Thou Sun so longed for,
  O'er this benighted sphere.
With hearts and hands uplifted,
  We plead, O Lord, to see
The day of earth's redemption
  That brings us unto Thee.

Laurentius Laurenti, 1700. Tr. Sarah B. Findlater, 1854

The Second Coming and Judgment

110 LANGTON S. M. *Charlotte S. Streatfeild, 1874*

1 Come, Lord, and tarry not; Bring the long-looked-for day;

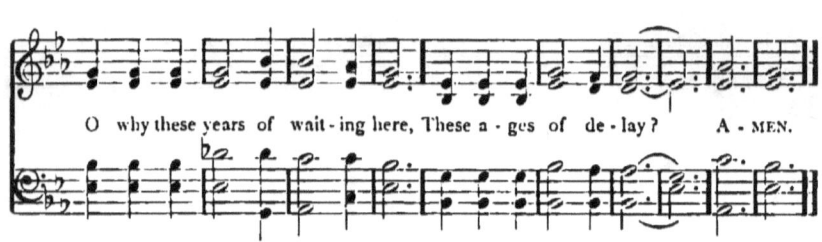

O why these years of waiting here, These ages of delay? A-MEN.

2 Come, for Thy saints still wait;
  Daily ascends their sigh:
The Spirit and the Bride say,"Come":
  Dost Thou not hear the cry?

3 Come, for creation groans,
  Impatient of Thy stay,
Worn out with these long years of ill,
  These ages of delay.

4 Come, and make all things new;
  Build up this ruined earth;
Restore our faded Paradise,
  Creation's second birth.

5 Come, and begin Thy reign
  Of everlasting peace;
Come, take the kingdom to Thyself,
  Great King of Righteousness.

Rev. Horatius Bonar, 1846

The Holy Ghost: Invocation and Praise

111 (LANGTON) S. M.

1 COME, Holy Spirit, come,
  Let Thy bright beams arise;
Dispel the darkness from our minds,
  And open all our eyes.

2 Cheer our desponding hearts,
  Thou heavenly Paraclete;
Give us to lie with humble hope
  At our Redeemer's feet.

3 Revive our drooping faith,
  Our doubts and fears remove,
And kindle in our breasts the flame
  Of never-dying love.

4 Convince us of our sin,
  Then lead to Jesus' blood,
And to our wondering view reveal
  The secret love of God.

5 'Tis Thine to cleanse the heart,
  To sanctify the soul,
To pour fresh life on every part,
  And new-create the whole.

6 Dwell therefore in our hearts,
  Our minds from bondage free;
Then we shall know, and praise, and
  The Father, Son, and Thee. [love

Rev. Joseph Hart, 1759

The Holy Ghost

112 SAXBY L. M.   Rev. Timothy R. Matthews (1826–)

1 Come, gracious Spirit, heavenly Dove, With light and comfort from above; Be Thou our Guardian, Thou our Guide; O'er every thought and step preside. A-MEN.

2 The light of truth to us display,
And make us know and choose Thy way:
Plant holy fear in every heart,
That we from God may ne'er depart.

3 Lead us to holiness, the road
Which we must take to dwell with God:

Lead us to Christ, the living Way,
Nor let us from His pastures stray.

4 Lead us to God, our final rest,
To be with Him for ever blest:
Lead us to heaven, that we may share
Fulness of joy for ever there.

Rev. Simon Browne, 1720: alt. Ash and Evans Coll. 1769, and elsewhere

FEDERAL STREET L. M.   Henry K. Oliver, 1832

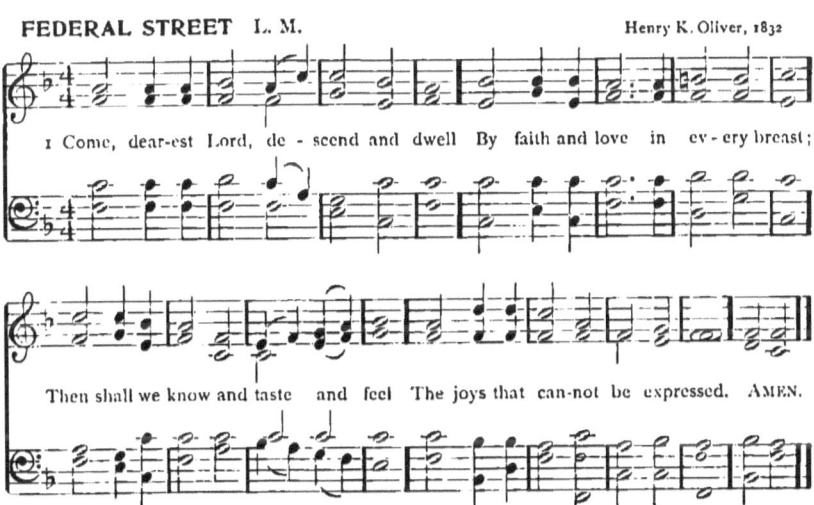

1 Come, dearest Lord, descend and dwell By faith and love in every breast; Then shall we know and taste and feel The joys that cannot be expressed. AMEN.

Invocation and Praise

113 FAITHFUL GUIDE 7.7.7.7. D. Marcus M. Wells, 1858

1. Holy Spirit, faithful Guide,
Ever near the Christian's side,
Gently lead us by the hand,
Pilgrims in a desert land:
Weary souls for e'er rejoice,
While they hear that sweetest voice
Whispering softly, "Wanderer, come!
Follow Me, I'll guide thee home."

2. Ever present, truest Friend,
Ever near Thine aid to lend,
Leave us not to doubt and fear,
Groping on in darkness drear:
When the storms are raging sore,
Hearts grow faint, and hopes give o'er,
Whisper softly, "Wanderer, come!
Follow Me, I'll guide thee home."

3. When our days of toil shall cease,
Waiting still for sweet release,
Nothing left but heaven and prayer,
Wondering if our names are there,
Wading deep the dismal flood,
Pleading naught but Jesus' blood,—
Whisper softly, "Wanderer, come!
Follow Me, I'll guide thee home."

Marcus M. Wells, 1858

114 (FEDERAL STREET) L. M.

1. COME, dearest Lord, descend and dwell
By faith and love in every breast;
Then shall we know and taste and feel
The joys that cannot be expressed.

2. Come, fill our hearts with inward strength;
Make our enlargèd souls possess
And learn the height, and breadth, and length
Of Thine unmeasurable grace.

3. Now to the God whose power can do
More than our thoughts or wishes know,
Be everlasting honors done
By all the Church, through Christ His Son.

Rev. Isaac Watts, 1709

The Holy Ghost

115 MERCY 7.7.7.7. Arr. from Louis M. Gottschalk, 1867

1 Holy Spirit, Truth Divine, Dawn upon this soul of mine; Word of God, and inward Light, Wake my spirit, clear my sight. A-MEN.

Copyright. By per. of Oliver Ditson Company

2 Holy Spirit, Love Divine,
Glow within this heart of mine;
Kindle every high desire;
Perish self in Thy pure fire!

3 Holy Spirit, Power Divine,
Fill and nerve this will of mine;
By Thee may I strongly live,
Bravely bear, and nobly strive.

4 Holy Spirit, Right Divine,
King within my conscience reign;
Be my Law, and I shall be
Firmly bound, for ever free.

5 Holy Spirit, Peace Divine,
Still this restless heart of mine;
Speak to calm this tossing sea,
Stayed in Thy tranquillity.

6 Holy Spirit, Joy Divine,
Gladden Thou this heart of mine;
In the desert ways I sing,
"Spring, O Well, for ever spring."

Rev. Samuel Longfellow, 1864

116 (MERCY) 7.7.7.7.

1 GRACIOUS Spirit, Dove Divine,
Let Thy light within me shine;
All my guilty fears remove,
Fill me full of heaven and love.

2 Speak Thy pardoning grace to me,
Set the burdened sinner free;
Lead me to the Lamb of God,
Wash me in His precious blood.

3 Life and peace to me impart;
Seal salvation on my heart;
Breathe Thyself into my breast,
Earnest of immortal rest.

4 Let me never from Thee stray,
Keep me in the narrow way,
Fill my soul with joy Divine,
Keep me, Lord, for ever Thine.

John Stocker, 1777

Invocation and Praise

117 MORECAMBE 10. 10. 10. 10.

1 Spirit of God, descend upon my heart;
Wean it from earth; through all its pulses move;
Stoop to my weakness, mighty as Thou art,
And make me love Thee as I ought to love. A-MEN.

2 I ask no dream, no prophet-ecstasies;
No sudden rending of the veil of clay;
No angel-visitant, no opening skies;
But take the dimness of my soul away.

3 Hast Thou not bid us love Thee, God and King?
All, all Thine own, soul, heart, and strength, and mind;
I see Thy cross—there teach my heart to cling:
O let me seek Thee, and O let me find.

4 Teach me to feel that Thou art always nigh;
Teach me the struggles of the soul to bear,
To check the rising doubt, the rebel sigh;
Teach me the patience of unanswered prayer.

5 Teach me to love Thee as Thine angels love,
One holy passion filling all my frame;
The baptism of the heaven-descended Dove,
My heart an altar, and Thy love the flame.

Rev. George Croly, 1854

The Holy Ghost

118 ST. CUTHBERT 8. 6. 8. 4.   Rev. John B. Dykes, 1861

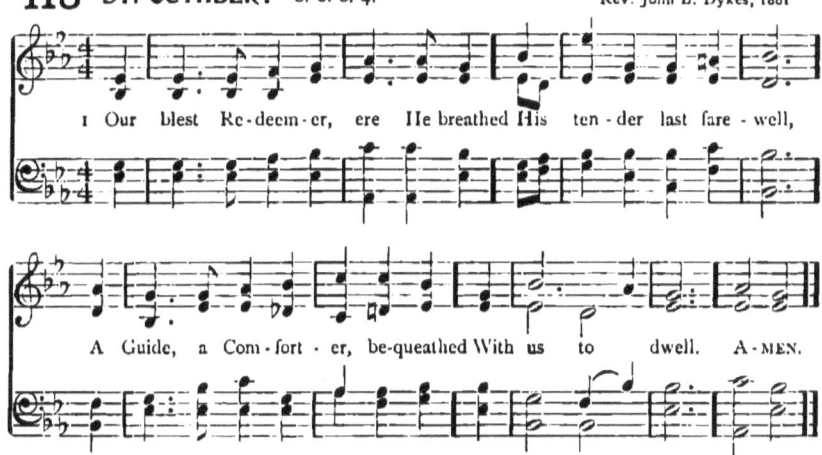

1 Our blest Redeemer, ere He breathed His tender last farewell,
A Guide, a Comforter, bequeathed With us to dwell. A-MEN.

2 He came in semblance of a dove,
 With sheltering wings outspread,
 The holy balm of peace and love
  On earth to shed.

3 He came sweet influence to impart,
  A gracious, willing Guest,
 While He can find one humble heart
  Wherein to rest.

4 And His that gentle voice we hear,
  Soft as the breath of even,
 That checks each thought, that calms each fear,
  And speaks of heaven.

5 And every virtue we possess,
  And every victory won,
 And every thought of holiness,
  Are His alone.

6 Spirit of purity and grace,
  Our weakness, pitying, see:
 O make our hearts Thy dwelling-place,
  And worthier Thee.

Harriet Auber, 1829

119 (LUX VESPERA) 7. 7. 7. 5.

1 GRACIOUS Spirit, Holy Ghost,
  Taught by Thee, we covet most,
  Of Thy gifts at Pentecost,
   Holy, heavenly love.

2 Faith, that mountains could remove,
  Tongues of earth or heaven above,
  Knowledge, all things, empty prove,
   Without heavenly love.

3 Love is kind, and suffers long;
  Love is meek, and thinks no wrong;
  Love than death itself more strong;
   Therefore, give us love.

4 Faith will vanish into sight;
  Hope be emptied in delight;
  Love in heaven will shine more bright;
   Therefore, give us love.

5 Faith and hope and love we see,
  Joining hand in hand, agree;
  But the greatest of the three,
   And the best, is love.

6 From the overshadowing
  Of Thy gold and silver wing,
  Shed on us who to Thee sing
   Holy, heavenly love.

Bishop Christopher Wordsworth, 1862

Invocation and Praise

120 ST. AGNES C. M. Rev. John B. Dykes, 1866

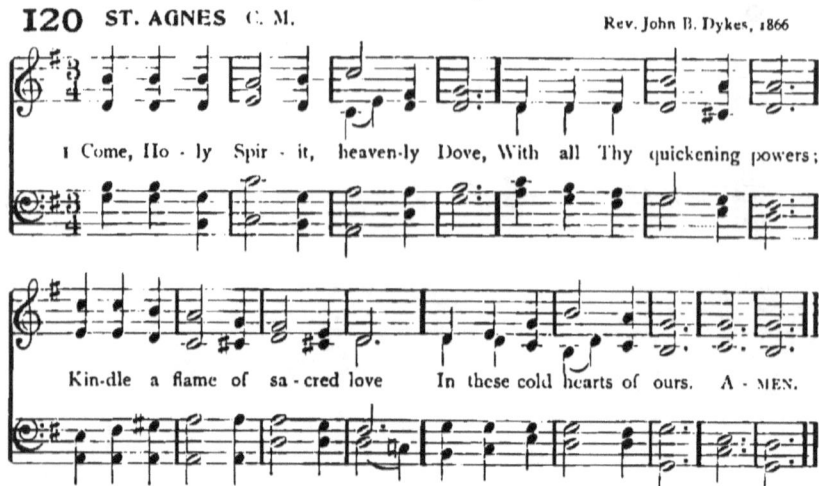

1 Come, Ho-ly Spir-it, heaven-ly Dove, With all Thy quickening powers;
Kin-dle a flame of sa-cred love In these cold hearts of ours. A-MEN.

2 Look how we grovel here below,
   Fond of these trifling toys;
   Our souls can neither fly nor go
   To reach eternal joys.

3 In vain we tune our formal songs,
   In vain we strive to rise;
   Hosannas languish on our tongues,
   And our devotion dies.

4 Dear Lord, and shall we ever live
   At this poor dying rate?
   Our love so faint, so cold to Thee,
   And Thine to us so great!

5 Come, Holy Spirit, heavenly Dove,
   With all Thy quickening powers;
   Come, shed abroad a Saviour's love,
   And that shall kindle ours.

Rev. Isaac Watts, 1707: verse 4, l. 1, alt.

LUX VESPERA 7. 7. 7. 5. Graham W. White, 1885

1 Gra-cious Spir-it, Ho-ly Ghost, Taught by Thee, we cov-et most,
Of Thy gifts at Pen-te-cost, Ho-ly, heaven-ly love. A-MEN.

The Holy Ghost

121 HERMON C. M. Lowell Mason, 1832

1 Thy home is with the humble, Lord; The simplest are the best;
Thy lodging is in childlike hearts; Thou makest there Thy rest. A-MEN.

2 Dear Comforter, eternal Love,
If Thou wilt stay with me,
Of lowly thoughts and simple ways
I'll build a house for Thee.

3 Who made this beating heart of mine
But Thou, my heavenly Guest?
Let no one have it, then, but Thee,
And let it be Thy rest.

Rev. Frederick W. Faber, 1849; verse 1, ll. 2, 4, verse 2, l. 4, verse 3, l. 4, alt.

Inspiration of the Holy Scriptures

122 DUNDEE C. M. Arr. from Christopher Tye, 1553

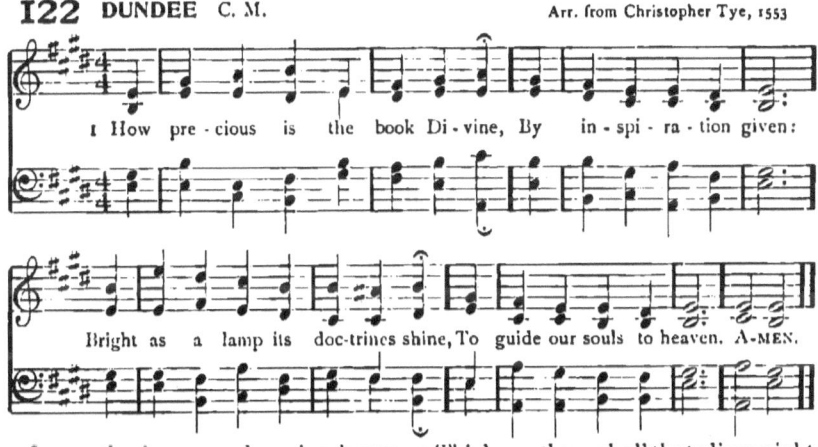

1 How precious is the book Divine, By inspiration given:
Bright as a lamp its doctrines shine, To guide our souls to heaven. A-MEN.

2 It sweetly cheers our drooping hearts,
In this dark vale of tears;
Life, light, and joy it still imparts,
And quells our rising fears.

3 This lamp, through all the tedious night
Of life, shall guide our way,
Till we behold the clearer light
Of an eternal day.

Rev. John Fawcett, 1782

Inspiration of the Holy Scriptures

123 MUNICH 7.6.7.6. D. J. G. C. Störl's Würtemberg Gesangbuch, 1711: Harmonized by Mendelssohn

1. O Word of God Incarnate, O Wisdom from on high,
O Truth unchanged, unchanging, O Light of our dark sky;
We praise Thee for the radiance That from the hallowed page,
A lantern to our footsteps, Shines on from age to age. A-MEN.

2. The Church from her dear Master Received the gift Divine,
And still that light she lifteth O'er all the earth to shine.
It is the golden casket, Where gems of truth are stored;
It is the heaven-drawn picture Of Christ, the living Word.

3. It floateth like a banner
Before God's host unfurled;
It shineth like a beacon
Above the darkling world.
It is the chart and compass
That o'er life's surging sea,
'Mid mists and rocks and quicksands,
Still guides, O Christ, to Thee.

4. O make Thy Church, dear Saviour,
A lamp of purest gold,
To bear before the nations
Thy true light, as of old.
O teach Thy wandering pilgrims
By this their path to trace,
Till, clouds and darkness ended,
They see Thee face to face.

Bishop William W. How, 1867

The Holy Ghost

124 ST. CYPRIAN 6. 6. 6. 6. Rev. Richard R. Chope, 1862

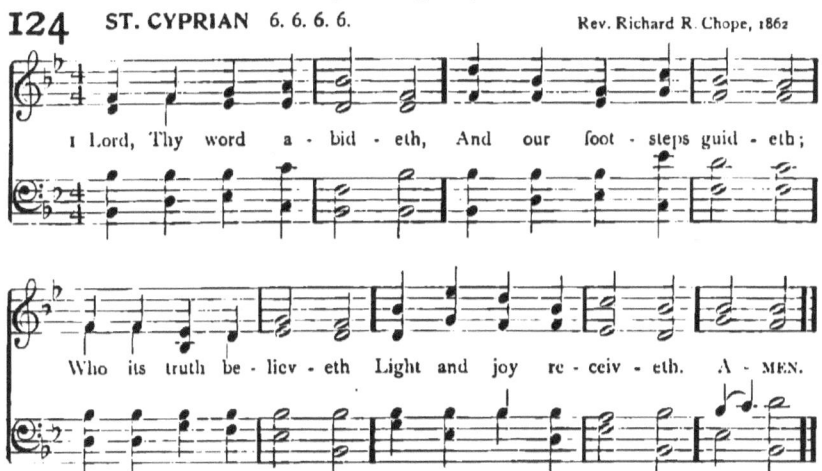

1 Lord, Thy word a-bid-eth, And our foot-steps guid-eth; Who its truth be-liev-eth Light and joy re-ceiv-eth. A-MEN.

2 When our foes are near us,
Then Thy word doth cheer us;
Word of consolation,
Message of salvation.

3 When the storms are o'er us,
And dark clouds before us,
Then its light directeth,
And our way protecteth.

4 Word of mercy, giving
Succor to the living;
Word of life, supplying
Comfort to the dying!

5 O that we, discerning
Its most holy learning,
Lord, may love and fear Thee,
Evermore be near Thee.

Rev. Sir Henry W. Baker, Bart., 1861

ORTONVILLE C. M. Thomas Hastings, 1837

1 The Spir-it breathes upon the word, And brings the truth to sight; Pre-cepts and prom-i-ses af-ford A sanc-ti-fy-ing light, A sanc-ti-fy-ing light. A-MEN.

Inspiration of the Holy Scriptures

125 BREAD OF LIFE 6.4.6.4.D. William F. Sherwin, 1877

1 Break Thou the bread of life, Dear Lord, to me, As Thou didst break the loaves Be-side the sea; Be-yond the sa-cred page I seek Thee, Lord; My spir-it pants for Thee, O liv-ing Word. A-MEN.

Copyright by J. H. Vincent

2 Bless Thou the truth, dear Lord,
  To me—to me—
As Thou didst bless the bread
  By Galilee;

Then shall all bondage cease,
  All fetters fall;
And I shall find my peace,
  My All in all.

Mary Ann Lathbury, 1877

126 (ORTONVILLE) C. M.

1 THE Spirit breathes upon the word,
    And brings the truth to sight;
  Precepts and promises afford
    A sanctifying light.

2 A glory gilds the sacred page,
    Majestic, like the sun:
  It gives a light to every age;
    It gives, but borrows none.

3 The Hand that gave it still supplies
    The gracious light and heat:

His truths upon the nations rise;
    They rise, but never set.

4 Let everlasting thanks be Thine
    For such a bright display
  As makes a world of darkness shine
    With beams of heavenly day.

5 My soul rejoices to pursue
    The steps of Him I love,
  Till glory break upon my view
    In brighter worlds above.

William Cowper, 1779

The Holy Ghost

127 UXBRIDGE L. M. Lowell Mason, 1830

1 The heavens declare Thy glory, Lord; In every star Thy wisdom shines; But when our eyes behold Thy word, We read Thy Name in fairer lines. A-MEN.

2 The rolling sun, the changing light,
And nights and days, Thy power confess;
But the blest volume Thou hast writ
Reveals Thy justice and Thy grace.

3 Sun, moon, and stars convey Thy praise
Round the whole earth, and never stand;
So when Thy truth began its race,
It touched and glanced on every land.

4 Nor shall Thy spreading gospel rest
Till through the world Thy truth has run;
Till Christ has all the nations blest
That see the light, or feel the sun.

5 Great Sun of Righteousness, arise;
Bless the dark world with heavenly light:
Thy gospel makes the simple wise,
Thy laws are pure, Thy judgments right.

Rev. Isaac Watts, 1719

The Church

128 (THE SEVEN WORDS) 7. 7. 7. 6.

1 JESUS, with Thy Church abide,
Be her Saviour, Lord, and Guide,
While on earth her faith is tried:
    We beseech Thee, hear us.

2 Keep her life and doctrine pure;
Grant her patience to endure,
Trusting in Thy promise sure:
    We beseech Thee, hear us.

3 Save her love from growing cold,
Make her watchmen strong and bold,
Fence her round, Thy peaceful fold:
    We beseech Thee, hear us.

4 May her lamp of truth be bright,
Bid her bear aloft its light
Through the realms of heathen night:
    We beseech Thee, hear us.

5 May she holy triumphs win,
Overthrow the hosts of sin,
Gather all the nations in:
    We beseech Thee, hear us.

6 May she soon all glorious be,
Spotless and from wrinkle free,
Pure and bright and worthy Thee:
    We beseech Thee, hear us.

Rev. Thomas B Pollock, 1871: alt. Hy. Anc. and Mod. 1875

The Church

129 SHIRLAND S. M.   Samuel Stanley, 1805

1 I love Thy kingdom, Lord, The house of Thine abode, The Church our blest Redeemer saved With His own precious blood. A-MEN.

2 I love Thy Church, O God:
Her walls before Thee stand,
Dear as the apple of Thine eye,
And graven on Thy hand.

3 For her my tears shall fall,
For her my prayers ascend;
To her my cares and toils be given,
Till toils and cares shall end.

4 Beyond my highest joy
I prize her heavenly ways,
Her sweet communion, solemn vows,
Her hymns of love and praise.

5 Sure as Thy truth shall last,
To Zion shall be given
The brightest glories earth can yield,
And brighter bliss of heaven.

Rev. Timothy Dwight, 1800

THE SEVEN WORDS 7. 7. 7. 6.   Arr. by Sir Arthur Sullivan, 1874

1 Jesus, with Thy Church abide, Be her Saviour, Lord, and Guide, While on earth her faith is tried: We beseech Thee, hear us. A-MEN.

The Church

130 AURELIA 7. 6. 7. 6. D.   Samuel S. Wesley, 1864

1. The Church's one Foundation
 Is Jesus Christ her Lord;
 She is His new creation
 By water and the word:
 From heaven He came and sought her
 To be His holy Bride;
 With His own blood He bought her,
 And for her life He died.

2. Elect from every nation,
 Yet one o'er all the earth,
 Her charter of salvation
 One Lord, one faith, one birth;
 One holy Name she blesses,
 Partakes one holy food,
 And to one hope she presses,
 With every grace endued.

3. Though with a scornful wonder
 Men see her sore oppressed,
 By schisms rent asunder,
 By heresies distressed,
 Yet saints their watch are keeping,
 Their cry goes up, "How long?"
 And soon the night of weeping
 Shall be the morn of song.

4. 'Mid toil and tribulation,
 And tumult of her war,
 She waits the consummation
 Of peace for evermore;
 Till with the vision glorious
 Her longing eyes are blest,
 And the great Church victorious
 Shall be the Church at rest.

                                        Rev. Samuel J. Stone, 1866

The Church

131 AUSTRIAN HYMN 8.7.8.7.D.   Joseph Haydn, 1797

1 Glorious things of thee are spoken, Zion, city of our God; He whose word cannot be broken Formed thee for His own abode: On the Rock of Ages founded, What can shake thy sure repose? With salvation's walls surrounded, Thou mayst smile at all thy foes. A-MEN.

2 See, the streams of living waters,
   Springing from eternal Love,
Well supply thy sons and daughters,
   And all fear of want remove:
Who can faint, while such a river
   Ever flows their thirst to assuage;
Grace, which, like the Lord the Giver,
   Never fails from age to age?

3 Round each habitation hovering,
   See the cloud and fire appear
For a glory and a covering,
   Showing that the Lord is near:
Thus deriving from their banner
   Light by night, and shade by day,
Safe they feed upon the manna
   Which He gives them when they pray.

Rev. John Newton, 1779

The Church

132 ST. ANNE C. M. William Croft, 1708

1 O where are kings and em-pires now Of old that went and came?
But, Lord, Thy Church is pray-ing yet, A thou-sand years the same. A-MEN.

2 We mark her goodly battlements,
 And her foundations strong ;
 We hear within the solemn voice
 Of her unending song.

3 For not like kingdoms of the world
 Thy holy Church, O God ;
 Though earthquake shocks are threat-
 And tempests are abroad ; [ening her,

4 Unshaken as eternal hills,
 Immovable she stands,
 A mountain that shall fill the earth,
 A house not made by hands.

Bishop A. Cleveland Coxe, 1839 : alt. and arr.

BROCKLESBURY 8. 7. 8. 7. Charlotte A. Barnard (1830–1869)

1 Sav-iour, who Thy flock art feed-ing With the shep herd's kind-est care,
All the fee-ble gen-tly lead-ing, While the lambs Thy bo-som share ; A-MEN.

Baptism

133 SILOAM C.M. Isaac B. Woodbury, 1842

1 By cool Siloam's shady rill How sweet the lily grows!
How sweet the breath beneath the hill Of Sharon's dewy rose! A-MEN.

2 Lo, such the child whose early feet
   The paths of peace have trod;
Whose secret heart, with influence sweet,
   Is upward drawn to God.

3 By cool Siloam's shady rill
   The lily must decay;
The rose that blooms beneath the hill
   Must shortly fade away:

4 And soon, too soon, the wintry hour
   Of man's maturer age
Will shake the soul with sorrow's power
   And stormy passion's rage.

5 O Thou, whose infant feet were found
   Within Thy Father's shrine,
Whose years, with changeless virtue crowned,
   Were all alike Divine;

6 Dependent on Thy bounteous breath,
   We seek Thy grace alone
In childhood, manhood, age, and death,
   To keep us still Thine own.

Bishop Reginald Heber, 1812 (Text of 1827)

134 (BROCKLESBURY) 8.7.8.7.

1 SAVIOUR, who Thy flock art feeding,
   With the shepherd's kindest care,
All the feeble gently leading,
   While the lambs Thy bosom share;

2 Now, these little ones receiving,
   Fold them in Thy gracious arm;
There, we know, Thy word believing,
   Only there secure from harm.

3 Never, from Thy pasture roving,
   Let them be the lion's prey;
Let Thy tenderness, so loving,
Keep them through life's dangerous [way.

4 Then, within Thy fold eternal,
   Let them find a resting-place,
Feed in pastures ever vernal,
   Drink the rivers of Thy grace.

Rev. William A Mühlenberg, 1826

7

The Church

135 BROOKFIELD L. M.
Thomas B. Southgate (1814-1868)

1 Jesus, and shall it ever be,
A mortal man ashamed of Thee?
Ashamed of Thee whom angels praise, Whose glories shine through endless days! A-MEN.

2 Ashamed of Jesus! sooner far
Let evening blush to own a star:
He sheds the beams of light Divine
O'er this benighted soul of mine.

3 Ashamed of Jesus! just as soon
Let midnight be ashamed of noon:
'Tis midnight with my soul till He,
Bright Morning Star, bid darkness flee.

4 Ashamed of Jesus, that dear Friend
On whom my hopes of heaven depend!
No; when I blush, be this my shame,
That I no more revere His Name.

5 Ashamed of Jesus! yes, I may
When I've no guilt to wash away,
No tear to wipe, no good to crave,
No fears to quell, no soul to save.

6 Till then—nor is my boasting vain—
Till then I boast a Saviour slain;
And O may this my glory be,
That Christ is not ashamed of me.

Rev. Joseph Grigg, 1765: alt. Rev. Benjamin Francis, 1787

136 (ROCKINGHAM NEW) L. M.

1 NOW I resolve with all my heart,
With all my powers, to serve the Lord;
Nor from His precepts e'er depart
Whose service is a rich reward.

2 O be His service all my joy;
Around let my example shine,
Till others love the blest employ,
And join in labors so Divine.

3 Be this the purpose of my soul,
My solemn, my determined choice,
To yield to His supreme control,
And in His kind commands rejoice.

4 O may I never faint nor tire, [ways:
Nor wandering leave His sacred
Great God, accept my soul's desire,
And give me strength to live Thy praise.

Anne Steele, 1760: verse 1, l. 1, alt.

Confession of Faith

137 DALLAS 7.7.7.7.   Arr. from Maria L. Cherubini (1760–1842)

1 Thine for ev-er! God of love, Hear us from Thy throne a-bove; Thine for ev-er may we be Here and in e-ter-ni-ty. A-MEN.

2 Thine for ever! Lord of life,
Shield us through our earthly strife;
Thou, the Life, the Truth, the Way,
Guide us to the realms of day.

3 Thine for ever! O how blest
They who find in Thee their rest!
Saviour, Guardian, heavenly Friend,
O defend us to the end.

4 Thine for ever! Saviour, keep
These Thy frail and trembling sheep;
Safe alone beneath Thy care,
Let us all Thy goodness share.

5 Thine for ever! Thou our Guide,
All our wants by Thee supplied,
All our sins by Thee forgiven,
Lead us, Lord, from earth to heaven.

Mary F. Maude, 1847

ROCKINGHAM NEW L. M.   Lowell Mason, 1830

1 Now I re-solve with all my heart, With all my powers, to serve the Lord; Nor from His pre-cepts e'er de-part Whose ser-vice is a rich re-ward. A-MEN.

The Church

138 EVAN C. M. Rev. William H. Havergal, 1846

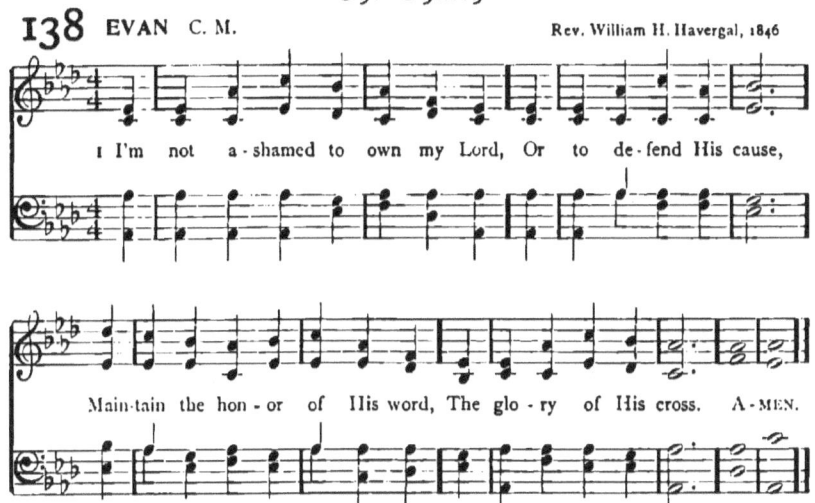

1. I'm not a-shamed to own my Lord, Or to de-fend His cause, Main-tain the hon-or of His word, The glo-ry of His cross. A-MEN.

2. Jesus, my God! I know His Name,
His Name is all my trust;
Nor will He put my soul to shame,
Nor let my hope be lost.

3. Firm as His throne His promise stands,
And He can well secure
What I've committed to His hands
Till the decisive hour.

4. Then will He own my worthless name
Before His Father's face,
And in the New Jerusalem
Appoint my soul a place.

Rev. Isaac Watts, 1709

The Lord's Supper

139 (EVAN) C. M.

1. ACCORDING to Thy gracious word,
In meek humility,
This will I do, my dying Lord,
I will remember Thee.

2. Thy body, broken for my sake,
My bread from heaven shall be;
Thy testamental cup I take,
And thus remember Thee.

3. Gethsemane can I forget?
Or there Thy conflict see,
Thine agony and bloody sweat,
And not remember Thee?

4. When to the cross I turn mine eyes,
And rest on Calvary,
O Lamb of God, my Sacrifice,
I must remember Thee;

5. Remember Thee, and all Thy pains,
And all Thy love to me:
Yea, while a breath, a pulse remains,
Will I remember Thee.

6. And when these failing lips grow dumb,
And mind and memory flee,
When Thou shalt in Thy kingdom come,
Jesus, remember me.

James Montgomery, 1825

The Lord's Supper

140 MORECAMBE 10. 10. 10. 10.

2 I am not worthy to be thought Thy child,
   Nor sit the last and lowest at Thy board;
   Too long a wanderer and too oft beguiled,
   I only ask one reconciling word.

3 One word from Thee, my Lord, one smile, one look,
   And I could face the cold, rough world again;
   And with that treasure in my heart could brook
   The wrath of devils and the scorn of men.

4 I hear Thy voice; Thou bidd'st me come and rest;
   I come, I kneel, I clasp Thy piercèd feet;
   Thou bidd'st me take my place, a welcome guest
   Among Thy saints, and of Thy banquet eat.

5 My praise can only breathe itself in prayer,
   My prayer can only lose itself in Thee;
   Dwell Thou for ever in my heart, and there,
   Lord, let me sup with Thee; sup Thou with me.

Bishop Edward H. Bickersteth, 1872

The Church

141 ST. AGNES C. M.
Rev. John B. Dykes, 1866

1 Shepherd of souls, refresh and bless Thy chosen pilgrim flock With manna in the wilderness, With water from the rock. A-MEN.

2 Hungry and thirsty, faint and weak,
As Thou when here below,
Our souls the joys celestial seek
Which from Thy sorrows flow.

3 We would not live by bread alone,
But by that word of grace,
In strength of which we travel on
To our abiding-place.

4 Be known to us in breaking bread,
But do not then depart;
Saviour, abide with us, and spread
Thy table in our heart.

5 There sup with us in love Divine;
Thy body and Thy blood,
That living bread, that heavenly wine,
Be our immortal food.

Verses 1, 2, 3, Anon.; verses 4, 5, James Montgomery, 1825

ROCKINGHAM OLD L. M.
Arr. by Edward Miller, 1790

1 My God, and is Thy table spread? And does Thy cup with love o'er-flow? Thither be all Thy children led, And let them all its sweetness know. A-MEN.

The Lord's Supper

142 QUEBEC L. M.   Henry Baker, 1866

1 Jesus, Thou Joy of loving hearts, Thou Fount of life, Thou Light of men,

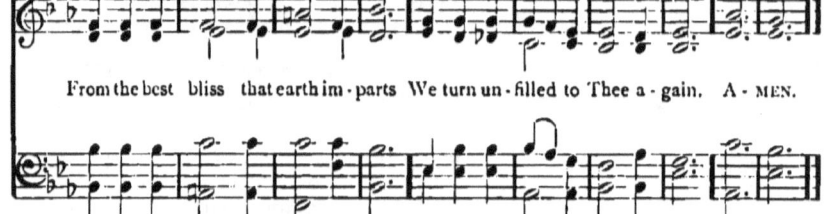

From the best bliss that earth imparts We turn unfilled to Thee again. A-MEN.

2 Thy truth unchanged hath ever stood;
Thou savest those that on Thee call;
To them that seek Thee Thou art good,
To them that find Thee All in all.

3 We taste Thee, O Thou living Bread,
And long to feast upon Thee still;
We drink of Thee, the Fountain-head,
And thirst our souls from Thee to fill.

4 Our restless spirits yearn for Thee,
Where'er our changeful lot is cast;
Glad when Thy gracious smile we see,
Blest when our faith can hold Thee fast.

5 O Jesus, ever with us stay,
Make all our moments calm and bright;
Chase the dark night of sin away,
Shed o'er the world Thy holy light.

         Bernard of Clairvaux, c. 1150: arr. Tr. Rev. Ray Palmer, 1858

---

143 (ROCKINGHAM OLD) L. M.

1 MY God, and is Thy table spread?
And does Thy cup with love o'erflow?
Thither be all Thy children led,
And let them all its sweetness know.

2 Hail, sacred feast which Jesus makes,
Rich banquet of His flesh and blood!
Thrice happy he who here partakes
That sacred stream, that heavenly food!

3 Why are its dainties all in vain
Before unwilling hearts displayed?
Was not for you the Victim slain?
Are you forbid the children's bread?

4 O let Thy table honored be,
And furnished well with joyful guests;
And may each soul salvation see
That here its sacred pledges tastes.

         Rev. Philip Doddridge, publ. 1755

The Church

144 THATCHER S. M.   Arr. from George F. Handel, 1732

1 How beau-teous are their feet Who stand on Zi-on's hill,
Who bring sal-va-tion on their tongues, And words of peace re-veal! A-MEN.

2 How charming is their voice!
  How sweet the tidings are!
  "Zion, behold thy Saviour King;
  He reigns and triumphs here."

3 How happy are our ears
  That hear this joyful sound,
  Which kings and prophets waited for,
  And sought, but never found!

4 How blessèd are our eyes
  That see this heavenly light!
  Prophets and kings desired it long,
  But died without the sight.

5 The watchmen join their voice,
  And tuneful notes employ;
  Jerusalem breaks forth in songs,
  And deserts learn the joy.

Rev. Isaac Watts, 1707

LABAN S. M.   Lowell Mason, 1830

1 Ye serv-ants of the Lord, Each in his of-fice wait,
Ob-serv-ant of His heaven-ly word, And watch-ful at His gate. A-MEN.

Consecration and Service

145 SOLDIERS OF CHRIST S. M.
Rev. William P. Merrill, 1895

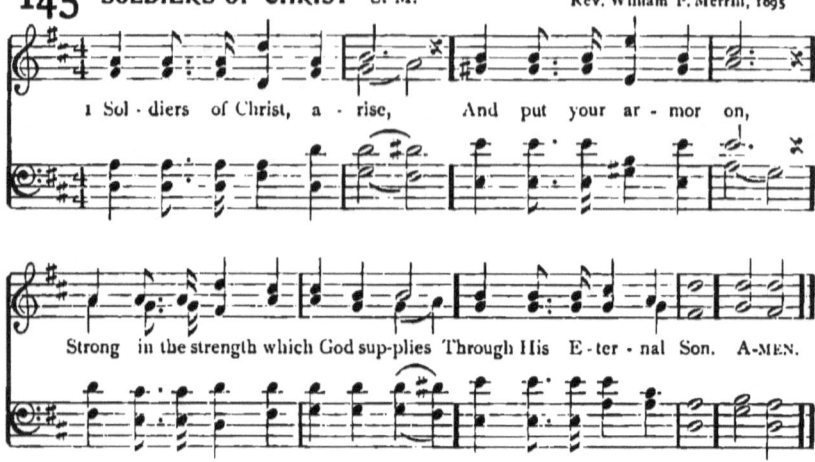

1 Soldiers of Christ, arise,
And put your armor on,
Strong in the strength which God supplies
Through His Eternal Son. A-MEN.

Copyright, 1895, by The Trustees of The Presbyterian Board of Publication and Sabbath-School Work

2 Strong in the Lord of hosts,
And in His mighty power,
Who in the strength of Jesus trusts
Is more than conqueror.

3 Stand then in His great might,
With all His strength endued;
But take, to arm you for the fight,
The panoply of God:

4 That, having all things done,
And all your conflicts passed,
Ye may o'ercome through Christ alone,
And stand entire at last.

5 From strength to strength go on;
Wrestle, and fight, and pray;
Tread all the powers of darkness down,
And win the well-fought day.

6 Still let the Spirit cry
In all His soldiers, "Come,"
Till Christ the Lord descends from high,
And takes the conquerors home.

Rev. Charles Wesley, 1749

146 (LABAN) S. M.

1 YE servants of the Lord,
Each in his office wait,
Observant of His heavenly word,
And watchful at His gate.

2 Let all your lamps be bright,
And trim the golden flame;
Gird up your loins, as in His sight,
For awful is His Name.

3 Watch: 'tis your Lord's command,
And while we speak, He's near;
Mark the first signal of His hand,
And ready all appear.

4 O happy servant he
In such a posture found!
He shall his Lord with rapture see,
And be with honor crowned.

5 Christ shall the banquet spread
With His own royal hand,
And raise that favorite servant's head
Amidst the angelic band.

Rev. Philip Doddridge, publ. 1755

The Church

147 CRUCIFER 8.7.8.7. D. — Henry Smart, 1867

1. Jesus, I my cross have taken, All to leave, and follow Thee;
Destitute, despised, forsaken, Thou, from hence, my all shalt be:
Perish every fond ambition, All I've sought, or hoped, or known;
Yet how rich is my condition, God and heaven are still my own. A-MEN.

2. Man may trouble and distress me,
   "'Twill but drive me to Thy breast;
Life with trials hard may press me,
   Heaven will bring me sweeter rest:
O 'tis not in grief to harm me
   While Thy love is left to me;
O 'twere not in joy to charm me,
   Were that joy unmixed with Thee.

3. Take, my soul, thy full salvation,
   Rise o'er sin and fear and care;
Joy to find in every station
   Something still to do or bear;
Think what Spirit dwells within thee,
   What a Father's smile is thine,
What a Saviour died to win thee;
   Child of heaven, shouldst thou repine?

Rev. Henry F. Lyte, 1824 (Text of 1833)

Consecration and Service

148 ELLESDIE 8.7.8.7. D.   Arr. from Mozart, by Joseph P. Holbrook, 1865

1 Hark! the voice of Jesus crying, "Who will go and work to-day?
Fields are white, and harvests waiting; Who will bear the sheaves away?"
Loud and long the Master calleth, Rich reward He offers free;
Who will answer, gladly saying, "Here am I; send me, send me." A-MEN.

2 If you cannot cross the ocean,
   And the heathen lands explore,
You can find the heathen nearer,
   You can help them at your door.
If you cannot give your thousands,
   You can give the widow's mite ;
And the least you give for Jesus
   Will be precious in His sight.

3 If you cannot speak like angels,
   If you cannot preach like Paul,
You can tell the love of Jesus,
   You can say He died for all.

If you cannot rouse the wicked
   With the judgment's dread alarms,
You can lead the little children
   To the Saviour's waiting arms.

4 Let none hear you idly saying,
   "There is nothing I can do,"
While the souls of men are dying,
   And the Master calls for you :
Take the task He gives you gladly,
   Let His work your pleasure be ;
Answer quickly when He calleth,
   "Here am I ; send me, send me."

Rev. Daniel March, 1868

The Church

149 WEBB 7. 6. 7. 6. D. George J. Webb, 1837

1. Stand up, stand up for Jesus, Ye soldiers of the cross;
Lift high His royal banner, It must not suffer loss:
From victory unto victory His army He shall lead,
Till every foe is vanquished, And Christ is Lord indeed. A-MEN.

2. Stand up, stand up for Jesus, The trumpet call obey;
Forth to the mighty conflict In this His glorious day:
Ye that are men now serve Him Against unnumbered foes;
Let courage rise with danger, And strength to strength oppose.

3. Stand up, stand up for Jesus,
   Stand in His strength alone;
   The arm of flesh will fail you,
   Ye dare not trust your own:
   Put on the gospel armor,
   Each piece put on with prayer;
   Where duty calls, or danger,
   Be never wanting there.

4. Stand up, stand up for Jesus,
   The strife will not be long;
   This day the noise of battle,
   The next the victor's song:
   To him that overcometh
   A crown of life shall be;
   He with the King of Glory
   Shall reign eternally.

Rev. George Duffield, 1858

Consecration and Service

150 LANCASHIRE 7. 6. 7. 6. D. — Henry Smart, 1836

1 O brothers, lift your voices, Triumphant songs to raise;
Till heaven on high rejoices, And earth is filled with praise;
Ten thousand hearts are bounding With holy hopes and free;
The gospel trump is sounding, The trump of Jubilee. A-MEN.

2 O Christian brothers, glorious
  Shall be the conflict's close;
The cross hath been victorious,
  And shall be o'er its foes:
Faith is our battle-token;
  Our Leader all controls;
Our trophies, fetters broken;
  Our captives, ransomed souls.

3 Not unto us, Lord Jesus,
  To Thee all praise be due,
Whose blood-bought mercy frees us,
  Has freed our brethren too.
Not unto us: in glory
  The angels catch the strain,
And cast their crowns before Thee
  Exultingly again.

Bishop Edward H. Bickersteth, 1848

The Church

151 FERGUSON S. M. — George Kingsley, 1843

1 Dear Lord and Master mine, Thy happy servant see;
My Conqueror, with what joy Divine Thy captive clings to Thee! A-MEN.

2 I love Thy yoke to wear,
  To feel Thy gracious bands;
Sweetly restrained by Thy care,
  And happy in Thy hands.

3 No bar would I remove,
  No bond would I unbind;
Within the limits of Thy love
  Full liberty I find.

4 I would not walk alone,
  But still with Thee, my God;
At every step my blindness own,
  And ask of Thee the road.

5 Dear Lord and Master mine,
  Still keep Thy servant true;
My Guardian and my Guide Divine,
  Bring, bring Thy pilgrim through.

Thomas H. Gill, 1868

ST. GEORGE S. M. — Henry J. Gauntlett, 1848

1 Revive Thy work, O Lord, Thy mighty arm make bare;
Speak with the voice that wakes the dead, And make Thy people hear. A-MEN.

Consecration and Service

152 PATMOS 7.7.7.7.   Rev. William H. Havergal, 1869

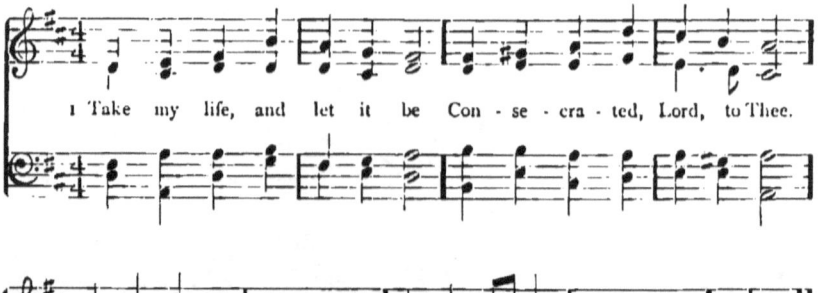
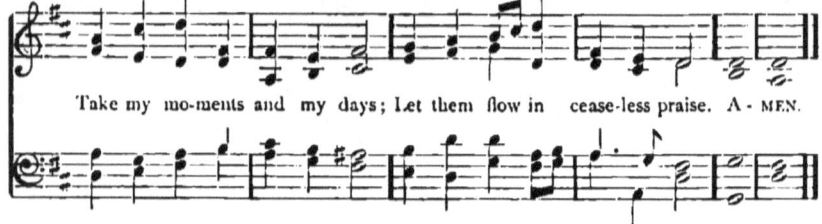

1 Take my life, and let it be Con-se-cra-ted, Lord, to Thee. Take my mo-ments and my days; Let them flow in cease-less praise. A-MEN.

2 Take my hands, and let them move
At the impulse of Thy love.
Take my feet, and let them be
Swift and beautiful for Thee.

3 Take my voice, and let me sing,
Always, only, for my King.
Take my lips, and let them be
Filled with messages from Thee.

4 Take my silver and my gold;
Not a mite would I withhold.

Take my intellect, and use
Every power as Thou shalt choose.

5 Take my will, and make it Thine;
It shall be no longer mine.
Take my heart, it is Thine own;
It shall be Thy royal throne.

6 Take my love; my Lord, I pour
At Thy feet its treasure-store.
Take myself, and I will be
Ever, only, all for Thee.

Frances R. Havergal, 1874

153 (ST. GEORGE) S. M.

1 REVIVE Thy work, O Lord,
Thy mighty arm make bare;
Speak with the voice that wakes the dead,
And make Thy people hear.

2 Revive Thy work, O Lord,
Disturb this sleep of death;
Quicken the smouldering embers now
By Thine almighty breath.

3 Revive Thy work, O Lord,
Create soul-thirst for Thee;
And hungering for the Bread of Life
O may our spirits be.

4 Revive Thy work, O Lord,
Exalt Thy precious Name;
And, by the Holy Ghost, our love
For Thee and Thine inflame.

5 Revive Thy work, O Lord,
Give pentecostal showers:
The glory shall be all Thine own,
The blessing, Lord, be ours.

Albert Midlane, 1858

The Church

154 LOWTON 8.7.8.7. *Albert Lowe, 1875*

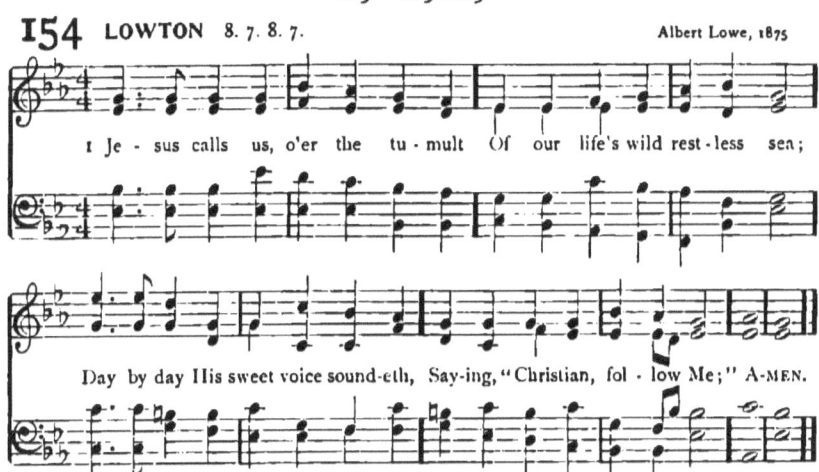

1 Jesus calls us, o'er the tumult Of our life's wild restless sea;
Day by day His sweet voice sound-eth, Saying, "Christian, follow Me;" A-MEN.

2 As, of old, apostles heard it
By the Galilean lake,
Turned from home and toil and kindred,
Leaving all for His dear sake.

3 Jesus calls us from the worship
Of the vain world's golden store,
From each idol that would keep us,
Saying, "Christian, love Me more."

4 In our joys and in our sorrows,
Days of toil and hours of ease,
Still He calls, in cares and pleasures,
"Christian, love Me more than these."

5 Jesus calls us: by Thy mercies,
Saviour, may we hear Thy call,
Give our hearts to Thy obedience,
Serve and love Thee best of all.

Cecil F. Alexander, 1852: verse 2, l. 1, alt.

STOCKWELL 8.7.8.7. *Darius E. Jones, 1851*

1 He that goeth forth with weeping, Bearing precious seed in love,
Never tiring, never sleeping, Findeth mercy from above: A-MEN.

Consecration and Service

155 UNIVERSITY COLLEGE 7. 7. 7. 7. Henry J. Gauntlett, 1848

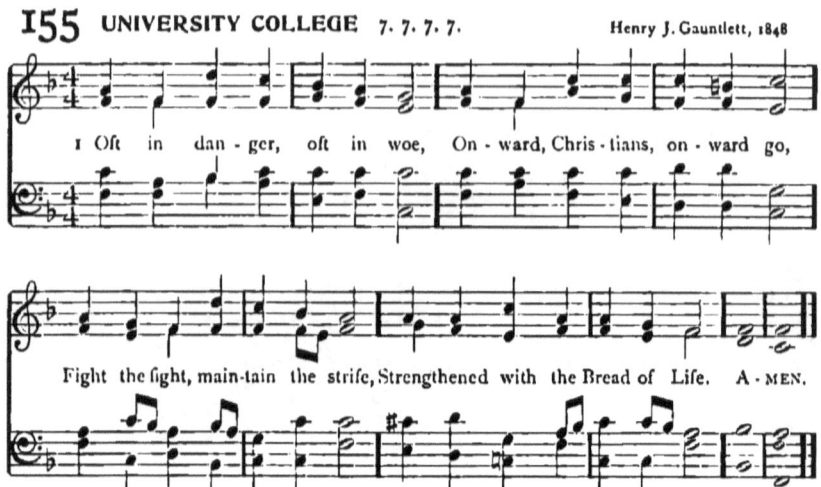

1 Oft in danger, oft in woe,
Onward, Christians, onward go,
Fight the fight, maintain the strife,
Strengthened with the Bread of Life. A-MEN.

2 Onward, Christians, onward go,
Join the war, and face the foe;
Faint not: much doth yet remain;
Dreary is the long campaign.

3 Shrink not, Christians: will ye yield?
Will ye quit the painful field?
Will ye flee in danger's hour?
Know ye not your Captain's power?

4 Let your drooping hearts be glad;
March, in heavenly armor clad;
Fight, nor think the battle long;
Victory soon shall tune your song.

5 Let not sorrow dim your eye,
Soon shall every tear be dry;
Let not woe your course impede,
Great your strength, if great your need.

6 Onward then to battle move;
More than conquerors ye shall prove:
Though opposed by many a foe,
Christian soldiers, onward go.

First 10 ll., Henry K. White, 1806; alt. Rev. Ed. Bickersteth, 1833, and Rev. W. J. Hall, 1836; the remainder, Frances S. Colquhoun, 1827

156 (STOCKWELL) 8. 7. 8. 7.

1 HE that goeth forth with weeping,
Bearing precious seed in love,
Never tiring, never sleeping,
Findeth mercy from above:

2 Soft descend the dews of heaven,
Bright the rays celestial shine;
Precious fruits will thus be given
Through an influence all Divine.

3 Sow thy seed; be never weary;
Let no fears thy soul annoy;
Be the prospect ne'er so dreary,
Thou shalt reap the fruits of joy.

4 Lo! the scene of verdure brightening,
See the rising grain appear;
Look again; the fields are whitening,
For the harvest-time is near.

Thomas Hastings, 1836

The Church

157 TRUE-HEARTED 11.10.11.10. with Refrain — Josiah Booth, 1890

1 True-hearted, whole-hearted, faithful and loyal, King of our lives, by Thy grace we will be; Under Thy standard, exalted and royal, Strong in Thy strength, we will battle for Thee.

REFRAIN.
Peal out the watchword, and silence it never, Song of our spirits rejoicing and free; "True-hearted, whole-hearted, now and for ever, King of our lives, by Thy grace we will be." A-MEN.

Consecration and Service

2 True-hearted, whole-hearted! fullest allegiance
   Yielding henceforth to our glorious King;
Valiant endeavor and loving obedience
   Freely and joyously now would we bring.—REF.

3 True-hearted! Saviour, Thou knowest our story;
   Weak are the hearts that we lay at Thy feet,
Sinful and treacherous; yet, for Thy glory,
   Heal them, and cleanse them from sin and deceit.—REF.

4 Whole-hearted! Saviour, belovèd and glorious,
   Take Thy great power and reign Thou alone,
Over our wills and affections victorious,
   Freely surrendered, and wholly Thine own.—REF.

Frances R. Havergal, 1874

158 HANFORD 8.8.8.4.   Sir Arthur Sullivan, 1874

1 Through good report and evil, Lord, Still guided by Thy faithful word,
Our staff, our buckler, and our sword, We follow Thee. A-MEN.

2 In silence of the lonely night,
   In the full glow of day's clear light,
Through life's strange windings, dark [or bright,
   We follow Thee.

3 With enemies on every side,
   We lean on Thee, the Crucified;
Forsaking all on earth beside,
   We follow Thee.

4 O Master, point Thou out the way,
   Nor suffer Thou our steps to stray;
Then in the path that leads to day
   We follow Thee.

5 Whom have we in the heaven above,
   Whom on this earth, save Thee, to love?
Still in Thy light we onward move;
   We follow Thee.

Rev. Horatius Bonar, 1866

The Church

159 WILLIAMS L. M. George Kingsley, 1853

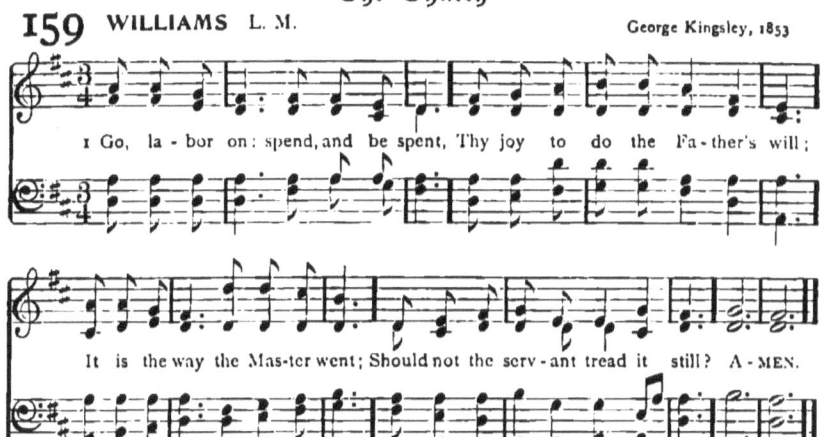

1 Go, labor on: spend, and be spent, Thy joy to do the Father's will;
It is the way the Master went; Should not the serv-ant tread it still? A-MEN.

2 Go, labor on: 'tis not for naught;
Thy earthly loss is heavenly gain;
Men heed thee, love thee, praise thee not;
The Master praises:—what are men?

3 Go, labor on: enough while here
If He shall praise thee, if He deign
Thy willing heart to mark and cheer;
No toil for Him shall be in vain.

4 Go, labor on while it is day:
The world's dark night is hastening on.
Speed, speed thy work, cast sloth away;
It is not thus that souls are won.

5 Toil on, and in thy toil rejoice;
For toil comes rest, for exile home;
Soon shalt thou hear the Bridegroom's voice,
The midnight peal, "Behold, I come."

Rev. Horatius Bonar, 1843

WAREHAM L. M. William Knapp, 1738

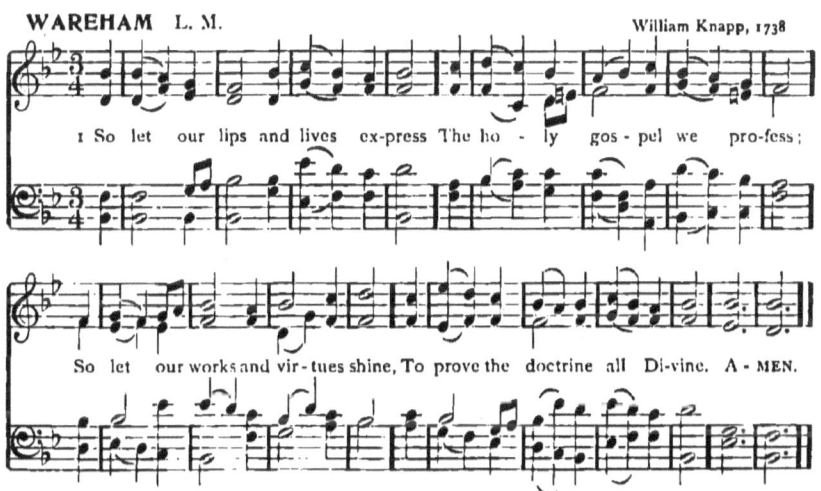

1 So let our lips and lives ex-press The ho-ly gos-pel we pro-fess;
So let our works and vir-tues shine, To prove the doctrine all Di-vine. A-MEN.

Consecration and Service

160 CANONBURY L. M. Arr. from Robert Schumann, 1839

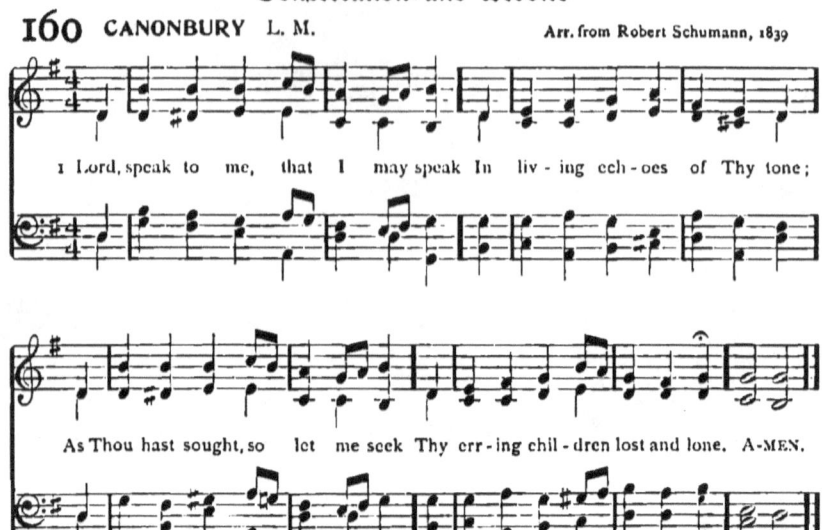

1 Lord, speak to me, that I may speak In living echoes of Thy tone; As Thou hast sought, so let me seek Thy erring children lost and lone. A-MEN.

2 O lead me, Lord, that I may lead
The wandering and the wavering feet;
O feed me, Lord, that I may feed
Thy hungering ones with manna sweet.

3 O strengthen me, that while I stand
Firm on the Rock, and strong in Thee,
I may stretch out a loving hand
To wrestlers with the troubled sea.

4 O teach me, Lord, that I may teach
The precious things Thou dost impart;
And wing my words, that they may reach
The hidden depths of many a heart.

5 O use me, Lord, use even me,
Just as Thou wilt, and when, and where;
Until Thy blessèd face I see,
Thy rest, Thy joy, Thy glory share.

Frances R. Havergal, 1872

161 (WAREHAM) L. M.

1 SO let our lips and lives express
The holy gospel we profess;
So let our works and virtues shine,
To prove the doctrine all Divine.

2 Thus shall we best proclaim abroad
The honors of our Saviour God;
When His salvation reigns within,
And grace subdues the power of sin.

3 Our flesh and sense must be denied,
Passion and envy, lust and pride;
While justice, temperance, truth, and love,
Our inward piety approve.

4 Religion bears our spirits up,
While we expect that blessèd hope,
The bright appearance of the Lord;
And faith stands leaning on His word.

Rev. Isaac Watts, 1709: verse 2, l. 3, alt.

The Church

162 ANGEL'S STORY 7. 6. 7. 6. D.   Arthur H. Mann, 1883

2 O let me feel Thee near me,
   The world is ever near;
   I see the sights that dazzle,
   The tempting sounds I hear:
   My foes are ever near me,
   Around me and within;
   But, Jesus, draw Thou nearer,
   And shield my soul from sin.

3 O Jesus, Thou hast promised
   To all who follow Thee
   That where Thou art in glory
   There shall Thy servant be;
   And, Jesus, I have promised
   To serve Thee to the end;
   O give me grace to follow
   My Master and my Friend.

   Rev. John E. Bode, 1869

Consecration and Service

163 TENNENT 7. 6. 7. 6. D. Uzziah C. Burnap, 1895

1 Lead on, O King Eternal, The day of march has come;
Henceforth in fields of conquest Thy tents shall be our home:
Through days of preparation Thy grace has made us strong,
And now, O King Eternal, We lift our battle-song. A-MEN.

Copyright, 1895, by The Trustees of The Presbyterian Board of Publication and Sabbath-School Work

2 Lead on, O King Eternal,
   Till sin's fierce war shall cease,
And Holiness shall whisper
   The sweet Amen of peace;
For not with swords loud clashing,
   Nor roll of stirring drums,
But deeds of love and mercy,
   The heavenly kingdom comes.

3 Lead on, O King Eternal:
   We follow, not with fears;
For gladness breaks like morning
   Where'er Thy face appears;
Thy cross is lifted o'er us;
   We journey in its light:
The crown awaits the conquest;
   Lead on, O God of might.

Rev. Ernest W. Shurtleff, 1888

The Church

164 ST. GERTRUDE 6. 5. 6. 5. 12l.   Sir Arthur Sullivan, 1871

1 Onward, Christian sol - diers, Marching as to war, With the cross of Je - sus Go - ing on be - fore: Christ the Roy - al Mas - ter Leads a - gainst the foe; For-ward in - to bat - tle, See, His ban-ners go. Onward, Christian sol - diers, Marching as to war, With the cross of Je - sus Go - ing on be - fore. A - MEN.

2 At the sign of triumph
   Satan's host doth flee;
On then, Christian soldiers,
   On to victory:
Hell's foundations quiver
   At the shout of praise;
Brothers, lift your voices,
   Loud your anthems raise.—REF.

3 Like a mighty army
   Moves the Church of God;
Brothers, we are treading
   Where the saints have trod;
We are not divided,
   All one body we,
One in hope and doctrine,
   One in charity.—REF.

Consecration and Service

4 Crowns and thrones may perish,
　　Kingdoms rise and wane,
　But the Church of Jesus
　　Constant will remain;
　Gates of hell can never
　　'Gainst that Church prevail;
　We have Christ's own promise,
　　And that cannot fail.—REF.

5 Onward, then, ye people,
　　Join our happy throng,
　Blend with ours your voices
　　In the triumph-song;
　Glory, laud, and honor
　　Unto Christ the King;
　This through countless ages
　　Men and angels sing.—REF.

　　　　　Rev. Sabine Baring-Gould, 1865

165　KOCHER 7. 6. 7. 6.　　　　　　Justin H. Knecht, 1799

1 O happy band of pilgrims,
　If onward ye will tread,
With Jesus as your Fellow,
　To Jesus as your Head. A-MEN.

2 O happy if ye labor
　　As Jesus did for men;
　O happy if ye hunger
　　As Jesus hungered then.

3 The cross that Jesus carried
　　He carried as your due;
　The crown that Jesus weareth
　　He weareth it for you.

4 The trials that beset you,
　　The sorrows ye endure,
　The manifold temptations
　　That death alone can cure,

5 What are they but His jewels
　　Of right celestial worth?
　What are they but the ladder
　　Set up to heaven on earth?

6 O happy band of pilgrims,
　　Look upward to the skies,
　Where such a light affliction
　　Shall win you such a prize.

　　　Rev. John M. Neale, 1862; based on Joseph the Hymnographer, c. 840

The Church

166 COLYTON 6. 5. 6. 5. D. William H. Monk, 1881

1. On our way rejoicing, As we homeward move,
   Hearken to our praises, O Thou God of love.
   Is there grief or sadness? Thou our Joy shalt be;
   Is our sky beclouded? There is light in Thee.

2. If with honest-hearted Love for God and man,
   Day by day Thou find us Doing all we can,
   Thou who giv'st the seed-time Wilt give large increase,
   Crown the head with blessings, Fill the heart with peace.

3. On our way rejoicing
   Gladly let us go;
   Victor is our Leader,
   Vanquished is the foe:
   Christ without, our safety;
   Christ within, our joy;
   Who, if we be faithful,
   Can our hope destroy?

4. Unto God the Father
   Joyful songs we sing;
   Unto God the Saviour
   Thankful hearts we bring;
   Unto God the Spirit
   Bow we and adore;
   On our way rejoicing
   Ever, evermore.

Rev. John S. B. Monsell, 1863, 1873: verse 1, ll. 6, 8, alt.

Consecration and Service

167 ALL SAINTS NEW C. M. D. — Henry S. Cutler, 1872

1 The Son of God goes forth to war, A kingly crown to gain;
His blood-red banner streams afar: Who follows in His train?
Who best can drink his cup of woe, Triumphant over pain,
Who patient bears his cross below, He follows in His train. A-MEN.

2 The martyr first, whose eagle eye Could pierce beyond the grave,
Who saw his Master in the sky, And called on Him to save:
Like Him, with pardon on his tongue In midst of mortal pain,
He prayed for them that did the wrong: Who follows in his train?

3 A glorious band, the chosen few
On whom the Spirit came,
Twelve valiant saints, their hope they knew,
And mocked the cross and flame:
They met the tyrant's brandished steel,
The lion's gory mane ;
They bowed their necks the death to feel :
Who follows in their train?

4 A noble army, men and boys,
The matron and the maid,
Around the Saviour's throne rejoice,
In robes of light arrayed:
They climbed the steep ascent of heaven
Through peril, toil, and pain ;
O God, to us may grace be given
To follow in their train.

Bishop Reginald Heber, publ. 1827

The Church

168 MAITLAND C. M. George N. Allen, 1850

1 Must Jesus bear the cross alone, And all the world go free? No, there's a cross for every one, And there's a cross for me. A-MEN.

2 How happy are the saints above,
Who once went sorrowing here ;
But now they taste unmingled love,
And joy without a tear.

3 The consecrated cross I'll bear
Till death shall set me free ;
And then go home my crown to wear,
For there's a crown for me.

4 Upon the crystal pavement, down
At Jesus' piercèd feet,
Joyful, I'll cast my golden crown,
And His dear Name repeat.

5 O precious cross! O glorious crown!
O resurrection day !
Ye angels, from the stars flash down,
And bear my soul away.

Verse 1, Rev. Thomas Shepherd, 1693, alt. ; verse 2, anon., c. 1810 ;
verse 3, anon., 1849 ; verses 4, 5, Rev. Charles Beecher, 1855

ST. MARK C. M. Henry J. Gauntlett (1805–1876)

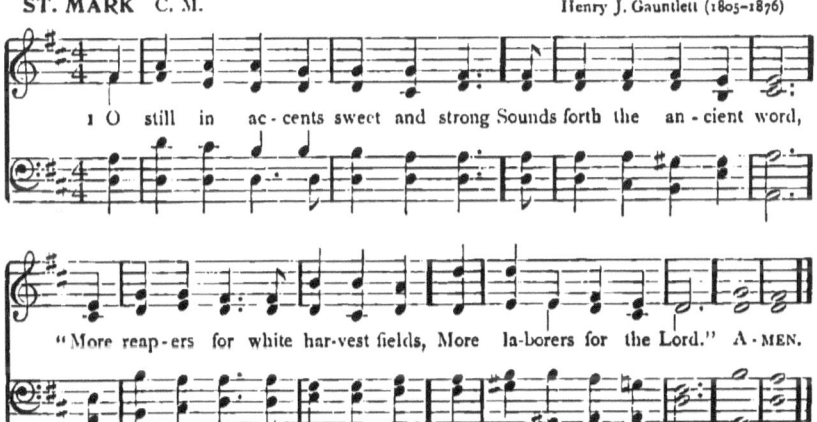

1 O still in accents sweet and strong Sounds forth the ancient word, "More reapers for white harvest fields, More laborers for the Lord." A-MEN.

Consecration and Service

169 WINTERTON 6. 4. 6. 4. 6. 6. 6. 4.   Sir Joseph Barnby, 1892

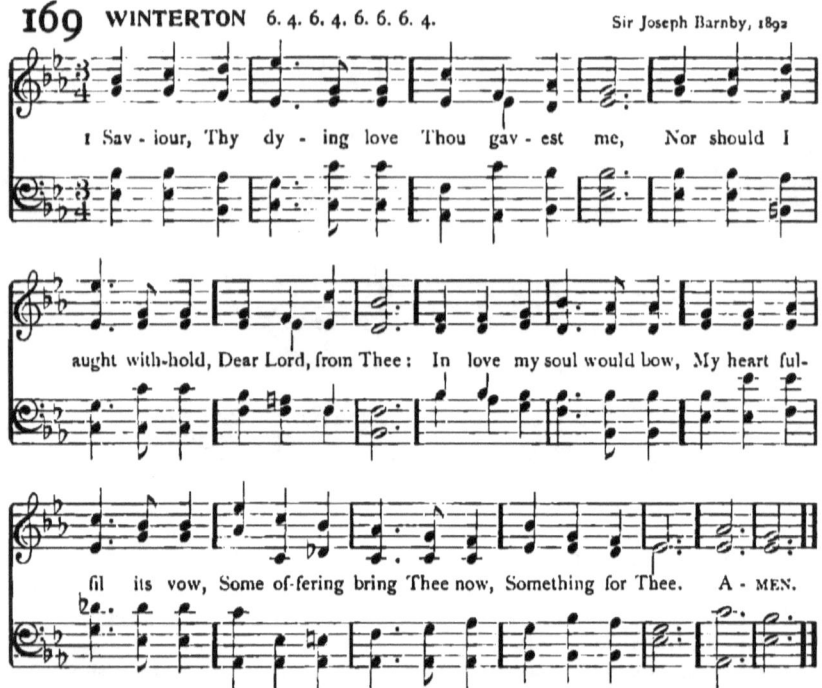

1 Saviour, Thy dying love Thou gavest me, Nor should I aught withhold, Dear Lord, from Thee: In love my soul would bow, My heart fulfil its vow, Some offering bring Thee now, Something for Thee. A-MEN.

2 O'er the blest mercy-seat
  Pleading for me,
Upward in faith I look,
  Jesus, to Thee:
Help me the cross to bear,
Thy wondrous love declare,
Some song to raise, or prayer,
  Something for Thee.

3 Give me a faithful heart,
  Likeness to Thee,
That each departing day
  Henceforth may see
Some work of love begun,
Some deed of kindness done,
Some wanderer sought and won,
  Something for Thee.

Rev. S. Dryden Phelps, 1862

170 (ST. MARK) C. M.

1 O STILL in accents sweet and strong
  Sounds forth the ancient word,
"More reapers for white harvest fields,
  More laborers for the Lord."

2 We hear the call; in dreams no more
  In selfish ease we lie,
But, girded for our Father's work,
  Go forth beneath His sky.

3 Where prophets' word, and martyrs' blood,
  And prayers of saints were sown,
We, to their labors entering in,
  Would reap where they have strown.

4 O Thou whose call our hearts has stirred,
  To do Thy will we come;
Thrust in our sickles at Thy word,
  And bear our harvest home.

Rev. Samuel Longfellow, 1864

The Church

171 WORK SONG 7. 6. 7. 5. D. — Lowell Mason, 1864

Copyright. By per. of Oliver Ditson Company

2 Work, for the night is coming :
  Work through the sunny noon ;
  Fill brightest hours with labor,
  Rest comes sure and soon ;
  Give every flying minute
  Something to keep in store ;
  Work, for the night is coming,
  When man works no more.

3 Work, for the night is coming :
  Under the sunset skies,
  While their bright tints are glowing,
  Work, for daylight flies ;
  Work till the last beam fadeth,
  Fadeth to shine no more ;
  Work while the night is darkening,
  When man's work is o'er.

Anna L. Coghill, c. 1860; alt.

Charities and Missions

172 FIAT LUX 6.6.4.6.6.6.4.   Rev. John B. Dykes, 1875

1 Christ for the world we sing; The world to Christ we bring With loving zeal; The poor and them that mourn, The faint and o-verborne, Sin-sick and sorrow-worn, Whom Christ doth heal. A-MEN.

2 Christ for the world we sing;
The world to Christ we bring
   With fervent prayer;
The wayward and the lost,
By restless passions tossed,
Redeemed at countless cost
   From dark despair.

3 Christ for the world we sing;
The world to Christ we bring
   With one accord;
With us the work to share,
With us reproach to dare,
With us the cross to bear,
   For Christ our Lord.

4 Christ for the world we sing;
The world to Christ we bring
   With joyful song;
The new-born souls whose days,
Reclaimed from error's ways,
Inspired with hope and praise,
   To Christ belong.

Rev. Samuel Wolcott, 1869

The Church

173 ELMHURST 8. 8. 8. 6.   Edwin Drewett, 1887

1 O God of mer-cy, God of might, In love and pit-y in-fi-nite, Teach us, as ev-er in Thy sight, To live our life to Thee. A-MEN.

2 And Thou who cam'st on earth to die,
That fallen man might live thereby,
O hear us, for to Thee we cry
 In hope, O Lord, to Thee.

3 Teach us the lesson Thou hast taught,
To feel for those Thy blood hath bought;
That every word and deed and thought
 May work a work for Thee.

4 For all are brethren, far and wide,
Since Thou, O Lord, for all hast died;
Then teach us, whatsoe'er betide,
 To love them all in Thee.

5 In sickness, sorrow, want, or care,
Whate'er it be, 'tis ours to share ;
May we, when help is needed, there
 Give help as unto Thee.

6 And may Thy Holy Spirit move
All those who live, to live in love,
Till Thou shalt greet in heaven above
 All those who live to Thee.
                    Rev. Godfrey Thring, 1877 : verse 6, l. 4, alt.

174 (REMSEN) C. M.

1 LORD, lead the way the Saviour went,
 By lane and cell obscure ;
And let love's treasures still be spent,
 Like His, upon the poor.

2 Like Him, through scenes of deep distress,
 Who bore the world's sad weight,
We, in their crowded loneliness,
 Would seek the desolate.

3 For Thou hast placed us side by side
 In this wide world of ill ;
And, that Thy followers may be tried,
 The poor are with us still.

4 Mean are all offerings we can make ;
 Yet Thou hast taught us, Lord,
If given for the Saviour's sake,
 They lose not their reward.
                    Rev. William Croswell, 1831

Charities and Missions

175 REDHEAD No. 45 7.7.7.7. Old French Melody: arr. by R. Redhead, 1853

1 Sol-diers of the cross, a-rise, Gird you with your ar-mor bright;
Might-y are your en-e-mies, Hard the bat-tle ye must fight. A-MEN.

2 O'er a faithless fallen world
  Raise your banner in the sky;
  Let it float there wide unfurled;
  Bear it onward; lift it high.

3 'Mid the homes of want and woe,
  Strangers to the living word,
  Let the Saviour's herald go,
  Let the voice of hope be heard.

4 Where the shadows deepest lie,
  Carry truth's unsullied ray;
  Where are crimes of blackest dye,
  There the saving sign display.

5 Be the banner still unfurled,
  Still unsheathed the Spirit's sword,
  Till the kingdoms of the world
  Are the kingdom of the Lord.

Bishop William W. How, 1854

REMSEN C. M. Joseph P. Holbrook, 1862

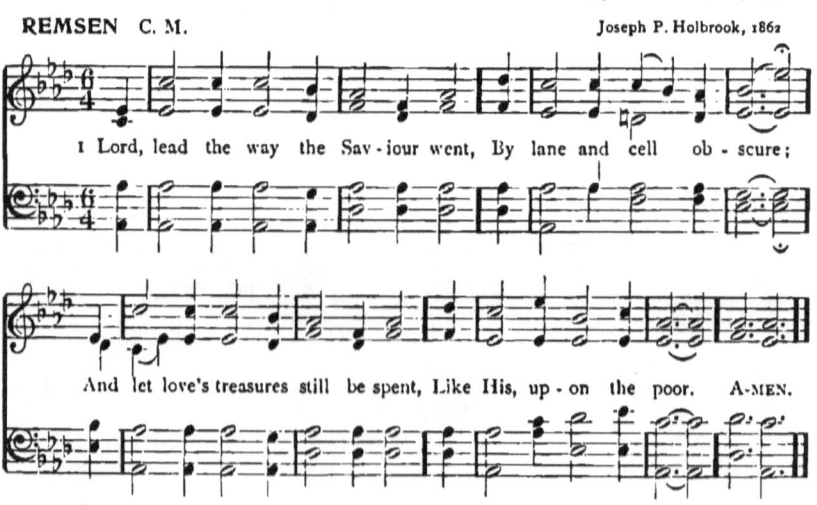

1 Lord, lead the way the Sav-iour went, By lane and cell ob-scure;
And let love's treasures still be spent, Like His, up-on the poor. A-MEN.

The Church

176 LENOX 6. 6. 6. 6. 8. 8.   Lewis Edson, 1782

1 Blow ye the trum-pet, blow, The glad-ly sol-emn sound; Let all the nations know, To earth's re-mot-est bound, The year of Ju-bi-lee is come, The year of Ju-bi-lee is come; Re-turn, ye ran-somed sin-ners, home. A-MEN.

2 Jesus, our Great High Priest,
   Hath full atonement made;
   Ye weary spirits, rest;
   Ye mournful souls, be glad:
The year of Jubilee is come;
Return, ye ransomed sinners, home.

3 Extol the Lamb of God,
   The all-atoning Lamb;
   Redemption in His blood
   Throughout the world proclaim:
The year of Jubilee is come;
Return, ye ransomed sinners, home.
                    Rev. Charles Wesley, 1750

177 (VIGIL) S. M.

1 O PRAISE our God to-day,
   His constant mercy bless,
Whose love hath helped us on our way,
   And granted us success.

2 His arm the strength imparts
   Our daily toil to bear;
His grace alone inspires our hearts
   Each other's load to share.

3 O happiest work below,
   Earnest of joy above,
To sweeten many a cup of woe
   By deeds of holy love!

4 Lord, may it be our choice
   This blessèd rule to keep,
"Rejoice with them that do rejoice,
   And weep with them that weep."
              Rev. Sir Henry W. Baker, Bart., 1861

Charities and Missions

178 SCHUMANN S. M.   Ascribed to Robert Schumann (1810–1856)

1 We give Thee but Thine own, What-e'er the gift may be: All that we have is Thine a-lone, A trust, O Lord, from Thee. A-MEN.

2 May we Thy bounties thus
   As stewards true receive,
And gladly, as Thou blessest us,
   To Thee our first-fruits give.

3 O hearts are bruised and dead,
   And homes are bare and cold,
And lambs for whom the Shepherd bled
   Are straying from the fold.

4 To comfort and to bless,
   To find a balm for woe,
To tend the lone and fatherless,
   Is angels' work below.

5 The captive to release,
   To God the lost to bring,
To teach the way of life and peace,—
   It is a Christ-like thing.

6 And we believe Thy word,
   Though dim our faith may be,
Whate'er for Thine we do, O Lord,
   We do it unto Thee.

Bishop William W. How, 1864

VIGIL S. M.   Arr. for St. Alban's Tune Book, 1865

1 O praise our God to-day, His con-stant mer-cy bless, Whose love hath helped us on our way, And grant-ed us suc-cess. A-MEN.

The Church

179 CALL THEM IN 8.7.8.7. D. with Refrain   Rev. Ethelbert W. Bullinger

1 Call them in! the poor, the wretched, Sin-stained wand-erers from the fold;
Peace and par-don free-ly of-fer; Can you weigh their worth with gold?
(alto) weigh their worth with gold?
Call them in! the Jew, the Gen-tile; Bid the stran-ger to the feast:
Call them in! the rich, the no-ble, From the high-est to the least.

REFRAIN.
Call them in! the weak, the wea-ry, La-den with the doom of sin;

Charities and Missions

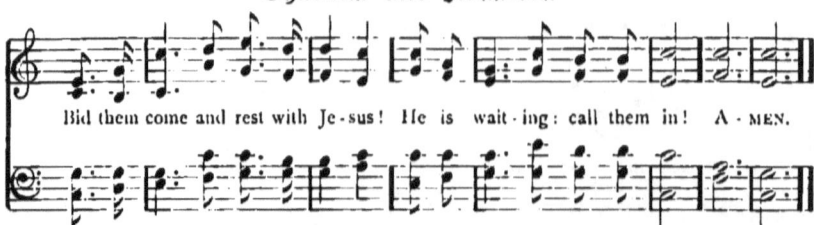

Bid them come and rest with Je-sus! He is wait-ing: call them in! A-MEN.

2 Call them in! the little children,
Ere they wander far away;
Wait, O wait not for to-morrow;
Christ would have them come to-day.
Follow on! the Lamb is leading;
He has conquered,—we shall win:
Bring the halt and blind to Jesus;
He will heal them: call them in!—REF.

3 Call them in! the broken-hearted,
Cowering 'neath the brand of shame:
Speak Love's message, low and tender;
'Twas for sinners Jesus came.
See! the shadows lengthen 'round us,
Soon the day-dawn will begin;
Can you leave the lost and lonely?
Christ is coming: call them in!—REF.

Anna Shipton, 1862; arr.

180 INASMUCH 8. 8. 8.

Uzziah C. Burnap, 1895

1 O daugh-ters blest of Gal-i-lee, With Je-sus chose ye well to be, Thrice hap-py ho-ly com-pan-y! A-MEN.

Copyright, 1895, by The Trustees of The Presbyterian Board of Publication and Sabbath-School Work

2 O joy, to see that Master dear!
O joy, to live with Him so near!
O joy, that gentle voice to hear!

3 O more than joy, to that dear Lord,
In purest, deepest love adored,
All lowly service to afford!

4 O Jesus, throned above the height,
Adoring troops of angels bright
Wait on Thy bidding day and night:

5 Thy sacred form we cannot see,
Yet, Lord, these hands may render Thee
Each lowly act of charity.

6 For while 'mid want and woe we move,
And tend Thy poor in gentle love,
We minister to Thee above.

7 O gracious Jesus, we confess
Our poor cold love, our nothingness:
Yet Thou wilt own, and Thou wilt bless.

Bishop William W. How, 1867

The Church

181 WEBB 7. 6. 7. 6. D.   George J. Webb, 1837

1. Hail to the Lord's Anointed, Great David's greater Son!
Hail, in the time appointed, His reign on earth begun!
He comes to break oppression, To set the captive free,
To take away transgression, And rule in equity.

2. He shall come down like showers Upon the fruitful earth;
And love, joy, hope, like flowers, Spring in His path to birth;
Before Him on the mountains Shall peace, the herald, go,
And righteousness, in fountains, From hill to valley flow. A-MEN.

3 Kings shall fall down before Him,
  And gold and incense bring;
All nations shall adore Him,
  His praise all people sing;
For He shall have dominion
  O'er river, sea, and shore,
Far as the eagle's pinion
  Or dove's light wing can soar.

4 O'er every foe victorious,
  He on His throne shall rest,
From age to age more glorious,
  All blessing and all-blest:
The tide of time shall never
  His covenant remove,
His Name shall stand for ever,—
  That Name to us is Love.

                       James Montgomery, 1821

Charities and Missions

182 (WEBB) 7.6.7.6. D.

1. THE morning light is breaking,
   The darkness disappears;
   The sons of earth are waking
   To penitential tears;
   Each breeze that sweeps the ocean
   Brings tidings from afar
   Of nations in commotion,
   Prepared for Zion's war.

2. See heathen nations bending
   Before the God we love,
   And thousand hearts ascending
   In gratitude above;
   While sinners, now confessing,
   The gospel call obey,
   And seek the Saviour's blessing,
   A nation in a day.

3. Blest river of salvation,
   Pursue thy onward way;
   Flow thou to every nation,
   Nor in thy richness stay:
   Stay not till all the lowly
   Triumphant reach their home;
   Stay not till all the holy
   Proclaim, "The Lord is come."

Rev. Samuel F. Smith, 1832

183 WALTHAM L. M.   J. Baptiste Calkin, 1872

1 Fling out the banner! let it float Skyward and seaward, high and wide;
The sun that lights its shining folds, The cross on which the Saviour died. A-MEN.

2. Fling out the banner! angels bend
   In anxious silence o'er the sign,
   And vainly seek to comprehend
   The wonder of the love Divine.

3. Fling out the banner! heathen lands
   Shall see from far the glorious sight,
   And nations, crowding to be born,
   Baptize their spirits in its light.

4. Fling out the banner! sin-sick souls,
   That sink and perish in the strife,
   Shall touch in faith its radiant hem,
   And spring immortal into life.

5. Fling out the banner! let it float
   Skyward and seaward, high and wide,
   Our glory, only in the cross;
   Our only hope, the Crucified!

Bishop George W. Doane, 1848

The Church

184 SCHUBERT 7.6.7.6.D.   Arr. from Schubert by William W. Gilchrist, 1895

1. And is the time ap-proach-ing, By proph-ets long fore-told,
   When all shall dwell to-geth-er, One Shep-herd and one fold?
   Shall ev-ery i-dol per-ish, To moles and bats be thrown?
   And ev-ery prayer be of-fered To God in Christ a-lone? A-MEN.

2. Shall Jew and Gen-tile meet-ing From many a dis-tant shore,
   A-round one al-tar kneel-ing, One com-mon Lord a-dore?
   Shall all that now di-vides us Re-move, and pass a-way
   Like shad-ows of the morn-ing Be-fore the blaze of day?

Copyright, 1895, by The Trustees of The Presbyterian Board of Publication and Sabbath-School Work

3 Shall all that now unites us
  More sweet and lasting prove,
  A closer bond of union
  In a blest land of love?
  Shall war be learned no longer?
  Shall strife and tumult cease?
  All earth His blessèd kingdom,
  The Lord and Prince of Peace!

4 O long-expected dawning,
  Come with thy cheering ray;
  When shall the morning brighten,
  The shadows flee away?
  O sweet anticipation!
  It cheers the watchers on
  To pray, and hope, and labor,
  Till the dark night be gone.

Jane Borthwick, 1859

Charities and Missions

185 MISSIONARY HYMN 7.6.7.6. D. Lowell Mason, 1823

1. From Greenland's icy mountains, From India's coral strand,
Where Afric's sunny fountains Roll down their golden sand,
From many an ancient river, From many a palmy plain,
They call us to deliver Their land from error's chain.

2. What though the spicy breezes Blow soft o'er Ceylon's isle;
Though every prospect pleases, And only man is vile:
In vain with lavish kindness The gifts of God are strown;
The heathen in his blindness Bows down to wood and stone.

3. Can we, whose souls are lighted
With wisdom from on high,
Can we to men benighted
The lamp of life deny?
Salvation! O salvation!
The joyful sound proclaim,
Till each remotest nation
Has learned Messiah's Name.

4. Waft, waft, ye winds, His story,
And you, ye waters, roll,
Till like a sea of glory
It spreads from pole to pole;
Till o'er our ransomed nature
The Lamb for sinners slain,
Redeemer, King, Creator,
In bliss returns to reign.

Bishop Reginald Heber, 1819

The Church

186 WILDERSMOUTH 8. 7. 8. 7. 4. 7.   Edward J. Hopkins, 1879

1 O'er the gloom-y hills of dark-ness, Cheered by no ce-les-tial ray,
Sun of Right-eous-ness, a-ris-ing, Bring the bright, the glo-rious day;
Send the gos-pel To the earth's re-mot-est bounds. A---MEN.

2 Kingdoms wide that sit in darkness,
　Grant them, Lord, the glorious light;
　And from eastern coast to western
　May the morning chase the night,
　　And redemption,
　Freely purchased, win the day.

3 Fly abroad, thou mighty gospel,
　Win and conquer, never cease;
　May thy lasting, wide dominions
　Multiply and still increase;
　　Sway Thy sceptre,
　Saviour, all the world around.

　　　　Rev. William Williams, 1772: verse 1, re-written; verse 2, l. 2, and verse 3, alt.

187 (MISSIONARY CHANT) L. M.

1 YE Christian heralds, go proclaim
　Salvation through Emmanuel's Name;
　To distant climes the tidings bear,
　And plant the Rose of Sharon there.

2 God shield you with a wall of fire,
　With flaming zeal your breasts inspire,
　Bid raging winds their fury cease,
　And hush the tempests into peace.

3 And when our labors all are o'er,
　Then we shall meet to part no more;
　Meet with the blood-bought throng to fall,
　And crown our Jesus Lord of all.

　　　　Rev. Bourne H. Draper, 1803: verse 1, ll. 1, 3, verse 2, l. 1, alt.

Charities and Missions

188 GRACE CHURCH L. M.
Arr. from Ignace Pleyel, 1815

1 Look from the sphere of end-less day, O God of mer-cy and of might;
In pit-y look on those who stray, Be-night-ed, in this land of light. A-MEN.

2 In peopled vale, in lonely glen,
In crowded mart by stream or sea,
How many of the sons of men
Hear not the message sent from Thee!

3 Send forth Thy heralds, Lord, to call
The thoughtless young, the hardened old,
A wandering flock, and bring them all
To the Good Shepherd's peaceful fold.

4 Send them Thy mighty word to speak,
Till faith shall dawn and doubt depart,
To awe the bold, to stay the weak,
And bind and heal the broken heart.

5 Then all these wastes, a dreary scene,
On which with sorrowing eyes we gaze,
Shall grow with living waters green,
And lift to heaven the voice of praise.

William Cullen Bryant, 1859

MISSIONARY CHANT L. M.
Charles Zeuner, 1832

1 Ye Chris-tian her-alds, go pro-claim Sal-va-tion through Em-man-uel's Name;
To dis-tant climes the tidings bear, And plant the Rose of Shar-on there. A-MEN.

The Church

189 WATCHMAN 7. 7, 7. 7. D. Lowell Mason, 1830

1 Watchman, tell us of the night, What its signs of promise are:
Traveller, o'er yon mountain's height, See that glory-beaming star!
Watchman, doth its beauteous ray Aught of joy or hope foretell?
Traveller, yes; it brings the day, Promised day of Israel. A-MEN.

2 Watchman, tell us of the night;
   Higher yet that star ascends:
Traveller, blessedness and light,
   Peace and truth, its course portends.
Watchman, will its beams alone
   Gild the spot that gave them birth?
Traveller, ages are its own,
   See, it bursts o'er all the earth.

3 Watchman, tell us of the night,
   For the morning seems to dawn:
Traveller, darkness takes its flight,
   Doubt and terror are withdrawn.
Watchman, let thy wanderings cease;
   Hie thee to thy quiet home:
Traveller, lo, the Prince of Peace,
   Lo, the Son of God is come!

Sir John Bowring, 1825 : verse 1, l. 6, verse 2, l. 8, alt.

Charities and Missions

190 LATTER DAY 8. 7. 8. 7. D.   Plymouth Collection, 1855

1 We are living, we are dwelling, In a grand and awful time;
In an age on ages telling, To be living is sublime.
Hark! the waking up of nations, Gog and Magog to the fray:
Hark! what soundeth is creation's Groaning for its latter day. A-MEN.

2 Worlds are charging, heaven beholding;
   Thou hast but an hour to fight;
Now, the blazoned cross unfolding,
   On, right onward, for the right!
On! let all the soul within you
   For the truth's sake go abroad;
Strike! let every nerve and sinew
   Tell on ages, tell for God.

Bishop A. Cleveland Coxe, 1840

The Church

191 PARK STREET L. M. Arr. from Frederick M. A. Venua, c. 1810

1 Jesus shall reign wher-e'er the sun Does his suc-ces-sive jour-neys run; His king-dom stretch from shore to shore, Till moons shall wax and wane no more, Till moons shall wax and wane no more. A-MEN.

2 For Him shall endless prayer be made,
And praises throng to crown His head:
His Name, like sweet perfume, shall rise
With every morning sacrifice;

3 People and realms of every tongue
Dwell on His love with sweetest song;
And infant voices shall proclaim
Their early blessings on His Name.

4 Blessings abound where'er He reigns;
The prisoner leaps to lose his chains,
The weary find eternal rest,
And all the sons of want are blest.

5 Let every creature rise and bring
Peculiar honors to our King,
Angels descend with songs again,
And earth repeat the loud Amen.

Rev. Isaac Watts, 1719

192 (GERMANY) L. M.

1 O CHRIST, our true and only Light,
Illumine those who sit in night;
Let those afar now hear Thy voice,
And in Thy fold with us rejoice.

2 And all who else have strayed from Thee,
O gently seek; Thy healing be
To every wounded conscience given;
And let them also share Thy heaven.

3 Shine on the darkened and the cold;
Recall the wanderers from Thy fold;
Unite those now who walk apart;
Confirm the weak and doubting heart:

4 So they with us may evermore
Such grace with wondering thanks adore,
And endless praise to Thee be given
By all the Church in earth and heaven.

Rev. Johann Heermann, 1630. Tr. Catherine Winkworth, 1858

The Communion of Saints

193 ALMSGIVING 8.8.8.4. Rev. John B. Dykes, 1865

1 Father of all, from land and sea
The nations sing, "Thine, Lord, are we;
Countless in number, but in Thee
May we be one." A-MEN.

2 O Son of God, whose love so free
For men did make Thee Man to be,
United to our God in Thee
　May we be one.

3 Thou, Lord, didst once for all atone;
Thee may both Jew and Gentile own
Of their two walls the Corner-stone,
　Making them one.

4 Join high with low, join young with old,
In love that never waxes cold;
Under one Shepherd, in one fold,
　Make us all one.

5 O Spirit blest, who from above
Cam'st gently gliding like a dove,
Calm all our strife, give faith and love;
　O make us one.

　　　　Bishop Christopher Wordsworth, 1871

GERMANY L. M. Wm. Gardiner's Sacred Melodies, 1815

1 O Christ, our true and only Light,
Illumine those who sit in night;
Let those afar now hear Thy voice,
And in Thy fold with us rejoice. A-MEN.

The Church

194 PLEYEL'S HYMN 7. 7. 7. 7. Arr. from Ignace Pleyel, 1790

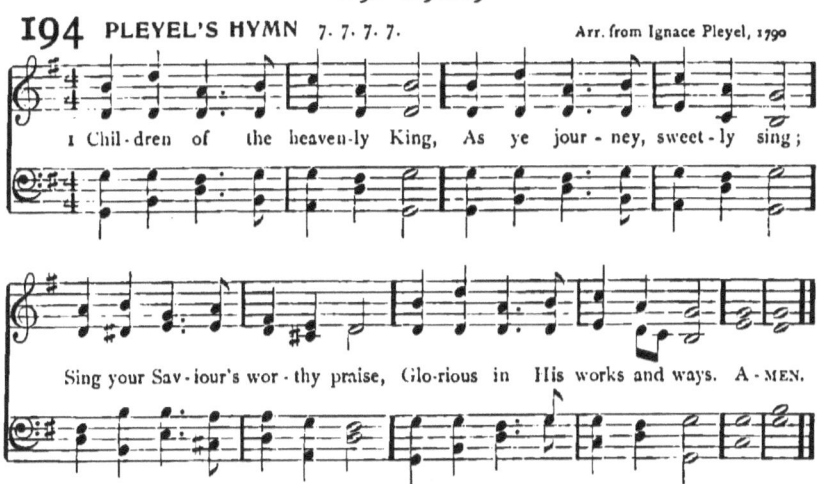

1 Children of the heavenly King, As ye journey, sweetly sing;
Sing your Saviour's worthy praise, Glorious in His works and ways. A-MEN.

2 We are travelling home to God
In the way the fathers trod;
They are happy now, and we
Soon their happiness shall see.

3 Shout, ye little flock and blest;
Ye on Jesus' throne shall rest;
There your seat is now prepared,
There your kingdom and reward.

4 Fear not, brethren; joyful stand
On the borders of your land;
Jesus Christ, your Father's Son,
Bids you undismayed go on.

5 Lord, obediently we go,
Gladly leaving all below;
Only Thou our Leader be,
And we still will follow Thee.

Rev. John Cennick, 1742

ROSEFIELD 7. 7. 7. 7. 7. 7. Rev. H. A. César Malan, 1834

1 {Blessed are the sons of God, They are bought with Christ's own blood;
 {They are ransomed from the grave, Life eternal they shall have:
With them numbered may we be, Here and in eternity. A-MEN.

The Communion of Saints

195 BOYLSTON S. M. Lowell Mason, 1832

1 Blest be the tie that binds Our hearts in Christian love:
The fellowship of kindred minds Is like to that above. A-MEN.

2 Before our Father's throne
  We pour our ardent prayers;
  Our fears, our hopes, our aims, are one,
  Our comforts and our cares.

3 We share our mutual woes,
  Our mutual burdens bear,
  And often for each other flows
  The sympathizing tear.

4 When we asunder part,
  It gives us inward pain;
  But we shall still be joined in heart,
  And hope to meet again.

5 This glorious hope revives
  Our courage by the way,
  While each in expectation lives,
  And longs to see the day.

6 From sorrow, toil, and pain,
  And sin, we shall be free;
  And perfect love and friendship reign
  Through all eternity.
                              Rev. John Fawcett, 1782

196 (ROSEFIELD) 7. 7. 7. 7. 7. 7.

1 BLESSÈD are the sons of God,
  They are bought with Christ's own blood;
  They are ransomed from the grave,
  Life eternal they shall have:
  With them numbered may we be,
  Here and in eternity.

2 They are justified by grace,
  They enjoy the Saviour's peace;
  All their sins are washed away,
  They shall stand in God's great day:
  With them numbered may we be,
  Here and in eternity.

3 They are lights upon the earth,
  Children of a heavenly birth;
  One with God, with Jesus one,
  Glory is in them begun:
  With them numbered may we be,
  Here and in eternity.
              Rev. Joseph Humphreys, 1743;
              arr. and verse 2, l. 2, alt.

The Church

197 BROWN C.M.
William B. Bradbury, 1844

1 Come, let us join our friends above That have obtained the prize, And on the eagle wings of love To joy celestial rise; A-MEN.

2 Let all the saints terrestrial sing
   With those to glory gone,
For all the servants of our King
   In earth and heaven are one.

3 One family we dwell in Him,
   One Church, above, beneath,
Though now divided by the stream,
   The narrow stream of death;

4 One army of the living God,
   To His command we bow;
Part of His host hath crossed the flood,
   And part is crossing now.

5 His militant, embodied host,
   With wishful looks we stand,
And long to see that happy coast,
   And reach that heavenly land:

6 E'en now by faith we join our hands
   With those that went before,
And greet the blood-besprinkled bands
   On the eternal shore.

Rev. Charles Wesley, 1759

198 (NORTHREPPS) C.M.

1 GIVE me the wings of faith to rise
   Within the veil, and see
The saints above, how great their joys,
   And bright their glories be.

2 Once they were mourning here below,
   And wet their couch with tears;
They wrestled hard, as we do now,
   With sins, and doubts, and fears.

3 I ask them whence their victory came;
   They, with united breath, .
Ascribe their conquest to the Lamb,
   Their triumph to His death.

4 They marked the footsteps that He trod,
   His zeal inspired their breast;
And, following their incarnate God,
   Possess the promised rest.

5 Our glorious Leader claims our praise
   For His own pattern given,
While the long cloud of witnesses
   Show the same path to heaven.

Rev. Isaac Watts, 1709

The Communion of Saints

199 WOOLWICH S. M.   Charles E. Kettle, 1876

1 O what, if we are Christ's, Is earth-ly shame or loss? Bright shall the crown of glo-ry be When we have borne the cross. A-MEN.

2 Keen was the trial once,
Bitter the cup of woe,
When martyred saints, baptized in blood,
Christ's sufferings shared below.

3 Bright is their glory now,
Boundless their joy above,
Where, on the bosom of their God,
They rest in perfect love.

4 Lord, may that grace be ours,
Like them in faith to bear
All that of sorrow, grief, or pain,
May be our portion here.

5 Enough, if Thou at last
The word of blessing give,
And let us rest beneath Thy feet,
Where saints and angels live.

Rev. Sir Henry W. Baker, Bart., 1852

NORTHREPPS C. M.   Josiah Booth, 1887

1 Give me the wings of faith to rise With-in the veil, and see The saints a-bove, how great their joys, And bright their glo-ries be. A-MEN.

The Church

200 SARUM 10. 10. 10. 4.   Sir Joseph Barnby, 1869

1 For all the saints who from their labors rest, Who Thee by faith before the world confessed, Thy Name, O Jesus, be forever blest. Alleluia! Alleluia! A-men.

2 Thou wast their Rock, their Fortress, and their Might;
Thou, Lord, their Captain in the well-fought fight;
Thou, in the darkness drear, their one true Light. Alleluia!

3 O may Thy soldiers, faithful, true, and bold,
Fight as the saints who nobly fought of old,
And win with them the victor's crown of gold. Alleluia!

4 O blest communion, fellowship Divine!
We feebly struggle, they in glory shine;
Yet all are one in Thee, for all are Thine. Alleluia!

5 And when the strife is fierce, the warfare long,
Steals on the ear the distant triumph-song,
And hearts are brave again, and arms are strong. Alleluia!

6 The golden evening brightens in the west;
Soon, soon to faithful warriors cometh rest;
Sweet is the calm of Paradise the blest. Alleluia!

7 But lo, there breaks a yet more glorious day;
The saints triumphant rise in bright array;
The King of Glory passes on His way. Alleluia!

The Grace of God in Christ

8 From earth's wide bounds, from ocean's farthest coast,
Through gates of pearl streams in the countless host,
Singing to Father, Son, and Holy Ghost. Alleluia!

Bishop William W. How, 1864

201 DEVOTION 6. 6. 6. 6. 6. 6. John H. Gower, 1895

1 Thy life was given for me, Thy blood, O Lord, was shed,
That I might ransomed be, And quickened from the dead:
Thy life was given for me; What have I given for Thee? A-MEN.

Copyright, 1895, by The Trustees of The Presbyterian Board of Publication and Sabbath-School Work

2 Long years were spent for me
  In weariness and woe,
That through eternity
  Thy glory I might know:
Long years were spent for me;
Have I spent one for Thee?

3 And Thou hast brought to me
  Down from Thy home above
Salvation full and free,
  Thy pardon and Thy love:

Great gifts Thou broughtest me;
What have I brought to Thee?

4 O let my life be given,
  My years for Thee be spent;
World-fetters all be riven,
  And joy with suffering blent:
Thou gav'st Thyself for me,
I give myself to Thee.

Frances R. Havergal, 1858;
recast, Church Hymns, 1871

Hymns of Salvation

202 COWPER C. M.
Lowell Mason, 1830

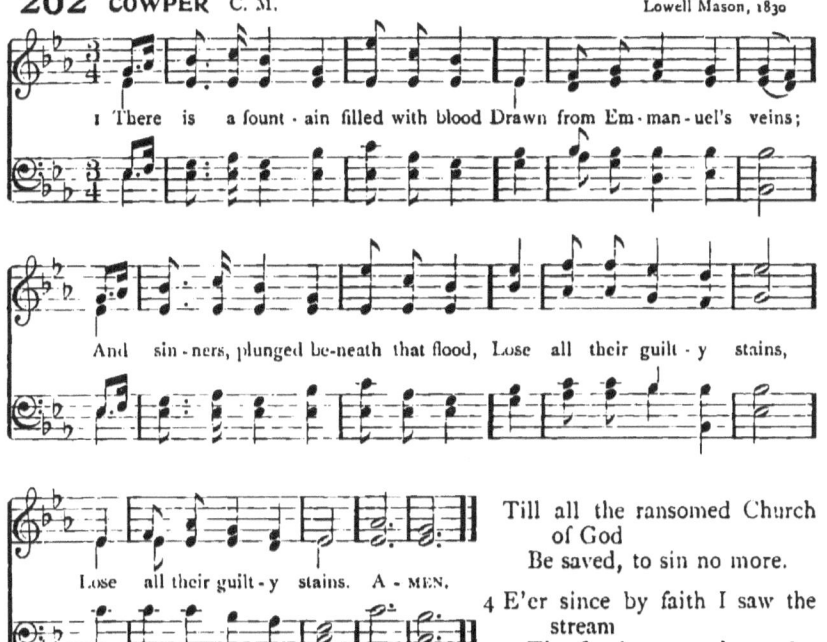

1 There is a fountain filled with blood Drawn from Emmanuel's veins; And sinners, plunged beneath that flood, Lose all their guilty stains, Lose all their guilty stains. A-MEN.

2 The dying thief rejoiced to see
   That fountain in his day;
And there have I, as vile as he,
   Washed all my sins away.

3 Dear dying Lamb, Thy precious blood
   Shall never lose its power
Till all the ransomed Church of God
   Be saved, to sin no more.

4 E'er since by faith I saw the stream
   Thy flowing wounds supply,
Redeeming love has been my theme,
   And shall be till I die.

5 Then in a nobler, sweeter song
   I'll sing Thy power to save,
When this poor lisping, stammering tongue
   Lies silent in the grave.

William Cowper, 1772

203 (OLMUTZ) S. M.

1 NOT all the blood of beasts
   On Jewish altars slain,
Could give the guilty conscience peace,
   Or wash away the stain:

2 But Christ, the heavenly Lamb,
   Takes all our sins away,
A sacrifice of nobler name
   And richer blood than they.

3 My faith would lay her hand
   On that dear head of Thine,
While like a penitent I stand,
   And there confess my sin.

4 My soul looks back to see
   The burdens Thou didst bear,
When hanging on the cursèd tree,
   And hopes her guilt was there.

Rev. Isaac Watts, 1709

The Grace of God in Christ

204 SILVER STREET S. M.
Isaac Smith, 1770

1 Grace! 'tis a charming sound, Harmonious to mine ear; Heaven with the echo shall resound, And all the earth shall hear. A-MEN.

2 Grace first contrived a way
To save rebellious man,
And all the steps that grace display
Which drew the wondrous plan.

3 Grace taught my wandering feet
To tread the heavenly road,
And new supplies each hour I meet
While pressing on to God.

4 Grace all the work shall crown
Through everlasting days;
It lays in heaven the topmost stone,
And well deserves the praise.

Rev. Philip Doddridge, publ. 1755

OLMUTZ S. M.
Arr. from a Gregorian Chant, by Lowell Mason, 1824

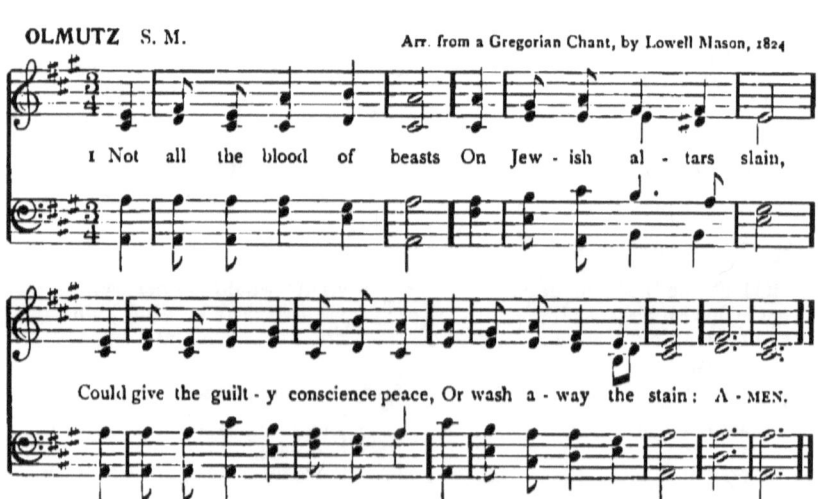

1 Not all the blood of beasts On Jewish altars slain, Could give the guilty conscience peace, Or wash away the stain: A-MEN.

Hymns of Salvation

205 CRUCIFER 8. 7. 8. 7. D.   Henry Smart, 1867

1 Was there ev-er kind-est shep-herd Half so gen-tle, half so sweet
As the Sav-iour who would have us Come and gath-er round His feet?
It is God; His love looks might-y, But is might-ier than it seems:
'Tis our Fa-ther; and His fond-ness Goes far out be-yond our dreams. A-MEN.

2 There's a wideness in God's mercy,
   Like the wideness of the sea ;
There's a kindness in His justice,
   Which is more than liberty.
There is welcome for the sinner,
   And more graces for the good ;
There is mercy with the Saviour,
   There is healing in His blood ;

3 There is plentiful redemption
   In the blood that has been shed ;
There is joy for all the members
   In the sorrows of the Head.
If our love were but more simple,
   We should take Him at His word ;
And our lives would be all sunshine
   In the sweetness of our Lord.
                    Rev. Frederick W. Faber, 1854

Invitation

206 SOFTLY AND TENDERLY 11.7.11.7. with Refrain Will L. Thompson, 1880

Copyright by Will L. Thompson & Co.

2 Why should we tarry when Jesus is pleading,
   Pleading for you and for me?
   Why should we linger and heed not His mercies,
   Mercies for you and for me?—REF.

3 O for the wonderful love He has promised,
   Promised for you and for me;
   Though we have sinned He has mercy and pardon,
   Pardon for you and for me.—REF.

Will L. Thompson, 1880

Hymns of Salvation

207 QUEBEC L. M.   Henry Baker, 1866

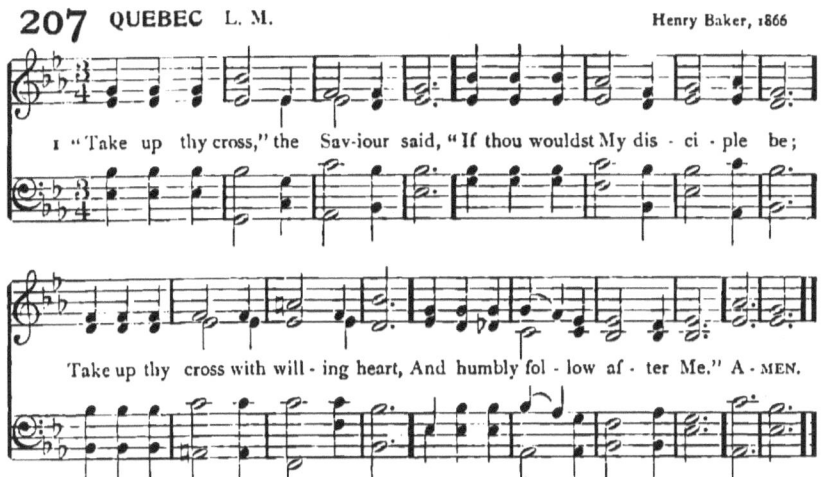

1 "Take up thy cross," the Saviour said, "If thou wouldst My disciple be; Take up thy cross with willing heart, And humbly follow after Me." A-MEN.

2 Take up thy cross; let not its weight
   Fill thy weak soul with vain alarm;
   His strength shall bear thy spirit up,
   And brace thy heart, and nerve thine arm.

3 Take up thy cross; nor heed the shame,
   And let thy foolish pride be still;
   Thy Lord refused not e'en to die
   Upon a cross, on Calvary's hill.

4 Take up thy cross, then, in His strength,
   And calmly sin's wild deluge brave;
   'Twill guide thee to a better home,
   It points to glory o'er the grave.

5 Take up thy cross, and follow on,
   Nor think till death to lay it down;
   For only he who bears the cross
   May hope to wear the glorious crown.

Rev. Charles W. Everest, 1833

ZEPHYR L. M.   William B. Bradbury, 1844

1 Behold! a Stranger's at the door; He gently knocks, has knocked before; Has waited long, is waiting still: You treat no other friend so ill. A-MEN.

Invitation

208 CLOLATA L. M.
W. St. Clair Palmer, 1893

1 God calling yet! shall I not hear? Earth's pleasures shall I still hold dear? Shall life's swift passing years all fly, And still my soul in slumbers lie? A-MEN.

2 God calling yet! shall I not rise?
Can I His loving voice despise,
And basely His kind care repay?
He calls me still; can I delay?

3 God calling yet! and shall He knock,
And I my heart the closer lock?
He still is waiting to receive,
And shall I dare His Spirit grieve?

4 God calling yet! and shall I give
No heed, but still in bondage live?
I wait, but He does not forsake;
He calls me still; my heart, awake!

5 God calling yet! I cannot stay;
My heart I yield without delay:
Vain world, farewell, from thee I part;
The voice of God hath reached my heart.

Gerhard Tersteegen, 1735: Tr. Sarah B. Findlater, 1855:
recast, Sabbath Hy. Bk., 1858

209 (ZEPHYR) L. M.

1 BEHOLD! a Stranger's at the door;
He gently knocks, has knocked before;
Has waited long, is waiting still:
You treat no other friend so ill.

2 But will He prove a friend indeed?
He will, the very Friend you need;
The Man of Nazareth, 'tis He,
With garments dyed at Calvary.

3 O lovely attitude! He stands
With melting heart and laden hands:
O matchless kindness! and He shows
This matchless kindness to His foes.

4 Rise, touched with gratitude Divine;
Turn out His enemy and thine,
That soul-destroying monster, sin,
And let the heavenly Stranger in.

5 Admit Him ere His anger burn;
His feet, departed, ne'er return:
Admit Him, or the hour's at hand
When at His door denied you'll stand.

Rev. Joseph Grigg, 1765: verse 4, l. 3, alt.

Hymns of Salvation

210 ST. EDITH 7.6.7.6. D.
Justin H. Knecht, 1799, and Rev. Edward Husband, 1871

1 O Jesus, Thou art standing Outside the fast-closed door, In lowly patience waiting To pass the threshold o'er: Shame on us, Christian brothers, His Name and sign who bear, O shame, thrice shame upon us, To keep Him standing there! A-MEN.

2 O Jesus, Thou art knocking;
And lo, that hand is scarred,
And thorns Thy brow encircle,
And tears Thy face have marred:
O love that passeth knowledge,
So patiently to wait!
O sin that hath no equal,
So fast to bar the gate!

3 O Jesus, Thou art pleading
In accents meek and low,
"I died for you, My children,
And will ye treat Me so?"
O Lord, with shame and sorrow
We open now the door;
Dear Saviour, enter, enter,
And leave us nevermore.

Bishop William W. How, 1867

Invitation

211 BLAIRGOWRIE 7.6.7.6. D.   Rev. John B. Dykes, 1872

1 To-day Thy mercy calls me
   To wash away my sin;
However great my trespass,
   Whate'er I may have been,
However long from mercy
   I may have turned away,
Thy blood, O Christ, can cleanse me,
   And make me white to-day.

2 To-day Thy gate is open,
   And all who enter in
Shall find a Father's welcome,
   And pardon for their sin;
The past shall be forgotten,
   A present joy be given,
A future grace be promised,
   A glorious crown in heaven.

3 To-day the Father calls me,
   The Holy Spirit waits,
The blessèd angels gather
   Around the heavenly gates:
No question will be asked me,
   How often I have come;
Although I oft have wandered,
   It is my Father's home.

4 O all-embracing mercy,
   Thou ever-open door,
What shall I do without thee
   When heart and eyes run o'er?
When all things seem against me,
   To drive me to despair,
I know one gate is open,
   One ear will hear my prayer.

                               Oswald Allen, 1861

Hymns of Salvation

212 INVITATION 6.6.6.6. D.   Frederick C. Maker, 1881

1. Come to the Saviour now, He gently calleth thee;
In true repentance bow, Before Him bend the knee;
He waiteth to bestow Salvation, peace, and love,
True joy on earth below, A home in heaven above. A-MEN.

2. Come to the Saviour now, Ye who have wandered far,
Renew your solemn vow, For His by right you are;
Come, like poor wandering sheep Returning to His fold;
His arm will safely keep, His love will ne'er grow cold.

3. Come to the Saviour, all,
Whate'er your burdens be;
Hear now His loving call,
"Cast all your care on Me."
Come, and for every grief
In Jesus you will find
A sure and safe relief,
A loving Friend, and kind.

John M. Wigner, 1871

213 (AZMON) C. M.

1. SALVATION! O the joyful sound;
'Tis pleasure to our ears,
A sovereign balm for every wound,
A cordial for our fears.

2. Buried in sorrow and in sin,
At hell's dark door we lay;
But we arise, by grace Divine,
To see a heavenly day.

3. Salvation! let the echo fly
The spacious earth around,
While all the armies of the sky
Conspire to raise the sound.

Rev. Isaac Watts, 1709

Invitation

214 VIGIL S. M. Arr. for St. Alban's Tune Book, 1865

1 To-mor-row, Lord, is Thine, Lodged in Thy sov-ereign hand;
And if its sun a-rise and shine, It shines by Thy com-mand. A-MEN.

2 The present moment flies,
   And bears our life away;
   O make Thy servants truly wise,
   That they may live to-day.

3 Since on this wingèd hour
   Eternity is hung,
   Waken, by Thine almighty power,
   The aged and the young.

4 One thing demands our care,
   O be it still pursued;
   Lest, slighted once, the season fair
   Should never be renewed.

5 To Jesus may we fly
   Swift as the morning light, [die
   Lest life's young golden beams should
   In sudden, endless night.

Rev. Philip Doddridge, publ. 1755

AZMON C. M. Arr. from Carl G Gläser, 1828, by Lowell Mason, 1839

1 Sal-va-tion! O the joy-ful sound; 'Tis pleas-ure to our ears,
A sovereign balm for ev-ery wound, A cor-dial for our fears. A-MEN.

Hymns of Salvation

215 STEPHANOS 8. 5. 8. 3.   Rev. Sir Henry W. Baker, Bart., 1868

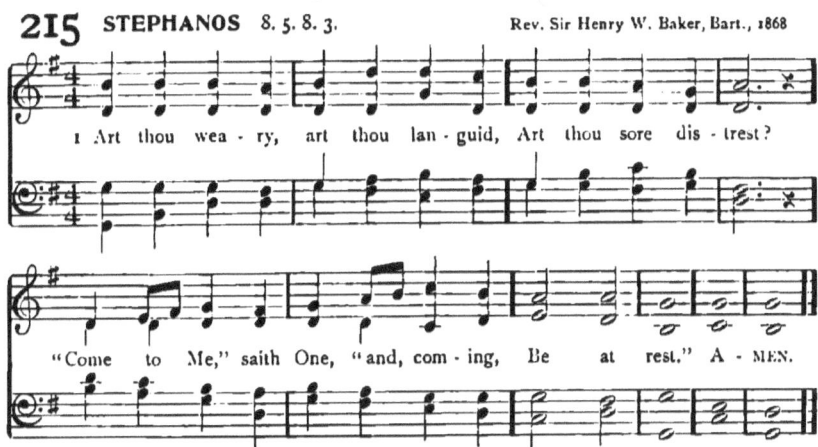

1 Art thou weary, art thou languid, Art thou sore distrest?
"Come to Me," saith One, "and, coming, Be at rest." A-MEN.

2 Hath He marks to lead me to Him,
   If He be my Guide?   [prints,
"In His feet and hands are wound-
   And His side."

3 Is there diadem, as Monarch,
   That His brow adorns?
"Yea, a crown, in very surety,
   But of thorns."

4 If I find Him, if I follow,
   What His guerdon here?
"Many a sorrow, many a labor,
   Many a tear."

5 If I still hold closely to Him,
   What hath He at last?
"Sorrow vanquished, labor ended,
   Jordan passed."

6 If I ask Him to receive me,
   Will He say me nay?
"Not till earth and not till heaven
   Pass away."

                                          Rev. John M. Neale, 1862

216 (ST. BEES) 7. 7. 7. 7.

1 Hark, my soul, it is the Lord!
'Tis thy Saviour, hear His word;
Jesus speaks, and speaks to thee,
"Say, poor sinner, lovest Thou Me?

2 "I delivered thee when bound,
And, when bleeding, healed thy wound;
Sought thee wandering, set thee right,
Turned thy darkness into light.

3 "Can a woman's tender care
Cease towards the child she bare?
Yes, she may forgetful be,
Yet will I remember thee.

4 "Mine is an unchanging love,
Higher than the heights above,
Deeper than the depths beneath,
Free and faithful, strong as death.

5 "Thou shalt see My glory soon,
When the work of grace is done;
Partner of My throne shalt be:
Say, poor sinner, lovest thou Me?"

6 Lord, it is my chief complaint,
That my love is weak and faint;
Yet I love Thee and adore;
O for grace to love Thee more!

                       William Cowper, 1768

Invitation

217 FORGIVENESS 7.7.7.7. George M. Garrett, 1872

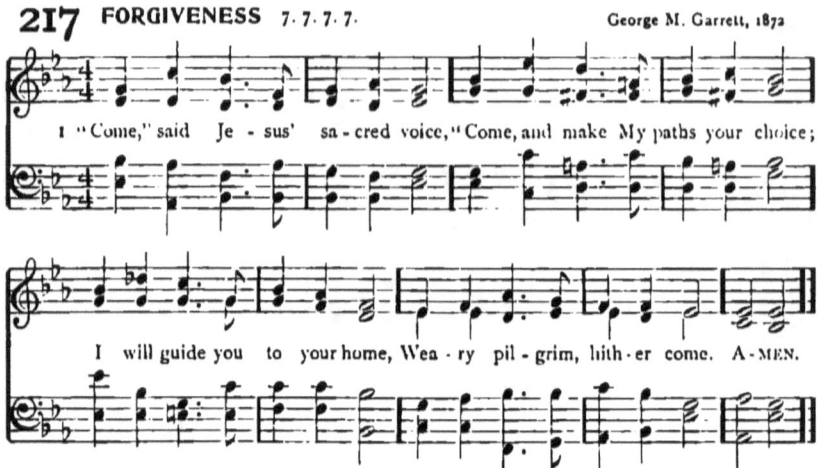

1 "Come," said Jesus' sacred voice, "Come, and make My paths your choice; I will guide you to your home, Weary pilgrim, hither come. A-MEN.

2 "Thou who, houseless, sole, forlorn,
Long hast borne the proud world's scorn,
Long hast roamed the barren waste,
Weary pilgrim, hither haste.

3 "Ye who, tossed on beds of pain,
Seek for ease, but seek in vain;

Ye, by fiercer anguish torn,
In remorse for guilt who mourn;

4 "Hither come, for here is found
Balm that flows for every wound,
Peace that ever shall endure,
Rest eternal, sacred, sure."

Anna L. Barbauld, 1792: verse 4, l. 1, alt.

ST. BEES 7.7.7.7. Rev. John B. Dykes, 1862

1 Hark, my soul, it is the Lord! 'Tis thy Saviour, hear His word; Jesus speaks, and speaks to thee, "Say, poor sinner, lovest thou Me? A-MEN.

Invitation

3 I love to tell the story;
  'Tis pleasant to repeat
What seems, each time I tell it,
  More wonderfully sweet.
I love to tell the story,
  For some have never heard
The message of salvation
  From God's own holy word.—REF.

4 I love to tell the story;
  For those who know it best
Seem hungering and thirsting
  To hear it, like the rest.
And when, in scenes of glory,
  I sing the new, new song,
'Twill be the old, old story
  That I have loved so long.—REF.
      Katherine Hankey, 1865: refrain added

219 ALMA 11. 10. 11. 10.　　　Arr. from Samuel Webbe, 1792

1 Come, ye disconsolate, where'er ye languish, Come to the mercy-seat, fervently kneel: Here bring your wounded hearts, here tell your anguish; Earth has no sorrows that heaven cannot heal. A-MEN.

2 Joy of the comfortless, light of the straying,
  Hope of the penitent, fadeless and pure!
Here speaks the Comforter, tenderly saying,
  "Earth has no sorrows that heaven cannot cure."

3 Here see the Bread of Life; see waters flowing
  Forth from the throne of God, pure from above:
Come to the feast prepared; come, ever knowing
  Earth has no sorrows but heaven can remove.
      Verses 1, 2, Thomas Moore, 1816, alt.; verse 3, Thomas Hastings, 1832

Invitation

2 Tell me the story softly,
   With earnest tones, and grave;
Remember, I'm the sinner
   Whom Jesus came to save:
Tell me the story always,
   If you would really be,
In any time of trouble,
   A comforter to me.—REF.

3 Tell me the same old story,
   When you have cause to fear
That this world's empty glory
   Is costing me too dear:
Yes, and when that world's glory
   Is dawning on my soul,
Tell me the old, old story,
   "Christ Jesus makes thee whole."—REF.

Katherine Hankey, 1866; refrain added

221 CANTUS 10. 10. 10.   Uzziah C. Burnap, 1895

1 "Yet there is room:" the Lamb's bright hall of song, With its fair glo-ry, beck-ons thee a-long: Room, room, still room! O en-ter, en-ter now. A-MEN.

Copyright, 1895, by The Trustees of The Presbyterian Board of Publication and Sabbath-School Work

2 Day is declining, and the sun is low;
  The shadows lengthen, light makes haste to go:
  Room, room, still room! O enter, enter now.

3 The bridal hall is filling for the feast;
  Pass in, pass in, and be the Bridegroom's guest:
  Room, room, still room! O enter, enter now.

4 Yet there is room: still open stands the gate,
  The gate of love; it is not yet too late:
  Room, room, still room! O enter, enter now.

5 Louder and sweeter sounds the loving call;
  Come, lingerer, come; enter that festal hall:
  Room, room, still room! O enter, enter now.

6 Ere night that gate may close, and seal thy doom;
  Then the last low, long cry, "No room, no room!"
  No room, no room! O woeful cry, "No room!"

Rev. Horatius Bonar, 1879

Hymns of Salvation

222 RAMOTH 7. 7. 7. 7. D. J. Baptiste Calkin, 1867

1 Lord, to Thee alone we turn, To Thy cross for safety fly;
There, as penitents, to learn How to live and how to die.
Sinful, on our knees we fall; Hear us, as for help we plead;
Hear us when on Thee we call; Aid us in our time of need. A-MEN.

2 In the midst of sin and strife,
In the depths of mortal woe,
Teach us, Lord, to live a life
Meet for sojourners below.
Though the road be oft-times dark,
Though the feet in weakness stray,
Lead us, Saviour, as the ark
Led Thy chosen on their way.

3 Weak and weary and alone
When the vale of death we tread,
Then be all Thy mercy shown,
Then be all Thy love displayed;
Guard us in that darksome hour,
Lead us to the land of rest,
Where, secure from Satan's power,
We may lie upon Thy breast.

Rev. Albert E. Evans, 1867

Repentance and Confession of Sin

223 LANGRAN 10. 10. 10. 10.   James Langran, 1862

1 Weary of earth, and laden with my sin,
I look at heaven and long to enter in;
But there no evil thing may find a home;
And yet I hear a voice that bids me "Come." A - MEN.

2 So vile I am, how dare I hope to stand
In the pure glory of that holy land?
Before the whiteness of that throne appear?
Yet there are hands stretched out to draw me near.

3 The while I fain would tread the heavenly way,
Evil is ever with me day by day;
Yet on mine ears the gracious tidings fall,
"Repent, confess, thou shalt be loosed from all."

4 It is the voice of Jesus that I hear;
His are the hands stretched out to draw me near,
And His the blood that can for all atone,
And set me faultless there before the throne.

5 Yea, Thou wilt answer for me, righteous Lord;
Thine all the merits, mine the great reward;
Thine the sharp thorns, and mine the golden crown;
Mine the life won, and Thine the life laid down.

Rev. Samuel J. Stone, 1866

Hymns of Salvation

224 BLUMENTHAL 7. 7. 7. 7. D. Arr. from Jacques Blumenthal, 1847

1 Saviour, when in dust to Thee
Low we bow the adoring knee,
When, repentant, to the skies
Scarce we lift our weeping eyes,
O by all the pains and woe
Suffered once for man below,—
Bending from Thy throne on high,
Hear our solemn litany. A-MEN.

2 By Thy helpless infant years,
By Thy life of want and tears,
By Thy days of sore distress
In the savage wilderness,
By the dread mysterious hour
Of the insulting tempter's power,—
Turn, O turn a favoring eye,
Hear our solemn litany.

3 By the sacred griefs that wept
O'er the grave where Lazarus slept,
By the boding tears that flowed
Over Salem's loved abode,
By the anguished sigh that told
Treachery lurked within Thy fold,—
From Thy seat above the sky
Hear our solemn litany.

Repentance and Confession of Sin

4 By Thine hour of dire despair,
By Thine agony of prayer,
By the cross, the nail, the thorn,
Piercing spear, and torturing scorn,
By the gloom that veiled the skies
O'er the dreadful sacrifice,—
Listen to our humble cry,
Hear our solemn litany.

5 By Thy deep expiring groan,
By the sad sepulchral stone,
By the vault whose dark abode
Held in vain the rising God,—
O from earth to heaven restored,
Mighty, re-ascended Lord,
Listen, listen to the cry
Of our solemn litany.

Sir Robert Grant, 1815

225 (BLUMENTHAL or SEYMOUR) 7. 7. 7. 7.

1 HOLY Father, hear my cry;
Holy Saviour, bend Thine ear;
Holy Spirit, come Thou nigh:
Father, Saviour, Spirit, hear.

2 Father, save me from my sin;
Saviour, I Thy mercy crave;
Gracious Spirit, make me clean:
Father, Son, and Spirit, save.

3 Father, let me taste Thy love;
Saviour, fill my soul with peace;
Spirit, come my heart to move:
Father, Son, and Spirit, bless.

4 Father, Son, and Spirit—Thou
One Jehovah, shed abroad
All Thy grace within me now;
Be my Father and my God.

Rev. Horatius Bonar, 1843

226 SEYMOUR 7. 7. 7. 7.

Arr. from Carl M. von Weber, 1826

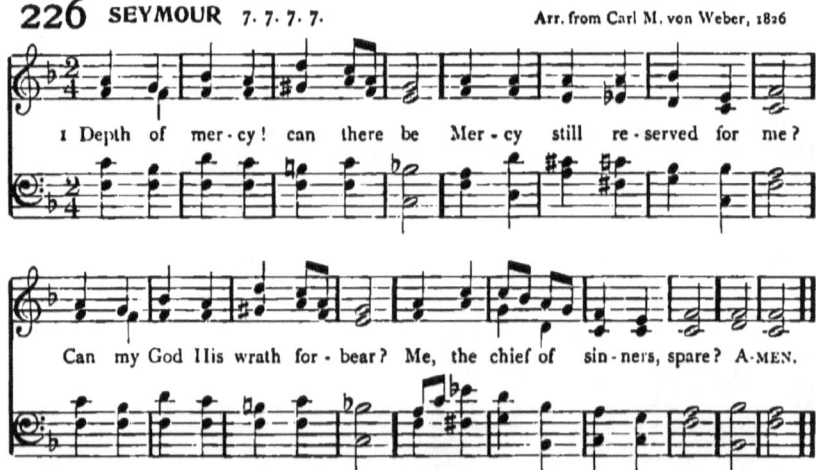

1 Depth of mercy! can there be
Mercy still reserved for me?
Can my God His wrath forbear?
Me, the chief of sinners, spare? A-MEN.

2 I have long withstood His grace,
Long provoked Him to His face,
Would not hearken to His calls,
Grieved Him by a thousand falls.

3 Kindled His relentings are;
Me He now delights to spare;
Cries, "How shall I give Thee up?"
Lets the lifted thunder drop.

4 There for me the Saviour stands,
Shows His wounds, and spreads His hands;
God is Love: I know, I feel;
Jesus weeps, but loves me still.

Rev. Charles Wesley, 1740

Hymns of Salvation

227 GOWER'S LITANY 7.7.7.6. John H. Gower, 1891

1 Fa-ther, hear Thy chil-dren's call; Hum-bly at Thy feet we fall,
Prod-i-gals, con-fess-ing all: We be-seech Thee, hear us. A-MEN.

2 Christ, be-neath Thy cross we blame All our life of sin and shame,
Pen-i-tent, we breathe Thy Name: We be-seech Thee, hear us.

Copyright by John H. Gower

3 Holy Spirit, grieved and tried,
Oft forgotten and defied,
Now we mourn our stubborn pride:
We beseech Thee, hear us.

4 Love that caused us first to be,
Love that bled upon the tree,
Love that draws us lovingly:
We beseech Thee, hear us.

5 Thou who hearest each contrite sigh,
Bidding sinful souls draw nigh,
Willing not that one should die,
We beseech Thee, hear us.

6 By the love that bids Thee spare,
By the heaven Thou dost prepare,
By Thy promises to prayer,
We beseech Thee, hear us.

Rev. Thomas B. Pollock, 1875

HAMBURG L. M. Arr. from a Gregorian Chant, by Lowell Mason, 1824

1 O Thou that hear'st when sin-ners cry, Though all my crimes be-fore Thee lie,
Be-hold them not with an-gry look, But blot their memory from Thy book. A-MEN.

Repentance and Confession of Sin

228 KEDRON 6. 4. 6. 4. 6. 6. 4. A. B. Spratt.

1 No, not despairingly
Come I to Thee;
No, not distrustingly
Bend I the knee:
Sin hath gone o'er me,
Yet is this still my plea,
Jesus hath died. A-MEN.

2 Lord, I confess to Thee
Sadly my sin;
All I am tell I Thee,
All I have been:
Purge Thou my sin away,
Wash Thou my soul this day;
Lord, make me clean.

3 Faithful and just art Thou,
Forgiving all;
Loving and kind art Thou
When poor ones call:
Lord, let the cleansing blood,
Blood of the Lamb of God,
Pass o'er my soul.

4 Then all is peace and light
This soul within;
Thus shall I walk with Thee,
The loved Unseen;
Leaning on Thee, my God,
Guided along the road,
Nothing between.

      Rev. Horatius Bonar, 1866

229 (HAMBURG) L. M.

1 O Thou that hear'st when sinners cry,
Though all my crimes before Thee lie,
Behold them not with angry look,
But blot their memory from Thy book.

2 Create my nature pure within,
And form my soul averse to sin;
Let Thy good Spirit ne'er depart,
Nor hide Thy presence from my heart.

3 I cannot live without Thy light,
Cast out and banished from Thy sight;
Thy holy joys, my God, restore,
And guard me, that I fall no more.

4 A broken heart, my God, my King,
Is all the sacrifice I bring;
The God of grace will ne'er despise
A broken heart for sacrifice.

      Rev. Isaac Watts, 1719

Hymns of Salvation

230 LEBANON S. M. D. John Zundel, 1855

1. I was a wand-ering sheep, I did not love the fold;
I did not love my Shep-herd's voice, I would not be con-trolled.
I was a way-ward child, I did not love my home;
I did not love my Fa-ther's voice, I loved a-far to roam. A-MEN.

2. The Shep-herd sought His sheep, The Fa-ther sought His child;
They fol-lowed me o'er vale and hill, O'er des-erts waste and wild:
They found me nigh to death, Famished and faint and lone;
They bound me with the bands of love, They saved the wand-ering one.

3 Jesus my Shepherd is;
 'Twas He that loved my soul,
 'Twas He that washed me in His blood,
 'Twas He that made me whole;
 'Twas He that sought the lost,
 That found the wandering sheep,
 'Twas He that brought me to the fold,
 'Tis He that still doth keep.

4 I was a wandering sheep,
 I would not be controlled;
 But now I love my Shepherd's voice,
 I love, I love the fold.
 I was a wayward child,
 I once preferred to roam;
 But now I love my Father's voice,
 I love, I love His home.

Rev. Horatius Bonar, 1843

Faith in Christ

231 THE HYMN TO JOY 8.7.8.7. D.   Arr. from Beethoven, 1824

1 Take me, O my Father, take me; Take me, save me, through Thy Son;
That which Thou wouldst have me, make me, Let Thy will in me be done.
Long from Thee my foot-steps stray-ing, Thorn-y proved the way I trod;
Wea-ry come I now, and pray-ing, Take me to Thy love, my God. A-MEN.

2 Fruitless years with grief recalling,
   Humbly I confess my sin;
At Thy feet, O Father, falling,
   To Thy household take me in.
Freely now to Thee I proffer
   This relenting heart of mine;
Freely life and soul I offer,
   Gift unworthy love like Thine.

3 Once the world's Redeemer, dying,
   Bore our sins upon the tree;
On that sacrifice relying,
   Now I look in hope to Thee:
Father, take me; all forgiving,
   Fold me to Thy loving breast;
In Thy love for ever living
   I must be for ever blest.

                                        Rev. Ray Palmer, 1864

Hymns of Salvation

232 MARGARET Irregular   Rev. Timothy R. Matthews (1826-)

1. Thou didst leave Thy throne And Thy kingly crown When Thou camest to earth for me, But in Bethlehem's home Was there found no room For Thy holy nativity: O come to my heart, Lord Jesus, There is room in my heart for Thee. A-MEN.

2. The foxes found rest, And the birds their nest, In the shade of the forest tree; But Thy couch was the sod, O Thou Son of God, In the deserts of Galilee: O come to my heart, Lord Jesus, There is room in my heart for Thee.

NOTE.—The ties and slurs are to be used as the syllables require.

3 Thou camest, O Lord,
  With the living word
That should set Thy people free;
  But with mocking scorn,
  And with crown of thorn,
They bore Thee to Calvary:
  O come to my heart, Lord Jesus,
  Thy cross is my only plea.

4 When heaven's arches shall ring,
  And her choirs shall sing,
At Thy coming to victory,
  Let Thy voice call me home,
  Saying, "Yet there is room,
There is room at My side for thee."
  And my heart shall rejoice, Lord Jesus,
  When Thou comest and callest for me.

Emily E. S. Elliott, 1864

Faith in Christ

233 OLIVET 6. 6. 4. 6. 6. 6. 4. Lowell Mason, 1832

1 My faith looks up to Thee, Thou Lamb of Calvary, Saviour Divine: Now hear me while I pray, Take all my guilt away, O let me from this day Be wholly Thine. A-MEN.

2 May Thy rich grace impart
　Strength to my fainting heart,
　　My zeal inspire;
　As Thou hast died for me,
　O may my love to Thee
　Pure, warm, and changeless be,
　　A living fire.

3 While life's dark maze I tread,
　And griefs around me spread,
　　Be Thou my Guide;
　Bid darkness turn to day,
　Wipe sorrow's tears away,
　Nor let me ever stray
　　From Thee aside.

4 When ends life's transient dream,
　When death's cold, sullen stream
　　Shall o'er me roll,
　Blest Saviour, then, in love,
　Fear and distrust remove;
　O bear me safe above,
　　A ransomed soul.

Rev. Ray Palmer, 1830

Hymns of Salvation

234 HOLLINGSIDE 7. 7. 7. 7. D.   Rev. John B. Dykes, 1861

1 Jesus, Lover of my soul,
    Let me to Thy bosom fly,
  While the nearer waters roll,
    While the tempest still is high:
  Hide me, O my Saviour, hide,
    Till the storm of life is past;
  Safe into the haven guide,
    O receive my soul at last. A-MEN.

2 Other refuge have I none;
    Hangs my helpless soul on Thee;
  Leave, ah! leave me not alone,
    Still support and comfort me.
  All my trust on Thee is stayed,
    All my help from Thee I bring;
  Cover my defenceless head
    With the shadow of Thy wing.

3 Wilt Thou not regard my call?
    Wilt Thou not accept my prayer?
  Lo, I sink, I faint, I fall!
    Lo, on Thee I cast my care;
  Reach me out Thy gracious hand!
    While I of Thy strength receive,
  Hoping against hope I stand,
    Dying, and behold I live!

4 Thou, O Christ, art all I want;
    More than all in Thee I find:
  Raise the fallen, cheer the faint,
    Heal the sick, and lead the blind.
  Just and holy is Thy Name;
    I am all unrighteousness;
  False and full of sin I am,
    Thou art full of truth and grace.

5 Plenteous grace with Thee is found,
    Grace to cover all my sin;
  Let the healing streams abound;
    Make and keep me pure within.
  Thou of life the Fountain art,
    Freely let me take of Thee;
  Spring Thou up within my heart,
    Rise to all eternity.

                              Rev. Charles Wesley, 1740

Faith in Christ

REFUGE 7.7.7.7. D.
Joseph P. Holbrook, 1862

1 Jesus, Lover of my soul, Let me to Thy bosom fly, While the nearer waters roll, While the tempest still is high: Hide me, O my Saviour, hide, Till the storm of life is past; Safe into the haven guide, O receive my soul at last. A-MEN.

MARTYN 7.7.7.7. D.
Simeon B. Marsh, 1834

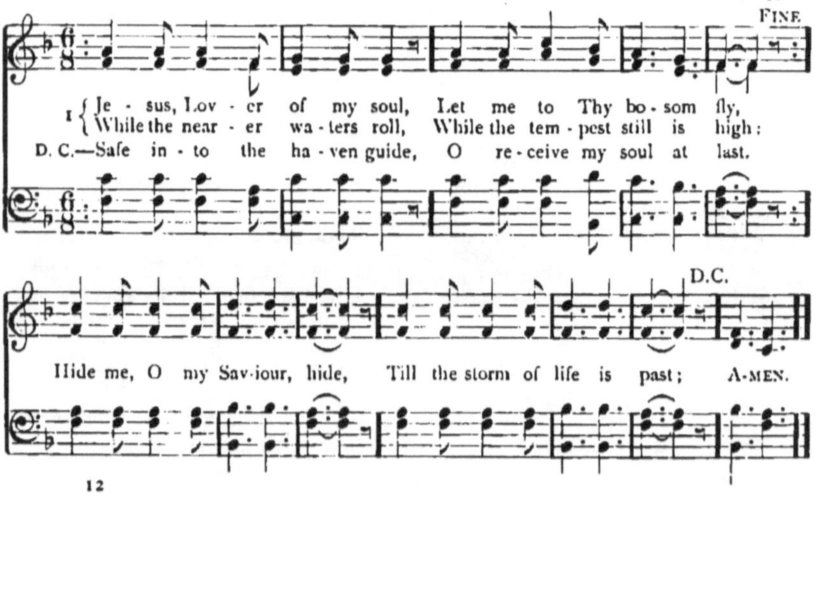

1 Jesus, Lover of my soul, Let me to Thy bosom fly,
While the nearer waters roll, While the tempest still is high:
D.C.—Safe into the haven guide, O receive my soul at last.

Hide me, O my Saviour, hide, Till the storm of life is past; A-MEN.

Hymns of Salvation

235 VOX DILECTI C. M. D.   Rev. John B. Dykes, 1868

1 I heard the voice of Jesus say, "Come unto Me and rest; Lay down, thou weary one, lay down Thy head upon My breast." I came to Jesus as I was, Weary and worn and sad, I found in Him a resting-place, And He has made me glad. A-MEN.

2 I heard the voice of Jesus say,
  "Behold, I freely give
The living water; thirsty one,
  Stoop down and drink, and live."
I came to Jesus, and I drank
  Of that life-giving stream;
My thirst was quenched, my soul re-
And now I live in Him. [vived,

3 I heard the voice of Jesus say,
  "I am this dark world's Light;
Look unto Me, thy morn shall rise,
  And all thy day be bright."
I looked to Jesus, and I found
  In Him my Star, my Sun;
And in that light of life I'll walk,
  Till travelling days are done.

Rev. Horatius Bonar, 1846

Faith in Christ

236 JUST AS I AM 8.8.8.6. Sir Joseph Barnby, 1893

2 Just as I am, and waiting not
To rid my soul of one dark blot,
To Thee, whose blood can cleanse each
O Lamb of God, I come. [spot,

3 Just as I am, though tossed about
With many a conflict, many a doubt,
Fightings and fears within, without,
O Lamb of God, I come.

4 Just as I am, poor, wretched, blind;
Sight, riches, healing of the mind,
Yea, all I need, in Thee to find,
O Lamb of God, I come.

5 Just as I am! Thou wilt receive,
Wilt welcome, pardon, cleanse, relieve;
Because Thy promise I believe,
O Lamb of God, I come.

Charlotte Elliott, 1836

WOODWORTH 8.8.8.6. William B. Bradbury, 1849

Hymns of Salvation

237 MIRIAM 7. 6. 7. 6. D.
Joseph P. Holbrook, 1865

1. I lay my sins on Jesus, The spotless Lamb of God;
He bears them all, and frees us From the accursed load:
I bring my guilt to Jesus, To wash my crimson stains
White in His blood most precious, Till not a spot remains. A-MEN.

2. I lay my wants on Jesus; All fulness dwells in Him;
He heals all my diseases, He doth my soul redeem:
I lay my griefs on Jesus, My burdens and my cares;
He from them all releases, He all my sorrows shares.

3. I rest my soul on Jesus,
This weary soul of mine;
His right hand me embraces,
I on His breast recline.
I love the Name of Jesus,
Emmanuel, Christ, the Lord;
Like fragrance on the breezes
His Name abroad is poured.

4. I long to be like Jesus,
Meek, loving, lowly, mild;
I long to be like Jesus,
The Father's holy Child:
I long to be with Jesus
Amid the heavenly throng,
To sing with saints His praises,
To learn the angels' song.

Rev. Horatius Bonar, 1843

Faith in Christ

238 WELCOME VOICE S. M. with Refrain — Rev. Lewis Hartsough (1828-)

1. I hear Thy welcome voice That calls me, Lord, to Thee For cleansing in Thy precious blood That flowed on Calvary.

REFRAIN.
I am coming, Lord; Coming now to Thee:
Wash me, cleanse me, in the blood That flowed on Calvary. A-MEN.

Used by arr. with the Biglow & Main Co., owners of copyright

2 Though coming weak and vile,
  Thou dost my strength assure;
 Thou dost my vileness fully cleanse,
  Till spotless all and pure.—REF.

3 'Tis Jesus calls me on
  To perfect faith and love,
 To perfect hope, and peace, and trust,
  For earth and heaven above.—REF.

4 'Tis Jesus who confirms
  The blessèd work within,
 By adding grace to welcomed grace,
  Where reigned the power of sin.—REF.

5 And He the witness gives
  To loyal hearts and free,
 That every promise is fulfilled,
  If faith but brings the plea.—REF.

Rev. Lewis Hartsough, (1828-)

Hymns of Salvation

239 TOPLADY 7.7.7.7.7.7. — Thomas Hastings, 1830

1 Rock of Ages, cleft for me, Let me hide myself in Thee; Let the water and the blood, From Thy riven side which flowed, A-MEN.

D.C.—Be of sin the double cure, Cleanse me from its guilt and power.

2 Not the labors of my hands
Can fulfil Thy law's demands;
Could my zeal no respite know,
Could my tears for ever flow,
All for sin could not atone;
Thou must save, and Thou alone.

3 Nothing in my hand I bring,
Simply to Thy cross I cling;
Naked, come to Thee for dress,
Helpless, look to Thee for grace;
Foul, I to the fountain fly;
Wash me, Saviour, or I die.

4 While I draw this fleeting breath,
When my eyelids close in death,
When I soar to worlds unknown,
See Thee on Thy judgment throne,
Rock of Ages, cleft for me,
Let me hide myself in Thee.

Rev. Augustus M. Toplady, 1776: verse 4, l. 2, alt. Rev. Thomas Cotterill, 1815

240 (TRUSTING) 7.7.7.7. with Refrain

1 I AM coming to the cross;
I am poor and weak and blind;
I am counting all but dross;
I shall full salvation find.

REF.—I am trusting, Lord, in Thee,
Blessèd Lamb of Calvary;
Humbly at Thy cross I bow;
Save me, Jesus, save me now.

2 Long my heart has sighed for Thee;
Long has evil reigned within;
Jesus sweetly speaks to me,
"I will cleanse you from all sin."—REF.

3 Here I give my all to Thee,—
Friends and time and earthly store;
Soul and body Thine to be,
Wholly Thine, for ever more.—REF.

4 In the promises I trust;
Now I feel the blood applied;
I am prostrate in the dust;
I with Christ am crucified.—REF.

Rev. William McDonald, 1869

Faith in Christ

241 LAMBETH C. M.

1 Lord, I be-lieve; Thy power I own, Thy word I would o-bey; I wan-der com-fort-less and lone When from Thy truth I stray. A-MEN.

2 Lord, I believe; but gloomy fears
  Sometimes bedim my sight;
  I look to Thee with prayers and tears,
  And cry for strength and light.

3 Lord, I believe; but Thou dost know
  My faith is cold and weak;
  Pity my frailty, and bestow
  The confidence I seek.

4 Yes, I believe; and only Thou
  Canst give my soul relief:
  Lord, to Thy truth my spirit bow;
  Help Thou mine unbelief.

Rev. John R. Wreford, 1837

TRUSTING 7. 7. 7. 7. with Refrain   William G. Fischer, 1869

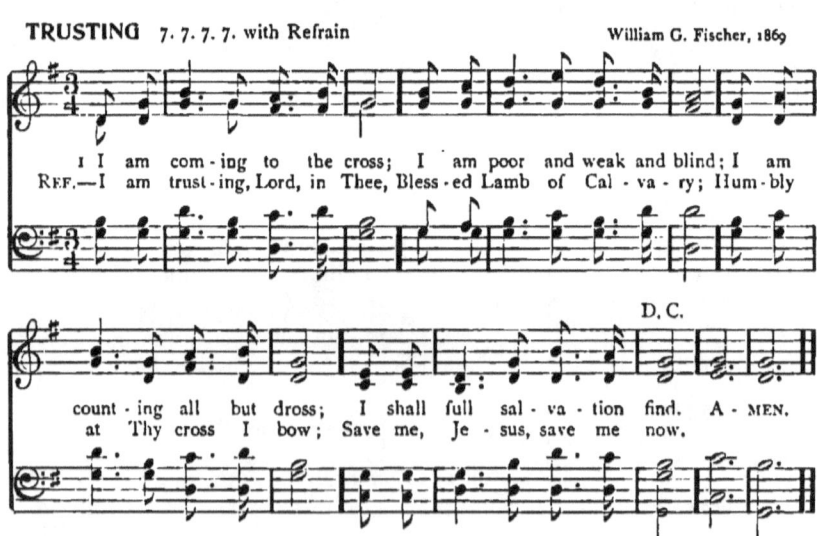

1 I am com-ing to the cross; I am poor and weak and blind; I am count-ing all but dross; I shall full sal-va-tion find. A-MEN.

REF.—I am trust-ing, Lord, in Thee, Bless-ed Lamb of Cal-va-ry; Hum-bly at Thy cross I bow; Save me, Je-sus, save me now.

Hymns of Salvation

242 CHRISTMAS C. M.   Arr. from George F. Handel, 1728

1 Awake, my soul, stretch every nerve, And press with vigor on; A heavenly race demands thy zeal, And an immortal crown, And an immortal crown. AMEN.

2 A cloud of witnesses around
Hold thee in full survey:
Forget the steps already trod,
And onward urge thy way.

3 'Tis God's all-animating voice
That calls thee from on high;
'Tis His own hand presents the prize
To thine aspiring eye:

4 That prize with peerless glories bright,
Which shall new lustre boast,
When victors' wreaths and monarchs' gems
Shall blend in common dust.

5 Blest Saviour, introduced by Thee,
Have I my race begun;
And, crowned with victory, at Thy feet
I'll lay my honors down.

Rev. Philip Doddridge, publ. 1755

243 (BELMONT) C. M.

1 O HELP us, Lord; each hour of need
Thy heavenly succor give:
Help us in thought, and word, and deed,
Each hour on earth we live.

2 O help us when our spirits bleed,
With contrite anguish sore;
And when our hearts are cold and dead,
O help us, Lord, the more.

3 O help us, through the prayer of faith
More firmly to believe;
For still, the more the servant hath,
The more shall he receive.

4 O help us, Jesus, from on high;
We know no help but Thee:
O help us so to live and die
As Thine in heaven to be.

Rev. Henry H. Milman, 1827

Conflict with Sin

244 MARTYRDOM C. M.   Hugh Wilson, c. 1825

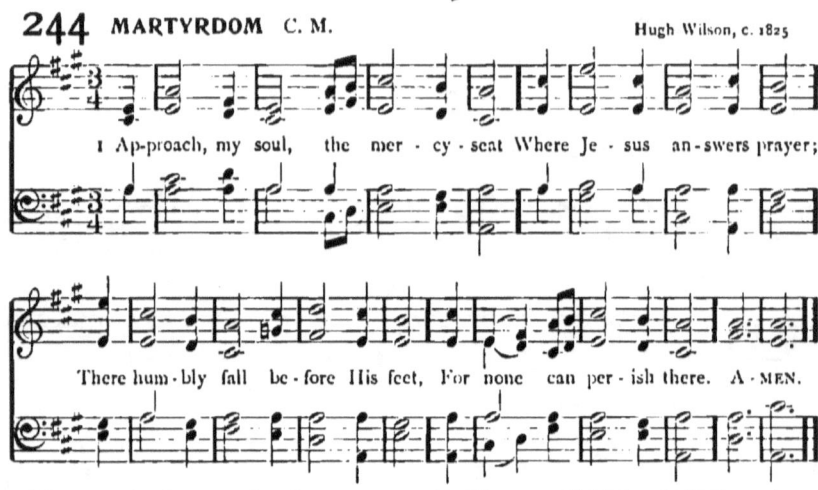

1 Ap-proach, my soul, the mer-cy-seat Where Je-sus an-swers prayer; There hum-bly fall be-fore His feet, For none can per-ish there. A-MEN.

2 Thy promise is my only plea;
   With this I venture nigh:
Thou callest burdened souls to Thee,
   And such, O Lord, am I.

3 Bowed down beneath a load of sin,
   By Satan sorely pressed,
By war without, and fears within,
   I come to Thee for rest.

4 Be Thou my Shield and Hiding-place,
   That, sheltered near Thy side,
I may my fierce accuser face,
   And tell him, Thou hast died.

5 O wondrous love! to bleed and die,
   To bear the cross and shame,
That guilty sinners, such as I,
   Might plead Thy gracious Name!

                 Rev. John Newton, 1779

BELMONT C. M.   Arr. from William Gardiner, 1812

1 O help us, Lord; each hour of need Thy heaven-ly suc-cor give: Help us in thought, and word, and deed, Each hour on earth we live. A-MEN.

Hymns of Salvation

245 PILOT 7.7.7.7.7.7.
John E. Gould, 1871

1 Jesus, Saviour, pilot me
Over life's tempestuous sea;
Unknown waves before me roll,
Hiding rock and treacherous shoal;
Chart and compass came from Thee:
Jesus, Saviour, pilot me. A-MEN.

2 As a mother stills her child,
Thou canst hush the ocean wild;
Boisterous waves obey Thy will
When thou sayest to them, "Be still."
Wondrous Sovereign of the sea,
Jesus, Saviour, pilot me.

3 When at last I near the shore,
And the fearful breakers roar
'Twixt me and the peaceful rest,
Then, while leaning on Thy breast,
May I hear Thee say to me,
"Fear not, I will pilot thee."

Rev. Edward Hopper, 1871

246 (VIGILATE) 7. 7. 7. 3.

1 Christian, seek not yet repose,
Cast thy dreams of ease away;
Thou art in the midst of foes:
Watch and pray.

2 Hear the victors who o'ercame;
Still they mark each warrior's way;
All with one sweet voice exclaim,
"Watch and pray."

3 Hear, above all, hear Thy Lord,
Him thou lovest to obey;
Hide within thy heart His word,
"Watch and pray."

4 Watch, as if on that alone
Hung the issue of the day;
Pray, that help may be sent down:
Watch and pray.

Charlotte Elliott, 1839: verse 1, l. 2, alt.

Conflict with Sin

247 MARLOW C. M. Rev. John Chetham's Psalmody, 1718

1 Am I a soldier of the cross, A follower of the Lamb, And shall I fear to own His cause, Or blush to speak His Name? A-MEN.

2 Must I be carried to the skies
On flowery beds of ease,
While others fought to win the prize,
And sailed through bloody seas?

3 Are there no foes for me to face?
Must I not stem the flood?
Is this vile world a friend to grace,
To help me on to God?

4 Sure I must fight if I would reign :
Increase my courage, Lord ;
I'll bear the toil, endure the pain,
Supported by Thy word.

5 Thy saints, in all this glorious war,
Shall conquer, though they die ;
They view the triumph from afar,
And seize it with their eye.

Rev. Isaac Watts, c. 1723

VIGILATE 7. 7. 7. 3. William H. Monk, 1868

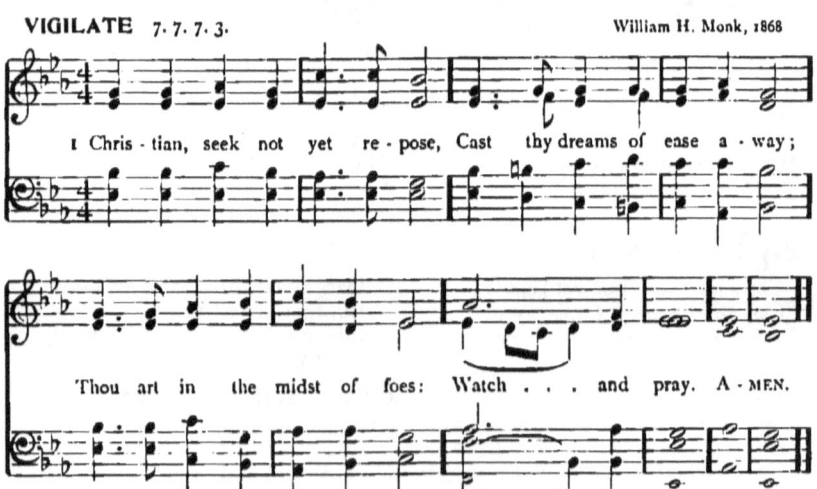

1 Christian, seek not yet repose, Cast thy dreams of ease away; Thou art in the midst of foes: Watch . . and pray. A-MEN.

Hymns of Salvation

248 MOZART L. M. — Arr. from Mozart (1756–1791)

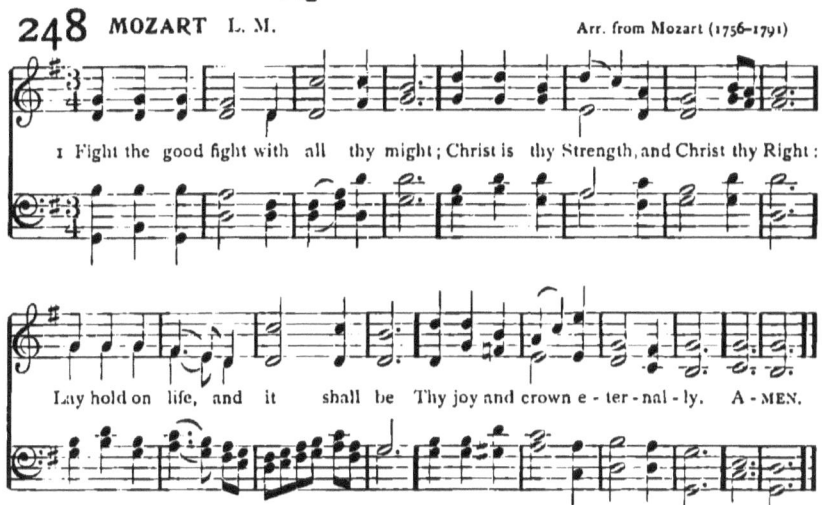

1 Fight the good fight with all thy might; Christ is thy Strength, and Christ thy Right:
Lay hold on life, and it shall be Thy joy and crown e-ter-nal-ly. A-MEN.

2 Run the straight race
Through God's good grace,
Lift up thine eyes, and seek His face;
Life with its way before us lies,
Christ is the Path, and Christ the Prize.

3 Cast care aside;
Upon thy Guide
Lean, and His mercy will provide;
Lean, and the trusting soul shall prove,
Christ is its Life, and Christ its Love.

4 Faint not, nor fear,
His arms are near;
He changeth not, and thou art dear;
Only believe, and thou shalt see
That Christ is All in all to thee.

Rev. John S. B. Monsell, 1863

249 (WAVERTREE) 8. 8. 8. 8. 8. 8.

1 SURROUNDED by unnumbered foes,
Against my soul the battle goes;
Yet though I weary, sore distrest,
I know that I shall reach my rest:
I lift my tearful eyes above,—
His banner over me is love.

2 Its sword my spirit will not yield,
Though flesh may faint upon the field;
He waves before my fading sight
The branch of palm, the crown of light:
I lift my brightening eyes above,—
His banner over me is love.

3 My cloud of battle-dust may dim,
His veil of splendor curtain Him;
And in the midnight of my fear
I may not feel Him standing near:
But, as I lift mine eyes above,
His banner over me is love.

Gerald Massey, 1869

Conflict with Sin

250 MENDON L. M.   German Melody: arr. by S. Dyer, 1824

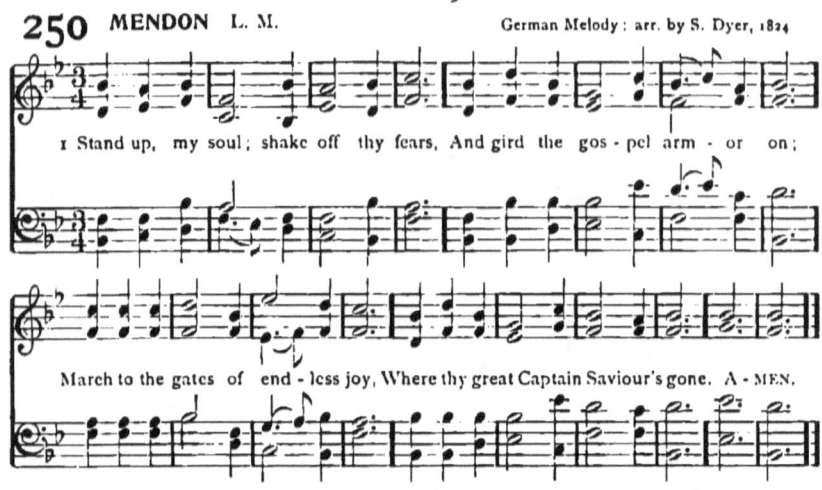

1 Stand up, my soul; shake off thy fears, And gird the gos-pel arm-or on; March to the gates of end-less joy, Where thy great Captain Saviour's gone. A-MEN.

2 Hell and thy sins resist thy course;
But hell and sin are vanquished foes:
Thy Jesus nailed them to the cross,
And sung the triumph when He rose.

3 Then let my soul march boldly on,
Press forward to the heavenly gate;

There peace and joy eternal reign,
And glittering robes for conquerors wait.

4 There shall I wear a starry crown,
And triumph in almighty grace;
While all the armies of the skies
Join in my glorious Leader's praise.

Rev. Isaac Watts, 1707

WAVERTREE 8. 8. 8. 8. 8. 8.   William Shore, 1840:
Har. by William W. Gilchrist, 1895

1 {Sur-round-ed by un-numbered foes, A-gainst my soul the bat-tle goes;
Yet though I wea-ry, sore dis-trest, I know that I shall reach my rest:}
I lift my tear-ful eyes a-bove,—His ban-ner o-ver me is love. A-MEN.

Copyright, 1895, by The Trustees of The Presbyterian Board of Publication and Sabbath-School Work

Hymns of Salvation

251 LABAN S. M.   Lowell Mason, 1830

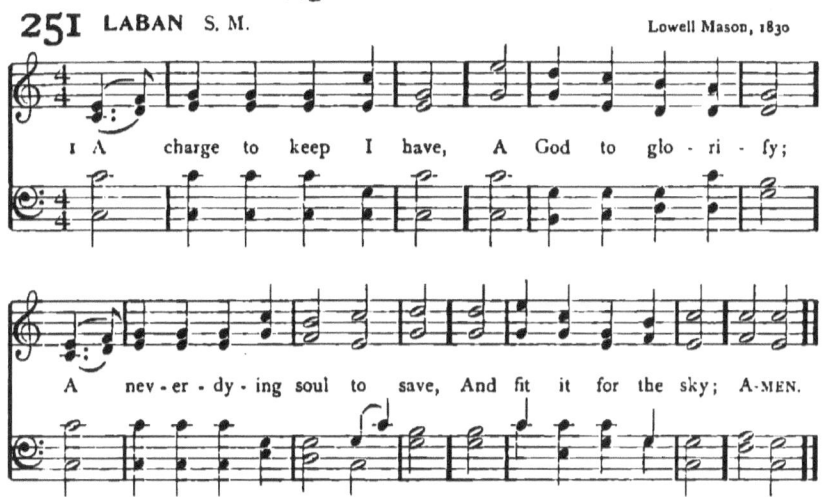

1. A charge to keep I have, A God to glorify;
A never-dying soul to save, And fit it for the sky; A-MEN.

2. To serve the present age,
My calling to fulfil,—
O may it all my powers engage
To do my Master's will.

3. Arm me with jealous care,
As in Thy sight to live;

And O, Thy servant, Lord, prepare
A strict account to give.

4. Help me to watch and pray,
And on Thyself rely,
Assured, if I my trust betray,
I shall for ever die.

                                                                          Rev. Charles Wesley, 1762

SCHUMANN S. M.   Ascribed to Robert Schumann (1810–1856)

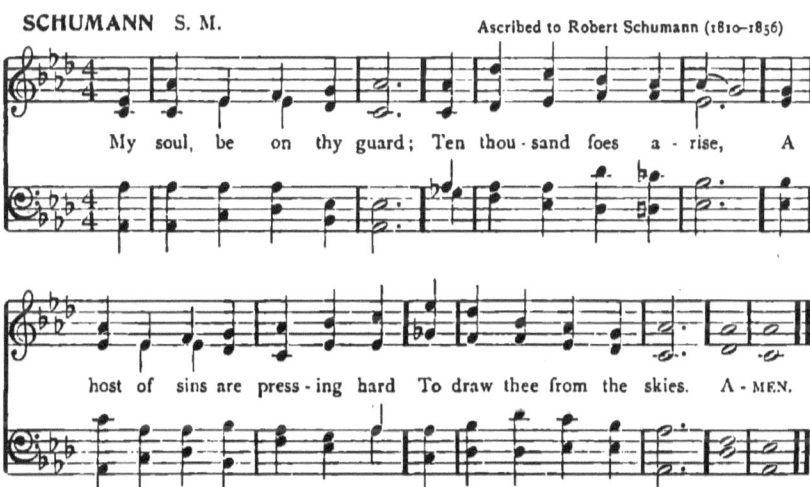

My soul, be on thy guard; Ten thousand foes arise, A host of sins are pressing hard To draw thee from the skies. A-MEN.

Conflict with Sin

252 ONWARD 5. 5. 5. 5. 6. 5. 6. 5. William C. Filby (1836–)

1 Breast the wave, Christian, When it is strong-est; Watch for day, Christian, When the night's long-est; On-ward and on-ward still Be thine en-deav-or; The rest that re-main-eth, Will be for ev-er. A-MEN.

2 Fight the fight, Christian,
   Jesus is o'er thee;
   Run the race, Christian,
   Heaven is before thee:
   He who hath promisèd
   Faltereth never;
   The love of eternity
   Flows on for ever.

3 Lift the eye, Christian,
   Just as it closeth;
   Raise the heart, Christian,
   Ere it reposeth;
   Thee from the love of Christ
   Nothing shall sever;
   And, when thy work is done,
   Praise Him for ever.

Joseph Stammers, 1830: verse 3, l. 7, alt.

253 (SCHUMANN or LABAN) S. M.

1 MY soul, be on thy guard;
   Ten thousand foes arise,
   A host of sins are pressing hard
   To draw thee from the skies.

2 O watch, and fight, and pray;
   The battle ne'er give o'er;
   Renew it boldly every day,
   And help Divine implore.

3 Ne'er think the victory won,
   Nor lay thine armor down;
   Thine arduous work will not be done,
   Till thou obtain thy crown.

4 Fight on, my soul, till death
   Shall bring thee to thy God;
   He'll take thee, at thy parting breath,
   Up to His blest abode.

Rev. George Heath, 1781: verse 3, ll. 2, 4, verse 4, alt.

Hymns of Salvation

254 AUTUMN 8.7.8.7.D. Louis Von Esch, c. 1810

1 Gently, Lord, O gently lead us, Pilgrims in this vale of tears,
Through the trials yet decreed us, Till our last great change appears.
When temptation's darts assail us, When in devious paths we stray,
Let Thy goodness never fail us, Lead us in Thy perfect way. A-MEN.

2 In the hour of pain and anguish,
In the hour when death draws near,
Suffer not our hearts to languish,
Suffer not our souls to fear;
And, when mortal life is ended,
Bid us in Thine arms to rest,
Till, by angel bands attended,
We awake among the blest.

Thomas Hastings, 1831, 1850

Conflict with Sin

255 NEED 6.4.6.4. with Refrain — Rev. Robert Lowry, 1872

1 I need Thee ev-ery hour, Most gra-cious Lord; No ten-der voice like Thine Can peace af-ford.

REFRAIN.
I need Thee, O I need Thee, Ev-ery hour I need Thee; O bless me now, my Sav-iour,—I come to Thee. A-MEN.

Copyright (words and music) by R. Lowry

2 I need Thee every hour;
  Stay Thou near by;
  Temptations lose their power
  When Thou art nigh.—REF.

3 I need Thee every hour,
  In joy or pain;
  Come quickly, and abide,
  Or life is vain.—REF.

4 I need Thee every hour;
  Teach me Thy will,
  And Thy rich promises
  In me fulfil.—REF.

5 I need Thee every hour,
  Most Holy One;
  O make me Thine indeed,
  Thou blessèd Son.—REF.

Annie S. Hawks, 1872: refrain added by Rev. Robert Lowry

Hymns of Salvation

256 PENITENCE 6. 5. 6. 5. D. — Spencer Lane

1. In the hour of trial, Jesus, plead for me;
Lest by base denial I depart from Thee:
When Thou seest me waver, With a look recall,
Nor for fear or favor Suffer me to fall.

2. With its witching pleasures Would this vain world charm,
Or its sordid treasures Spread to work me harm,
Bring to my remembrance Sad Gethsemane,
Or, in darker semblance, Cross-crowned Calvary.

A-MEN.

By per. of Rev. C. L. Hutchins

3 If with sore affliction
Thou in love chastise,
Pour Thy benediction
On the sacrifice;
Then, upon Thine altar
Freely offered up,
Though the flesh may falter,
Faith shall drink the cup.

4 When in dust and ashes
To the grave I sink,
While heaven's glory flashes
O'er the shelving brink,
On Thy truth relying
Through that mortal strife,
Lord, receive me, dying,
To eternal life.

James Montgomery, 1834: verse 1, l. 2, alt.

Conflict with Sin

257 HANFORD 8.8.8.4. Sir Arthur Sullivan, 1874

1 Jesus, my Saviour, look on me, For I am weary and opprest; I come to cast myself on Thee: Thou art my Rest. A-MEN.

2 Look down on me, for I am weak;
I feel the toilsome journey's length;
Thine aid omnipotent I seek:
  Thou art my Strength.

3 I am bewildered on my way,
Dark and tempestuous is the night;
O send Thou forth some cheering ray:
  Thou art my Light.

4 I hear the storms around me rise;
But when I dread the impending shock,
My spirit to the refuge flies:
  Thou art my Rock.

5 Standing alone on Jordan's brink,
In that tremendous latest strife,
Thou wilt not suffer me to sink:
  Thou art my Life.

6 Thou wilt my every want supply,
E'en to the end, whate'er befall;
Through life, in death, eternally,
  Thou art my All.
Charlotte Elliott, 1869

Trust

258 (HANFORD) 8.8.8.4.

1 MY God and Father, while I stray
Far from my home in life's rough way,
O teach me from my heart to say,
  Thy will be done.

2 Though dark my path and sad my lot,
Let me be still and murmur not,
Or breathe the prayer Divinely taught,
  Thy will be done.

3 If thou shouldst call me to resign
What most I prize, it ne'er was mine;
I only yield Thee what was Thine:
  Thy will be done.

4 If but my fainting heart be blest
With Thy sweet Spirit for its guest,
My God, to Thee I leave the rest;
  Thy will be done.

5 Renew my will from day to day;
Blend it with Thine, and take away
All that now makes it hard to say,
  Thy will be done.

6 Then, when on earth I breathe no more
The prayer oft mixed with tears before,
I'll sing upon a happier shore,
  Thy will be done.
Charlotte Elliott, 1834

Hymns of Salvation

259 DOMINUS REGIT ME 8.7.8.7.
Rev. John B. Dykes, 1868

1 The King of love my Shepherd is, Whose goodness faileth never;
I nothing lack if I am His And He is mine for ever. A-MEN.

2 Where streams of living water flow
My ransomed soul He leadeth,
And, where the verdant pastures grow,
With food celestial feedeth.

3 Perverse and foolish oft I strayed,
But yet in love He sought me,
And on His shoulder gently laid,
And home, rejoicing, brought me.

4 In death's dark vale I fear no ill
With Thee, dear Lord, beside me;
Thy rod and staff my comfort still,
Thy cross before to guide me.

5 Thou spread'st a table in my sight;
Thy unction grace bestoweth;
And O what transport of delight
From Thy pure chalice floweth.

6 And so through all the length of days
Thy goodness faileth never:
Good Shepherd, may I sing Thy praise
Within Thy house for ever.

Rev. Sir Henry W. Baker, Bart., 1868

260 (BULLINGER) 8.5.8.3.

1 I AM trusting Thee, Lord Jesus,
Trusting only Thee;
Trusting Thee for full salvation,
Great and free.

2 I am trusting Thee for pardon;
At Thy feet I bow;
For Thy grace and tender mercy,
Trusting now.

3 I am trusting Thee for cleansing
In the crimson flood;
Trusting Thee to make me holy
By Thy blood.

4 I am trusting Thee to guide me;
Thou alone shalt lead,
Every day and hour supplying
All my need.

5 I am trusting Thee for power,
Thine can never fail;
Words which Thou Thyself shalt give me
Must prevail.

6 I am trusting Thee, Lord Jesus;
Never let me fall;
I am trusting Thee for ever,
And for all.

Frances R. Havergal, 1874

Trust

261 HOLY GUIDE 6.6.6.6. Uzziah C. Burnap, 1895

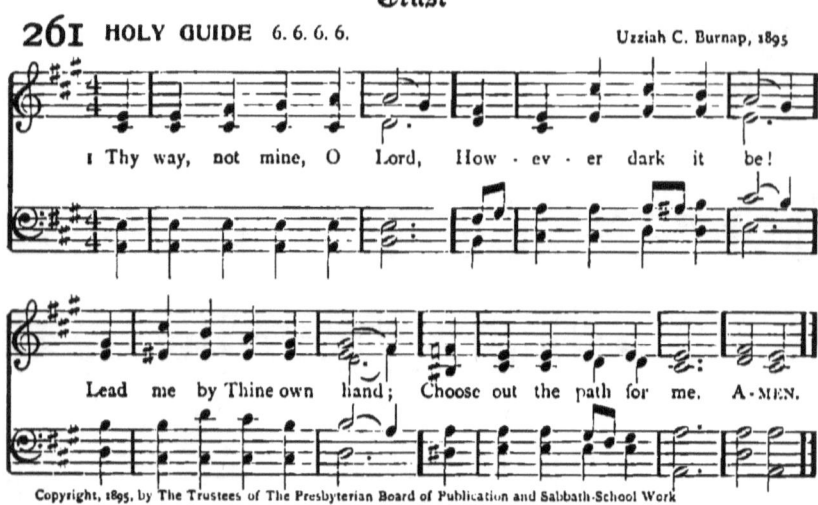

1 Thy way, not mine, O Lord, How-ev-er dark it be! Lead me by Thine own hand; Choose out the path for me. A-MEN.

Copyright, 1895, by The Trustees of The Presbyterian Board of Publication and Sabbath-School Work

2 Smooth let it be or rough,
　It will be still the best;
　Winding or straight, it leads
　Right onward to Thy rest.

3 I dare not choose my lot;
　I would not, if I might;
　Choose Thou for me, my God,
　So shall I walk aright.

4 The kingdom that I seek
　Is Thine; so let the way
　That leads to it be Thine,
　Else I must surely stray.

5 Not mine, not mine the choice,
　In things or great or small;
　Be Thou my Guide, my Strength,
　My Wisdom, and my All.

Rev. Horatius Bonar, 1857

BULLINGER 8.5.8.3. Rev. Ethelbert W. Bullinger, 1877

1 I am trust-ing Thee, Lord Je-sus, Trust-ing on-ly Thee; Trust-ing Thee for full sal-va-tion, Great and free. A-MEN.

Hymns of Salvation

262 BEATITUDO C. M. Rev. John B. Dykes, 1875

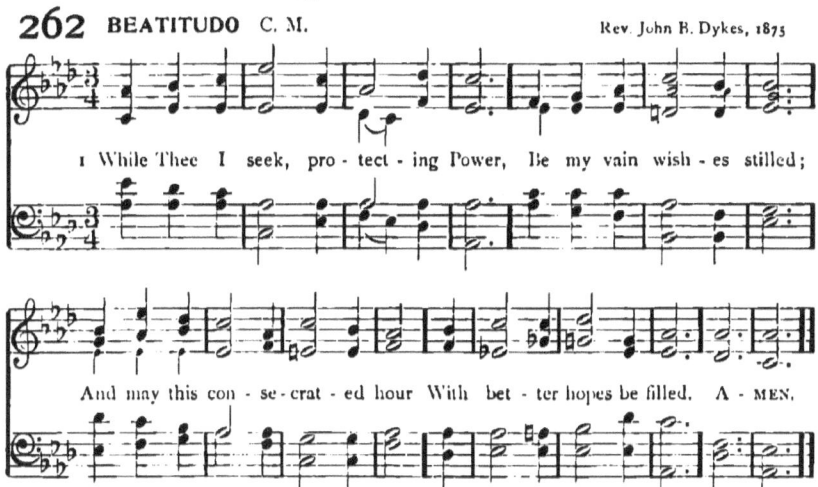

1 While Thee I seek, pro-tect-ing Power, Be my vain wish-es stilled;
And may this con-se-crat-ed hour With bet-ter hopes be filled. A - MEN.

2 Thy love the powers of thought bestowed;
To Thee my thoughts would soar:
Thy mercy o'er my life has flowed;
That mercy I adore.

3 In each event of life, how clear
Thy ruling hand I see;
Each blessing to my soul more dear
Because conferred by Thee.

4 In every joy that crowns my days,
In every pain I bear,
My heart shall find delight in praise,
Or seek relief in prayer.

5 When gladness wings my favored hour,
Thy love my thoughts shall fill;
Resigned, when storms of sorrow lower,
My soul shall meet Thy will.

6 My lifted eye, without a tear,
The lowering storm shall see;
My steadfast heart shall know no fear;
That heart will rest on Thee.

Helen M. Williams, 1786

263 (BEATITUDO) C. M.

1 FATHER of Love, our Guide and Friend,
O lead us gently on,
Until life's trial time shall end,
And heavenly peace be won.

2 We know not what the path may be
As yet by us untrod;
But we can trust our all to Thee,
Our Father and our God.

3 If called, like Abraham's child, to climb
The hill of sacrifice,
Some angel may be there in time;
Deliverance shall arise:

4 Or, if some darker lot be good,
O teach us to endure
The sorrow, pain, or solitude,
That make the spirit pure.

5 Christ by no flowery pathway came;
And we, His followers here,
Must do Thy will and praise Thy Name,
In hope, and love, and fear.

6 And, till in heaven we sinless bow,
And faultless anthems raise,
O Father, Son, and Spirit, now
Accept our feeble praise.

Rev. William J. Irons, 1844

Trust

264 BALERMA C. M.   Arr. by Robert Simpson, 1833

1 The Lord's my Shep-herd, I'll not want; He makes me down to lie
In pas-tures green, He lead-eth me The qui-et wa-ters by. A-MEN.

2 My soul He doth restore again;
And me to walk doth make
Within the paths of righteousness,
Ev'n for His own Name's sake.

3 Yea, though I walk in death's dark vale,
Yet will I fear none ill;
For Thou art with me, and Thy rod
And staff me comfort still.

4 My table Thou hast furnishèd
In presence of my foes;
My head Thou dost with oil anoint,
And my cup overflows.

5 Goodness and mercy all my life
Shall surely follow me;
And in God's house for evermore
My dwelling-place shall be.

Scottish Psalter, 1650: based on Francis Rous, Sir William Mure, and others

265 (BALERMA) C. M.

1 O GOD of Bethel, by whose hand
Thy people still are fed,
Who through this weary pilgrimage
Hast all our fathers led,

2 Our vows, our prayers, we now present
Before Thy throne of grace;
God of our fathers, be the God
Of their succeeding race.

3 Through each perplexing path of life
Our wandering footsteps guide;
Give us each day our daily bread,
And raiment fit provide.

4 O spread Thy covering wings around
Till all our wanderings cease,
And at our Father's loved abode
Our souls arrive in peace.

5 Such blessings from Thy gracious hand
Our humble prayers implore;
And Thou shalt be our chosen God,
And portion evermore.

*Verses 1-4, Rev. Philip Doddridge, 1737, recast by Rev. John Logan, 1781:
verse 1, l. 1, alt. and verse 5, added, Scottish Trs. and Paraphs., 1781*

Hymns of Salvation

266 JEWETT 6. 6. 6. 6. D.
Arr. from C. M. von Weber, by Joseph P. Holbrook, 1862

1 My Jesus, as Thou wilt! O may Thy will be mine;
In - to Thy hand of love I would my all re - sign.
Through sor - row, or through joy, Con - duct me as Thine own;
And help me still to say, My Lord, Thy will be done. A-MEN.

2 My Jesus, as Thou wilt!
  Though seen through many a tear,
  Let not my star of hope
    Grow dim or disappear.
  Since Thou on earth hast wept
    And sorrowed oft alone,
  If I must weep with Thee,
    My Lord, Thy will be done.

3 My Jesus, as Thou wilt!
    All shall be well for me;
  Each changing future scene
    I gladly trust with Thee.
  Straight to my home above
    I travel calmly on,
  And sing, in life or death,
    My Lord, Thy will be done.

Rev. Benjamin Schmolck, c. 1704. Tr. Jane Borthwick, 1854

Trust

267 HE LEADETH ME L. M. D. — William B. Bradbury, 1864

1 He leadeth me: O blessed thought! O words with heavenly comfort fraught!
Whate'er I do, where'er I be, Still 'tis God's hand that leadeth me.

REFRAIN.
He leadeth me, He leadeth me; By His own hand He leadeth me:
His faithful follower I would be, For by His hand He leadeth me. A-MEN.

Used by arr. with the Biglow & Main Co., owners of copyright

2 Sometimes 'mid scenes of deepest gloom,
Sometimes where Eden's bowers bloom,
By waters calm, o'er troubled sea,—
Still 'tis His hand that leadeth me.—REF.

3 Lord, I would clasp Thy hand in mine,
Nor ever murmur nor repine;
Content, whatever lot I see,
Since 'tis my God that leadeth me.—REF.

4 And when my task on earth is done,
When, by Thy grace, the victory's won,
E'en death's cold wave I will not flee,
Since God through Jordan leadeth me.—REF.

Rev Joseph H. Gilmore, 1862: ll. 3, 4, of refrain added

Hymns of Salvation

268 BENTLEY 7. 6. 7. 6. D. John Hullah, 1867

1. Sometimes a light surprises
   The Christian while he sings;
   It is the Lord, who rises
   With healing in His wings:
   When comforts are declining,
   He grants the soul again
   A season of clear shining,
   To cheer it after rain. A-MEN.

2. In holy contemplation
   We sweetly then pursue
   The theme of God's salvation,
   And find it ever new;
   Set free from present sorrow,
   We cheerfully can say,
   Let the unknown to-morrow
   Bring with it what it may.

3. It can bring with it nothing
   But He will bear us through;
   Who gives the lilies clothing
   Will clothe His people too:
   Beneath the spreading heavens
   No creature but is fed;
   And He who feeds the ravens
   Will give His children bread.

4. Though vine nor fig-tree neither
   Their wonted fruit shall bear,
   Though all the field should wither,
   Nor flocks nor herds be there;
   Yet God the same abiding,
   His praise shall tune my voice,
   For, while in Him confiding,
   I cannot but rejoice.

William Cowper, 1779

Trust

269 (BENTLEY) 7.6.7.6.D.

1 IN heavenly love abiding,
   No change my heart shall fear,
And safe is such confiding,
   For nothing changes here.
The storm may roar without me,
   My heart may low be laid;
But God is round about me,
   And can I be dismayed?

2 Wherever He may guide me,
   No want shall turn me back;
My Shepherd is beside me,
   And nothing can I lack.
His wisdom ever waketh,
   His sight is never dim;
He knows the way He taketh,
   And I will walk with Him.

3 Green pastures are before me,
   Which yet I have not seen;
Bright skies will soon be o'er me,
   Where the dark clouds have been.
My hope I cannot measure,
   The path to life is free;
My Saviour has my treasure,
   And He will walk with me.

Anna L. Waring, 1850

270 OLIPHANT 8.7.8.7.4.7.

Arr from Pierre M. F. de S. Baillot, 1830, by Lowell Mason, 1832

1 Guide me, O Thou Great Jehovah,
   Pilgrim through this barren land;
I am weak, but Thou art mighty,
   Hold me with Thy powerful hand:
Bread of heaven, Bread of heaven,
   Feed me till I want no more. AMEN.

2 Open now the crystal fountain,
   Whence the healing stream doth flow;
Let the fire and cloudy pillar
   Lead me all my journey through:
Strong Deliverer,
   Be Thou still my Strength and Shield.

3 When I tread the verge of Jordan,
   Bid my anxious fears subside;
Death of deaths and hell's Destruction,
   Land me safe on Canaan's side:
Songs of praises
   I will ever give to Thee.

Rev. William Williams (Welsh), 1745. Tr. verse 1, Rev. Peter Williams, 1771; verses 2, 3, Rev. Wm. Williams, c. 1772

Hymns of Salvation

271 ADESTE FIDELES 11. 11. 11. 11.

1 How firm a foun-da-tion, ye saints of the Lord, Is laid for your faith in His ex-cel-lent word! What more can He say than to you He hath said,— You who un-to Je-sus for ref-uge have fled? You who un-to Je-sus for ref-uge have fled? A-MEN.

2 " Fear not, I am with thee, O be not dismayed;
I, I am thy God, and will still give thee aid;
I'll strengthen thee, help thee, and cause thee to stand,
Upheld by My righteous, omnipotent hand.

3 " When through the deep waters I call thee to go,
The rivers of woe shall not thee overflow;
For I will be with thee thy troubles to bless,
And sanctify to thee thy deepest distress.

Trust

4 "When through fiery trials thy pathway shall lie,
My grace, all-sufficient, shall be thy supply;
The flame shall not hurt thee; I only design
Thy dross to consume, and thy gold to refine.

5 "The soul that on Jesus hath leaned for repose,
I will not, I will not desert to his foes;
That soul, though all hell should endeavor to shake,
I'll never, no, never, no, never forsake."

"K," in Rippon's Selection, 1787

272 NEWLAND S. M. Henry J. Gauntlett, 1858

1 The Lord my Shepherd is, I shall be well supplied;
Since He is mine and I am His, What can I want beside? A-MEN.

2 He leads me to the place
  Where heavenly pasture grows,
  Where living waters gently pass,
  And full salvation flows.

3 If e'er I go astray,
  He doth my soul reclaim;
  And guides me in His own right way,
  For His most holy Name.

4 While He affords His aid
  I cannot yield to fear;
  Though I should walk through death's dark shade,
  My Shepherd's with me there.

5 The bounties of Thy love
  Shall crown my following days;
  Nor from Thy house will I remove,
  Nor cease to speak Thy praise.

Rev. Isaac Watts, 1719

273 (NEWLAND) S. M.

1 MY times are in Thy hand;
  My God, I wish them there;
  My life, my friends, my soul, I leave
  Entirely to Thy care.

2 My times are in Thy hand,
  Whatever they may be;
  Pleasing or painful, dark or bright,
  As best may seem to Thee.

3 My times are in Thy hand;
  Why should I doubt or fear?
  A Father's hand will never cause
  His child a needless tear.

4 My times are in Thy hand,
  Jesus the crucified;
  The hand my cruel sins had pierced
  Is now my guard and guide.

William F. Lloyd, c. 1838

Hymns of Salvation

274 LUX BENIGNA 10. 4. 10. 4. 10. 10. Rev. John B. Dykes (1823-1876)

1 Lead, kindly Light, amid the encircling gloom, Lead Thou me on;
  The night is dark, and I am far from home; Lead Thou me on:
  Keep Thou my feet; I do not ask to see
  The distant scene,—one step enough for me. A-MEN.

2 I was not ever thus, nor prayed that Thou Shouldst lead me on;
  I loved to choose and see my path; but now Lead Thou me on.
  I loved the garish day, and, spite of fears,
  Pride ruled my will: remember not past years.

3 So long Thy power hath blest me, sure it still
  Will lead me on
  O'er moor and fen, o'er crag and torrent, till
  The night is gone;
  And with the morn those angel faces smile,
  Which I have loved long since, and lost awhile.

Cardinal John H. Newman, 1833

Trust

275 CHESTER C. M. D. Oratory Hymns, 1868

1 Thou art my Hiding-place, O Lord,
  In Thee I put my trust;
Encouraged by Thy holy word,
  A feeble child of dust:
I have no argument beside,
  I urge no other plea;
And 'tis enough my Saviour died,
  My Saviour died for me. A-MEN.

2 When storms of fierce temptation beat,
  And furious foes assail,
My refuge is the mercy-seat,
  My hope within the veil.
From strife of tongues and bitter words
  My spirit flies to Thee:
Joy to my heart the thought affords,
  My Saviour died for me.

Rev. Thomas Raffles, 1833

Hymns of Salvation

276 VESPERS L. M.
James W. Elliott (1816-)

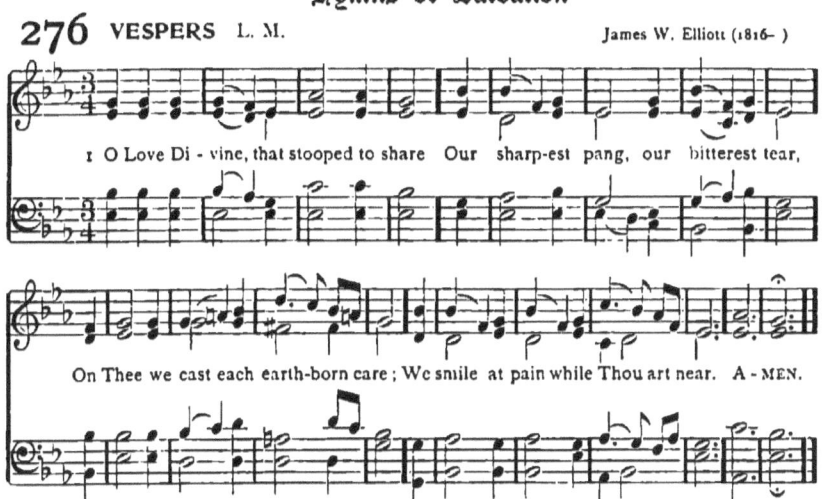

1 O Love Di-vine, that stooped to share Our sharp-est pang, our bitterest tear, On Thee we cast each earth-born care; We smile at pain while Thou art near. A-MEN.

2 Though long the weary way we tread,
And sorrow crown each lingering year,
No path we shun, no darkness dread,
Our hearts still whispering, Thou art near.

3 When drooping pleasure turns to grief,
And trembling faith is changed to fear,
The murmuring wind, the quivering leaf,
Shall softly tell us, Thou art near.

4 On Thee we fling our burdening woe,
O Love Divine, for ever dear;
Content to suffer while we know,
Living and dying, Thou art near.

Oliver Wendell Holmes, 1859

GREEN HILL C. M.
Albert L. Peace, 1885

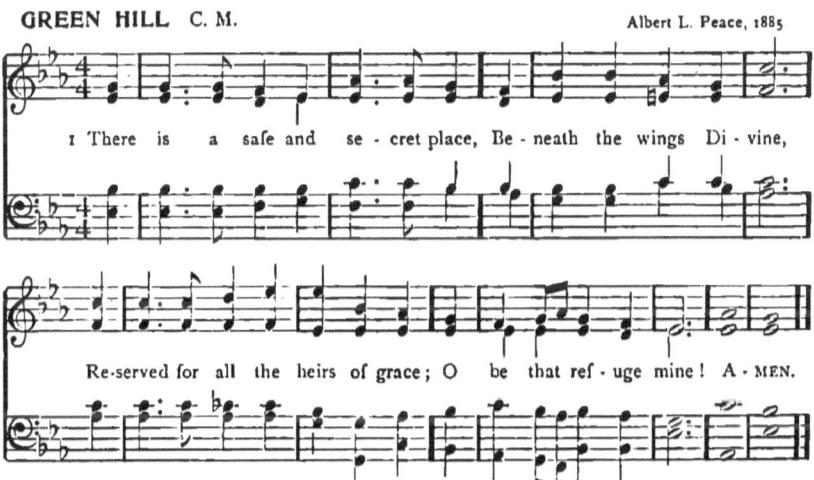

1 There is a safe and se-cret place, Be-neath the wings Di-vine, Re-served for all the heirs of grace; O be that ref-uge mine! A-MEN.

Trust

277 SUBMISSION 10. 4. 10. 4.   Albert L. Peace, 1889

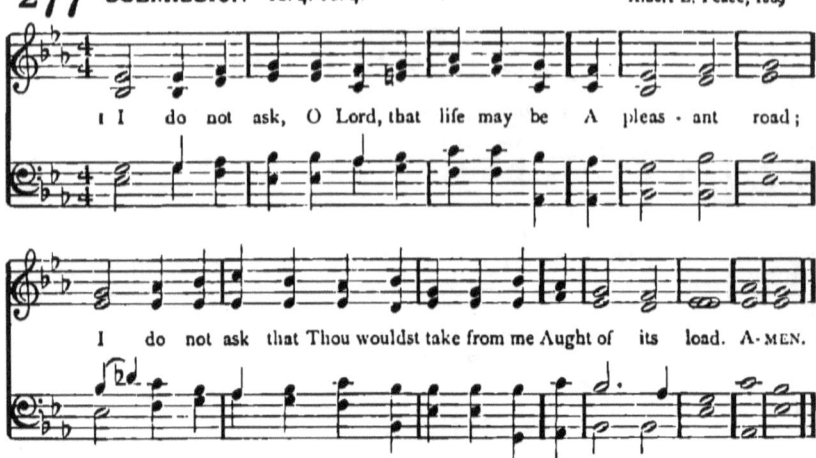

1 I do not ask, O Lord, that life may be
   A pleasant road;
I do not ask that Thou wouldst take from me
   Aught of its load. A-MEN.

2 I do not ask that flowers should always spring
    Beneath my feet;
  I know too well the poison and the sting
    Of things too sweet.

3 For one thing only, Lord, dear Lord,
    I plead:
  Lead me aright,
  Though strength should falter and though heart should bleed,
    Through peace to light.

4 I do not ask, O Lord, that Thou shouldst shed
    Full radiance here;
  Give but a ray of peace, that I may tread
    Without a fear.

5 I do not ask my cross to understand,
    My way to see;
  Better in darkness just to feel Thy hand,
    And follow Thee.

6 Joy is like restless day; but peace Divine
    Like quiet night:
  Lead me, O Lord, till perfect day shall shine,
    Through peace to light.
                    Adelaide A. Procter, 1862

278 (GREEN HILL) C. M.

1 THERE is a safe and secret place,
    Beneath the wings Divine,
  Reserved for all the heirs of grace;
    O be that refuge mine!

2 The least and feeblest there may bide,
    Uninjured and unawed;
  While thousands fall on every side,
    He rests secure in God.

3 He feeds in pastures, large and fair,
    Of love and truth Divine:
  O child of God, O glory's heir,
    How rich a lot is thine!

4 A hand almighty to defend,
    An ear for every call,
  An honored life, a peaceful end,
    And heaven to crown it all!
                    Rev. Henry F. Lyte, 1834

Hymns of Salvation

279 WARD L. M. Old Scotch Melody; arr. by Lowell Mason, 1830

1 God is the Ref-uge of His saints When storms of sharp dis-tress in-vade: Ere we can of-fer our complaints, Be-hold Him pres-ent with His aid. A-MEN.

2 Let mountains from their seats be hurled
Down to the deep, and buried there,
Convulsions shake the solid world,
Our faith shall never yield to fear.

3 Loud may the troubled ocean roar;
In sacred peace our souls abide,
While every nation, every shore,
Trembles, and dreads the swelling tide.

4 There is a stream whose gentle flow
Supplies the city of our God;
Life, love, and joy, still gliding through,
And watering our Divine abode.

5 That sacred stream, Thy holy word,
Our grief allays, our fear controls;
Sweet peace Thy promises afford,
And give new strength to fainting souls.

6 Zion enjoys her Monarch's love,
Secure against a threatening hour;
Nor can her firm foundations move,
Built on His truth, and armed with power.

Rev. Isaac Watts, 1719: verse 5, l. 2, alt.

280 (DENNIS) S. M.

1 HOW gentle God's commands,
How kind His precepts are!
Come, cast your burdens on the Lord,
And trust His constant care.

2 While Providence supports,
Let saints securely dwell;
That hand, which bears all nature up,
Shall guide His children well.

3 Why should this anxious load
Press down your weary mind?
Haste to your heavenly Father's throne,
And sweet refreshment find.

4 His goodness stands approved,
Down to the present day;
I'll drop my burden at His feet,
And bear a song away.

Rev. Philip Doddridge, publ. 1755

Trust

281 GREENWOOD S. M. — Joseph E. Sweetser, 1849

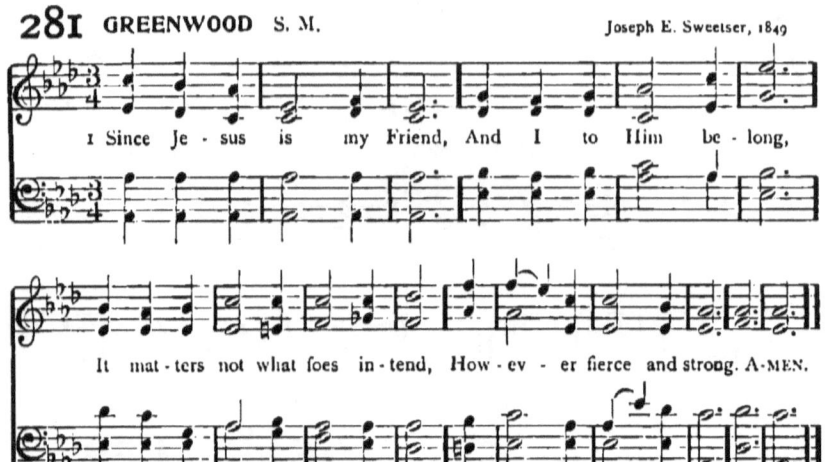

1 Since Jesus is my Friend, And I to Him belong,
It matters not what foes intend, However fierce and strong. A-MEN.

2 He whispers in my breast
  Sweet words of holy cheer,
How they who seek in God their rest
  Shall ever find Him near;

3 How God hath built above
  A city fair and new,   [prove
Where eye and heart shall see and
  What faith has counted true.

4 My heart for gladness springs;
  It cannot more be sad;
For very joy it laughs and sings,—
  Sees naught but sunshine glad.

5 The sun that lights mine eyes
  Is Christ, the Lord I love;
I sing for joy of that which lies
  Stored up for us above.

Rev. Paul Gerhardt, 1656. Tr. Catherine Winkworth, 1855; alt. and arr.

DENNIS S. M. — Arr. from Hans G Nägeli, by Lowell Mason, 1845

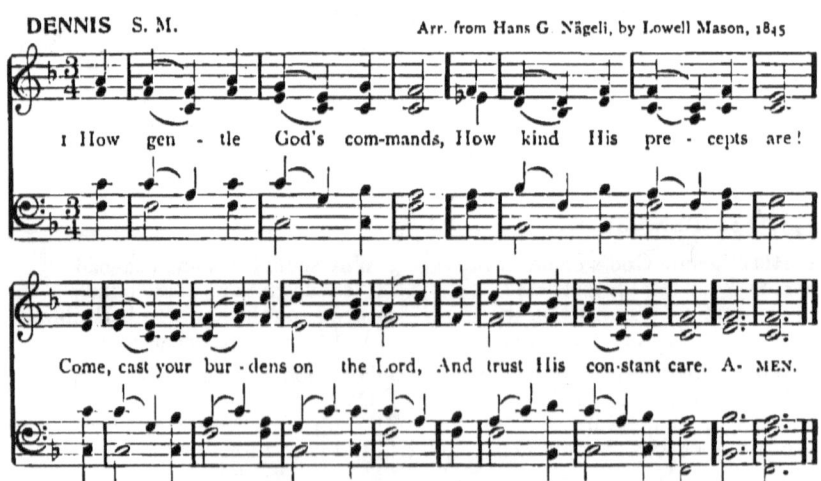

1 How gentle God's commands, How kind His precepts are!
Come, cast your burdens on the Lord, And trust His constant care. A- MEN.

Hymns of Salvation

282 MERCY 7. 7. 7. 7. Arr. from Louis M. Gottschalk, 1867

1 Cast thy bur-den on the Lord, On-ly lean up-on His word;
Thou wilt soon have cause to bless His e-ter-nal faith-ful-ness. A-MEN.

Copyright: by per. of Oliver Ditson Company

2 He sustains thee by His hand,
He enables thee to stand;
Those whom Jesus once hath loved
From His grace are never moved.

3 Human counsels come to naught;
That shall stand which God hath wrought;
His compassion, love, and power
Are the same for evermore.

4 Heaven and earth may pass away,
God's free grace shall not decay;
He hath promised to fulfil
All the pleasure of His will.

5 Jesus, Guardian of Thy flock,
Be Thyself our constant Rock;
Make us, by Thy powerful hand,
Strong as Zion's mountain stand.

Anon. in Rowland Hill's Ps. and Hy., 1783

NAOMI C. M. Arr. from Hans G Nägeli, by Lowell Mason, 1836

1 Fa-ther, what-e'er of earth-ly bliss Thy sove-reign will de-nies,
Ac-cept-ed at Thy throne of grace, Let this pe-ti-tion rise: A-MEN.

Trust

283 WOODWARD'S LITANY 7.7.7.7.   W. W. Woodward, 1863

1 Day by day the manna fell;
O to learn this lesson well!
Still by constant mercy fed,
Give me, Lord, my daily bread. A-MEN.

2 "Day by day" the promise reads;
Daily strength for daily needs:
Cast foreboding fears away,
Take the manna of to-day.

3 Lord, my times are in Thy hand;
All my sanguine hopes have planned
To Thy wisdom I resign,
And would make Thy purpose mine.

4 Thou my daily task shalt give;
Day by day to Thee I live;
So shall added years fulfil,
Not my own, my Father's will.

                                             Josiah Conder, 1836

284 (WOODWARD'S LITANY) 7.7.7.7.

1 WAIT, my soul, upon the Lord,
To His gracious promise flee,
Laying hold upon His word,
"As thy days thy strength shall be."

2 If the sorrows of thy case
Seem peculiar still to thee,
God has promised needful grace:
"As thy days thy strength shall be."

3 Days of trial, days of grief,
In succession thou mayst see;
This is still thy sweet relief:
"As thy days thy strength shall be."

4 Rock of Ages, I'm secure,
With Thy promise, full and free,
Faithful, positive, and sure,
"As thy days thy strength shall be."

                                        William F. Lloyd (1791-1853)

285 (NAOMI) C. M.

1 FATHER, whate'er of earthly bliss
Thy sovereign will denies,
Accepted at Thy throne of grace,
Let this petition rise:

2 Give me a calm, a thankful heart,
From every murmur free;
The blessings of Thy grace impart,
And make me live to Thee.

3 Let the sweet hope that Thou art mine
My life and death attend;
Thy presence through my journey shine,
And crown my journey's end.

                     Anne Steele, 1760; alt. Rev. A. M. Toplady, 1776

Hymns of Salvation

286   FAITH   C. M.
Rev. John B. Dykes, 1867

1 Im-mor-tal Love, for ev-er full, For ev-er flow-ing free, For ev-er shared, for ev-er whole, A nev-er-ebb-ing sea! A-MEN.

2 We may not climb the heavenly steeps
   To bring the Lord Christ down;
In vain we search the lowest deeps,
   For Him no depths can drown:

3 But warm, sweet, tender, even yet
   A present Help is He;
And faith has still its Olivet,
   And love its Galilee.

4 The healing of His seamless dress
   Is by our beds of pain;
We touch Him in life's throng and press,
   And we are whole again.

5 Through Him the first fond prayers are said
   Our lips of childhood frame;
The last low whispers of our dead
   Are burdened with His Name.

6 Our Lord, and Master of us all,
   Whate'er our name or sign,
We own Thy sway, we hear Thy call,
   We test our lives by Thine.

John G. Whittier, 1866

287   (ORTONVILLE or FAITH)   C. M.

1 MAJESTIC sweetness sits enthroned
   Upon the Saviour's brow;
His head with radiant glories crowned,
   His lips with grace o'erflow.

2 No mortal can with Him compare,
   Among the sons of men;
Fairer is He than all the fair
   That fill the heavenly train.

3 He saw me plunged in deep distress,
   He flew to my relief;
For me He bore the shameful cross,
   And carried all my grief.

4 To Him I owe my life and breath,
   And all the joys I have;
He makes me triumph over death,
   And saves me from the grave.

5 To heaven, the place of His abode,
   He brings my weary feet;
Shows me the glories of my God,
   And makes my joys complete.

6 Since from His bounty I receive
   Such proofs of love Divine,
Had I a thousand hearts to give,
   Lord, they should all be Thine.

Rev. Samuel Stennett, 1787: verse 1, l. 2, alt.

Love, and Communion with Christ

288 HOLY CROSS C. M.   Arr. by James C. Wade, 1865

2 When once Thou visitest the heart,
   Then truth begins to shine,
   Then earthly vanities depart,
   Then kindles love Divine.

3 O Jesus, Light of all below,
   Thou Fount of life and fire,
   Surpassing all the joys we know,
   And all we can desire !

4 May every heart confess Thy Name,
   And ever Thee adore ;
   And seeking Thee, itself inflame
   To seek Thee more and more.

5 Thee may our tongues for ever bless ;
   Thee may we love alone ;
   And ever in our lives express
   The image of Thine own.

        Bernard of Clairvaux (1091–1153.) Tr. Rev. Edward Caswall, 1849

ORTONVILLE C. M.   Thomas Hastings, 1837

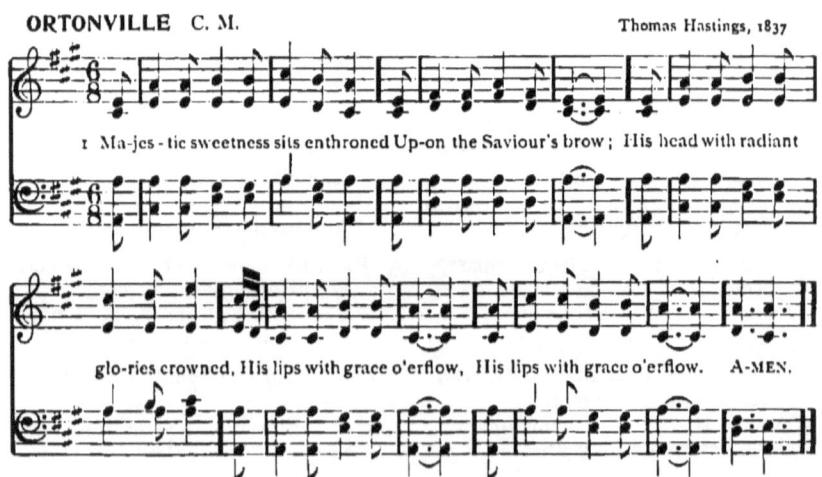

Hymns of Salvation

289 ST. PETER C. M.
Alexander R. Reinagle, 1826

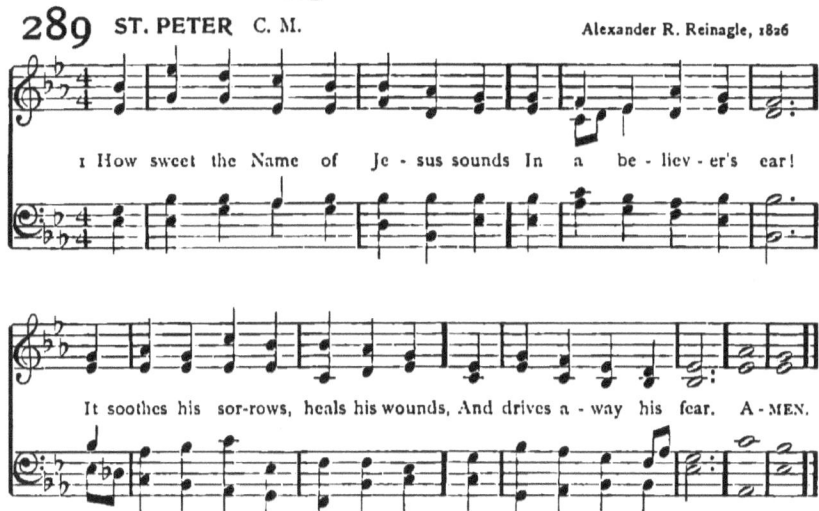

1. How sweet the Name of Jesus sounds In a believer's ear!
It soothes his sorrows, heals his wounds, And drives away his fear. A-MEN.

2. It makes the wounded spirit whole,
   And calms the troubled breast;
   'Tis Manna to the hungry soul,
   And to the weary Rest.

3. Dear Name! the Rock on which I build,
   My Shield and Hiding-place,
   My never-failing Treasury, filled
   With boundless stores of grace;

4. Jesus, my Shepherd, Brother, Friend,
   My Prophet, Priest, and King,
   My Lord, my Life, my Way, my End,
   Accept the praise I bring.

5. Weak is the effort of my heart,
   And cold my warmest thought;
   But when I see Thee as Thou art,
   I'll praise Thee as I ought.

6. Till then I would Thy love proclaim
   With every fleeting breath;
   And may the music of Thy Name
   Refresh my soul in death.

Rev. John Newton, 1779: verse 4, l. 1, alt.

290 (HEBER) C. M.

1. JESUS, I love Thy charming Name,
   'Tis music to mine ear;
   Fain would I sound it out so loud
   That earth and heaven should hear.

2. Yes, Thou art precious to my soul,
   My Transport and my Trust;
   Jewels to Thee are gaudy toys,
   And gold is sordid dust.

3. All my capacious powers can wish
   In Thee doth richly meet;
   Not to mine eyes is light so dear,
   Nor friendship half so sweet.

4. Thy grace still dwells upon my heart,
   And sheds its fragrance there;
   The noblest balm of all its wounds,
   The cordial of its care.

Rev. Philip Doddridge, 1717

Love, and Communion with Christ

291 HOLY TRINITY C. M.   Sir Joseph Barnby, 1861

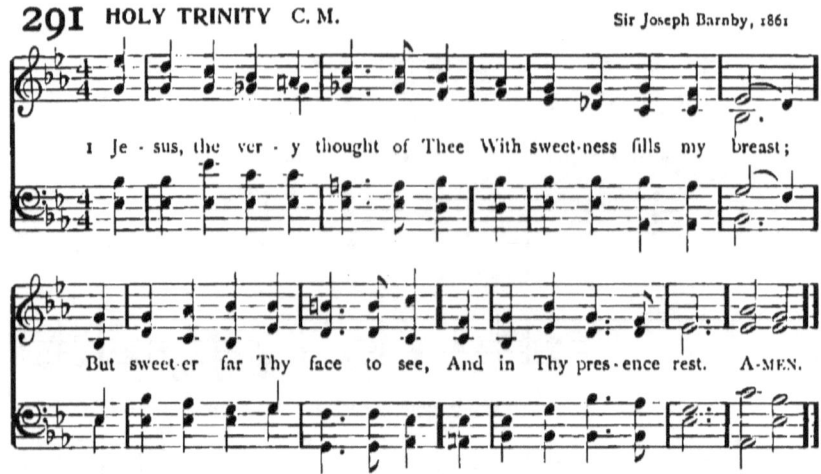

1 Jesus, the very thought of Thee With sweetness fills my breast; But sweeter far Thy face to see, And in Thy presence rest. A-MEN.

2 Nor voice can sing, nor heart can frame,
   Nor can the memory find,
A sweeter sound than Thy blest Name,
   O Saviour of mankind.

3 O Hope of every contrite heart,
   O Joy of all the meek,
To those who fall, how kind Thou art!
   How good to those who seek!

4 But what to those who find? Ah, this
   Nor tongue nor pen can show:
The love of Jesus, what it is
   None but His loved ones know.

5 Jesus, our only Joy be Thou,
   As Thou our Prize wilt be;
Jesus, be Thou our Glory now,
   And through eternity.

Bernard of Clairvaux (1091-1153.)   Tr. Rev. Edward Caswall, 1849; verse 4, l. 4, alt.

HEBER C. M.   George Kingsley, 1838

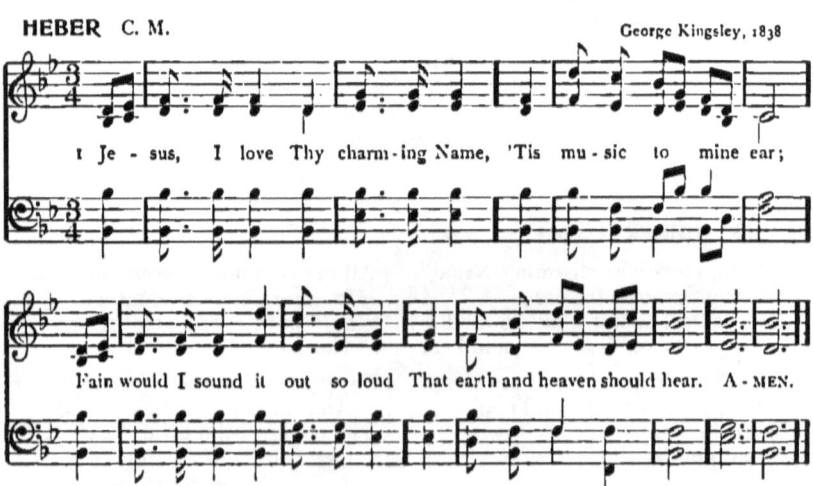

1 Jesus, I love Thy charming Name, 'Tis music to mine ear; Fain would I sound it out so loud That earth and heaven should hear. A-MEN.

Hymns of Salvation

292 JESU, MAGISTER BONE 7. 6. 7. 6. D.   Rev. John B. Dykes, 1875

1. I know no life divided, O Lord of life, from Thee;
In Thee is life provided For all mankind and me:
I know no death, O Jesus, Because I live in Thee;
Thy death it is which frees us From death eternally. A-MEN.

2 I fear no tribulation,
  Since, whatsoe'er it be,
It makes no separation
  Between my Lord and me.
If Thou, my God and Teacher,
  Vouchsafe to be my own,
Though poor, I shall be richer
  Than monarch on his throne.

3 If, while on earth I wander,
  My heart is light and blest,
Ah, what shall I be yonder,
  In perfect peace and rest?
O blessèd thought in dying!
  We go to meet the Lord,
Where there shall be no sighing,
  A kingdom our reward.

Rev. Carl J. P. Spitta, 1833. Tr. Richard Massie, 1860

Love, and Communion with Christ

293 HODNET 7.6.7.6.D. Arr. from Sigismund Thalberg (1812–1871)

1 O Lamb of God, still keep me
  Near to Thy wound-ed side;
'Tis on-ly there in safe-ty
  And peace I can a-bide.
What foes and snares sur-round me,
  What doubts and fears with-in!
The grace that sought and found me
  A-lone can keep me clean. A-MEN.

2 'Tis only in Thee hiding,
    I know my life secure;
  Only in Thee abiding,
    The conflict can endure:
  Thine arm the victory gaineth
    O'er every hateful foe;
  Thy love my heart sustaineth
    In all its care and woe.

3 Soon shall my eyes behold Thee,
    With rapture, face to face;
  One half hath not been told me
    Of all Thy power and grace;
  Thy beauty, Lord, and glory,
    The wonders of Thy love,
  Shall be the endless story
    Of all Thy saints above.

Rev. James G. Deck, 1842

Hymns of Salvation

294 LOVE DIVINE 8.7.8.7. D. George F. Le Jeune, 1887

1. Love Divine, all loves excelling, Joy of heaven, to earth come down;
Fix in us Thy humble dwelling, All Thy faithful mercies crown:
Jesus, Thou art all compassion, Pure, unbounded love Thou art;
Visit us with Thy salvation, Enter every trembling heart. A-MEN.

2. Breathe, O breathe Thy loving Spirit Into every troubled breast;
Let us all in Thee inherit, Let us find the promised rest:
Take away the love of sinning; Alpha and Omega be;
End of faith, as its Beginning, Set our hearts at liberty.

3 Come, Almighty to deliver,
Let us all Thy life receive;
Suddenly return, and never,
Never more Thy temples leave.
Thee we would be always blessing,
Serve Thee as Thy hosts above,
Pray, and praise Thee without ceasing,
Glory in Thy perfect love.

4 Finish, then, Thy new creation;
Pure and spotless let us be:
Let us see Thy great salvation
Perfectly restored in Thee;
Changed from glory into glory,
Till in heaven we take our place,
Till we cast our crowns before Thee,
Lost in wonder, love, and praise.

Rev. Charles Wesley, 1747: verse 2, ll. 4, 5, alt.

Love, and Communion with Christ

295 SAVOY CHAPEL 7.6.7.6. D.   J. Baptiste Calkin (1827–)

1. To Thee, O dear, dear Saviour, My spirit turns for rest, My peace is in Thy favor, My pillow on Thy breast; Though all the world deceive me, I know that I am Thine, And Thou wilt never leave me, O blessed Saviour mine. A-MEN.

2. In Thee my trust abideth, On Thee my hope relies, O Thou whose love provideth For all beneath the skies; O Thou whose mercy found me, From bondage set me free, And then for ever bound me, With three-fold cords to Thee.

3. My grief is in the dulness
With which this sluggish heart
Doth open to the fulness
Of all Thou wouldst impart;
My joy is in Thy beauty
Of holiness Divine,
My comfort in the duty
That binds my life in Thine.

4. Alas, that I should ever
Have failed in love to Thee,
The only One who never
Forgat or slighted me!
O for a heart to love Thee
More truly as I ought,
And nothing place above Thee
In deed, or word, or thought.

Rev. John S. B. Monsell, 1863

Hymns of Salvation

296 CONSTANCE 8. 7. 8. 7. D. Sir Arthur Sullivan, 1875

1. I've found a Friend; O such a Friend! He loved me ere I knew Him;
He drew me with the cords of love, And thus He bound me to Him;
And round my heart still close-ly twine Those ties which naught can sev-er,
For I am His, and He is mine, For ev-er and for ev-er. A-MEN.

2 I've found a Friend; O such a Friend!
   He bled, He died to save me;
And not alone the gift of life,
   But His own self He gave me.
Naught that I have mine own I'll call,
   I'll hold it for the Giver;
My heart, my strength, my life, my all,
   Are His, and His for ever.

3 I've found a Friend; O such a Friend,
   So kind and true and tender!
So wise a Counsellor and Guide,
   So mighty a Defender!
From Him who loves me now so well
   What power my soul shall sever?
Shall life or death, shall earth or hell?
   No: I am His for ever.

Rev. James G. Small, 1866

Love, and Communion with Christ

297 SAWLEY C. M.   *James Walch, 1860*

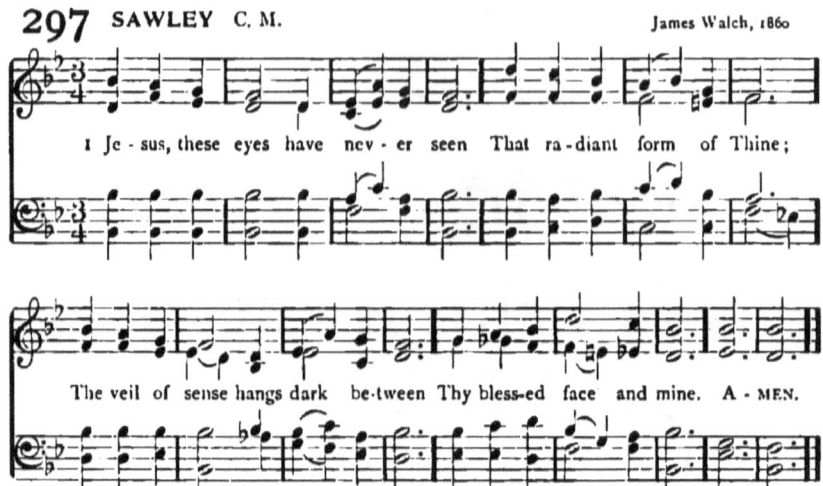

1 Jesus, these eyes have never seen That radiant form of Thine;
The veil of sense hangs dark between Thy blessed face and mine. A-MEN.

2 I see Thee not, I hear Thee not,
   Yet art Thou oft with me;
And earth hath ne'er so dear a spot
   As where I meet with Thee.

3 Like some bright dream that comes unsought,
   When slumbers o'er me roll,
Thine image ever fills my thought,
   And charms my ravished soul.

4 Yet though I have not seen, and still
   Must rest in faith alone;
I love Thee, dearest Lord, and will,
   Unseen, but not unknown.

5 When death these mortal eyes shall seal,
   And still this throbbing heart,
The rending veil shall Thee reveal,
   All glorious as Thou art.
               Rev. Ray Palmer, 1858

298 (SAWLEY) C. M.

1 JESUS, Thou art the sinner's Friend;
   As such I look to Thee;
Now, in the fulness of Thy love,
   O Lord, remember me.

2 Remember Thy pure word of grace,
   Remember Calvary's tree,
Remember all Thy dying groans,
   And then remember me.

3 Thou wondrous Advocate with God,
   I yield my soul to Thee;
While Thou art pleading on the throne,
   Dear Lord, remember me.

4 Lord, I am guilty, I am vile,
   But Thy salvation's free;
Then, in Thine all-abounding grace,
   Dear Lord, remember me.

5 Howe'er forsaken or despised,
   Howe'er oppressed I be,
Howe'er forgotten here on earth,
   Do Thou remember me.

6 And when I close my eyes in death,
   And human help shall flee,
Then, then, my dear redeeming God,
   O then remember me.
          Rev. Richard Burnham, 1796: verses 1, 4, alt.

Hymns of Salvation

299 SOLITUDE 7.7.7.7.   Lewis T. Downes, 1851

1 Sav-iour, teach me, day by day, Love's sweet les-son,— to o-bey;
Sweet-er les-son can-not be, Lov-ing Him who first loved me. A-MEN.

2 With a child's glad heart of love,
At Thy bidding may I move;
Prompt to serve and follow Thee,
Loving Him who first loved me.

3 Teach me thus Thy steps to trace,
Strong to follow in Thy grace;
Learning how to love from Thee,
Loving Him who first loved me.

4 Love in loving finds employ,
In obedience all her joy;
Ever new that joy will be,
Loving Him who first loved me.

5 Though a foolish child and weak,
More than this I need not seek;
Singing, till Thy face I see,
Of His love who first loved me.

                                  Jane E. Leeson, 1842

GORTON S. M.   Arr. from Beethoven (1770-1827)

1 My spir-it on Thy care, Blest Sav-iour, I re-cline;
Thou wilt not leave me to de-spair, For Thou art Love Di-vine. A-MEN.

Love, and Communion with Christ

300 PAX TECUM 10. 10. G. T. Caldbeck, 1877

2 Peace, perfect peace, by thronging duties pressed?
  To do the will of Jesus, this is rest.

3 Peace, perfect peace, with sorrows surging round?
  On Jesus' bosom naught but calm is found.

4 Peace, perfect peace, with loved ones far away?
  In Jesus' keeping we are safe, and they.

5 Peace, perfect peace, our future all unknown?
  Jesus we know, and He is on the throne.

6 Peace, perfect peace, death shadowing us and ours?
  Jesus has vanquished death and all its powers.

7 It is enough: earth's struggles soon shall cease,
  And Jesus call us to heaven's perfect peace.
  Bishop Edward H. Bickersteth, 1875

301 (GORTON) S. M.

1 MY spirit on Thy care,
  Blest Saviour, I recline;
Thou wilt not leave me to despair,
  For Thou art Love Divine.

2 In Thee I place my trust,
  On Thee I calmly rest;
I know Thee good, I know Thee just,
  And count Thy choice the best.

3 Whate'er events betide,
  Thy will they all perform;
Safe in Thy breast my head I hide,
  Nor fear the coming storm.

4 Let good or ill befall,
  It must be good for me;
Secure of having Thee in all,
  Of having all in Thee.
  Rev. Henry F. Lyte, 1834

Hymns of Salvation

302 FLEMMING 8.8.8.6. Arr. from Friedrich F. Flemming, 1810

1 O Holy Saviour, Friend unseen, Since on Thine arm Thou bidd'st me lean, Help me, throughout life's varying scene, By faith to cling to Thee. A-MEN.

2 Blest with this fellowship Divine,
Take what Thou wilt, I'll ne'er repine;
E'en as the branches to the vine,
My soul would cling to Thee.

3 What though the world deceitful prove,
And earthly friends and joys remove,
With patient, uncomplaining love
Still would I cling to Thee.

4 Though faith and hope may long be tried,
I ask not, need not aught beside;
How safe, how calm, how satisfied,
The souls that cling to Thee!

5 Blest is my lot, whate'er befall;
What can disturb me, who appal,
While as my Strength, my Rock, my Saviour, I cling to Thee? [All,

Charlotte Elliott, 1834

ECKHARDTSHEIM C. M. Charles Zeuner, 1833

1 If Christ is mine, then all is mine, And more than angels know; Both present things and things to come, And grace and glory too. . . . A-MEN.

Love, and Communion with Christ

303 ALBERT 8. 7. 8. 7. 7. 7. Heinrich Albert, 1643

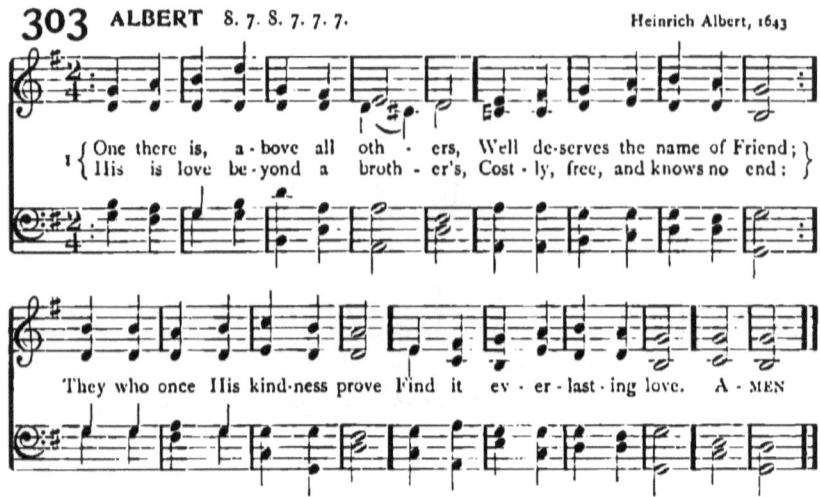

1. One there is, above all others, Well deserves the name of Friend;
   His is love beyond a brother's, Costly, free, and knows no end:
   They who once His kindness prove Find it everlasting love. A-MEN

2 Which of all our friends, to save us,
Could or would have shed their blood?
But our Jesus died to have us
Reconciled in Him to God:
This was boundless love indeed;
Jesus is a Friend in need.

3 When He lived on earth abased,
"Friend of sinners" was His name;
Now above all glory raised,
He rejoices in the same;
Still He calls them brethren, friends,
And to all their wants attends.

4 O for grace our hearts to soften!
Teach us, Lord, at length to love;
We, alas! forget too often
What a Friend we have above:
But when home our souls are brought,
We will love Thee as we ought.

Rev. John Newton, 1779

304 (ECKHARDTSHEIM) C. M.

1 IF Christ is mine, then all is mine,
And more than angels know;
Both present things and things to come,
And grace and glory too.

2 If He is mine, then, though He frown,
He never will forsake;
His chastisements all work for good,
And but His love bespeak.

3 If he is mine, I need not fear
The rage of earth and hell;
He will support my feeble frame,
And all their power repel.

4 If He is mine, let friends forsake,
And earthly comforts flee;
He, the Dispenser of all good,
Is more than these to me.

5 If He is mine, I'll fearless pass
Through death's tremendous vale;
He'll be my Comfort and my Stay
When heart and flesh shall fail.

6 Let Jesus tell me He is mine,
I nothing want beside;
My soul shall at the Fountain live
When all the streams are dried.

Rev. Benjamin Beddome, publ. 1817

2 Consecrate me now to Thy service, Lord,
By the power of grace Divine;
Let my soul look up with a steadfast hope,
And my will be lost in Thine.—REF.

3 O the pure delight of a single hour
That before Thy throne I spend,
When I kneel in prayer, and with Thee, my God,
I commune as friend with friend! REF.

4 There are depths of love that I cannot know
Till I cross the narrow sea,
There are heights of joy that I may not reach
Till I rest in peace with Thee.—REF.

Fanny J. (Crosby) Van Alstyne, 1875

Love, and Communion with Christ

306 ST. JUDE 8.7.8.8.7. Charles J. Vincent, 1877

1 O the bitter shame and sorrow
   That a time could ever be,
When I let the Saviour's pity
   Plead in vain, and proudly answered,
"All of self, and none of Thee." A-MEN.

2 Yet He found me; I beheld Him
   Bleeding on the accursèd tree,
Heard Him pray, "Forgive them, Father!"
And my wistful heart said faintly,
   "Some of self, and some of Thee."

3 Day by day His tender mercy,
   Healing, helping, full and free,
Sweet and strong, and, ah! so patient,
Brought me lower, while I whispered,
   "Less of self, and more of Thee."

4 Higher than the highest heavens,
   Deeper than the deepest sea,
Lord, Thy love at last hath conquered;
Grant me now my soul's desire,
   "None of self, and all of Thee."

Rev. Theodore Monod, 1874

Hymns of Salvation

307 MESSIAH 7. 7. 7. 7. D.
Arr. from L. J. F. Herold, by Geo. Kingsley, 1838

1 Jesus, merciful and mild, Lead me as a helpless child:
On no other arm but Thine Would my weary soul recline.
Thou art ready to forgive, Thou canst bid the sinner live;
Guide the wanderer, day by day, In the strait and narrow way. A-MEN.

2 Thou canst fit me by Thy grace
For the heavenly dwelling-place;
All Thy promises are sure,
Ever shall Thy love endure;
Then what more could I desire,
How to greater bliss aspire?
All I need, in Thee I see;
Thou art All in all to me.

3 Jesus, Saviour all Divine,
Hast Thou made me truly Thine?
Hast Thou bought me by Thy blood?
Reconciled my heart to God?
Hearken to my tender prayer,
Let me Thine own image bear,
Let me love Thee more and more
Till I reach heaven's blissful shore.

Thomas Hastings, 1858

Love, and Communion with Christ

308 SPANISH HYMN 7. 7. 7. 7. 7. 7.   Arr. by Benjamin Carr, 1824

1 Blessed Saviour, Thee I love,
All my other joys above;
All my hopes in Thee abide,
Thou my hope, and naught beside:
Ever let my glory be,
Only, only, only Thee. A-MEN.

2 Once again beside the cross,
  All my gain I count but loss;
  Earthly pleasures fade away,—
  Clouds they are that hide my day:
  Hence, vain shadows! let me see
  Jesus crucified for me.

3 Blessèd Saviour, Thine am I,
  Thine to live, and Thine to die;
  Height or depth, or creature power,
  Ne'er shall hide my Saviour more:
  Ever shall my glory be,
  Only, only, only Thee.

Rev. George Duffield, 1851

309 (SPANISH HYMN) 7. 7. 7. 7. 7. 7.

1 JESUS, Master, whose I am,
  Purchased Thine alone to be,
  By Thy blood, O spotless Lamb,
    Shed so willingly for me;
  Let my heart be all Thine own,
  Let me live to Thee alone.

2 Other lords have long held sway;
  Now Thy Name alone to bear,
  Thy dear voice alone obey
Is my daily, hourly prayer.
Whom have I in heaven but Thee?
Nothing else my joy can be.

3 Jesus, Master, I am Thine;
  Keep me faithful, keep me near;
  Let Thy presence in me shine
    All my homeward way to cheer.
  Jesus, at Thy feet I fall,
  O be Thou my All in all.

Frances R. Havergal, 1865

3 Let me love Thee more and more,
Till this fleeting, fleeting life is o'er;
Till my soul is lost in love,
In a brighter, brighter world above.—REF.

Fanny J. (Crosby) Van Alstyne, 1875

Copyright, 1875, by Biglow & Main. Used by per.

Love, and Communion with Christ

311 LOVING-KINDNESS L. M. American Melody

1 Awake, my soul, in joyful lays,
And sing thy great Redeemer's praise;
He justly claims a song from me,
His loving-kindness is so free;
Loving-kindness, loving-kindness, His loving-kindness is so free. A-MEN.

2 He saw me ruined in the fall,
Yet loved me notwithstanding all,
And saved me from my lost estate,
His loving-kindness is so great.

3 Through mighty hosts of cruel foes,
Where earth and hell my way oppose,
He safely leads my soul along,
His loving-kindness is so strong.

4 So when I pass death's gloomy vale,
And life and mortal powers shall fail,
O may my last expiring breath
His loving-kindness sing in death.

5 Then shall I mount, and soar away
To the bright world of endless day;
There shall I sing, with sweet surprise,
His loving-kindness in the skies.

Rev. Samuel Medley, 1782

Hymns of Salvation

312 ST. MARGARET 8.8.8.8.6.
Albert L. Peace, 1885

1 O Love that wilt not let me go,
I rest my weary soul in Thee;
I give Thee back the life I owe,
That in Thine ocean depths its flow

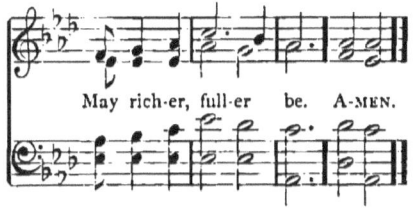

May richer, fuller be. A-MEN.

2 O Light that followest all my way,
  I yield my flickering torch to Thee;
  My heart restores its borrowed ray,
  That in Thy sunshine's blaze its day
    May brighter, fairer be.

3 O Joy that seekest me through pain,
  I cannot close my heart to Thee;
  I trace the rainbow through the rain,
  And feel the promise is not vain
    That morn shall tearless be.

4 O Cross that liftest up my head,
  I dare not ask to fly from Thee;
  I lay in dust life's glory dead,
  And from the ground there blossoms red
    Life that shall endless be.
        Rev. George Matheson, 1882

313 (HENDON) 7.7.7.7.

1 CHRIST, of all my hopes the Ground,
    Christ, the Spring of all my joy,
  Still in Thee may I be found,
    Still for Thee my powers employ.

2 Fountain of o'erflowing grace,
    Freely from Thy fulness give;
  Till I close my earthly race,
    May I prove it "Christ to live."

3 Firmly trusting in Thy blood,
    Nothing shall my heart confound;
  Safely I shall pass the flood,
    Safely reach Emmanuel's ground.

4 When I touch the blessèd shore,
    Back the closing waves shall roll;
  Death's dark stream shall nevermore
    Part from Thee my ravished soul.

5 Thus, O thus, an entrance give
    To the land of cloudless sky;
  Having known it "Christ to live,"
    Let me know it "gain to die."
        Rev. Ralph Wardlaw, 1817

Love, and Communion with Christ

314 NETTLETON 8. 7. 8. 7. D. Rev. Asahel Nettleton, 1825

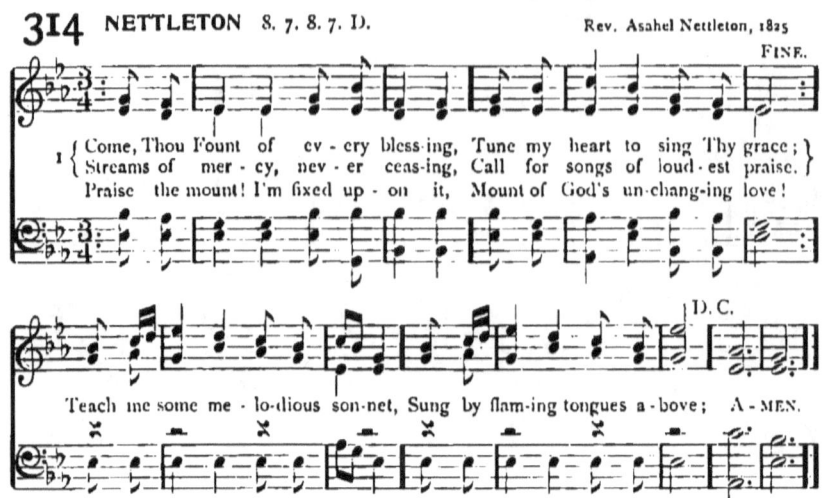

1. Come, Thou Fount of ev-ery bless-ing, Tune my heart to sing Thy grace;
   Streams of mer-cy, nev-er ceas-ing, Call for songs of loud-est praise.
   Praise the mount! I'm fixed up-on it, Mount of God's un-chang-ing love!
   Teach me some me-lo-dious son-net, Sung by flam-ing tongues a-bove; A-MEN.

2. Here I raise my Ebenezer;
   Hither by Thy help I'm come;
   And I hope, by Thy good pleasure,
   Safely to arrive at home.
   Jesus sought me when a stranger,
   Wandering from the fold of God;
   He, to rescue me from danger,
   Interposed with precious blood.

3. O to grace how great a debtor
   Daily I'm constrained to be!
   Let that grace now, like a fetter,
   Bind my wandering heart to Thee.
   Prone to wander, Lord, I feel it;
   Prone to leave the God I love;
   Here's my heart; O take and seal it,
   Seal it from Thy courts above.

   Rev. Robert Robinson, 1758

HENDON 7. 7. 7. 7. Rev. H. A. César Malan, 1827

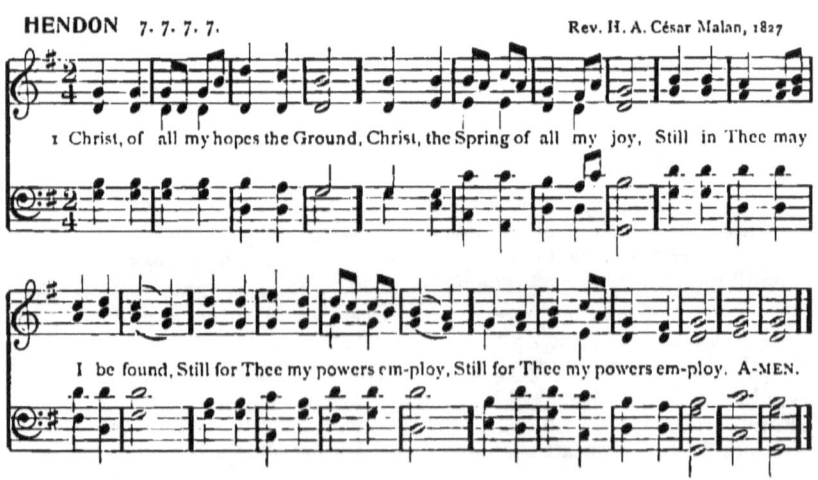

1. Christ, of all my hopes the Ground, Christ, the Spring of all my joy, Still in Thee may I be found, Still for Thee my powers em-ploy, Still for Thee my powers em-ploy. A-MEN.

Hymns of Salvation

315 ERIE 8.7.8.7. D. C. Crozat Converse, 1868

1 What a Friend we have in Jesus, All our sins and griefs to bear! What a privilege to carry Everything to God in prayer! O what peace we often forfeit, O what needless pain we bear, All because we do not carry Everything to God in prayer. A-MEN.

By per. of C. C. Converse, owner of copyright

2 Have we trials and temptations?
　Is there trouble anywhere?
We should never be discouraged:
　Take it to the Lord in prayer!
Can we find a friend so faithful,
　Who will all our sorrows share?
Jesus knows our every weakness—
　Take it to the Lord in prayer!

3 Are we weak and heavy laden,
　Cumbered with a load of care?
Precious Saviour, still our Refuge,—
　Take it to the Lord in prayer!
Do thy friends despise, forsake thee?
　Take it to the Lord in prayer!
In His arms He'll take and shield thee,
　Thou wilt find a solace there.

　　　　Joseph Scriven (c. 1820–1886)

Hymns of Salvation

317 RETREAT L. M.
Thomas Hastings, 1842

1 From ev-ery storm-y wind that blows, From ev-ery swell-ing tide of woes, There is a calm, a sure re-treat; 'Tis found be-neath the mer-cy-seat. A-MEN.

2 There is a place where Jesus sheds
The oil of gladness on our heads,
A place than all besides more sweet;
It is the blood-stained mercy-seat.

3 There is a spot where spirits blend,
Where friend holds fellowship with friend,
Though sundered far; by faith they meet,
Around the common mercy-seat.

4 Ah, whither could we flee for aid,
When tempted, desolate, dismayed,
Or how the hosts of hell defeat,
Had suffering saints no mercy-seat?

5 There, there on eagle wings we soar,
And time and sense seem all no more,
And heaven comes down our souls to greet,
And glory crowns the mercy-seat.

6 O may my hand forget her skill,
My tongue be silent, cold, and still,
This bounding heart forget to beat,
If I forget the mercy-seat.

Rev. Hugh Stowell, 1827, 1831

318 (STATE STREET) S. M.

1 BEHOLD the throne of grace!
The promise calls me near:
There Jesus shows a smiling face,
And waits to answer prayer.

2 My soul, ask what thou wilt;
Thou canst not be too bold;
Since His own blood for thee He spilt,
What else can He withhold?

3 Thine image, Lord, bestow,
Thy presence and Thy love;
I ask to serve Thee here below,
And reign with Thee above.

4 Teach me to live by faith;
Conform my will to Thine;
Let me victorious be in death,
And then in glory shine.

Rev. John Newton, 1779

Prayer

319 ST. ANDREW S. M. *Sir Joseph Barnby, 1866*

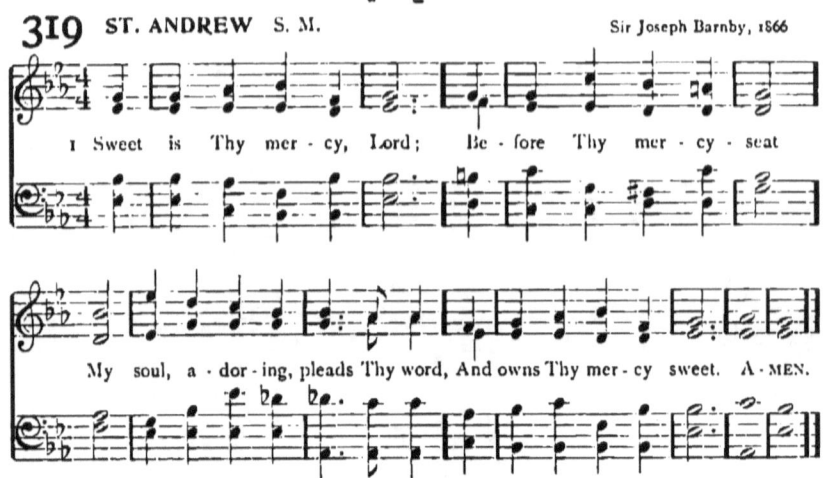

1 Sweet is Thy mercy, Lord;
  Before Thy mercy-seat
My soul, adoring, pleads Thy word,
  And owns Thy mercy sweet. A-MEN.

2 My need and Thy desires
   Are all in Christ complete;
  Thou hast the justice truth requires,
   And I Thy mercy sweet.

3 Where'er Thy Name is blest,
   Where'er Thy people meet,
  There I delight in Thee to rest,
   And find Thy mercy sweet.

4 Light Thou my weary way,
   Lead Thou my wandering feet,
  That while I stay on earth I may
   Still find Thy mercy sweet.

5 Thus shall the heavenly host
   Hear all my songs repeat
  To Father, Son, and Holy Ghost,
   My joy, Thy mercy sweet.
     Rev. John S. B. Monsell, 1862

STATE STREET S. M. *Jonathan C. Woodman, 1844*

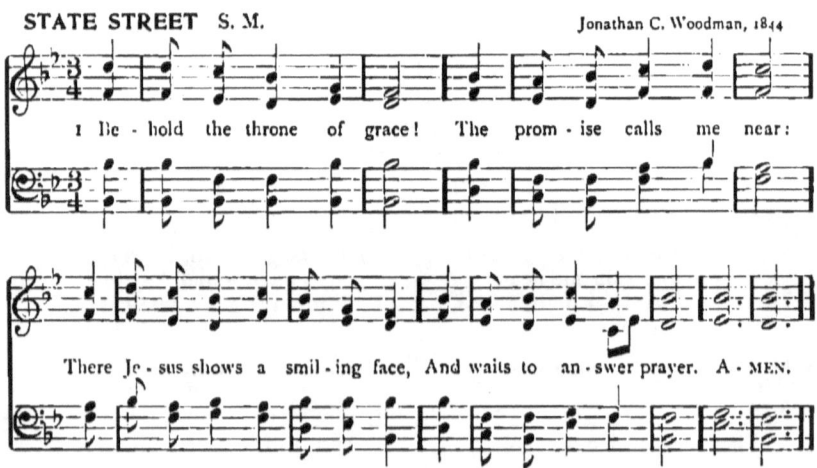

1 Behold the throne of grace! The promise calls me near:
  There Jesus shows a smiling face, And waits to answer prayer. A-MEN.

Hymns of Salvation

320 HORTON 7. 7. 7. 7. Arr. from Xavier Schnyder (1786-1868)

1 Come, my soul, thy suit prepare: Jesus loves to answer prayer; He Himself has bid thee pray, Therefore will not say thee nay. A-MEN.

2 Thou art coming to a King,
Large petitions with thee bring;
For His grace and power are such,
None can ever ask too much.

3 With my burden I begin:
Lord, remove this load of sin;
Let Thy blood, for sinners spilt,
Set my conscience free from guilt.

4 Lord, I come to Thee for rest,
Take possession of my breast;
There Thy blood-bought right maintain,
And without a rival reign.

5 While I am a pilgrim here,
Let Thy love my spirit cheer;
As my Guide, my Guard, my Friend,
Lead me to my journey's end.

Rev. John Newton, 1779

ELIZABETHTOWN C. M. George Kingsley, 1838

1 When cold our hearts, and far from Thee Our wandering spirits stray, And thoughts and lips move heavily, Lord, teach us how to pray. A-MEN.

Prayer

321 ELMHURST 8.8.8.6. Edwin Drewett, 1887

1 O Thou, the contrite sinners' Friend, Who, loving, lov'st them to the end, On this alone my hopes depend, That Thou wilt plead for me. A-MEN.

2 When, weary in the Christian race,
Far off appears my resting-place,
And, fainting, I mistrust Thy grace,
Then, Saviour, plead for me.

3 When I have erred and gone astray,
Afar from Thine and wisdom's way,
And see no glimmering guiding ray,
Still, Saviour, plead for me.

4 When Satan, by my sins made bold,
Strives from Thy cross to loose my hold,
Then with Thy pitying arms enfold,
And plead, O plead for me.

5 And when my dying hour draws near,
O'ercast with sorrow, pain, and fear,
Then to my fainting sight appear,
Pleading in heaven for me.

6 When the full light of heavenly day
Reveals my sins in dread array,
Say Thou hast washed them all away;
O say Thou plead'st for me.

Charlotte Elliott, 1835: verse 5, l. 2, alt.

322 (ELIZABETHTOWN) C. M.

1 WHEN cold our hearts, and far from Thee
Our wandering spirits stray,
And thoughts and lips move heavily,
Lord, teach us how to pray.

2 Too vile to venture near Thy Throne,
Too poor to turn away;
Our only voice,—Thy Spirit's groan,—
Lord, teach us how to pray.

3 We know not how to seek Thy face,
Unless Thou lead the way;
We have no words, unless Thy grace,
Lord, teach us how to pray.

4 Here every thought and fond desire
We on Thine altar lay;
And when our souls have caught Thy fire,
Lord, teach us how to pray.

Rev. John S. B. Monsell, 1837

Hymns of Salvation

323 HERBERT 8.8.8.4.   Rev. Richard R. Chope, 1862

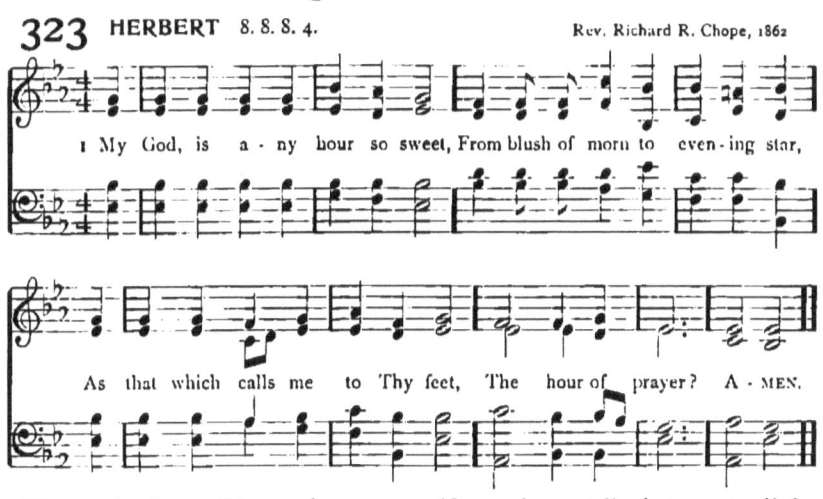

1 My God, is any hour so sweet, From blush of morn to evening star, As that which calls me to Thy feet, The hour of prayer? A-MEN.

2 Blest is that tranquil hour of morn,
And blest that solemn hour of eve,
When, on the wings of prayer upborne,
The world I leave.

3 Then is my strength by Thee renewed;
Then are my sins by Thee forgiven;
Then dost Thou cheer my solitude
With hopes of heaven.

4 No words can tell what sweet relief
There for my every want I find;
What strength for warfare, balm for grief,
What piece of mind!

5 Lord, till I reach yon blissful shore,
No privilege so dear shall be
As thus my inmost soul to pour
In prayer to Thee.

Charlotte Elliott, 1835 (text of 1836)

BYEFIELD C. M.   Thomas Hastings, 1840

1 Prayer is the soul's sincere desire, Uttered or unexpressed, The motion of a hidden fire That trembles in the breast. A-MEN.

Prayer

324 EVAN C. M. Rev. William H. Havergal, 1846

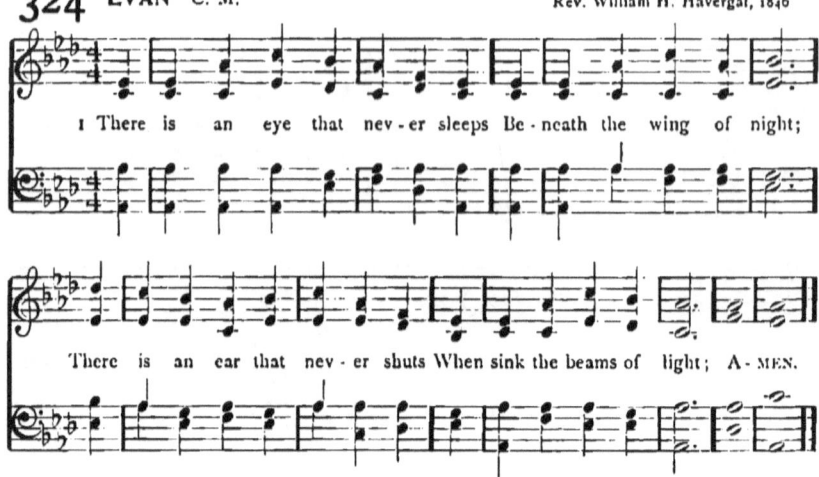

1 There is an eye that nev-er sleeps Be-neath the wing of night;
There is an ear that nev-er shuts When sink the beams of light; A-MEN.

2 There is an arm that never tires
   When human strength gives way;
   There is a love that never fails
   When earthly loves decay.

3 That eye is fixed on seraph throngs;
   That arm upholds the sky;
   That ear is filled with angel songs;
   That love is throned on high.

4 But there's a power which man can wield
   When mortal aid is vain,
   That eye, that arm, that love to reach,
   That listening ear to gain.

5 That power is prayer, which soars on high,
   Through Jesus, to the throne,
   And moves the hand which moves the world,
   To bring salvation down.
                Rev. James C. Wallace (c. 1793–1841)

325 (BYEFIELD) C. M.

1 PRAYER is the soul's sincere desire,
   Uttered or unexpressed,
   The motion of a hidden fire
   That trembles in the breast.

2 Prayer is the burden of a sigh,
   The falling of a tear,
   The upward glancing of an eye
   When none but God is near.

3 Prayer is the simplest form of speech
   That infant lips can try;
   Prayer the sublimest strains that reach
   The Majesty on high.

4 Prayer is the contrite sinner's voice
   Returning from his ways,
   While angels in their songs rejoice,
   And cry, "Behold, he prays."

5 Prayer is the Christian's vital breath,
   The Christian's native air,
   His watchword at the gates of death;
   He enters heaven with prayer.

6 O Thou, by whom we come to God,
   The Life, the Truth, the Way,
   The path of prayer Thyself hast trod;
   Lord, teach us how to pray.
                James Montgomery, 1819

Hymns of Salvation

326 EVEN ME 8.7.8.7. with Refrain — William B. Bradbury, 1862

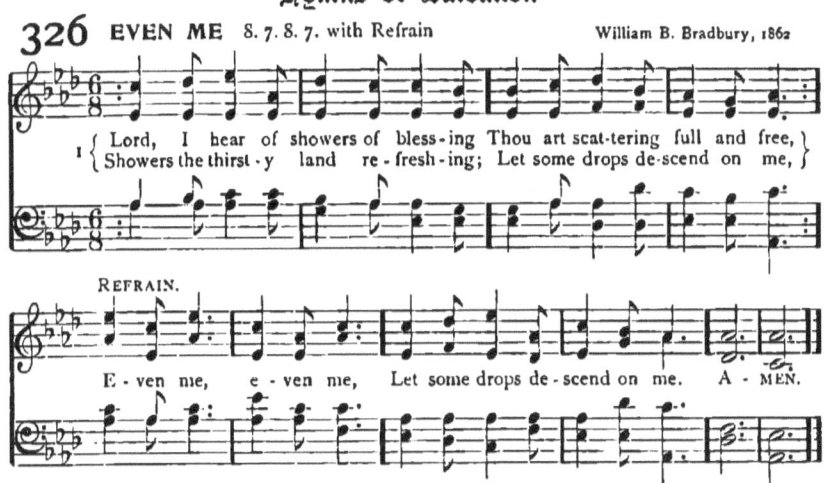

1. Lord, I hear of showers of blessing Thou art scattering full and free,
Showers the thirsty land refreshing; Let some drops descend on me,

REFRAIN.
E-ven me, e-ven me, Let some drops descend on me. A-MEN.

Used by arr. with the Biglow & Main Co., owners of copyright

2 Pass me not, O gracious Father,
Sinful though my heart may be;
Thou might'st pass me, but the rather
Let Thy mercy light on me.—REF.

3 Pass me not, O tender Saviour,
Let me love and cling to Thee;
I am longing for Thy favor;
When Thou comest, call for me.—REF.

4 Pass me not, O mighty Spirit,
Thou canst make the blind to see;
Witnesser of Jesus' merit,
Speak the word of power to me.—REF.

5 Have I long in sin been sleeping,
Long been slighting, grieving Thee?
Has the world my heart been keeping?
O forgive and rescue me.—REF.

Elizabeth Codner, 1860; verse 1, l. 4, verse 2, l, 3, alt.

BEATRICE 8.7.8.7. — Rev. William W. Coe, 1895

The Refrain is to be omitted

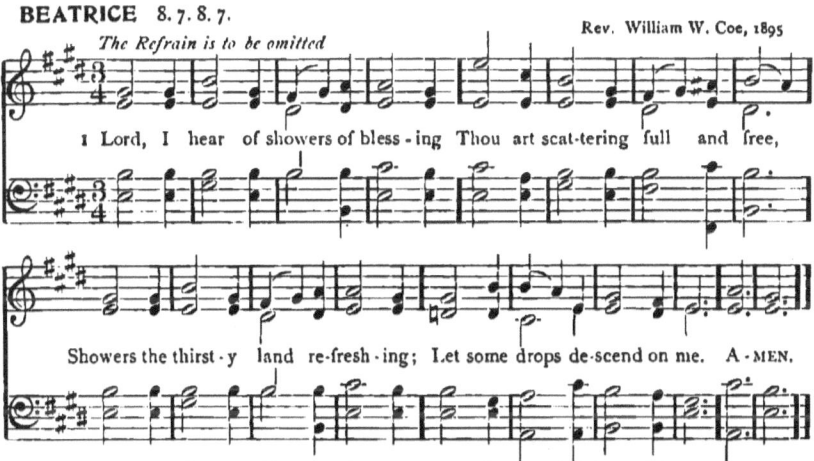

1 Lord, I hear of showers of blessing Thou art scattering full and free,
Showers the thirsty land refreshing; Let some drops descend on me. A-MEN.

Copyright, 1895, by The Trustees of The Presbyterian Board of Publication and Sabbath-School Work

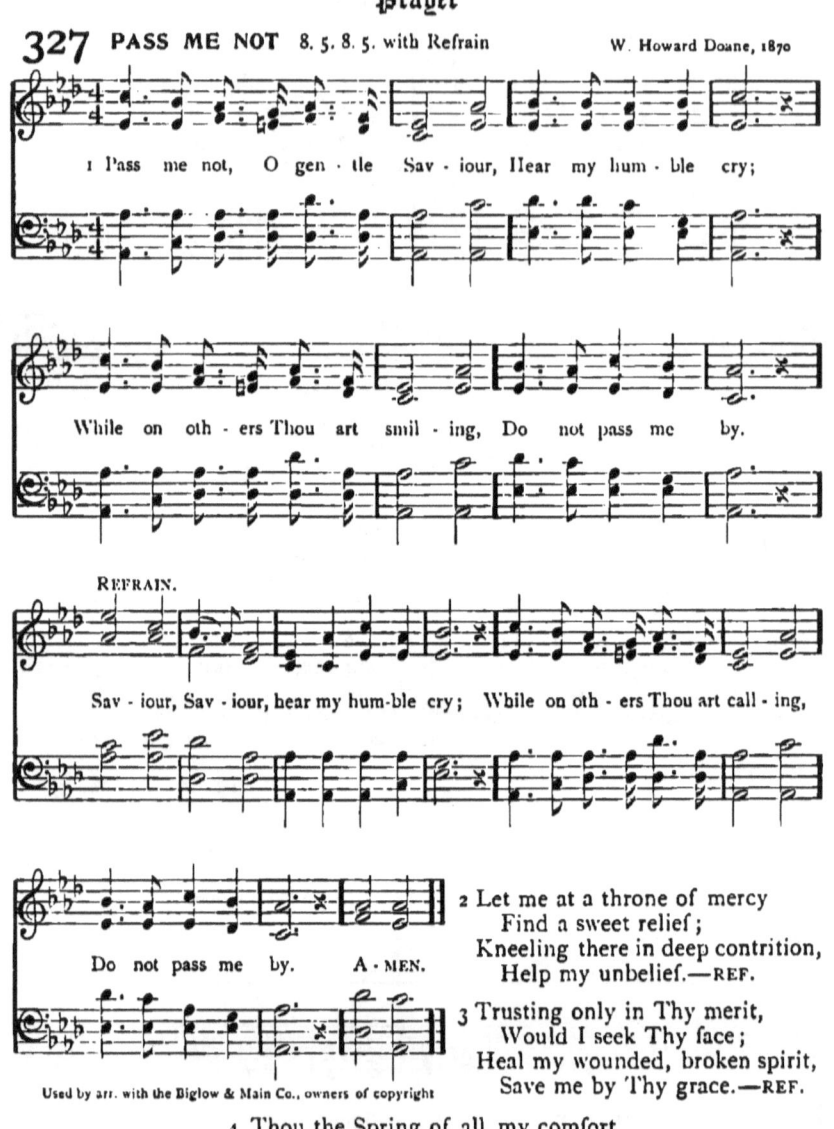

2 Let me at a throne of mercy
Find a sweet relief;
Kneeling there in deep contrition,
Help my unbelief.—REF.

3 Trusting only in Thy merit,
Would I seek Thy face;
Heal my wounded, broken spirit,
Save me by Thy grace.—REF.

4 Thou the Spring of all my comfort,
More than life to me,
Whom have I on earth beside Thee?
Whom in heaven but Thee?—REF.

Fanny J. (Crosby) Van Alstyne, 1868

Hymns of Salvation

328 BETHANY 6. 4. 6. 4. 6. 6. 4. Arr. by Lowell Mason, 1856

1 Nearer, my God, to Thee, Nearer to Thee! E'en though it be a cross That raiseth me; Still all my song shall be, Nearer, my God, to Thee, Nearer, my God, to Thee, Nearer to Thee! A-MEN.

Used by arr. with Oliver Ditson Company, owners of copyright

2 Though like the wanderer,
The sun gone down,
Darkness be over me,
My rest a stone;
Yet in my dreams I'd be
Nearer, my God, to Thee,
Nearer to Thee!

3 There let the way appear,
Steps unto heaven:
All that Thou send'st to me
In mercy given:
Angels to beckon me
Nearer, my God, to Thee,
Nearer to Thee!

4 Then, with my waking thoughts
Bright with Thy praise,
Out of my stony griefs
Bethel I'll raise:
So by my woes to be
Nearer, my God, to Thee,
Nearer to Thee!

5 Or if on joyful wing
Cleaving the sky,
Sun, moon, and stars forgot,
Upwards I fly,
Still all my song shall be,
Nearer, my God, to Thee,
Nearer to Thee!

Sarah F. Adams, 1841: verse 1, l. 5, alt.

Aspiration

329 NEARER TO THEE 6. 4. 6. 4. 6. 6. 4.   William R. Braine, 1861

1 More love to Thee, O Christ, More love to Thee! Hear Thou the prayer I make On bend-ed knee; This is my ear-nest plea, More love, O Christ, to Thee, More love, O Christ, to Thee, More love to Thee! A-MEN.

2 Once earthly joy I craved,
   Sought peace and rest;
Now Thee alone I seek,
   Give what is best:
This all my prayer shall be,
More love, O Christ, to Thee,
   More love to Thee!

3 Let sorrow do its work,
   Send grief and pain;
Sweet are Thy messengers,
   Sweet their refrain,
When they can sing with me,
More love, O Christ, to Thee,
   More love to Thee!

4 Then shall my latest breath
   Whisper Thy praise;
This be the parting cry
   My heart shall raise,
This still its prayer shall be,
More love, O Christ, to Thee,
   More love to Thee!

Elizabeth P. Prentiss, 1869

Hymns of Salvation

330 ALEXANDRIA C. M. William Arnold, c. 1800

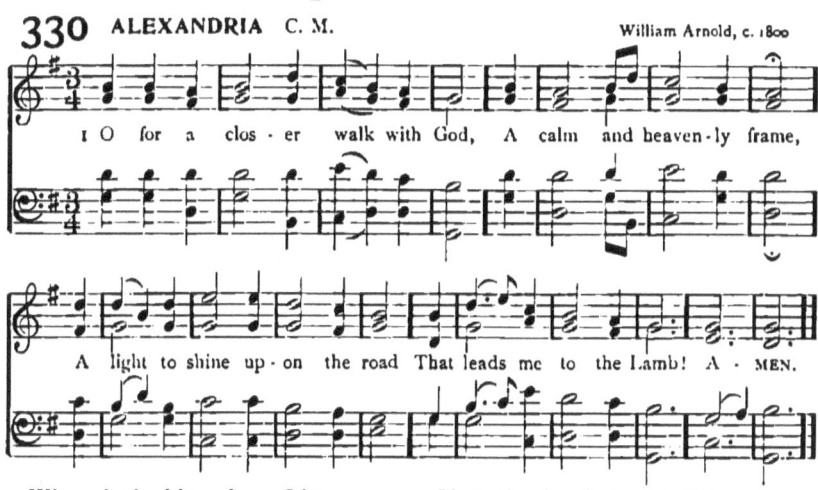

1 O for a clos-er walk with God, A calm and heaven-ly frame,
A light to shine up-on the road That leads me to the Lamb! A-MEN.

2 Where is the blessedness I knew
When first I saw the Lord?
Where is the soul-refreshing view
Of Jesus and His word?

3 What peaceful hours I once enjoyed!
How sweet their memory still!
But they have left an aching void
The world can never fill.

4 Return, O Holy Dove; return,
Sweet Messenger of rest:

I hate the sins that made Thee mourn
And drove Thee from my breast.

5 The dearest idol I have known,
Whate'er that idol be,
Help me to tear it from Thy throne,
And worship only Thee.

6 So shall my walk be close with God,
Calm and serene my frame;
So purer light shall mark the road
That leads me to the Lamb.

William Cowper, 1772

DALEHURST C. M. Arthur Cottman, 1872

1 O for a clos-er walk with God, A calm and heaven-ly frame,
A light to shine up-on the road That leads me to the Lamb! A-MEN.

Aspiration

331 BELMONT C. M.   Arr. from William Gardiner, 1812

1 When I can read my ti-tle clear To man-sions in the skies, I bid fare-well to ev-ery fear, And wipe my weep-ing eyes. A-MEN.

2 Should earth against my soul engage,
   And hellish darts be hurled,
   Then I can smile at Satan's rage,
   And face a frowning world.

3 Let cares like a wild deluge come,
   And storms of sorrow fall,
   May I but safely reach my home,
   My God, my heaven, my all:

4 There shall I bathe my weary soul
   In seas of heavenly rest,
   And not a wave of trouble roll
   Across my peaceful breast.

Rev. Isaac Watts, 1707

332 (BELMONT or DALEHURST) C. M.

1 O FOR a heart to praise my God,
   A heart from sin set free;
   A heart that always feels Thy blood,
   So freely spilt for me!

2 A heart resigned, submissive, meek,
   My great Redeemer's throne;
   Where only Christ is heard to speak,
   Where Jesus reigns alone;

3 A humble, lowly, contrite heart,
   Believing, true, and clean,
   Which neither life nor death can part
   From Him that dwells within;

4 A heart in every thought renewed,
   And full of love Divine;
   Perfect, and right, and pure, and good,
   A copy, Lord, of Thine.

5 Thy nature, gracious Lord, impart;
   Come quickly from above;
   Write Thy new Name upon my heart,
   Thy new, best Name of Love.

Rev. Charles Wesley, 1742 (Text of 1782)

Hymns of Salvation

333 COVENTRY C. M. Arr. by Lowell Mason, 1841

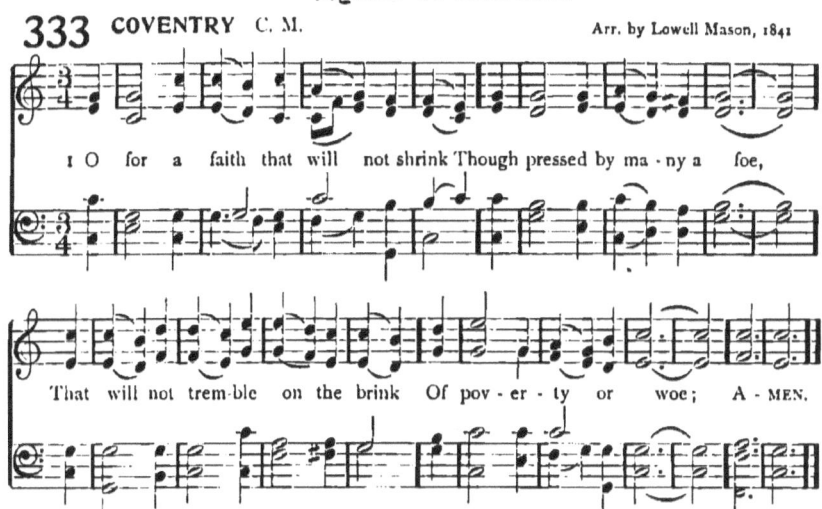

1 O for a faith that will not shrink Though pressed by ma-ny a foe, That will not trem-ble on the brink Of pov-er-ty or woe; A-MEN.

2 That will not murmur nor complain
Beneath the chastening rod,
But in the hour of grief or pain
Can lean upon its God;

3 A faith that shines more bright and clear
When tempests rage without,
That, when in danger, knows no fear,
In darkness feels no doubt;

4 A faith that keeps the narrow way
Till life's last spark is fled,
And with a pure and heavenly ray
Lights up a dying bed.

5 Lord, give me such a faith as this,
And then, whate'er may come,
I taste e'en now the hallowed bliss
Of an eternal home.

Rev. William H. Bathurst, 1831

LYTE S. M. John B. Wilkes, 1861

1 Far from my heaven-ly home, Far from my Fa-ther's breast, Faint-ing I cry, "Blest Spir-it, come And speed me to my rest." A-MEN.

Aspiration

334 WHITTIER 8. 6. 8. 8. 6. Frederick C. Maker (1844–)

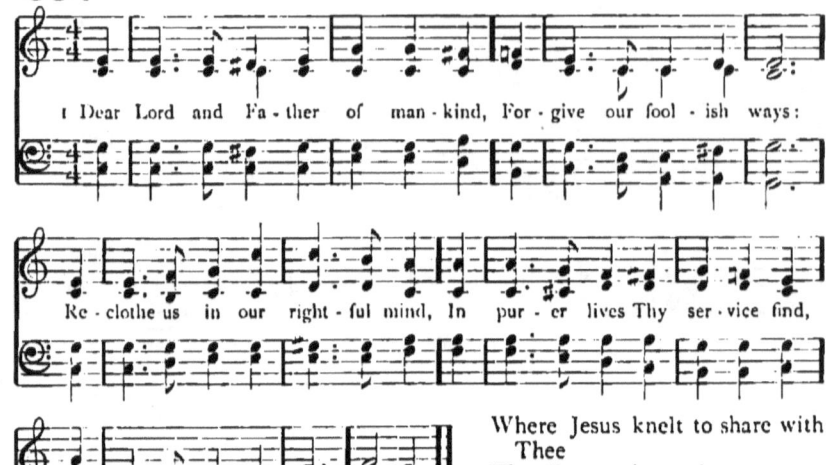

1 Dear Lord and Father of mankind, Forgive our foolish ways;
Re-clothe us in our rightful mind, In purer lives Thy service find,
In deeper reverence, praise. A-MEN.

2 In simple trust like theirs who heard,
 Beside the Syrian sea,
The gracious calling of the Lord,
Let us, like them, without a word,
 Rise up and follow Thee.

3 O Sabbath rest by Galilee!
 O calm of hills above,
Where Jesus knelt to share with Thee
The silence of eternity,
 Interpreted by love!

4 With that deep hush subduing all
Our words and works that drown
The tender whisper of Thy call,
As noiseless let Thy blessing fall
 As fell Thy manna down.

5 Drop Thy still dews of quietness,
 Till all our strivings cease;
Take from our souls the strain and stress,
And let our ordered lives confess
 The beauty of Thy peace.

John G. Whittier, 1872

335 (LYTE) S. M.

1 FAR from my heavenly home,
 Far from my Father's breast,
Fainting I cry, "Blest Spirit, come
 And speed me to my rest."

2 Upon the willows long
 My harp has silent hung:
How should I sing a cheerful song
 Till thou inspire my tongue?

3 My spirit homeward turns,
 And fain would thither flee:
My heart, O Zion, droops and yearns
 When I remember thee.

4 To thee, to thee I press,
 A dark and toilsome road:
When shall I pass the wilderness,
 And reach the saints' abode?

5 God of my life, be near;
 On Thee my hopes I cast:
O guide me through the desert here,
 And bring me home at last.

Rev. Henry F. Lyte, 1834

Hymns of Salvation

336 BERA L. M. — John E. Gould, 1849

1 O Thou, to whose all-search-ing sight The darkness shin-eth as the light, Search, prove my heart; it pants for Thee; O burst these bands, and set it free. A-MEN.

2 Wash out its stains, refine its dross;
Nail my affections to the cross;
Hallow each thought; let all within
Be clean, as Thou, my Lord, art clean.

3 If in this darksome wild I stray,
Be Thou my Light, be Thou my Way;
No foes, no violence I fear,
No harm, while Thou, my God, art near.

4 When rising floods my head o'erflow,
When sinks my heart in waves of woe,
Jesus, Thy timely aid impart,
And raise my head, and cheer my heart.

5 Saviour, where'er Thy steps I see,
Dauntless, untired, I follow Thee:
O let Thy hand support me still,
And lead me to Thy holy hill.

6 If rough and thorny be my way,
My strength proportion to my day;
Till toil and grief and pain shall cease
Where all is calm and joy and peace.

Count N. L. von Zinzendorf, 1721 (verse 4, Rev. J. A. Freylinghausen, 1704). Tr. Rev. John Wesley, 1738: verse 3, l. 4, alt.

337 (BERA) L. M.

1 MY God, permit me not to be
A stranger to myself and Thee;
Amidst a thousand thoughts I rove,
Forgetful of my highest love.

2 Why should my passions mix with earth,
And thus debase my heavenly birth?
Why should I cleave to things below,
And let my God, my Saviour, go?

3 Call me away from flesh and sense:
One sovereign word can draw me thence;
I would obey the voice Divine,
And all inferior joys resign.

4 Be earth, with all her scenes, withdrawn,
Let noise and vanity be gone;
In secret silence of the mind
My heaven, and there my God, I find.

Rev. Isaac Watts, 1709

Aspiration

338 AMSTERDAM 7. 6. 7. 6. 7. 7. 7. 6. The Foundery Collection, 1742

1 Rise, my soul, and stretch thy wings, Thy better portion trace;
Rise from transitory things Towards heaven, thy native place.
Sun and moon and stars decay, Time shall soon this earth remove;
Rise, my soul, and haste away To seats prepared above. A-MEN.

2 Rivers to the ocean run,
　Nor stay in all their course ;
　Fire ascending seeks the sun ;
　Both speed them to their source :
So my soul, derived from God,
　Pants to view His glorious face,
　Forward tends to His abode,
　To rest in His embrace.

3 Cease, ye pilgrims, cease to mourn,
　Press onward to the prize ;
　Soon our Saviour will return
　Triumphant in the skies :
Yet a season, and you know
　Happy entrance will be given,
　All our sorrows left below,
　And earth exchanged for heaven.

　　　　　Rev. Robert Seagrave, 1742

Hymns of Salvation

339 COOLING C. M.
Alonzo J. Abbey, 1858

1 O could I find, from day to day,
A nearness to my God,
Then would my hours glide sweet away,
While leaning on His word. A-MEN.

2 Lord, I desire with Thee to live,
Anew from day to day,
In joys the world can never give,
Nor ever take away.

3 Blest Jesus, come and rule my heart,
And make me wholly Thine,
That I may never more depart,
Nor grieve Thy love Divine.

4 Thus, till my last expiring breath,
Thy goodness I'll adore;
And when my frame dissolves in death,
My soul shall love Thee more.

Benjamin Cleveland, c. 1790 : alt.

340 (CANONBURY) L. M.

1 FORTH in Thy Name, O Lord, I go,
My daily labor to pursue;
Thee, only Thee, resolved to know
In all I think, or speak, or do.

2 The task Thy wisdom hath assigned
O let me cheerfully fulfil;
In all my works Thy presence find,
And prove Thy good and perfect will.

3 Preserve me from my calling's snare,
And hide my simple heart above;
Above the thorns of choking care,
The gilded baits of worldly love.

4 Thee may I set at my right hand,
Whose eyes mine inmost substance see,
And labor on at Thy command,
And offer all my works to Thee.

5 Give me to bear Thy easy yoke,
And every moment watch and pray;
And still to things eternal look,
And hasten to Thy glorious day:

6 For Thee delightfully employ
Whate'er Thy bounteous grace hath given,
And run my course with even joy,
And closely walk with Thee to heaven.

Rev. Charles Wesley, 1749 : verse 2, l. 4, alt.

Aspiration

341 NORTHREPPS C. M. Josiah Booth, 1887

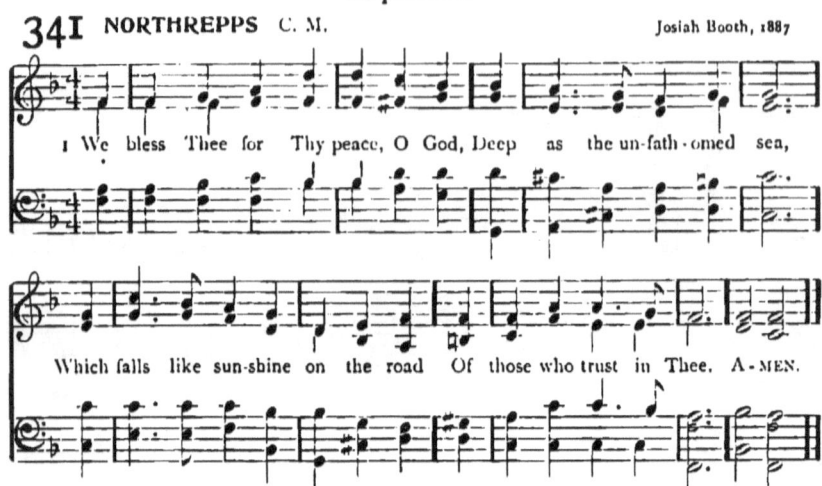

1 We bless Thee for Thy peace, O God, Deep as the un-fath-omed sea, Which falls like sun-shine on the road Of those who trust in Thee. A-MEN.

2 We ask not, Father, for repose
Which comes from outward rest,
If we may have through all life's woes
Thy peace within our breast:

3 That peace which suffers and is strong,
Trusts where it cannot see,
Deems not the trial-way too long,
But leaves the end with Thee:

4 That peace which flows serene and deep,
A river in the soul,
Whose banks a living verdure keep,
God's sunshine o'er the whole.

5 O Father, give our hearts this peace,
Whate'er the outward be,
Till all life's discipline shall cease,
And we go home to Thee.

Anon.

CANONBURY L. M. Arr. from Robert Schumann, 1839

1 Forth in Thy Name, O Lord, I go, My dai-ly la-bor to pur-sue; Thee, on-ly Thee, re-solved to know In all I think, or speak, or do. A-MEN.

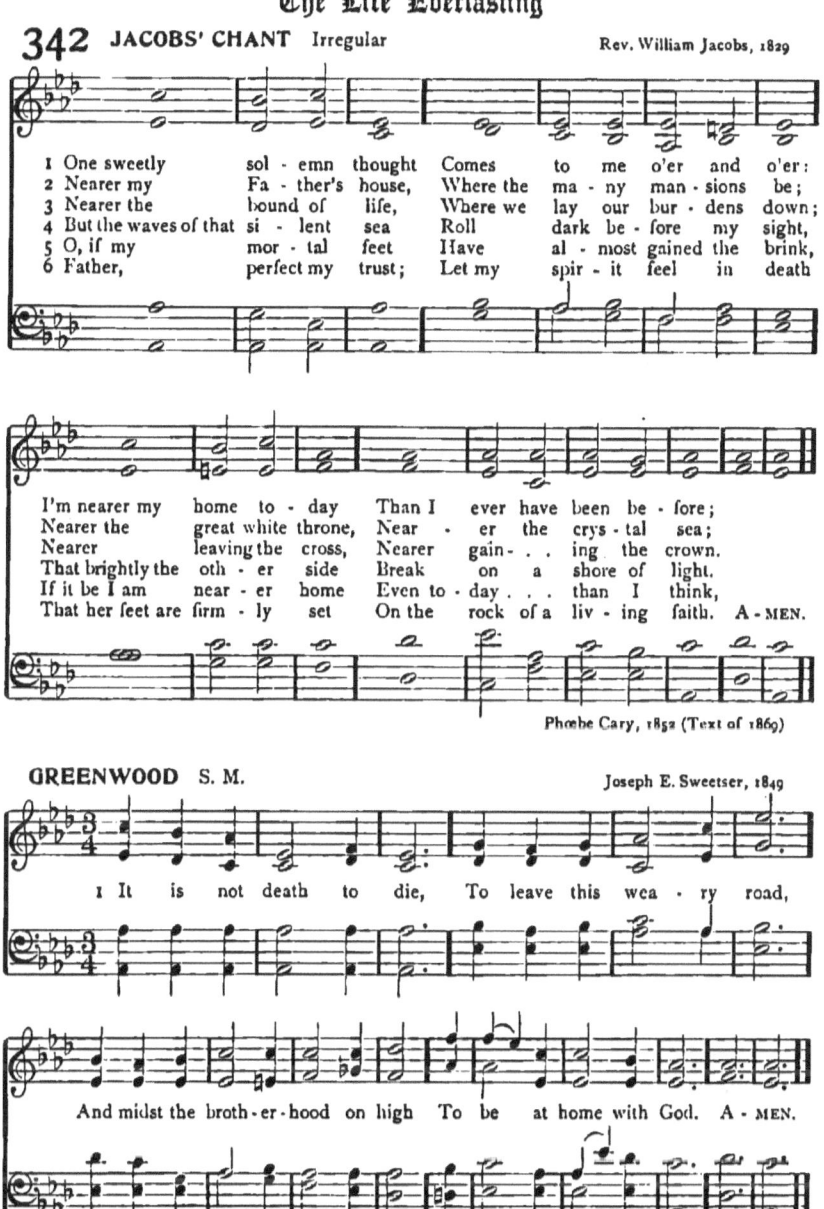

Death

343 REST L. M. — William B. Bradbury, 1843

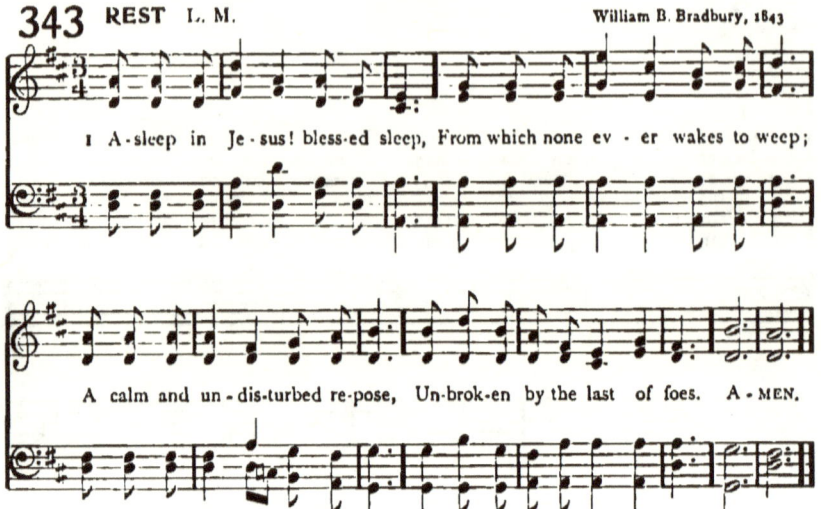

1 A-sleep in Je-sus! bless-ed sleep, From which none ev-er wakes to weep; A calm and un-dis-turbed re-pose, Un-brok-en by the last of foes. A-MEN.

2 Asleep in Jesus! O how sweet
  To be for such a slumber meet;
  With holy confidence to sing
  That death hath lost his venomed sting.

3 Asleep in Jesus! peaceful rest,
  Whose waking is supremely blest;
  No fear, no woe, shall dim that hour
  That manifests the Saviour's power.

4 Asleep in Jesus! O for me
  May such a blissful refuge be;
  Securely shall my ashes lie,
  Waiting the summons from on high.

5 Asleep in Jesus! far from thee
  Thy kindred and their graves may be;
  But thine is still a blessèd sleep,
  From which none ever wakes to weep.

  Margaret Mackay, 1832

344 (GREENWOOD) S. M.

1 IT is not death to die,
    To leave this weary road,
  And midst the brotherhood on high
    To be at home with God.

2 It is not death to close
    The eye long dimmed by tears,
  And wake, in glorious repose
    To spend eternal years.

3 It is not death to bear
    The wrench that sets us free
  From dungeon chain, to breathe the air
    Of boundless liberty.

4 It is not death to fling
    Aside this sinful dust,
  And rise, on strong exulting wing,
    To live among the just.

5 Jesus, Thou Prince of Life,
    Thy chosen cannot die:
  Like Thee, they conquer in the strife,
    To reign with Thee on high.

   Rev. H. A. César Malan, 1832. Tr. Rev. George W. Bethune, 1847

The Life Everlasting

345 FREDERICK 11. 11. 11. 11. George Kingsley, 1833

1 I would not live alway; I ask not to stay
Where storm after storm rises dark o'er the way;
The few lurid mornings that dawn on us here
Are enough for life's woes, full enough for its cheer. A-MEN.

2 I would not live alway, thus fettered by sin;
Temptation without, and corruption within:
E'en the rapture of pardon is mingled with fears,
And the cup of thanksgiving with penitent tears.

3 I would not live alway; no, welcome the tomb:
Since Jesus hath lain there, I dread not its gloom;
There sweet be my rest, till He bid me arise
To hail Him in triumph descending the skies.

Death

4 Who, who would live alway, away from his God,
  Away from yon heaven, that blissful abode,
  Where the rivers of pleasure flow o'er the bright plains,
  And the noontide of glory eternally reigns;

5 Where the saints of all ages in harmony meet,
  Their Saviour and brethren, transported, to greet;
  While the anthems of rapture unceasingly roll,
  And the smile of the Lord is the feast of the soul?

  Rev. William A. Mühlenberg, c. 1824 (Text of 1826)

346 WAKEFIELD 7. 6. 7. 7. 6.   William W. Gilchrist, 1895

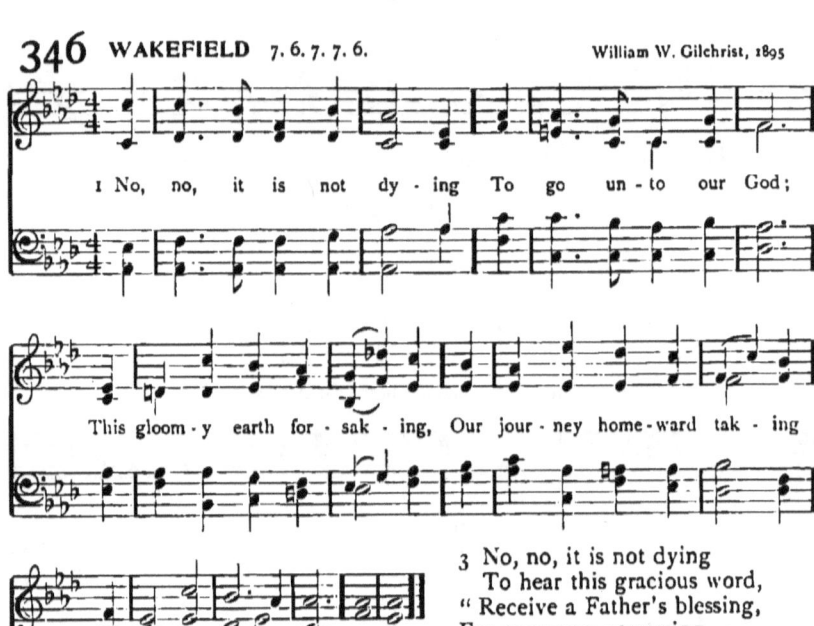

1 No, no, it is not dying
  To go unto our God;
  This gloomy earth forsaking,
  Our journey homeward taking
  Along the starry road. A-MEN.

Copyright, 1895, by The Trustees of The Presbyterian Board
of Publication and Sabbath-School Work

2 No, no, it is not dying
  Heaven's citizen to be;
  A crown immortal wearing,
  And rest unbroken sharing,
  From care and conflict free.

3 No, no, it is not dying
  To hear this gracious word,
  "Receive a Father's blessing,
  For evermore possessing
  The favor of Thy Lord."

4 No, no, it is not dying
  The Shepherd's voice to know:
  His sheep He ever leadeth,
  His peaceful flock He feedeth
  Where living pastures grow.

5 No, no, it is not dying
  To wear a lordly crown;
  Among God's people dwelling,
  The glorious triumph swelling
  Of Him whose sway we own.

  Rev. H. A. César Malan, 1832. Tr. Rev. Robinson P. Dunn, 1859

The Life Everlasting

347 HEAVEN IS MY HOME 6. 4. 6. 4. 6. 6. 6. 4.   Sir Arthur Sullivan, 1872

1. I'm but a stranger here, Heaven is my home; Earth is a desert drear, Heaven is my home: Danger and sorrow stand Round me on every hand; Heaven is my fatherland, Heaven is my home. A-MEN.

2. What though the tempest rage,
Heaven is my home;
Short is my pilgrimage,
Heaven is my home:
And time's wild wintry blast
Soon shall be overpast;
I shall reach home at last,
Heaven is my home.

3. There, at my Saviour's side,
Heaven is my home;
I shall be glorified,
Heaven is my home.
There are the good and blest,
Those I love most and best;
And there I too shall rest,
Heaven is my home.

4. Therefore I murmur not,
Heaven is my home;
Whate'er my earthly lot,
Heaven is my home:
And I shall surely stand
There at my Lord's right hand;
Heaven is my fatherland,
Heaven is my home.

Rev. Thomas R. Taylor, publ. 1836

The Life Everlasting

348 SHINING SHORE 8. 7. 8. 7. D. — George F. Root, 1859

1 My days are glid-ing swift-ly by, And I, a pil-grim stran-ger,
Would not de-tain them as they fly, Those hours of toil and dan-ger:

REFRAIN.
For O we stand on Jor-dan's strand, Our friends are pass-ing o-ver;
And, just be-fore, the shin-ing shore We may al-most dis-cov-er. A-MEN.

Used by arr. with Oliver Ditson Company, owners of copyright

2 We'll gird our loins, my brethren dear,
   Our distant home discerning;
   Our absent Lord has left us word,
   "Let every lamp be burning."—REF.

3 Should coming days be cold and dark,
   We need not cease our singing;
   That perfect rest naught can molest,
   Where golden harps are ringing. REF.

4 Let sorrow's rudest tempest blow,
   Each cord on earth to sever;
   Our King says, "Come," and there's our home,
   For ever, O for ever.—REF.

Rev. David Nelson, 1835

The Life Everlasting

349 PARADISE 8.6.8.6.6.6.6.6.   Sir Joseph Barnby, 1866

1 O Par-a-dise! O Par-a-dise! Who doth not crave for rest?
Who would not seek the hap-py land Where they that loved are blest?

REFRAIN.
Where loy-al hearts and true Stand ev-er in the light,
All rap-ture through and through, In God's most ho-ly sight. A-MEN.

2 O Paradise! O Paradise!
   The world is growing old;
Who would not be at rest and free
   Where love is never cold?—REF.

3 O Paradise! O Paradise!
   I want to sin no more;

I want to be as pure on earth
   As on thy spotless shore;—REF.

4 Lord Jesus, King of Paradise,
   O keep me in Thy love,
And guide me to that happy land
   Of perfect rest above;—REF.

Rev. Frederick W. Faber, 1862: verse 4, added, Hy. Anc. and Mod. 1868

The Life Everlasting

350 EWING 7.6.7.6. D.   Alexander Ewing, 1853

1. Jerusalem the golden, With milk and honey blest!
Beneath thy contemplation Sink heart and voice oprest.
I know not, O I know not, What joys await us there;
What radiancy of glory, What bliss beyond compare. A-MEN.

2. They stand, those halls of Zion, All jubilant with song,
And bright with many an angel, And all the martyr throng.
The Prince is ever in them, The daylight is serene;
The pastures of the blessed Are decked in glorious sheen.

3. There is the throne of David;
And there, from care released,
The song of them that triumph,
The shout of them that feast;
And they, who with their Leader
Have conquered in the fight,
For ever and for ever
Are clad in robes of white.

4. Exult, O dust and ashes,
The Lord shall be thy part:
His only and for ever,
Thou shalt be, and thou art.
Exult, O dust and ashes,
The Lord shall be thy part:
His only and for ever,
Thou shalt be, and thou art.

Bernard of Cluny, c. 1145. Tr. Rev. John M. Neale, 1851: verse 1, ll. 6, 8, verse 2, l. 2, alt.

The Life Everlasting

351 HOLY CROSS C. M.
Arr. by James C. Wade, 1865

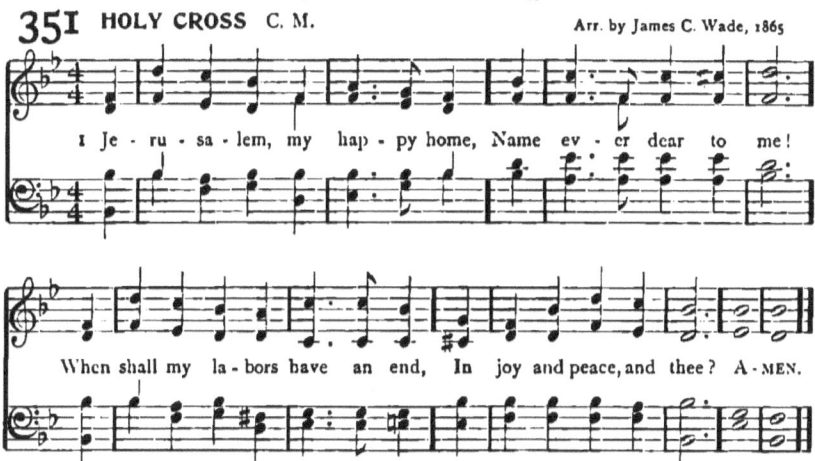

1 Jerusalem, my happy home, Name ever dear to me! When shall my labors have an end, In joy and peace, and thee? A-MEN.

2 When shall these eyes thy heaven-built walls
  And pearly gates behold?
Thy bulwarks with salvation strong,
  And streets of shining gold?

3 There happier bowers than Eden's bloom,
  Nor sin nor sorrow know:
Blest seats! through rude and stormy scenes
  I onward press to you.

4 Why should I shrink at pain and woe,
  Or feel at death dismay?
I've Canaan's goodly land in view,
  And realms of endless day.

5 Apostles, martyrs, prophets, there
  Around my Saviour stand;
And soon my friends in Christ below
  Will join the glorious band.

6 Jerusalem, my happy home!
  My soul still pants for thee:
Then shall my labors have an end,
  When I thy joys shall see.

Anon. (ascribed to J. Montgomery,) Eckington Coll., c. 1796 (based on " F. B. P.," in MS. of 16th or 17th cent.)

352 (ST. PAUL'S COLLEGE) S. M.

1 O WHERE shall rest be found,
  Rest for the weary soul?
'Twere vain the ocean-depths to sound,
  Or pierce to either pole:

2 The world can never give
  The bliss for which we sigh;
'Tis not the whole of life to live,
  Nor all of death to die.

3 Beyond this vale of tears
  There is a life above,
Unmeasured by the flight of years,
  And all that life is love:

4 There is a death whose pang
  Outlasts the fleeting breath;
O what eternal horrors hang
  Around the second death!

5 Lord God of truth and grace,
  Teach us that death to shun,
Lest we be banished from Thy face,
  And evermore undone.

6 Here would we end our quest:
  Alone are found in Thee
The life of perfect love, the rest
  Of immortality.

James Montgomery, 1818 (text of 1825)

The Life Everlasting

353 ST. MARGUERITE C. M. Rev. Edward C. Walker, 1876

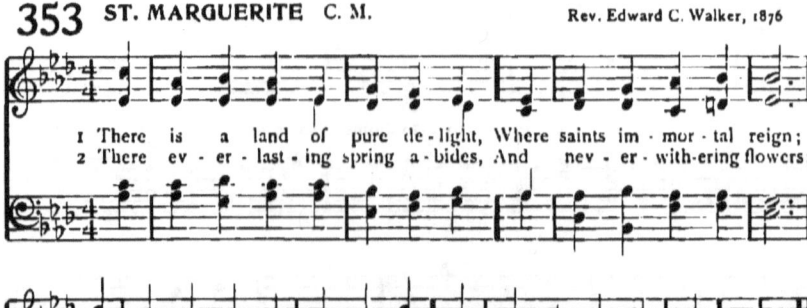

1 There is a land of pure de-light, Where saints im-mor-tal reign;
In-fi-nite day ex-cludes the night, And pleas-ures ban-ish pain. A-MEN.

2 There ev-er-last-ing spring a-bides, And nev-er-with-ering flowers;
Death, like a nar-row sea, di-vides This heaven-ly land from ours.

3 Sweet fields beyond the swelling flood
 Stand dressed in living green;
 So to the Jews old Canaan stood,
 While Jordan rolled between.

4 But timorous mortals start and shrink
 To cross this narrow sea;
 And linger, shivering, on the brink,
 And fear to launch away.

5 O could we make our doubts remove,
 Those gloomy doubts that rise,
 And see the Canaan that we love
 With unbeclouded eyes;

6 Could we but climb where Moses stood,
 And view the landscape o'er, [flood,
 Not Jordan's stream, nor death's cold
 Should fright us from the shore.

Rev. Isaac Watts, 1707

ST. PAUL'S COLLEGE S. M. George Lomas, 1876

1 O where shall rest be found, Rest for the wea-ry soul?
'Twere vain the o-cean-depths to sound, Or pierce to ei-ther pole: A-MEN.

The Life Everlasting

354 RUTHERFORD 7.6.7.6.7.6.7.5.
Arr. from Chrétien Urhan, 1834,
by Edw. F. Rimbault, 1867

1. The sands of time are sinking, The dawn of heaven breaks,
The summer morn I've sighed for, The fair sweet morn awakes:
Dark, dark hath been the midnight, But day-spring is at hand,
And glory, glory dwelleth In Emmanuel's land. A-MEN.

2. The King there in His beauty Without a veil is seen;
It were a well-spent journey, Though seven deaths lay between:
The Lamb with His fair army Doth on Mount Zion stand,
And glory, glory dwelleth In Emmanuel's land.

3. O Christ, He is the Fountain,
The deep sweet Well of love!
The streams on earth I've tasted
More deep I'll drink above:
There to an ocean fulness
His mercy doth expand,
And glory, glory dwelleth
In Emmanuel's land.

4. With mercy and with judgment
My web of time He wove,
And aye the dews of sorrow
Were lustred by His love:
I'll bless the hand that guided,
I'll bless the heart that planned,
When throned where glory dwelleth
In Emmanuel's land.

Anne R. Cousin, 1857

The Life Everlasting

355 MATERNA C. M. D.   Samuel A. Ward, 1882

1 O Mother dear, Jerusalem, When shall I come to thee?
When shall my sorrows have an end? Thy joys when shall I see?
O happy harbor of the saints! O sweet and pleasant soil!
In thee no sorrow may be found, No grief, no care, no toil. A-MEN.

2 Thy walls are made of precious stones, Thy bulwarks diamonds square;
Thy gates are of right orient pearl, Exceeding rich and rare.
Thy turrets and thy pinnacles With carbuncles do shine;
Thy very streets are paved with gold, Surpassing clear and fine.

3 Thy gardens and thy gallant walks
   Continually are green,   [flowers
There grow such sweet and pleasant
   As nowhere else are seen.
Quite through the streets, with silver
   The flood of life doth flow; [sound,
Upon whose banks on every side
   The wood of life doth grow.

4 There trees for evermore bear fruit,
   And evermore do spring;
There evermore the angels sit,
   And evermore do sing.
Jerusalem, my happy home,
   Would God I were in thee!
Would God my woes were at an end,
   Thy joys that I might see!

"F. B. P.," in MS. of 16th or 17th cent.; verse 1, l. 1, from W. Prid, 1585

The Life Everlasting

356 PILGRIMS 11. 10. 11. 10. 9. 11.   Henry Smart, 1868

1 Hark! hark, my soul! Angelic songs are swelling O'er earth's green fields and ocean's wave-beat shore: How sweet the truth those blessed strains are telling Of that new life when sin shall be no more. *REFRAIN.* Angels of Jesus, Angels of light, Singing to welcome the pilgrims of the night! A-MEN.

  2 Onward we go, for still we hear them singing,
     "Come, weary souls, for Jesus bids you come;"
    And through the dark, its echoes sweetly ringing,
     The music of the gospel leads us home.—REF.

  3 Far, far away, like bells at evening pealing,
     The voice of Jesus sounds o'er land and sea;
    And laden souls, by thousands meekly stealing,
     Kind Shepherd, turn their weary steps to Thee.—REF.

The Life Everlasting

4 Rest comes at length: though life be long and dreary,
    The day must dawn, and darksome night be past;
    Faith's journeys end in welcomes to the weary,
        And heaven, the heart's true home, will come at last.—REF.

5 Angels, sing on, your faithful watches keeping;
    Sing us sweet fragments of the songs above;
    Till morning's joy shall end the night of weeping,
        And life's long shadows break in cloudless love.—REF.

Rev. Frederick W. Faber, 1854: verse 4, l. 3, verse 5, ll. 3, 4, alt.

357 WOODLAND 8.6.8.8.6.   Nathaniel D. Gould, 1832

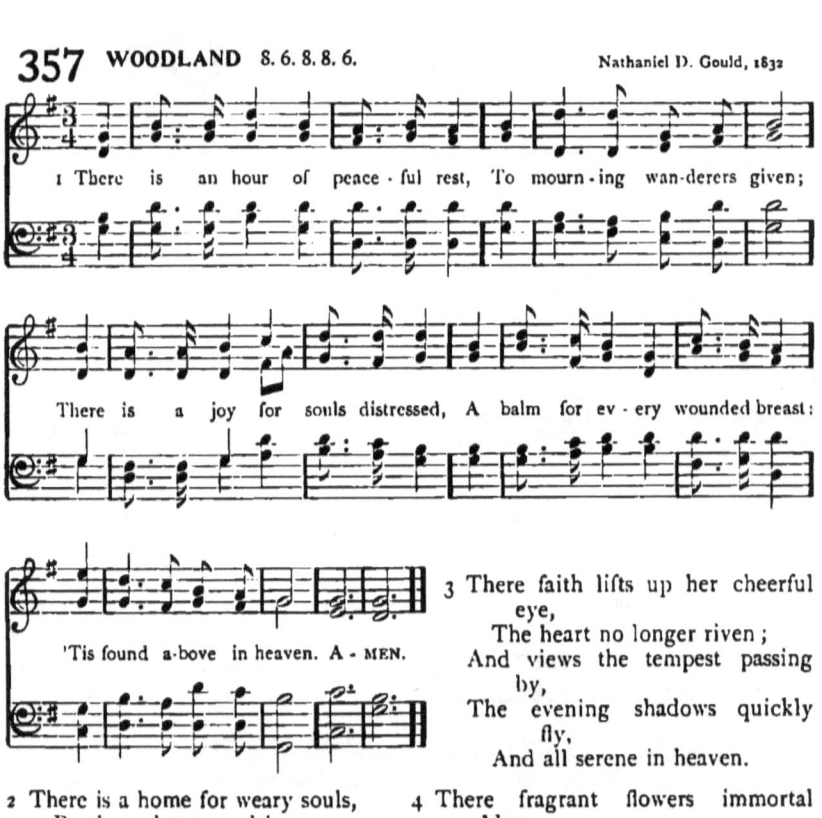

1 There is an hour of peaceful rest, To mourning wanderers given;
There is a joy for souls distressed, A balm for every wounded breast:
'Tis found above in heaven. A-MEN.

2 There is a home for weary souls,
    By sin and sorrow driven,
When tossed on life's tempestuous shoals,
    Where storms arise and ocean rolls,
    And all is drear—'tis heaven.

3 There faith lifts up her cheerful eye,
    The heart no longer riven;
And views the tempest passing by,
    The evening shadows quickly fly,
    And all serene in heaven.

4 There fragrant flowers immortal bloom,
    And joys supreme are given;
There rays Divine disperse the gloom;
    Beyond the confines of the tomb
    Appears the dawn of heaven.

William B. Tappan, 1818

The Life Everlasting

358 DAILY, DAILY 8. 7. 8. 7. D.   Henri F. Hemy, 1865

1 Daily, daily sing the praises Of the city God hath made;
In the beauteous fields of Eden Its foundation-stones are laid.

REFRAIN.
O that I had wings of angels, Here to spread and heaven-ward fly!
I would seek the gates of Zion, Far beyond the starry sky. A-MEN.

2 All the walls of that dear city
   Are of bright and burnished gold;
It is matchless in its beauty,
   And its treasures are untold.—REF.

3 In the midst of that dear city
   Christ is reigning on His seat,
And the angels swing their censers
   In a ring about His feet.—REF.

4 There the meadows green and dewy
   Shine with lilies wondrous fair;
Thousand, thousand are the colors
   Of the waving flowers there.—REF.

5 There the wind is sweetly fragrant,
   And is laden with the song
Of the seraphs, and the elders,
   And the great redeemèd throng.—REF.

Rev. Sabine Baring-Gould, 1865

The Opening and Closing of the Year

359 BENEVENTO 7. 7. 7. 7. D.   Arr. from Samuel Webbe, 1792

1 While with ceaseless course the sun
    Hasted through the former year,
Many souls their race have run,
    Never more to meet us here:
Fixed in an eternal state,
    They have done with all below;
We a little longer wait,
    But how little none can know. A-MEN.

2 As the wingèd arrow flies
    Speedily the mark to find,
As the lightning from the skies
    Darts, and leaves no trace behind,—
Swiftly thus our fleeting days
    Bear us down life's rapid stream;
Upward, Lord, our spirits raise,
    All below is but a dream.

3 Thanks for mercies past receive;
    Pardon of our sins renew;
Teach us henceforth how to live
    With eternity in view;
Bless Thy word to young and old;
    Fill us with a Saviour's love;
And when life's short tale is told,
    May we dwell with Thee above.

Rev. John Newton, 1774

The Opening and Closing of the Year

360 ST. SYLVESTER 8. 7. 8. 7. Rev. John B. Dykes, 1862

1 Days and moments quickly flying
Speed us onward to the dead:
O how soon shall we be lying
Each within his narrow bed! A-MEN.

2 Jesus, merciful Redeemer,
Rouse dead souls to hear Thy voice;
Wake, O wake each idle dreamer
Now to make the eternal choice.

3 As a shadow life is fleeting;
As a vapor so it flies;
For the old year now retreating
Pardon grant, and make us wise;

4 Wise that we our days may number,
Strive and wrestle with our sin,
Stay not in our work, nor slumber
Till Thy glorious rest we win.

5 Soon before the Judge all glorious
We with all the dead shall stand:
Saviour, over death victorious,
Place us then on Thy right hand.

Rev. Edward Caswall, 1858; recast in Church Hymns, 1871

361 (GERMANY) L. M.

1 GREAT God, we sing that mighty hand
By which supported still we stand;
The opening year Thy mercy shows;
That mercy crowns it till it close.

2 By day, by night, at home, abroad,
Still are we guarded by our God;
By His incessant bounty fed,
By His unerring counsel led.

3 With grateful hearts the past we own;
The future, all to us unknown,
We to Thy guardian care commit,
And peaceful leave before Thy feet.

4 In scenes exalted or depressed,
Thou art our Joy, and Thou our Rest;
Thy goodness all our hopes shall raise,
Adored through all our changing days.

5 When death shall interrupt these songs,
And seal in silence mortal tongues;
Our Helper God, in whom we trust,
In better worlds our souls shall boast.

Rev. Philip Doddridge, publ. 1755

Harvest and Thanksgiving

362 NUREMBERG 7.7.7.7.
Alt. from Johann R. Ahle, 1664

1 Praise to God, immortal praise, For the love that crowns our days:
Bounteous Source of every joy, Let Thy praise our tongues employ. A-MEN.

2 Flocks that whiten all the plain;
Yellow sheaves of ripened grain;
Clouds that drop their fattening dews,
Suns that temperate warmth diffuse;

3 All that Spring with bounteous hand
Scatters o'er the smiling land;

All that liberal Autumn pours
From her rich o'erflowing stores;—

4 These to Thee, my God, we owe,
Source whence all our blessings flow;
And for these my soul shall raise
Grateful vows and solemn praise.

Anna L. Barbauld, 1772

GERMANY L. M.
Wm. Gardiner's Sacred Melodies, 1815

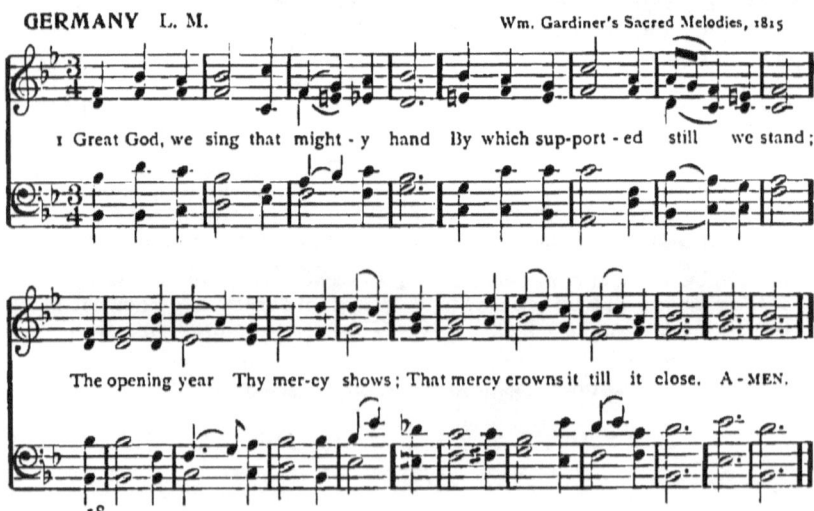

1 Great God, we sing that mighty hand By which supported still we stand;
The opening year Thy mercy shows; That mercy crowns it till it close. A-MEN.

Harvest and Thanksgiving

363 ST. GEORGE'S, WINDSOR 7. 7. 7. 7. D. Sir George J. Elvey 1859

1 Come, ye thankful people, come,
Raise the song of harvest-home:
All is safely gathered in,
Ere the winter storms begin;
God, our Maker, doth provide
For our wants to be supplied:
Come to God's own temple, come,
Raise the song of harvest-home.

2 All the world is God's own field,
Fruit unto His praise to yield;
Wheat and tares together sown,
Unto joy or sorrow grown:
First the blade, and then the ear,
Then the full corn shall appear:
Lord of harvest, grant that we
Wholesome grain and pure may be.

3 For the Lord our God shall come,
And shall take His harvest home;
From His field shall in that day
All offences purge away;
Give His angels charge at last
In the fire the tares to cast,
But the fruitful ears to store
In His garner evermore.

4 Even so, Lord, quickly come
To Thy final harvest-home;
Gather Thou Thy people in,
Free from sorrow, free from sin;
There for ever purified,
In Thy presence to abide:
Come, with all Thine angels, come,
Raise the glorious harvest-home.

Rev. Henry Alford, 1844

Harvest and Thanksgiving

364 REGENT SQUARE 8. 7. 8. 7. 4. 7. Henry Smart, 1867

1 Praise, my soul, the King of heaven, To His feet Thy tribute bring; Ransomed, healed, restored, forgiven, Who, like me, His praise should sing? Praise Him, praise Him, Praise Him, praise Him, Praise the Everlasting King. A-MEN.

2 Praise Him for His grace and favor
  To our fathers in distress;
Praise Him, still the same for ever,
  Slow to chide, and swift to bless;
    Praise Him, praise Him,
  Glorious in His faithfulness.

3 Father-like, He tends and spares us;
  Well our feeble frame He knows;
In His hands He gently bears us,
  Rescues us from all our foes;
    Praise Him, praise Him,
  Widely as His mercy goes.

4 Angels, help us to adore Him;
  Ye behold Him face to face;
Sun and moon, bow down before Him,
  Dwellers all in time and space,
    Praise Him, praise Him,
  Praise with us the God of grace.

Rev. Henry F. Lyte, 1834

Anniversary

365 ST. MARTIN'S C. M. — William Tans'ur, 1735

1 Let chil-dren hear the might-y deeds Which God per-formed of old;
Which in our young-er years we saw, And which our fa-thers told. A-MEN.

2 He bids us make His glories known,
His works of power and grace;
And we'll convey His wonders down,
Through every rising race.

3 Our lips shall tell them to our sons,
And they again to theirs;

That generations yet unborn
May teach them to their heirs.

4 Thus shall they learn in God alone
Their hope securely stands,
That they may ne'er forget His works,
But practise His commands.

Rev. Isaac Watts, 1719

WAREHAM L. M. — William Knapp, 1738

1 O God, be-neath Thy guid-ing hand, Our ex-iled fa-thers crossed the sea;
And when they trod the wintry strand, With prayer and psalm they worshipped Thee. AMEN.

National

366 DORT 6.6.4.6.6.6.4. Lowell Mason, 1832

1 God bless our na-tive land; Firm may she ev-er stand Through storm and night: When the wild tem-pests rave, Rul-er of wind and wave, Do Thou our coun-try save By Thy great might.

2 For her our prayers shall rise To God a-bove the skies; On Him we wait; Thou who art ev-er nigh, Guard-ing with watch-ful eye, To Thee a-loud we cry, God save the State. A-MEN.

1st 5 ll. Rev. Charles T. Brooks, c. 1833;
the remainder, Rev. John S. Dwight, 1844

367 (WAREHAM) L. M.

1 O GOD, beneath Thy guiding hand,
Our exiled fathers crossed the sea;
And when they trod the wintry strand,
With prayer and psalm they worshipped Thee.

2 Thou heard'st, well pleased, the song, the prayer:
Thy blessing came; and still its power
Shall onward, through all ages, bear
The memory of that holy hour.

3 Laws, freedom, truth, and faith in God
Came with those exiles o'er the waves;
And where their pilgrim feet have trod,
The God they trusted guards their graves.

4 And here Thy Name, O God of love,
Their children's children shall adore,
Till these eternal hills remove,
And spring adorns the earth no more.

Rev. Leonard Bacon, 1833 (text of 1845)

National

368 AMERICA 6. 6. 4. 6. 6. 6. 4.

Harmonia Anglicana, 1744

1 My country, 'tis of thee, Sweet land of liberty, Of thee I sing; Land where my fathers died, Land of the pilgrim's pride, From every mountain side Let freedom ring. A-MEN.

2 My native country, thee,
  Land of the noble free,
   Thy name I love;
  I love thy rocks and rills,
  Thy woods and templed hills;
  My heart with rapture thrills
   Like that above.

3 Let music swell the breeze,
  And ring from all the trees
   Sweet freedom's song:
  Let mortal tongues awake;
  Let all that breathe partake;
  Let rocks their silence break,
   The sound prolong.

4 Our fathers' God, to Thee,
  Author of liberty,
   To Thee we sing:
  Long may our land be bright
  With freedom's holy light;
  Protect us by Thy might,
   Great God, our King.

Rev. Samuel F. Smith, 1832

Temperance

369. JESU, MAGISTER BONE 7.6.7.6. D.
Rev. John B. Dykes, 1875

1. O Thou, before whose presence Naught evil may come in,
Yet who dost look in mercy Down on this world of sin,
O give us noble purpose To set the sin-bound free,
And Christ-like tender pity To seek the lost for Thee. A-MEN.

2. Fierce is our subtle foeman: The forces at his hand
With woes that none can number Despoil the pleasant land;
All they who war against them, In strife so keen and long,
Must in their Saviour's armor Be stronger than the strong.

3. So hast Thou wrought among us
The great things that we see!
For things that are we thank Thee,
And for the things to be:
For bright hope is uplifting
Faint hands and feeble knees,
To strive beneath Thy blessing
For greater things than these.

4. Lead on, O Love and Mercy,
O Purity and Power;
Lead on till peace eternal
Shall close this battle-hour:
Till all who prayed and struggled
To set their brethren free,
In triumph meet to praise Thee,
Most Holy Trinity.

Rev. Samuel J. Stone, 1889

Farewell Service

370 GOD BE WITH YOU 9. 8. 8. 9. with Refrain   William G. Tomer, 1882

1. God be with you till we meet a-gain, By His coun-sels guide, up-hold you, With His sheep se-cure-ly fold you, God be with you till we meet a-gain.

REFRAIN.
Till we meet, ... till we meet, Till we meet at Je-sus' feet;
Till we meet, ... till we meet, God be with you till we meet a-gain. A-MEN.

Copyright, by J. E. Rankin.

2 God be with you till we meet again,
  'Neath His wings protecting hide you,
  Daily manna still divide you,
  God be with you till we meet again. REF.

3 God be with you till we meet again,
  When life's perils thick confound you,
  Put His arms unfailing round you,
  God be with you till we meet again. REF.

4 God be with you till we meet again,
  Keep love's banner floating o'er you,
  Smite death's threatening wave before you,
  God be with you till we meet again. REF.

Rev. Jeremiah E. Rankin, 1882

Doxologies

OLD HUNDREDTH L. M.   Genevan Psalter, 1551

1 Praise God, from whom all blessings flow; Praise Him, all creatures here below; Praise Him above, ye heavenly host: Praise Father, Son, and Holy Ghost. A-MEN.

Bishop Thomas Ken, 1693

S. M.

WE give Thee glory, Lord,
  Thy majesty adore;
Thee, Father, Son, and Holy Ghost,
  We bless for evermore.

Rev. Horatius Bonar, 1866

C. M.

To Father, Son, and Holy Ghost,
  The God whom we adore,
Be glory, as it was, is now,
  And shall be evermore.

Tate and Brady's New Version, 1696

7. 6. 7. 6. D.

GREAT God of earth and heaven,
  To Thee our songs we raise;
To Thee be glory given
  And everlasting praise:
We joyfully confess Thee,
  Eternal Triune God;
We magnify, we bless Thee,
  And spread Thy praise abroad.

Rev. Edwin F. Hatfield, 1872

7. 7. 7. 7.

SING we to our God above
Praise eternal as His love;
Praise Him, all ye heavenly host,
Father, Son, and Holy Ghost.

Rev. Charles Wesley, 1740

8. 7. 8. 7.

PRAISE the Father, earth and heaven,
  Praise the Son, the Spirit praise;
As it was, and is, be given
  Glory through eternal days.

Anon., 1827

8. 7. 8. 7. D.

PRAISE the God of all creation,
  Praise the Father's boundless love;
Praise the Lamb, our Expiation,
  Priest and King enthroned above;
Praise the Fountain of salvation,
  Him by whom our spirits live:
Undivided adoration
  To the One Jehovah give.

Josiah Conder, 1836

Selections from

The Psalter

For Use in the Services of the Churches

Arranged by the

Rev. Elijah R. Craven, D. D., LL.D.

and the

Rev. Louis F. Benson, D. D.

✠

Philadelphia
The Presbyterian Board of Publication
and Sabbath-School Work
1898

Copyright, 1895, by The Trustees of
The Presbyterian Board of Publication and Sabbath-School Work.

PREFACE

IN obedience to a continuous demand, these Selections from the Psalter have been prepared for use in the services of the churches. The text is that of the standard of the American Bible Society, except that words there printed in italics are here given in the roman type, and that the verses included in any selection are numbered consecutively, with a note to show their numbering in the original Psalm. It has seemed best, on the whole, that these Selections should be arranged for reading verse by verse, rather than by the structural divisions within the verse. It is by verses, and not by antiphons, that the Psalms have been learned; and the verse-divisions, while originally artificial, no doubt, now mark the natural and familiar breaks in the rhythm of the Psalm, not only in the English Bible, but in the memory and the heart. This arrangement has been decided upon with the further thought, also, that if in the future a like selection from the Psalter, pointed for chanting, shall be issued by the Board, this arrangement for reading may correspond with that; for the proper pointing of the Psalms for chanting requires the verse-divisions.

The Psalms are here given in the order in which they occur in the Scriptures. But, within the limits imposed by such an arrangement, the effort has been made to give a certain unity, or at least manifest progression, of thought to each selection. The Gloria Patri is printed after the Selections, and is arranged so that it may be either read or sung, in such churches as desire to use it at the close of the reading.

The Psalter

Selection 1

PSALM 1

1 BLESSED is the man that walketh not in the counsel of the ungodly, nor standeth in the way of sinners, nor sitteth in the seat of the scornful.

2 But his delight is in the law of the LORD; and in his law doth he meditate day and night.

3 And he shall be like a tree planted by the rivers of water, that bringeth forth his fruit in his season; his leaf also shall not wither; and whatsoever he doeth shall prosper.

4 The ungodly are not so: but are like the chaff which the wind driveth away.

5 Therefore the ungodly shall not stand in the judgment, nor sinners in the congregation of the righteous.

6 For the LORD knoweth the way of the righteous: but the way of the ungodly shall perish.

PSALM 2

7 WHY do the heathen rage, and the people imagine a vain thing?

8 The kings of the earth set themselves, and the rulers take counsel together, against the LORD, and against his Anointed, saying,

9 Let us break their bands asunder, and cast away their cords from us.

10 He that sitteth in the heavens shall laugh: the LORD shall have them in derision.

11 Then shall he speak unto them in his wrath, and vex them in his sore displeasure.

12 Yet have I set my King upon my holy hill of Zion.

13 I will declare the decree: the LORD hath said unto me, Thou art my Son; this day have I begotten thee.

14 Ask of me, and I shall give thee the heathen for thine inheritance, and the uttermost parts of the earth for thy possession.

15 Thou shalt break them with a rod of iron; thou shalt dash them in pieces like a potter's vessel.

16 Be wise now therefore, O ye kings: be instructed, ye judges of the earth.

17 Serve the LORD with fear, and rejoice with trembling.

18 Kiss the Son, lest he be angry, and ye perish from the way, when his wrath is kindled but a little. Blessed are all they that put their trust in him.

PSALM 4

19 HEAR me when I call, O God of my righteousness: thou hast enlarged me when I was in distress; have mercy upon me, and hear my prayer.

20 O ye sons of men, how long will ye turn my glory into shame? how long will ye love vanity, and seek after leasing?

21 But know that the LORD hath set apart him that is godly for himself: the LORD will hear when I call unto him.

22 Stand in awe, and sin not; commune with your own heart upon your bed, and be still.

23 Offer the sacrifices of righteousness, and put your trust in the LORD.

24 There be many that say, Who will show us any good? LORD, lift thou up the light of thy countenance upon us.

25 Thou hast put gladness in my heart, more than in the time that their corn and their wine increased.

26 I will both lay me down in peace, and sleep: for thou, LORD, only makest me dwell in safety.

The Psalter

Selection 2

Psalm 5 : 1-7

1 GIVE ear to my words, O LORD; consider my meditation.

2 Hearken unto the voice of my cry, my King, and my God: for unto thee will I pray.

3 My voice shalt thou hear in the morning, O LORD; in the morning will I direct my prayer unto thee, and will look up.

4 For thou art not a God that hath pleasure in wickedness: neither shall evil dwell with thee.

5 The foolish shall not stand in thy sight: thou hatest all workers of iniquity.

6 Thou shalt destroy them that speak leasing: the LORD will abhor the bloody and deceitful man.

7 But as for me, I will come into thy house in the multitude of thy mercy: and in thy fear will I worship toward thy holy temple.

Psalm 8

8 O LORD our Lord, how excellent is thy name in all the earth! who hast set thy glory above the heavens.

9 Out of the mouth of babes and sucklings hast thou ordained strength because of thine enemies, that thou mightest still the enemy and the avenger.

10 When I consider thy heavens, the work of thy fingers, the moon and the stars, which thou hast ordained;

11 What is man, that thou art mindful of him? and the son of man, that thou visitest him?

12 For thou hast made him a little lower than the angels, and hast crowned him with glory and honor.

13 Thou madest him to have dominion over the works of thy hands; thou hast put all things under his feet:

14 All sheep and oxen, yea, and the beasts of the field;

15 The fowl of the air, and the fish of the sea, and whatsoever passeth through the paths of the seas.

16 O LORD our Lord, how excellent is thy name in all the earth!

Psalm 11

17 IN the LORD put I my trust: how say ye to my soul, Flee as a bird to your mountain?

18 For, lo, the wicked bend their bow, they make ready their arrow upon the string, that they may privily shoot at the upright in heart.

19 If the foundations be destroyed, what can the righteous do?

20 The LORD is in his holy temple, the LORD'S throne is in heaven: his eyes behold, his eyelids try, the children of men.

21 The LORD trieth the righteous: but the wicked and him that loveth violence his soul hateth.

22 Upon the wicked he shall rain snares, fire and brimstone, and a horrible tempest: this shall be the portion of their cup.

23 For the righteous LORD loveth righteousness; his countenance doth behold the upright.

Selection 3

Psalm 13

1 HOW long wilt thou forget me, O LORD? for ever? how long wilt thou hide thy face from me?

2 How long shall I take counsel in my soul, having sorrow in my heart daily? how long shall mine enemy be exalted over me?

3 Consider and hear me, O LORD my God: lighten mine eyes, lest I sleep the sleep of death;

4 Lest mine enemy say, I have prevailed against him; and those that trouble me rejoice when I am moved.

The Psalter

5 But I have trusted in thy mercy; my heart shall rejoice in thy salvation.

6 I will sing unto the LORD, because he hath dealt bountifully with me.

PSALM 15

7 LORD, who shall abide in thy tabernacle? who shall dwell in thy holy hill?

8 He that walketh uprightly, and worketh righteousness, and speaketh the truth in his heart.

9 He that backbiteth not with his tongue, nor doeth evil to his neighbor, nor taketh up a reproach against his neighbor.

10 In whose eyes a vile person is contemned; but he honoreth them that fear the LORD. He that sweareth to his own hurt, and changeth not.

11 He that putteth not out his money to usury, nor taketh reward against the innocent. He that doeth these things shall never be moved.

PSALM 16

12 PRESERVE me, O God: for in thee do I put my trust.

13 O my soul, thou hast said unto the LORD, Thou art my Lord: my goodness extendeth not to thee;

14 But to the saints that are in the earth and to the excellent, in whom is all my delight.

15 Their sorrows shall be multiplied that hasten after another god: their drink offerings of blood will I not offer, nor take up their names into my lips.

16 The LORD is the portion of mine inheritance and of my cup: thou maintainest my lot.

17 The lines are fallen unto me in pleasant places; yea, I have a goodly heritage.

18 I will bless the LORD, who hath given me counsel: my reins also instruct me in the night seasons.

19 I have set the LORD always before me: because he is at my right hand, I shall not be moved.

20 Therefore my heart is glad, and my glory rejoiceth: my flesh also shall rest in hope.

21 For thou wilt not leave my soul in hell; neither wilt thou suffer thine Holy One to see corruption.

22 Thou wilt show me the path of life: in thy presence is fulness of joy; at thy right hand there are pleasures for evermore.

Selection 4
PSALM 17 : 1–9, 15

1 HEAR the right, O LORD, attend unto my cry; give ear unto my prayer, that goeth not out of feigned lips.

2 Let my sentence come forth from thy presence; let thine eyes behold the things that are equal.

3 Thou hast proved mine heart; thou hast visited me in the night; thou hast tried me, and shalt find nothing: I am purposed that my mouth shall not transgress.

4 Concerning the works of men, by the word of thy lips I have kept me from the paths of the destroyer.

5 Hold up my goings in thy paths, that my footsteps slip not.

6 I have called upon thee, for thou wilt hear me, O God: incline thine ear unto me, and hear my speech.

7 Show thy marvellous loving-kindness, O thou that savest by thy right hand them which put their trust in thee from those that rise up against them.

8 Keep me as the apple of the eye; hide me under the shadow of thy wings,

9 From the wicked that oppress me, from my deadly enemies, who compass me about.

10 As for me, I will behold thy face in righteousness: I shall be satisfied, when I awake, with thy likeness.

The Psalter

Psalm 18 : 1-19

11 I WILL love thee, O Lord, my strength.

12 The Lord is my rock, and my fortress, and my deliverer; my God, my strength, in whom I will trust; my buckler, and the horn of my salvation, and my high tower.

13 I will call upon the Lord, who is worthy to be praised: so shall I be saved from mine enemies.

14 The sorrows of death compassed me, and the floods of ungodly men made me afraid.

15 The sorrows of hell compassed me about: the snares of death prevented me.

16 In my distress I called upon the Lord, and cried unto my God: he heard my voice out of his temple, and my cry came before him, even into his ears.

17 Then the earth shook and trembled; the foundations also of the hills moved and were shaken, because he was wroth.

18 There went up a smoke out of his nostrils, and fire out of his mouth devoured: coals were kindled by it.

19 He bowed the heavens also, and came down: and darkness was under his feet.

20 And he rode upon a cherub, and did fly: yea, he did fly upon the wings of the wind.

21 He made darkness his secret place; his pavilion round about him were dark waters and thick clouds of the skies.

22 At the brightness that was before him his thick clouds passed, hail stones and coals of fire.

23 The Lord also thundered in the heavens, and the Highest gave his voice; hail stones and coals of fire.

24 Yea, he sent out his arrows, and scattered them; and he shot out lightnings, and discomfited them.

25 Then the channels of waters were seen, and the foundations of the world were discovered at thy rebuke, O Lord, at the blast of the breath of thy nostrils.

26 He sent from above, he took me, he drew me out of many waters.

27 He delivered me from my strong enemy, and from them which hated me; for they were too strong for me.

28 They prevented me in the day of my calamity: but the Lord was my stay.

29 He brought me forth also into a large place; he delivered me, because he delighted in me.

Selection 5

Psalm 18 : 25-35

1 WITH the merciful thou wilt show thyself merciful; with an upright man thou wilt show thyself upright;

2 With the pure thou wilt show thyself pure; and with the froward thou wilt show thyself froward.

3 For thou wilt save the afflicted people; but wilt bring down high looks.

4 For thou wilt light my candle: the Lord my God will enlighten my darkness.

5 For by thee I have run through a troop; and by my God have I leaped over a wall.

6 As for God, his way is perfect: the word of the Lord is tried; he is a buckler to all those that trust in him.

7 For who is God save the Lord? or who is a rock save our God?

8 It is God that girdeth me with strength, and maketh my way perfect.

9 He maketh my feet like hinds' feet, and setteth me upon my high places.

10 He teacheth my hands to war, so that a bow of steel is broken by mine arms.

11 Thou hast also given me the shield of thy salvation; and thy right hand hath holden me up, and thy gentleness hath made me great.

The Psalter

Psalm 19

12 THE heavens declare the glory of God; and the firmament showeth his handywork.

13 Day unto day uttereth speech, and night unto night showeth knowledge.

14 There is no speech nor language, where their voice is not heard.

15 Their line is gone out through all the earth, and their words to the end of the world. In them hath he set a tabernacle for the sun,

16 Which is as a bridegroom coming out of his chamber, and rejoiceth as a strong man to run a race.

17 His going forth is from the end of the heaven, and his circuit unto the ends of it: and there is nothing hid from the heat thereof.

18 The law of the LORD is perfect, converting the soul: the testimony of the LORD is sure, making wise the simple.

19 The statutes of the LORD are right, rejoicing the heart: the commandment of the LORD is pure, enlightening the eyes.

20 The fear of the LORD is clean, enduring for ever: the judgments of the LORD are true and righteous altogether.

21 More to be desired are they than gold, yea, than much fine gold: sweeter also than honey and the honeycomb.

22 Moreover by them is thy servant warned: and in keeping of them there is great reward.

23 Who can understand his errors? cleanse thou me from secret faults.

24 Keep back thy servant also from presumptuous sins; let them not have dominion over me: then shall I be upright, and I shall be innocent from the great transgression.

25 Let the words of my mouth, and the meditation of my heart, be acceptable in thy sight, O LORD, my strength, and my redeemer.

Selection 6

Psalm 20

1 THE LORD hear thee in the day of trouble; the name of the God of Jacob defend thee;

2 Send thee help from the sanctuary, and strengthen thee out of Zion;

3 Remember all thy offerings, and accept thy burnt sacrifice;

4 Grant thee according to thine own heart, and fulfil all thy counsel.

5 We will rejoice in thy salvation, and in the name of our God we will set up our banners: the LORD fulfil all thy petitions.

6 Now know I that the LORD saveth his anointed; he will hear him from his holy heaven with the saving strength of his right hand.

7 Some trust in chariots, and some in horses: but we will remember the name of the LORD our God.

8 They are brought down and fallen: but we are risen, and stand upright.

9 Save, LORD: let the king hear us when we call.

Psalm 23

10 THE LORD is my shepherd; I shall not want.

11 He maketh me to lie down in green pastures: he leadeth me beside the still waters.

12 He restoreth my soul: he leadeth me in the paths of righteousness for his name's sake.

13 Yea, though I walk through the valley of the shadow of death, I will fear no evil: for thou art with me; thy rod and thy staff they comfort me.

14 Thou preparest a table before me in the presence of mine enemies: thou anointest my head with oil; my cup runneth over.

15 Surely goodness and mercy shall follow me all the days of my life: and I will dwell in the house of the LORD for ever.

The Psalter

Psalm 24

16 THE earth is the LORD'S, and the fulness thereof; the world, and they that dwell therein.

17 For he hath founded it upon the seas, and established it upon the floods.

18 Who shall ascend into the hill of the LORD? or who shall stand in his holy place?

19 He that hath clean hands, and a pure heart; who hath not lifted up his soul unto vanity, nor sworn deceitfully.

20 He shall receive the blessing from the LORD, and righteousness from the God of his salvation.

21 This is the generation of them that seek him, that seek thy face, O Jacob.

22 Lift up your heads, O ye gates; and be ye lifted up, ye everlasting doors; and the King of glory shall come in.

23 Who is this King of glory? The LORD strong and mighty, the LORD mighty in battle.

24 Lift up your heads, O ye gates; even lift them up, ye everlasting doors; and the King of glory shall come in.

25 Who is this King of glory? The LORD of hosts, he is the King of glory.

Selection 7

Psalm 25

1 UNTO thee, O LORD, do I lift up my soul.

2 O my God, I trust in thee: let me not be ashamed, let not mine enemies triumph over me.

3 Yea, let none that wait on thee be ashamed: let them be ashamed which transgress without cause.

4 Show me thy ways, O LORD; teach me thy paths.

5 Lead me in thy truth, and teach me: for thou art the God of my salvation; on thee do I wait all the day.

6 Remember, O LORD, thy tender mercies and thy loving-kindnesses; for they have been ever of old.

7 Remember not the sins of my youth, nor my transgressions: according to thy mercy remember thou me for thy goodness' sake, O LORD.

8 Good and upright is the LORD: therefore will he teach sinners in the way.

9 The meek will he guide in judgment: and the meek will he teach his way.

10 All the paths of the LORD are mercy and truth unto such as keep his covenant and his testimonies.

11 For thy name's sake, O LORD, pardon mine iniquity; for it is great.

12 What man is he that feareth the LORD? him shall he teach in the way that he shall choose.

13 His soul shall dwell at ease; and his seed shall inherit the earth.

14 The secret of the LORD is with them that fear him; and he will show them his covenant.

15 Mine eyes are ever toward the LORD; for he shall pluck my feet out of the net.

16 Turn thee unto me, and have mercy upon me; for I am desolate and afflicted.

17 The troubles of my heart are enlarged: O bring thou me out of my distresses.

18 Look upon mine affliction and my pain; and forgive all my sins.

19 Consider mine enemies; for they are many; and they hate me with cruel hatred.

20 O keep my soul, and deliver me: let me not be ashamed; for I put my trust in thee.

21 Let integrity and uprightness preserve me; for I wait on thee.

22 Redeem Israel, O God, out of all his troubles.

The Psalter

Selection 8

Psalm 26 : 8-12

1 LORD, I have loved the habitation of thy house, and the place where thine honor dwelleth.

2 Gather not my soul with sinners, nor my life with bloody men :

3 In whose hands is mischief, and their right hand is full of bribes.

4 But as for me, I will walk in mine integrity : redeem me, and be merciful unto me.

5 My foot standeth in an even place : in the congregations will I bless the LORD.

Psalm 27

6 THE LORD is my light and my salvation ; whom shall I fear ? the LORD is the strength of my life ; of whom shall I be afraid ?

7 When the wicked, even mine enemies and my foes, came upon me to eat up my flesh, they stumbled and fell.

8 Though a host should encamp against me, my heart shall not fear : though war should rise against me, in this will I be confident.

9 One thing have I desired of the LORD, that will I seek after ; that I may dwell in the house of the LORD all the days of my life, to behold the beauty of the LORD, and to inquire in his temple.

10 For in the time of trouble he shall hide me in his pavilion : in the secret of his tabernacle shall he hide me ; he shall set me up upon a rock.

11 And now shall mine head be lifted up above mine enemies round about me : therefore will I offer in his tabernacle sacrifices of joy ; I will sing, yea, I will sing praises unto the LORD.

12 Hear, O LORD, when I cry with my voice : have mercy also upon me, and answer me.

13 When thou saidst, Seek ye my face ; my heart said unto thee, Thy face, LORD, will I seek.

14 Hide not thy face far from me ; put not thy servant away in anger : thou hast been my help ; leave me not, neither forsake me, O God of my salvation.

15 When my father and my mother forsake me, then the LORD will take me up.

16 Teach me thy way, O LORD, and lead me in a plain path, because of mine enemies.

17 Deliver me not over unto the will of mine enemies : for false witnesses are risen up against me, and such as breathe out cruelty.

18 I had fainted, unless I had believed to see the goodness of the LORD in the land of the living.

19 Wait on the LORD : be of good courage, and he shall strengthen thine heart ; wait, I say, on the LORD.

Psalm 28 : 6-9

20 BLESSED be the LORD, because he hath heard the voice of my supplications.

21 The LORD is my strength and my shield ; my heart trusted in him, and I am helped : therefore my heart greatly rejoiceth ; and with my song will I praise him.

22 The LORD is their strength, and he is the saving strength of his anointed.

23 Save thy people, and bless thine inheritance : feed them also, and lift them up for ever.

Selection 9

Psalm 29

1 GIVE unto the LORD, O ye mighty, give unto the LORD glory and strength.

2 Give unto the LORD the glory due unto his name ; worship the LORD in the beauty of holiness.

3 The voice of the LORD is upon the waters : the God of glory thundereth : the LORD is upon many waters.

The Psalter

4 The voice of the LORD is powerful; the voice of the LORD is full of majesty.
5 The voice of the LORD breaketh the cedars; yea, the LORD breaketh the cedars of Lebanon.
6 He maketh them also to skip like a calf; Lebanon and Sirion like a young unicorn.
7 The voice of the LORD divideth the flames of fire.
8 The voice of the LORD shaketh the wilderness; the LORD shaketh the wilderness of Kadesh.
9 The voice of the LORD maketh the hinds to calve, and discovereth the forests: and in his temple doth every one speak of his glory.
10 The LORD sitteth upon the flood; yea, the LORD sitteth King for ever.
11 The LORD will give strength unto his people; the LORD will bless his people with peace.

Psalm 30

12 I WILL extol thee, O LORD; for thou hast lifted me up, and hast not made my foes to rejoice over me.
13 O LORD my God, I cried unto thee, and thou hast healed me.
14 O LORD, thou hast brought up my soul from the grave: thou hast kept me alive, that I should not go down to the pit.
15 Sing unto the LORD, O ye saints of his, and give thanks at the remembrance of his holiness.
16 For his anger endureth but a moment; in his favor is life: weeping may endure for a night, but joy cometh in the morning.
17 And in my prosperity I said, I shall never be moved.
18 LORD, by thy favor thou hast made my mountain to stand strong: thou didst hide thy face, and I was troubled.
19 I cried to thee, O LORD; and unto the LORD I made supplication.
20 What profit is there in my blood, when I go down to the pit? Shall the dust praise thee? shall it declare thy truth?
21 Hear, O LORD, and have mercy upon me: LORD, be thou my helper.
22 Thou hast turned for me my mourning into dancing: thou hast put off my sackcloth, and girded me with gladness;
23 To the end that my glory may sing praise to thee, and not be silent. O LORD my God, I will give thanks unto thee for ever.

Selection 10

Psalm 31 : 1-5, 15-16, 19-24

1 IN thee, O LORD, do I put my trust; let me never be ashamed: deliver me in thy righteousness.
2 Bow down thine ear to me; deliver me speedily: be thou my strong rock, for a house of defence to save me.
3 For thou art my rock and my fortress; therefore for thy name's sake lead me, and guide me.
4 Pull me out of the net that they have laid privily for me: for thou art my strength.
5 Into thine hand I commit my spirit: thou hast redeemed me, O LORD God of truth.
6 My times are in thy hand: deliver me from the hand of mine enemies, and from them that persecute me.
7 Make thy face to shine upon thy servant: save me for thy mercies' sake.
8 Oh how great is thy goodness, which thou hast laid up for them that fear thee; which thou hast wrought for them that trust in thee before the sons of men!
9 Thou shalt hide them in the secret of thy presence from the pride of man: thou shalt keep them secretly in a pavilion from the strife of tongues.

The Psalter

10 Blessed be the LORD: for he hath showed me his marvellous kindness in a strong city.

11 For I said in my haste, I am cut off from before thine eyes: nevertheless thou heardest the voice of my supplications when I cried unto thee.

12 O love the LORD, all ye his saints: for the LORD preserveth the faithful, and plentifully rewardeth the proud doer.

13 Be of good courage, and he shall strengthen your heart, all ye that hope in the LORD.

PSALM 32

14 BLESSED is he whose transgression is forgiven, whose sin is covered.

15 Blessed is the man unto whom the LORD imputeth not iniquity, and in whose spirit there is no guile.

16 When I kept silence, my bones waxed old through my roaring all the day long.

17 For day and night thy hand was heavy upon me: my moisture is turned into the drought of summer.

18 I acknowledged my sin unto thee, and mine iniquity have I not hid. I said, I will confess my transgressions unto the LORD; and thou forgavest the iniquity of my sin.

19 For this shall every one that is godly pray unto thee in a time when thou mayest be found: surely in the floods of great waters they shall not come nigh unto him.

20 Thou art my hiding place; thou shalt preserve me from trouble; thou shalt compass me about with songs of deliverance.

21 I will instruct thee and teach thee in the way which thou shalt go: I will guide thee with mine eye.

22 Be ye not as the horse, or as the mule, which have no understanding: whose mouth must be held in with bit and bridle, lest they come near unto thee.

23 Many sorrows shall be to the wicked: but he that trusteth in the LORD, mercy shall compass him about.

24 Be glad in the LORD, and rejoice, ye righteous: and shout for joy, all ye that are upright in heart.

Selection 11

PSALM 33

1 REJOICE in the LORD, O ye righteous: for praise is comely for the upright.

2 Praise the LORD with harp: sing unto him with the psaltery and an instrument of ten strings.

3 Sing unto him a new song; play skilfully with a loud noise.

4 For the word of the LORD is right; and all his works are done in truth.

5 He loveth righteousness and judgment: the earth is full of the goodness of the LORD.

6 By the word of the LORD were the heavens made; and all the host of them by the breath of his mouth.

7 He gathereth the waters of the sea together as a heap: he layeth up the depth in storehouses.

8 Let all the earth fear the LORD: let all the inhabitants of the world stand in awe of him.

9 For he spake, and it was done; he commanded, and it stood fast.

10 The LORD bringeth the counsel of the heathen to naught: he maketh the devices of the people of none effect.

11 The counsel of the LORD standeth for ever, the thoughts of his heart to all generations.

12 Blessed is the nation whose God is the LORD; and the people whom he hath chosen for his own inheritance.

13 The LORD looketh from heaven; he beholdeth all the sons of men.

14 From the place of his habitation he looketh upon all the inhabitants of the earth.

The Psalter

15 He fashioneth their hearts alike; he considereth all their works.

16 There is no king saved by the multitude of a host : a mighty man is not delivered by much strength.

17 A horse is a vain thing for safety : neither shall he deliver any by his great strength.

18 Behold, the eye of the LORD is upon them that fear him, upon them that hope in his mercy;

19 To deliver their soul from death, and to keep them alive in famine.

20 Our soul waiteth for the LORD: he is our help and our shield.

21 For our heart shall rejoice in him, because we have trusted in his holy name.

22 Let thy mercy, O LORD, be upon us, according as we hope in thee.

Selection 12

Psalm 34

1 I WILL bless the LORD at all times: his praise shall continually be in my mouth.

2 My soul shall make her boast in the LORD: the humble shall hear thereof, and be glad.

3 O magnify the LORD with me, and let us exalt his name together.

4 I sought the LORD, and he heard me, and delivered me from all my fears.

5 They looked unto him, and were lightened : and their faces were not ashamed.

6 This poor man cried, and the LORD heard him, and saved him out of all his troubles.

7 The angel of the LORD encampeth round about them that fear him, and delivereth them.

8 O taste and see that the LORD is good : blessed is the man that trusteth in him.

9 O fear the LORD, ye his saints : for there is no want to them that fear him.

10 The young lions do lack, and suffer hunger; but they that seek the LORD shall not want any good thing.

11 Come, ye children, hearken unto me : I will teach you the fear of the LORD.

12 What man is he that desireth life, and loveth many days, that he may see good ?

13 Keep thy tongue from evil, and thy lips from speaking guile.

14 Depart from evil, and do good; seek peace, and pursue it.

15 The eyes of the LORD are upon the righteous, and his ears are open unto their cry.

16 The face of the LORD is against them that do evil, to cut off the remembrance of them from the earth.

17 The righteous cry, and the LORD heareth, and delivereth them out of all their troubles.

18 The LORD is nigh unto them that are of a broken heart; and saveth such as be of a contrite spirit.

19 Many are the afflictions of the righteous : but the LORD delivereth him out of them all.

20 He keepeth all his bones: not one of them is broken.

21 Evil shall slay the wicked : and they that hate the righteous shall be desolate.

22 The LORD redeemeth the soul of his servants: and none of them that trust in him shall be desolate.

Psalm 36 : 5–10

23 Thy mercy, O LORD, is in the heavens; and thy faithfulness reacheth unto the clouds.

24 Thy righteousness is like the great mountains; thy judgments are a great deep: O LORD, thou preservest man and beast.

25 How excellent is thy loving-kindness,

The Psalter

O God! therefore the children of men put their trust under the shadow of thy wings.

26 They shall be abundantly satisfied with the fatness of thy house; and thou shalt make them drink of the river of thy pleasures.

27 For with thee is the fountain of life: in thy light shall we see light.

28 O continue thy loving-kindness unto them that know thee; and thy righteousness to the upright in heart.

Selection 13
PSALM 37 : 1-9, 23-40

1 FRET not thyself because of evil doers, neither be thou envious against the workers of iniquity.

2 For they shall soon be cut down like the grass, and wither as the green herb.

3 Trust in the LORD, and do good; so shalt thou dwell in the land, and verily thou shalt be fed.

4 Delight thyself also in the LORD; and he shall give thee the desires of thine heart.

5 Commit thy way unto the LORD; trust also in him; and he shall bring it to pass.

6 And he shall bring forth thy righteousness as the light, and thy judgment as the noonday.

7 Rest in the LORD, and wait patiently for him: fret not thyself because of him who prospereth in his way, because of the man who bringeth wicked devices to pass.

8 Cease from anger, and forsake wrath: fret not thyself in any wise to do evil.

9 For evil doers shall be cut off: but those that wait upon the LORD, they shall inherit the earth.

10 The steps of a good man are ordered by the LORD; and he delighteth in his way.

11 Though he fall, he shall not be utterly cast down: for the LORD upholdeth him with his hand.

12 I have been young, and now am old; yet have I not seen the righteous forsaken, nor his seed begging bread.

13 He is ever merciful, and lendeth; and his seed is blessed.

14 Depart from evil, and do good; and dwell for evermore.

15 For the LORD loveth judgment, and forsaketh not his saints; they are preserved for ever; but the seed of the wicked shall be cut off.

16 The righteous shall inherit the land, and dwell therein for ever.

17 The mouth of the righteous speaketh wisdom, and his tongue talketh of judgment.

18 The law of his God is in his heart; none of his steps shall slide.

19 The wicked watcheth the righteous, and seeketh to slay him.

20 The LORD will not leave him in his hand, nor condemn him when he is judged.

21 Wait on the LORD, and keep his way, and he shall exalt thee to inherit the land: when the wicked are cut off, thou shalt see it.

22 I have seen the wicked in great power, and spreading himself like a green bay tree.

23 Yet he passed away, and, lo, he was not: yea, I sought him, but he could not be found.

24 Mark the perfect man, and behold the upright: for the end of that man is peace.

25 But the transgressors shall be destroyed together: the end of the wicked shall be cut off.

26 But the salvation of the righteous is of the LORD: he is their strength in the time of trouble.

27 And the LORD shall help them, and deliver them; he shall deliver them from the wicked, and save them, because they trust in him.

The Psalter

Selection 14
Psalm 39

1 I SAID, I will take heed to my ways, that I sin not with my tongue: I will keep my mouth with a bridle, while the wicked is before me.

2 I was dumb with silence, I held my peace, even from good; and my sorrow was stirred.

3 My heart was hot within me; while I was musing the fire burned: then spake I with my tongue,

4 Lord, make me to know mine end, and the measure of my days, what it is; that I may know how frail I am.

5 Behold, thou hast made my days as a handbreath; and mine age is as nothing before thee: verily every man at his best state is altogether vanity.

6 Surely every man walketh in a vain show; surely they are disquieted in vain: he heapeth up riches, and knoweth not who shall gather them.

7 And now, Lord, what wait I for? my hope is in thee.

8 Deliver me from all my transgressions: make me not the reproach of the foolish.

9 I was dumb, I opened not my mouth; because thou didst it.

10 Remove thy stroke away from me: I am consumed by the blow of thine hand.

11 When thou with rebukes dost correct man for iniquity, thou makest his beauty to consume away like a moth: surely every man is vanity.

12 Hear my prayer, O Lord, and give ear unto my cry; hold not thy peace at my tears: for I am a stranger with thee, and a sojourner, as all my fathers were.

13 O spare me, that I may recover strength, before I go hence, and be no more.

Psalm 40 : 1–13, 16–17

14 I WAITED patiently for the Lord; and he inclined unto me, and heard my cry.

15 He brought me up also out of a horrible pit, out of the miry clay, and set my feet upon a rock, and established my goings.

16 And he hath put a new song in my mouth, even praise unto our God: many shall see it, and fear, and shall trust in the Lord.

17 Blessed is that man that maketh the Lord his trust, and respecteth not the proud, nor such as turn aside to lies.

18 Many, O Lord my God, are thy wonderful works which thou hast done, and thy thoughts which are to us-ward:

19 They cannot be reckoned up in order unto thee: if I would declare and speak of them, they are more than can be numbered.

20 Sacrifice and offering thou didst not desire; mine ears hast thou opened: burnt offering and sin offering hast thou not required.

21 Then said I, Lo, I come: in the volume of the book it is written of me,

22 I delight to do thy will, O my God, yea, thy law is within my heart.

23 I have preached righteousness in the great congregation: lo, I have not refrained my lips, O Lord, thou knowest.

24 I have not hid thy righteousness within my heart; I have declared thy faithfulness and thy salvation: I have not concealed thy loving-kindness and thy truth from the great congregation.

25 Withhold not thou thy tender mercies from me, O Lord: let thy lovingkindness and thy truth continually preserve me.

26 For innumerable evils have compassed me about: mine iniquities have taken hold upon me, so that I am not able to look up; they are more than the

The Psalter

hairs of mine head: therefore my heart faileth me.

27 Be pleased, O LORD, to deliver me: O LORD, make haste to help me.

28 Let all those that seek thee rejoice and be glad in thee: let such as love thy salvation say continually, The LORD be magnified.

29 But I am poor and needy; yet the LORD thinketh upon me: thou art my help and my deliverer; make no tarrying, O my God.

Selection 15

PSALM 42

1 AS the hart panteth after the water brooks, so panteth my soul after thee, O God.

2 My soul thirsteth for God, for the living God: when shall I come and appear before God?

3 My tears have been my meat day and night, while they continually say unto me, Where is thy God?

4 When I remember these things, I pour out my soul in me: for I had gone with the multitude, I went with them to the house of God, with the voice of joy and praise, with a multitude that kept holyday.

5 Why art thou cast down, O my soul? and why art thou disquieted in me? hope thou in God; for I shall yet praise him for the help of his countenance.

6 O my God, my soul is cast down within me: therefore will I remember thee from the land of Jordan, and of the Hermonites, from the hill Mizar.

7 Deep calleth unto deep at the noise of thy waterspouts: all thy waves and thy billows are gone over me.

8 Yet the LORD will command his lovingkindness in the daytime, and in the night his song shall be with me, and my prayer unto the God of my life.

9 I will say unto God my rock, Why hast thou forgotten me? why go I mourning because of the oppression of the enemy?

10 As with a sword in my bones, mine enemies reproach me; while they say daily unto me, Where is thy God?

11 Why art thou cast down, O my soul? and why art thou disquieted within me? hope thou in God: for I shall yet praise him, who is the health of my countenance, and my God.

PSALM 43

12 JUDGE me, O God, and plead my cause against an ungodly nation: O deliver me from the deceitful and unjust man.

13 For thou art the God of my strength: why dost thou cast me off? why go I mourning because of the oppression of the enemy?

14 O send out thy light and thy truth: let them lead me; let them bring me unto thy holy hill, and to thy tabernacles.

15 Then will I go unto the altar of God, unto God my exceeding joy: yea, upon the harp will I praise thee, O God my God.

16 Why art thou cast down, O my soul? and why art thou disquieted within me? hope in God: for I shall yet praise him, who is the health of my countenance, and my God.

PSALM 44 : 1–8

17 WE have heard with our ears, O God, our fathers have told us, what work thou didst in their days, in the times of old.

18 How thou didst drive out the heathen with thy hand, and plantedst them; how thou didst afflict the people, and cast them out.

19 For they got not the land in possession by their own sword, neither did their own arm save them: but thy

The Psalter

right hand, and thine arm, and the light of thy countenance, because thou hadst a favor unto them.

20 Thou art my King, O God: command deliverances for Jacob.

21 Through thee will we push down our enemies: through thy name will we tread them under that rise up against us.

22 For I will not trust in my bow, neither shall my sword save me.

23 But thou hast saved us from our enemies, and hast put them to shame that hated us.

24 In God we boast all the day long, and praise thy name forever.

Selection 16
PSALM 45

1 MY heart is inditing a good matter: I speak of the things which I have made touching the King: my tongue is the pen of a ready writer.

2 Thou art fairer than the children of men: grace is poured into thy lips: therefore God hath blessed thee for ever.

3 Gird thy sword upon thy thigh, O most Mighty, with thy glory and thy majesty.

4 And in thy majesty ride prosperously, because of truth and meekness and righteousness; and thy right hand shall teach thee terrible things.

5 Thine arrows are sharp in the heart of the King's enemies; whereby the people fall under thee.

6 Thy throne, O God, is for ever and ever: the sceptre of thy kingdom is a right sceptre.

7 Thou lovest righteousness, and hatest wickedness: therefore God, thy God, hath anointed thee with the oil of gladness above thy fellows.

8 All thy garments smell of myrrh, and aloes, and cassia, out of the ivory palaces, whereby they have made thee glad.

9 Kings' daughters were among thy honorable women: upon thy right hand did stand the queen in gold of Ophir.

10 Hearken, O daughter, and consider, and incline thine ear; forget also thine own people, and thy father's house;

11 So shall the King greatly desire thy beauty: for he is thy Lord; and worship thou him.

12 And the daughter of Tyre shall be there with a gift; even the rich among the people shall entreat thy favor.

13 The King's daughter is all glorious within: her clothing is of wrought gold.

14 She shall be brought unto the King in raiment of needlework: the virgins her companions that follow her shall be brought unto thee.

15 With gladness and rejoicing shall they be brought: they shall enter into the King's palace.

16 Instead of thy fathers shall be thy children, whom thou mayest make princes in all the earth.

17 I will make thy name to be remembered in all generations: therefore shall the people praise thee for ever and ever.

PSALM 46

18 GOD is our refuge and strength, a very present help in trouble.

19 Therefore will we not fear, though the earth be removed, and though the mountains be carried into the midst of the sea;

20 Though the waters thereof roar and be troubled, though the mountains shake with the swelling thereof.

21 There is a river, the streams whereof shall make glad the city of God, the holy place of the tabernacles of the Most High.

22 God is in the midst of her; she shall not be moved: God shall help her, and that right early.

23 The heathen raged, the kingdoms were moved: he uttered his voice, the earth melted.

The Psalter

24 The LORD of hosts is with us; the God of Jacob is our refuge.

25 Come, behold the works of the LORD, what desolations he hath made in the earth.

26 He maketh wars to cease unto the end of the earth; he breaketh the bow, and cutteth the spear in sunder; he burneth the chariot in the fire.

27 Be still, and know that I am God: I will be exalted among the heathen, I will be exalted in the earth.

28 The LORD of hosts is with us; the God of Jacob is our refuge.

Selection 17

PSALM 47

1 O CLAP your hands, all ye people; shout unto God with the voice of triumph.

2 For the LORD most high is terrible; he is a great King over all the earth.

3 He shall subdue the people under us, and the nations under our feet.

4 He shall choose our inheritance for us, the excellency of Jacob whom he loved.

5 God is gone up with a shout, the LORD with the sound of a trumpet.

6 Sing praises to God, sing praises: sing praises unto our King, sing praises.

7 For God is the King of all the earth: sing ye praises with understanding.

8 God reigneth over the heathen: God sitteth upon the throne of his holiness.

9 The princes of the people are gathered together, even the people of the God of Abraham: for the shields of the earth belong unto God: he is greatly exalted.

PSALM 48

10 GREAT is the LORD, and greatly to be praised in the city of our God, in the mountain of his holiness.

11 Beautiful for situation, the joy of the whole earth, is mount Zion, on the sides of the north, the city of the great King.

12 God is known in her palaces for a refuge.

13 For, lo, the kings were assembled, they passed by together.

14 They saw it, and so they marvelled; they were troubled, and hasted away.

15 Fear took hold upon them there, and pain, as of a woman in travail.

16 Thou breakest the ships of Tarshish with an east wind.

17 As we have heard, so have we seen in the city of the LORD of hosts, in the city of our God: God will establish it for ever.

18 We have thought of thy lovingkindness, O God, in the midst of thy temple.

19 According to thy name, O God, so is thy praise unto the ends of the earth: thy right hand is full of righteousness.

20 Let mount Zion rejoice, let the daughters of Judah be glad, because of thy judgments.

21 Walk about Zion, and go round about her: tell the towers thereof.

22 Mark ye well her bulwarks, consider her palaces; that ye may tell it to the generation following.

23 For this God is our God for ever and ever: he will be our guide even unto death.

Selection 18

PSALM 51

1 HAVE mercy upon me, O God, according to thy lovingkindness: according unto the multitude of thy tender mercies blot out my transgressions.

2 Wash me thoroughly from mine iniquity, and cleanse me from my sin.

3 For I acknowledge my transgressions: and my sin is ever before me.

The Psalter

4 Against thee, thee only, have I sinned, and done this evil in thy sight: that thou mightest be justified when thou speakest, and be clear when thou judgest.

5 Behold, I was shapen in iniquity; and in sin did my mother conceive me.

6 Behold, thou desirest truth in the inward parts: and in the hidden part thou shalt make me to know wisdom.

7 Purge me with hyssop, and I shall be clean: wash me, and I shall be whiter than snow.

8 Make me to hear joy and gladness; that the bones which thou hast broken may rejoice.

9 Hide thy face from my sins, and blot out all mine iniquities.

10 Create in me a clean heart, O God; and renew a right spirit within me.

11 Cast me not away from thy presence; and take not thy Holy Spirit from me.

12 Restore unto me the joy of thy salvation; and uphold me with thy free Spirit.

13 Then will I teach transgressors thy ways; and sinners shall be converted unto thee.

14 Deliver me from bloodguiltiness, O God, thou God of my salvation: and my tongue shall sing aloud of thy righteousness.

15 O LORD, open thou my lips; and my mouth shall show forth thy praise.

16 For thou desirest not sacrifice; else would I give it; thou delightest not in burnt offering.

17 The sacrifices of God are a broken spirit: a broken and a contrite heart, O God, thou wilt not despise.

18 Do good in thy good pleasure unto Zion: build thou the walls of Jerusalem.

19 Then shalt thou be pleased with the sacrifices of righteousness, with burnt offering and whole burnt offering: then shall they offer bullocks upon thine altar.

Selection 19

PSALM 53

1 THE fool hath said in his heart, There is no God. Corrupt are they, and have done abominable iniquity: there is none that doeth good.

2 God looked down from heaven upon the children of men, to see if there were any that did understand, that did seek God.

3 Every one of them is gone back: they are altogether become filthy; there is none that doeth good, no, not one.

4 Have the workers of iniquity no knowledge? who eat up my people as they eat bread: they have not called upon God.

5 There were they in great fear, where no fear was: for God hath scattered the bones of him that encampeth against thee: thou hast put them to shame, because God hath despised them.

6 Oh that the salvation of Israel were come out of Zion! When God bringeth back the captivity of his people, Jacob shall rejoice, and Israel shall be glad.

PSALM 56: 3-4, 8-13

7 WHAT time I am afraid, I will trust in thee.

8 In God I will praise his word, in God I have put my trust; I will not fear what flesh can do unto me.

9 Thou tellest my wanderings: put thou my tears into thy bottle: are they not in thy book?

10 When I cry unto thee, then shall mine enemies turn back: this I know; for God is for me.

11 In God will I praise his word: in the LORD will I praise his word.

12 In God have I put my trust: I will not be afraid what man can do unto me.

13 Thy vows are upon me, O God: I will render praises unto thee.

The Psalter

14 For thou hast delivered my soul from death: wilt not thou deliver my feet from falling, that I may walk before God in the light of the living?

Psalm 57

15 BE merciful unto me, O God, be merciful unto me: for my soul trusteth in thee: yea, in the shadow of thy wings will I make my refuge, until these calamities be overpast.

16 I will cry unto God most high; unto God that performeth all things for me.

17 He shall send from heaven, and save me from the reproach of him that would swallow me up. God shall send forth his mercy and his truth.

18 My soul is among lions: and I lie even among them that are set on fire, even the sons of men, whose teeth are spears and arrows, and their tongue a sharp sword.

19 Be thou exalted, O God, above the heavens; let thy glory be above all the earth.

20 They have prepared a net for my steps; my soul is bowed down: they have digged a pit before me, into the midst whereof they are fallen themselves.

21 My heart is fixed, O God, my heart is fixed: I will sing and give praise.

22 Awake up, my glory; awake, psaltery and harp: I myself will awake early.

23 I will praise thee, O Lord, among the people: I will sing unto thee among the nations.

24 For thy mercy is great unto the heavens, and thy truth unto the clouds.

25 Be thou exalted, O God, above the heavens: let thy glory be above all the earth.

Selection 20

Psalm 61

1 HEAR my cry, O God; attend unto my prayer.

2 From the end of the earth will I cry unto thee, when my heart is overwhelmed: lead me to the rock that is higher than I.

3 For thou hast been a shelter for me, and a strong tower from the enemy.

4 I will abide in thy tabernacle for ever: I will trust in the covert of thy wings.

5 For thou, O God, hast heard my vows: thou hast given me the heritage of those that fear thy name.

6 Thou wilt prolong the king's life: and his years as many generations.

7 He shall abide before God for ever: O prepare mercy and truth, which may preserve him.

8 So will I sing praise unto thy name for ever, that I may daily perform my vows.

Psalm 62

9 TRULY my soul waiteth upon God: from him cometh my salvation.

10 He only is my rock and my salvation; he is my defence; I shall not be greatly moved.

11 How long will ye imagine mischief against a man? ye shall be slain all of you: as a bowing wall shall ye be, and as a tottering fence.

12 They only consult to cast him down from his excellency: they delight in lies: they bless with their mouth, but they curse inwardly.

13 My soul, wait thou only upon God: for my expectation is from him.

14 He only is my rock and my salvation: he is my defence; I shall not be moved.

15 In God is my salvation and my glory: the rock of my strength, and my refuge, is in God.

16 Trust in him at all times; ye people, pour out your heart before him: God is a refuge for us.

The Psalter

17 Surely men of low degree are vanity, and men of high degree are a lie : to be laid in the balance, they are altogether lighter than vanity.

18 Trust not in oppression, and become not vain in robbery : if riches increase, set not your heart upon them.

19 God hath spoken once ; twice have I heard this ; that power belongeth unto God.

20 Also unto thee, O Lord, belongeth mercy : for thou renderest to every man according to his work.

Selection 21

PSALM 63

1 O GOD, thou art my God ; early will I seek thee : my soul thirsteth for thee, my flesh longeth for thee in a dry and thirsty land, where no water is ;

2 To see thy power and thy glory, so as I have seen thee in the sanctuary.

3 Because thy loving-kindness is better than life, my lips shall praise thee.

4 Thus will I bless thee while I live : I will lift up my hands in thy name.

5 My soul shall be satisfied as with marrow and fatness ; and my mouth shall praise thee with joyful lips :

6 When I remember thee upon my bed, and meditate on thee in the night watches.

7 Because thou hast been my help, therefore in the shadow of thy wings will I rejoice.

8 My soul followeth hard after thee : thy right hand upholdeth me.

9 But those that seek my soul, to destroy it, shall go into the lower parts of the earth.

10 They shall fall by the sword : they shall be a portion for foxes.

11 But the king shall rejoice in God ; every one that sweareth by him shall glory : but the mouth of them that speak lies shall be stopped.

PSALM 65

12 PRAISE waiteth for thee, O God, in Zion : and unto thee shall the vow be performed.

13 O thou that hearest prayer, unto thee shall all flesh come.

14 Iniquities prevail against me : as for our transgressions, thou shalt purge them away.

15 Blessed is the man whom thou choosest, and causest to approach unto thee, that he may dwell in thy courts : we shall be satisfied with the goodness of thy house, even of thy holy temple.

16 By terrible things in righteousness wilt thou answer us, O God of our salvation ; who art the confidence of all the ends of the earth, and of them that are afar off upon the sea :

17 Which by his strength setteth fast the mountains ; being girded with power :

18 Which stilleth the noise of the seas, the noise of their waves, and the tumult of the people.

19 They also that dwell in the uttermost parts are afraid at thy tokens : thou makest the outgoings of the morning and evening to rejoice.

20 Thou visitest the earth, and waterest it : thou greatly enrichest it with the river of God, which is full of water : thou preparest them corn, when thou hast so provided for it.

21 Thou waterest the ridges thereof abundantly : thou settlest the furrows thereof : thou makest it soft with showers : thou blessest the springing thereof.

22 Thou crownest the year with thy goodness ; and thy paths drop fatness.

23 They drop upon the pastures of the wilderness : and the little hills rejoice on every side.

24 The pastures are clothed with flocks ; the valleys also are covered over with corn ; they shout for joy, they also sing.

The Psalter

Selection 22

Psalm 66

1 MAKE a joyful noise unto God, all ye lands :

2 Sing forth the honor of his name : make his praise glorious.

3 Say unto God, How terrible art thou in thy works! through the greatness of thy power shall thine enemies submit themselves unto thee.

4 All the earth shall worship thee, and shall sing unto thee ; they shall sing to thy name.

5 Come and see the works of God : he is terrible in his doing toward the children of men.

6 He turned the sea into dry land : they went through the flood on foot: there did we rejoice in him.

7 He ruleth by his power for ever ; his eyes behold the nations : let not the rebellious exalt themselves.

8 O bless our God, ye people, and make the voice of his praise to be heard :

9 Which holdeth our soul in life, and suffereth not our feet to be moved.

10 For thou, O God, hast proved us : thou hast tried us, as silver is tried.

11 Thou broughtest us into the net ; thou laidst affliction upon our loins.

12 Thou hast caused men to ride over our heads ; we went through fire and through water : but thou broughtest us out into a wealthy place.

13 I will go into thy house with burnt offerings : I will pay thee my vows,

14 Which my lips have uttered, and my mouth hath spoken, when I was in trouble.

15 I will offer unto thee burnt sacrifices of fatlings, with the incense of rams: I will offer bullocks with goats.

16 Come and hear, all ye that fear God, and I will declare what he hath done for my soul.

17 I cried unto him with my mouth, and he was extolled with my tongue.

18 If I regard iniquity in my heart, the Lord will not hear me :

19 But verily God hath heard me ; he hath attended to the voice of my prayer.

20 Blessed be God, which hath not turned away my prayer, nor his mercy from me.

Psalm 67

21 GOD be merciful unto us, and bless us ; and cause his face to shine upon us ;

22 That thy way may be known upon earth, thy saving health among all nations.

23 Let the people praise thee, O God ; let all the people praise thee.

24 O let the nations be glad and sing for joy : for thou shalt judge the people righteously, and govern the nations upon earth.

25 Let the people praise thee, O God ; let all the people praise thee.

26 Then shall the earth yield her increase ; and God, even our own God, shall bless us.

27 God shall bless us ; and all the ends of the earth shall fear him.

Selection 23

Psalm 68 : 1-19, 28-29, 31-35

1 LET God arise, let his enemies be scattered : let them also that hate him flee before him.

2 As smoke is driven away, so drive them away : as wax melteth before the fire, so let the wicked perish at the presence of God.

3 But let the righteous be glad ; let them rejoice before God : yea, let them exceedingly rejoice.

4 Sing unto God, sing praises to his name : extol him that rideth upon the heavens by his name JAH, and rejoice before him.

5 A father of the fatherless, and a judge of the widows, is God in his holy habitation.

The Psalter

6 God setteth the solitary in families: he bringeth out those which are bound with chains: but the rebellious dwell in a dry land.

7 O God, when thou wentest forth before thy people, when thou didst march through the wilderness;

8 The earth shook, the heavens also dropped at the presence of God: even Sinai itself was moved at the presence of God, the God of Israel.

9 Thou, O God, didst send a plentiful rain, whereby thou didst confirm thine inheritance, when it was weary.

10 Thy congregation hath dwelt therein: thou, O God, hast prepared of thy goodness for the poor.

11 The Lord gave the word: great was the company of those that published it.

12 Kings of armies did flee apace: and she that tarried at home divided the spoil.

13 Though ye have lain among the pots, yet shall ye be as the wings of a dove covered with silver, and her feathers with yellow gold.

14 When the Almighty scattered kings in it, it was white as snow in Salmon.

15 The hill of God is as the hill of Bashan; a high hill as the hill of Bashan.

16 Why leap ye, ye high hills? this is the hill which God desireth to dwell in; yea, the LORD will dwell in it for ever.

17 The chariots of God are twenty thousand, even thousands of angels: the Lord is among them, as in Sinai, in the holy place.

18 Thou hast ascended on high, thou hast led captivity captive: thou hast received gifts for men; yea, for the rebellious also, that the LORD God might dwell among them.

19 Blessed be the Lord, who daily loadeth us with benefits, even the God of our salvation.

20 Thy God hath commanded thy strength: strengthen, O God, that which thou hast wrought for us.

21 Because of thy temple at Jerusalem shall kings bring presents unto thee.

22 Princes shall come out of Egypt; Ethiopia shall soon stretch out her hands unto God.

23 Sing unto God, ye kingdoms of the earth; O sing praises unto the Lord;

24 To him that rideth upon the heavens of heavens, which were of old; lo, he doth send out his voice, and that a mighty voice.

25 Ascribe ye strength unto God: his excellency is over Israel, and his strength is in the clouds.

26 O God, thou art terrible out of thy holy places: the God of Israel is he that giveth strength and power unto his people. Blessed be God.

Selection 24

PSALM 70

1 MAKE haste, O God, to deliver me; make haste to help me, O LORD.

2 Let them be ashamed and confounded that seek after my soul: let them be turned backward, and put to confusion, that desire my hurt.

3 Let them be turned back for a reward of their shame that say, Aha, aha.

4 Let all those that seek thee rejoice and be glad in thee: and let such as love thy salvation say continually, Let God be magnified.

5 But I am poor and needy; make haste unto me, O God: thou art my help and my deliverer; O LORD, make no tarrying.

PSALM 71 : 1–5, 8–9, 12, 14–24

6 IN thee, O LORD, do I put my trust: let me never be put to confusion.

7 Deliver me in thy righteousness, and cause me to escape; incline thine ear unto me, and save me.

The Psalter

8 Be thou my strong habitation, whereunto I may continually resort : thou hast given commandment to save me ; for thou art my rock and my fortress.

9 Deliver me, O my God, out of the hand of the wicked, out of the hand of the unrighteous and cruel man.

10 For thou art my hope, O Lord GOD: thou art my trust from my youth.

11 Let my mouth be filled with thy praise and with thy honor all the day.

12 Cast me not off in the time of old age; forsake me not when my strength faileth.

13 O God, be not far from me : O my God, make haste for my help.

14 But I will hope continually, and will yet praise thee more and more.

15 My mouth shall show forth thy righteousness and thy salvation all the day ; for I know not the numbers thereof.

16 I will go in the strength of the Lord GOD : I will make mention of thy righteousness, even of thine only.

17 O God, thou hast taught me from my youth : and hitherto have I declared thy wondrous works.

18 Now also when I am old and grayheaded, O God, forsake me not ; until I have showed thy strength unto this generation, and thy power to every one that is to come.

19 Thy righteousness also, O God, is very high, who hast done great things : O God, who is like unto thee !

20 Thou, which hast showed me great and sore troubles, shalt quicken me again, and shalt bring me up again from the depths of the earth.

21 Thou shalt increase my greatness, and comfort me on every side.

22 I will also praise thee with the psaltery, even thy truth, O my God : unto thee will I sing with the harp, O thou Holy One of Israel.

23 My lips shall greatly rejoice when I sing unto thee ; and my soul, which thou hast redeemed.

24 My tongue shall also talk of thy righteousness all the day long : for they are confounded, for they are brought unto shame, that seek my hurt.

Selection 25

PSALM 72

1 GIVE the king thy judgments, O God, and thy righteousness unto the king's son.

2 He shall judge thy people with righteousness, and thy poor with judgment.

3 The mountains shall bring peace to the people, and the little hills, by righteousness.

4 He shall judge the poor of the people, he shall save the children of the needy, and shall break in pieces the oppressor.

5 They shall fear thee as long as the sun and moon endure, throughout all generations.

6 He shall come down like rain upon the mown grass: as showers that water the earth.

7 In his days shall the righteous flourish ; and abundance of peace so long as the moon endureth.

8 He shall have dominion also from sea to sea, and from the river unto the ends of the earth.

9 They that dwell in the wilderness shall bow before him ; and his enemies shall lick the dust.

10 The kings of Tarshish and of the isles shall bring presents: the kings of Sheba and Seba shall offer gifts.

11 Yea, all kings shall fall down before him : all nations shall serve him.

12 For he shall deliver the needy when he crieth ; the poor also, and him that hath no helper.

The Psalter

13 He shall spare the poor and needy, and shall save the souls of the needy.

14 He shall redeem their soul from deceit and violence: and precious shall their blood be in his sight.

15 And he shall live, and to him shall be given of the gold of Sheba: prayer also shall be made for him continually; and daily shall he be praised.

16 There shall be a handful of corn in the earth upon the top of the mountains; the fruit thereof shall shake like Lebanon: and they of the city shall flourish like grass of the earth.

17 His name shall endure for ever: his name shall be continued as long as the sun: and men shall be blessed in him: all nations shall call him blessed.

18 Blessed be the LORD God, the God of Israel, who only doeth wondrous things.

19 And blessed be his glorious name for ever: and let the whole earth be filled with his glory. Amen, and Amen.

Selection 26

PSALM 73 : 1-26

1 TRULY God is good to Israel, even to such as are of a clean heart.

2 But as for me, my feet were almost gone; my steps had well nigh slipped.

3 For I was envious at the foolish, when I saw the prosperity of the wicked.

4 For there are no bands in their death: but their strength is firm.

5 They are not in trouble as other men; neither are they plagued like other men.

6 Therefore pride compasseth them about as a chain; violence covereth them as a garment.

7 Their eyes stand out with fatness: they have more than heart could wish.

8 They are corrupt, and speak wickedly concerning oppression: they speak loftily.

9 They set their mouth against the heavens, and their tongue walketh through the earth.

10 Therefore his people return hither: and waters of a full cup are wrung out to them.

11 And they say, How doth God know? and is there knowledge in the Most High?

12 Behold, these are the ungodly, who prosper in the world; they increase in riches.

13 Verily I have cleansed my heart in vain, and washed my hands in innocency.

14 For all the day long have I been plagued, and chastened every morning.

15 If I say, I will speak thus; behold, I should offend against the generation of thy children.

16 When I thought to know this, it was too painful for me;

17 Until I went into the sanctuary of God; then understood I their end.

18 Surely thou didst set them in slippery places: thou castedst them down into destruction.

19 How are they brought into desolation, as in a moment! they are utterly consumed with terrors.

20 As a dream when one awaketh; so, O Lord, when thou awakest, thou shalt despise their image.

21 Thus my heart was grieved, and I was pricked in my reins.

22 So foolish was I, and ignorant: I was as a beast before thee.

23 Nevertheless I am continually with thee: thou hast holden me by my right hand.

24 Thou shalt guide me with thy counsel, and afterward receive me to glory.

25 Whom have I in heaven but thee? and there is none upon earth that I desire besides thee.

26 My flesh and my heart faileth: but God is the strength of my heart, and my portion for ever.

The Psalter

Selection 27
Psalm 77

1 I CRIED unto God with my voice, even unto God with my voice; and he gave ear unto me.

2 In the day of my trouble I sought the Lord: my sore ran in the night, and ceased not: my soul refused to be comforted.

3 I remembered God, and was troubled: I complained, and my spirit was overwhelmed.

4 Thou holdest mine eyes waking: I am so troubled that I cannot speak.

5 I have considered the days of old, the years of ancient times.

6 I call to remembrance my song in the night: I commune with mine own heart: and my spirit made diligent search.

7 Will the Lord cast off for ever? and will he be favorable no more?

8 Is his mercy clean gone for ever? doth his promise fail for evermore?

9 Hath God forgotten to be gracious? hath he in anger shut up his tender mercies?

10 And I said, This is my infirmity: but I will remember the years of the right hand of the Most High.

11 I will remember the works of the LORD: surely I will remember thy wonders of old.

12 I will meditate also of all thy work, and talk of thy doings.

13 Thy way, O God, is in the sanctuary: who is so great a God as our God?

14 Thou art the God that doest wonders: thou hast declared thy strength among the people.

15 Thou hast with thine arm redeemed thy people, the sons of Jacob and Joseph.

16 The waters saw thee, O God, the waters saw thee; they were afraid: the depths also were troubled.

17 The clouds poured out water: the skies sent out a sound: thine arrows also went abroad.

18 The voice of thy thunder was in the heaven: the lightnings lightened the world: the earth trembled and shook.

19 Thy way is in the sea, and thy path in the great waters, and thy footsteps are not known.

20 Thou leddest thy people like a flock by the hand of Moses and Aaron.

Selection 28
Psalm 80

1 GIVE ear, O Shepherd of Israel, thou that leadest Joseph like a flock; thou that dwellest between the cherubim, shine forth.

2 Before Ephraim and Benjamin and Manasseh stir up thy strength, and come and save us.

3 Turn us again, O God, and cause thy face to shine; and we shall be saved.

4 O LORD God of hosts, how long wilt thou be angry against the prayer of thy people?

5 Thou feedest them with the bread of tears; and givest them tears to drink in great measure.

6 Thou makest us a strife unto our neighbors: and our enemies laugh among themselves.

7 Turn us again, O God of hosts, and cause thy face to shine; and we shall be saved.

8 Thou hast brought a vine out of Egypt: thou hast cast out the heathen, and planted it.

9 Thou preparedst room before it, and didst cause it to take deep root, and it filled the land.

10 The hills were covered with the shadow of it, and the boughs thereof were like the goodly cedars.

11 She sent out her boughs unto the sea, and her branches unto the river.

The Psalter

12 Why hast thou then broken down her hedges, so that all they which pass by the way do pluck her?

13 The boar out of the wood doth waste it, and the wild beast of the field doth devour it.

14 Return, we beseech thee, O God of hosts: look down from heaven, and behold, and visit this vine;

15 And the vineyard which thy right hand hath planted, and the branch that thou madest strong for thyself.

16 It is burned with fire, it is cut down: they perish at the rebuke of thy countenance.

17 Let thy hand be upon the man of thy right hand, upon the son of man whom thou madest strong for thyself.

18 So will not we go back from thee: quicken us, and we will call upon thy name.

19 Turn us again, O LORD God of hosts, cause thy face to shine; and we shall be saved.

Selection 29

PSALM 84

1 HOW amiable are thy tabernacles, O LORD of hosts!

2 My soul longeth, yea, even fainteth for the courts of the LORD: my heart and my flesh crieth out for the living God.

3 Yea, a sparrow hath found a house, and the swallow a nest for herself, where she may lay her young, even thine altars, O LORD of hosts, my King, and my God.

4 Blessed are they that dwell in thy house: they will be still praising thee.

5 Blessed is the man whose strength is in thee; in whose heart are the ways of them.

6 Who passing through the valley of Baca make it a well; the rain also filleth the pools.

7 They go from strength to strength, every one of them in Zion appeareth before God.

8 O LORD God of hosts, hear my prayer: give ear, O God of Jacob.

9 Behold, O God our shield, and look upon the face of thine anointed.

10 For a day in thy courts is better than a thousand. I had rather be a doorkeeper in the house of my God, than to dwell in the tents of wickedness.

11 For the LORD God is a sun and shield: the LORD will give grace and glory: no good thing will he withhold from them that walk uprightly.

12 O LORD of hosts, blessed is the man that trusteth in thee.

PSALM 85

13 LORD, thou hast been favorable unto thy land: thou hast brought back the captivity of Jacob.

14 Thou hast forgiven the iniquity of thy people; thou hast covered all their sin.

15 Thou hast taken away all thy wrath: thou hast turned thyself from the fierceness of thine anger.

16 Turn us, O God of our salvation, and cause thine anger toward us to cease.

17 Wilt thou be angry with us for ever? wilt thou draw out thine anger to all generations?

18 Wilt thou not revive us again: that thy people may rejoice in thee?

19 Show us thy mercy, O LORD, and grant us thy salvation.

20 I will hear what God the LORD will speak: for he will speak peace unto his people, and to his saints: but let them not turn again to folly.

21 Surely his salvation is nigh them that fear him; that glory may dwell in our land.

22 Mercy and truth are met together; righteousness and peace have kissed each other.

23 Truth shall spring out of the earth; and righteousness shall look down from heaven.

The Psalter

24 Yea, the LORD shall give that which is good; and our land shall yield her increase.

25 Righteousness shall go before him; and shall set us in the way of his steps.

Selection 30

PSALM 86

1 BOW down thine ear, O LORD, hear me: for I am poor and needy.

2 Preserve my soul; for I am holy: O thou my God, save thy servant that trusteth in thee.

3 Be merciful unto me, O Lord: for I cry unto thee daily.

4 Rejoice the soul of thy servant: for unto thee, O Lord, do I lift up my soul.

5 For thou, Lord, art good, and ready to forgive; and plenteous in mercy unto all them that call upon thee.

6 Give ear, O LORD, unto my prayer; and attend to the voice of my supplications.

7 In the day of my trouble I will call upon thee: for thou wilt answer me.

8 Among the gods there is none like unto thee, O Lord; neither are there any works like unto thy works.

9 All nations whom thou hast made shall come and worship before thee, O Lord; and shall glorify thy name.

10 For thou art great, and doest wondrous things: thou art God alone.

11 Teach me thy way, O LORD; I will walk in thy truth: unite my heart to fear thy name.

12 I will praise thee, O Lord my God, with all my heart: and I will glorify thy name for evermore.

13 For great is thy mercy toward me: and thou hast delivered my soul from the lowest hell.

14 O God, the proud are risen against me, and the assemblies of violent men have sought after my soul; and have not set thee before them.

15 But thou, O Lord, art a God full of compassion, and gracious, longsuffering, and plenteous in mercy and truth.

16 O turn unto me, and have mercy upon me; give thy strength unto thy servant, and save the son of thine handmaid.

17 Show me a token for good; that they which hate me may see it, and be ashamed: because thou, LORD, hast holpen me, and comforted me.

PSALM 87

18 HIS foundation is in the holy mountains.

19 The LORD loveth the gates of Zion more than all the dwellings of Jacob.

20 Glorious things are spoken of thee, O city of God.

21 I will make mention of Rahab and Babylon to them that know me: behold Philistia, and Tyre, with Ethiopia; this man was born there.

22 And of Zion it shall be said, This and that man was born in her: and the Highest himself shall establish her.

23 The LORD shall count, when he writeth up the people, that this man was born there.

24 As well the singers as the players on instruments shall be there: all my springs are in thee.

Selection 31

PSALM 89 : 1-37

1 I WILL sing of the mercies of the LORD for ever: with my mouth will I make known thy faithfulness to all generations.

2 For I have said, Mercy shall be built up for ever: thy faithfulness shalt thou establish in the very heavens.

3 I have made a covenant with my chosen, I have sworn unto David my servant.

4 Thy seed will I establish for ever, and build up thy throne to all generations.

The Psalter

5 And the heavens shall praise thy wonders, O LORD: thy faithfulness also in the congregation of the saints.

6 For who in the heaven can be compared unto the LORD? who among the sons of the mighty can be likened unto the LORD?

7 God is greatly to be feared in the assembly of the saints, and to be had in reverence of all them that are about him.

8 O LORD God of hosts, who is a strong LORD like unto thee? or to thy faithfulness round about thee?

9 Thou rulest the raging of the sea: when the waves thereof arise, thou stillest them.

10 Thou hast broken Rahab in pieces, as one that is slain; thou hast scattered thine enemies with thy strong arm.

11 The heavens are thine, the earth also is thine: as for the world and the fulness thereof, thou hast founded them.

12 The north and the south thou hast created them: Tabor and Hermon shall rejoice in thy name.

13 Thou hast a mighty arm: strong is thy hand, and high is thy right hand.

14 Justice and judgment are the habitation of thy throne: mercy and truth shall go before thy face.

15 Blessed is the people that know the joyful sound: they shall walk, O LORD, in the light of thy countenance.

16 In thy name shall they rejoice all the day: and in thy righteousness shall they be exalted.

17 For thou art the glory of their strength: and in thy favor our horn shall be exalted.

18 For the LORD is our defence; and the Holy One of Israel is our King.

19 Then thou spakest in vision to thy Holy One, and saidst, I have laid help upon one that is mighty; I have exalted one chosen out of the people.

20 I have found David my servant; with my holy oil have I anointed him:

21 With whom my hand shall be established: mine arm also shall strengthen him.

22 The enemy shall not exact upon him; nor the son of wickedness afflict him.

23 And I will beat down his foes before his face, and plague them that hate him.

24 But my faithfulness and my mercy shall be with him: and in my name shall his horn be exalted.

25 I will set his hand also in the sea, and his right hand in the rivers.

26 He shall cry unto me, Thou art my Father, my God, and the Rock of my salvation.

27 Also I will make him my firstborn, higher than the kings of the earth.

28 My mercy will I keep for him for evermore, and my covenant shall stand fast with him.

29 His seed also will I make to endure for ever, and his throne as the days of heaven.

30 If his children forsake my law, and walk not in my judgments;

31 If they break my statutes, and keep not my commandments;

32 Then will I visit their transgression with the rod, and their iniquity with stripes.

33 Nevertheless my loving-kindness will I not utterly take from him, nor suffer my faithfulness to fail.

34 My covenant will I not break, nor alter the thing that is gone out of my lips.

35 Once have I sworn by my holiness that I will not lie unto David.

36 His seed shall endure for ever, and his throne as the sun before me.

37 It shall be established for ever as the moon, and as a faithful witness in heaven.

The Psalter

Selection 32
Psalm 90

1 LORD, thou hast been our dwelling-place in all generations.

2 Before the mountains were brought forth, or ever thou hadst formed the earth and the world, even from everlasting to everlasting, thou art God.

3 Thou turnest man to destruction; and sayest, Return, ye children of men.

4 For a thousand years in thy sight are but as yesterday when it is past, and as a watch in the night.

5 Thou carriest them away as with a flood; they are as a sleep: in the morning they are like grass which groweth up.

6 In the morning it flourisheth, and groweth up; in the evening it is cut down, and withereth.

7 For we are consumed by thine anger, and by thy wrath are we troubled.

8 Thou hast set our iniquities before thee, our secret sins in the light of thy countenance.

9 For all our days are passed away in thy wrath: we spend our years as a tale that is told.

10 The days of our years are three-score years and ten; and if by reason of strength they be fourscore years, yet is their strength labor and sorrow; for it is soon cut off, and we fly away.

11 Who knoweth the power of thine anger? even according to thy fear, so is thy wrath.

12 So teach us to number our days, that we may apply our hearts unto wisdom.

13 Return, O LORD, how long? and let it repent thee concerning thy servants.

14 O satisfy us early with thy mercy; that we may rejoice and be glad all our days.

15 Make us glad according to the days wherein thou hast afflicted us, and the years wherein we have seen evil.

16 Let thy work appear unto thy servants, and thy glory unto their children.

17 And let the beauty of the LORD our God be upon us: and establish thou the work of our hands upon us; yea, the work of our hands establish thou it.

Selection 33
Psalm 91

1 HE that dwelleth in the secret place of the Most High shall abide under the shadow of the Almighty.

2 I will say of the LORD, He is my refuge and my fortress: my God; in him will I trust.

3 Surely he shall deliver thee from the snare of the fowler, and from the noisome pestilence.

4 He shall cover thee with his feathers, and under his wings shalt thou trust: his truth shall be thy shield and buckler.

5 Thou shalt not be afraid for the terror by night; nor for the arrow that flieth by day;

6 Nor for the pestilence that walketh in darkness; nor for the destruction that wasteth at noonday.

7 A thousand shall fall at thy side, and ten thousand at thy right hand; but it shall not come nigh thee.

8 Only with thine eyes shalt thou behold and see the reward of the wicked.

9 Because thou hast made the LORD, which is my refuge, even the Most High, thy habitation;

10 There shall no evil befall thee, neither shall any plague come nigh thy dwelling.

11 For he shall give his angels charge over thee, to keep thee in all thy ways.

12 They shall bear thee up in their hands, lest thou dash thy foot against a stone.

13 Thou shalt tread upon the lion and adder: the young lion and the dragon shalt thou trample under feet.

The Psalter

14 Because he hath set his love upon me, therefore will I deliver him: I will set him on high, because he hath known my name.

15 He shall call upon me, and I will answer him: I will be with him in trouble; I will deliver him, and honor him.

16 With long life will I satisfy him, and show him my salvation.

Selection 34
PSALM 92

1 IT is a good thing to give thanks unto the LORD, and to sing praises unto thy name, O Most High:

2 To show forth thy loving-kindness in the morning, and thy faithfulness every night,

3 Upon an instrument of ten strings, and upon the psaltery; upon the harp with a solemn sound.

4 For thou, LORD, hast made me glad through thy work: I will triumph in the works of thy hands.

5 O LORD, how great are thy works! and thy thoughts are very deep.

6 A brutish man knoweth not; neither doth a fool understand this.

7 When the wicked spring as the grass, and when all the workers of iniquity do flourish; it is that they shall be destroyed for ever:

8 But thou, LORD, art most high for evermore.

9 For, lo, thine enemies, O LORD, for, lo, thine enemies shall perish; all the workers of iniquity shall be scattered.

10 But my horn shalt thou exalt like the horn of a unicorn: I shall be anointed with fresh oil.

11 Mine eye also shall see my desire on mine enemies, and mine ears shall hear my desire of the wicked that rise up against me.

12 The righteous shall flourish like the palm tree: he shall grow like a cedar in Lebanon.

13 Those that be planted in the house of the LORD shall flourish in the courts of our God.

14 They shall still bring forth fruit in old age; they shall be fat and flourishing;

15 To show that the LORD is upright: he is my rock, and there is no unrighteousness in him.

PSALM 93

16 THE LORD reigneth, he is clothed with majesty; the LORD is clothed with strength, wherewith he hath girded himself: the world also is stablished, that it cannot be moved.

17 Thy throne is established of old: thou art from everlasting.

18 The floods have lifted up, O LORD, the floods have lifted up their voice; the floods lift up their waves.

19 The LORD on high is mightier than the noise of many waters, yea, than the mighty waves of the sea.

20 Thy testimonies are very sure: holiness becometh thine house, O LORD, for ever.

Selection 35
PSALM 95

1 O COME, let us sing unto the LORD: let us make a joyful noise to the Rock of our salvation.

2 Let us come before his presence with thanksgiving, and make a joyful noise unto him with psalms.

3 For the LORD is a great God, and a great King above all gods.

4 In his hands are the deep places of the earth: the strength of the hills is his also.

5 The sea is his, and he made it: and his hands formed the dry land.

6 O come, let us worship and bow down: let us kneel before the LORD our maker.

The Psalter

7 For he is our God; and we are the people of his pasture, and the sheep of his hand. To day if ye will hear his voice,

8 Harden not your heart, as in the provocation, and as in the day of temptation in the wilderness:

9 When your fathers tempted me, proved me, and saw my work.

10 Forty years long was I grieved with this generation, and said, It is a people that do err in their heart, and they have not known my ways:

11 Unto whom I sware in my wrath that they should not enter into my rest.

Psalm 96

12 O SING unto the Lord a new song: sing unto the Lord, all the earth.

13 Sing unto the Lord, bless his name; show forth his salvation from day to day.

14 Declare his glory among the heathen, his wonders among all people.

15 For the Lord is great, and greatly to be praised: he is to be feared above all gods.

16 For all the gods of the nations are idols: but the Lord made the heavens.

17 Honor and majesty are before him: strength and beauty are in his sanctuary.

18 Give unto the Lord, O ye kindreds of the people, give unto the Lord glory and strength.

19 Give unto the Lord the glory due unto his name: bring an offering, and come into his courts.

20 O worship the Lord in the beauty of holiness: fear before him, all the earth.

21 Say among the heathen that the Lord reigneth: the world also shall be established that it shall not be moved: he shall judge the people righteously.

22 Let the heavens rejoice, and let the earth be glad; let the sea roar, and the fulness thereof.

23 Let the field be joyful, and all that is therein: then shall all the trees of the wood rejoice

24 Before the Lord: for he cometh, for he cometh to judge the earth: he shall judge the world with righteousness, and the people with his truth.

Selection 36
Psalm 97

1 THE Lord reigneth; let the earth rejoice; let the multitude of isles be glad thereof.

2 Clouds and darkness are round about him: righteousness and judgment are the habitation of his throne.

3 A fire goeth before him, and burneth up his enemies round about.

4 His lightnings enlightened the world: the earth saw, and trembled.

5 The hills melted like wax at the presence of the Lord, at the presence of the Lord of the whole earth.

6 The heavens declare his righteousness, and all the people see his glory.

7 Confounded be all they that serve graven images, that boast themselves of idols: worship him, all ye gods.

8 Zion heard, and was glad; and the daughters of Judah rejoiced because of thy judgments, O Lord.

9 For thou, Lord, art high above all the earth: thou art exalted far above all gods.

10 Ye that love the Lord, hate evil: he preserveth the souls of his saints; he delivereth them out of the hand of the wicked.

11 Light is sown for the righteous, and gladness for the upright in heart.

12 Rejoice in the Lord, ye righteous; and give thanks at the remembrance of his holiness.

The Psalter

Psalm 98

13 O SING unto the Lord a new song; for he hath done marvellous things: his right hand, and his holy arm, hath gotten him the victory.

14 The Lord hath made known his salvation: his righteousness hath he openly showed in the sight of the heathen.

15 He hath remembered his mercy and his truth toward the house of Israel: all the ends of the earth have seen the salvation of our God.

16 Make a joyful noise unto the Lord, all the earth: make a loud noise, and rejoice, and sing praise.

17 Sing unto the Lord with the harp; with the harp, and the voice of a psalm.

18 With trumpets and sound of cornet make a joyful noise before the Lord, the King.

19 Let the sea roar, and the fulness thereof; the world, and they that dwell therein.

20 Let the floods clap their hands: let the hills be joyful together

21 Before the Lord; for he cometh to judge the earth: with righteousness shall he judge the world, and the people with equity.

Psalm 99

22 THE Lord reigneth; let the people tremble: he sitteth between the cherubim; let the earth be moved.

23 The Lord is great in Zion; and he is high above all the people.

24 Let them praise thy great and terrible name; for it is holy.

25 The king's strength also loveth judgment; thou dost establish equity, thou executest judgment and righteousness in Jacob.

26 Exalt ye the Lord our God, and worship at his footstool; for he is holy.

27 Moses and Aaron among his priests, and Samuel among them that call upon his name; they called upon the Lord, and he answered them.

28 He spake unto them in the cloudy pillar: they kept his testimonies, and the ordinance that he gave them.

29 Thou answeredst them, O Lord our God: thou wast a God that forgavest them, though thou tookest vengeance of their inventions.

30 Exalt the Lord our God, and worship at his holy hill; for the Lord our God is holy.

Selection 37

Psalm 100

1 MAKE a joyful noise unto the Lord, all ye lands.

2 Serve the Lord with gladness: come before his presence with singing.

3 Know ye that the Lord he is God: it is he that hath made us, and not we ourselves; we are his people, and the sheep of his pasture.

4 Enter into his gates with thanksgiving, and into his courts with praise: be thankful unto him, and bless his name.

5 For the Lord is good; his mercy is everlasting; and his truth endureth to all generations.

Psalm 103

6 BLESS the Lord, O my soul: and all that is within me, bless his holy name.

7 Bless the Lord, O my soul, and forget not all his benefits:

8 Who forgiveth all thine iniquities; who healeth all thy diseases;

9 Who redeemeth thy life from destruction; who crowneth thee with lovingkindness and tender mercies;

10 Who satisfieth thy mouth with good things; so that thy youth is renewed like the eagle's.

11 The Lord executeth righteousness and judgment for all that are oppressed.

12 He made known his ways unto Moses, his acts unto the children of Israel.

13 The LORD is merciful and gracious, slow to anger, and plenteous in mercy.

14 He will not always chide: neither will he keep his anger for ever.

15 He hath not dealt with us after our sins; nor rewarded us according to our iniquities.

16 For as the heaven is high above the earth, so great is his mercy toward them that fear him.

17 As far as the east is from the west, so far hath he removed our transgressions from us.

18 Like as a father pitieth his children, so the LORD pitieth them that fear him.

19 For he knoweth our frame; he remembereth that we are dust.

20 As for man, his days are as grass: as a flower of the field, so he flourisheth.

21 For the wind passeth over it, and it is gone; and the place thereof shall know it no more.

22 But the mercy of the LORD is from everlasting to everlasting upon them that fear him, and his righteousness unto children's children;

23 To such as keep his covenant, and to those that remember his commandments to do them.

24 The LORD hath prepared his throne in the heavens; and his kingdom ruleth over all.

25 Bless the LORD, ye his angels, that excel in strength, that do his commandments, hearkening unto the voice of his word.

26 Bless ye the LORD, all ye his hosts; ye ministers of his, that do his pleasure.

27 Bless the LORD, all his works in all places of his dominion: bless the LORD, O my soul.

Selection 38
PSALM 104

1 BLESS the LORD, O my soul. O LORD my God, thou art very great; thou art clothed with honor and majesty:

2 Who coverest thyself with light as with a garment: who stretchest out the heavens like a curtain:

3 Who layeth the beams of his chambers in the waters: who maketh the clouds his chariot: who walketh upon the wings of the wind:

4 Who maketh his angels spirits; his ministers a flaming fire:

5 Who laid the foundations of the earth, that it should not be removed for ever.

6 Thou coveredst it with the deep as with a garment: the waters stood above the mountains.

7 At thy rebuke they fled; at the voice of thy thunder they hasted away.

8 They go up by the mountains; they go down by the valleys unto the place which thou hast founded for them.

9 Thou has set a bound that they may not pass over; that they turn not again to cover the earth.

10 He sendeth the springs into the valleys, which run among the hills.

11 They give drink to every beast of the field: the wild asses quench their thirst.

12 By them shall the fowls of the heaven have their habitation, which sing among the branches.

13 He watereth the hills from his chambers: the earth is satisfied with the fruit of thy works.

14 He causeth the grass to grow for the cattle, and herb for the service of man: that he may bring forth food out of the earth;

15 And wine that maketh glad the heart of man, and oil to make his face to shine, and bread which strengtheneth man's heart.

16 The trees of the LORD are full of sap; the cedars of Lebanon, which he hath planted;

17 Where the birds make their nests:

The Psalter

as for the stork, the fir trees are her house.

18 The high hills are a refuge for the wild goats; and the rocks for the conies.

19 He appointed the moon for seasons: the sun knoweth his going down.

20 Thou makest darkness, and it is night: wherein all the beasts of the forest do creep forth.

21 The young lions roar after their prey, and seek their meat from God.

22 The sun ariseth, they gather themselves together, and lay them down in their dens.

23 Man goeth forth unto his work and to his labor until the evening.

24 O LORD, how manifold are thy works! in wisdom hast thou made them all: the earth is full of thy riches.

25 So is this great and wide sea, wherein are things creeping innumerable, both small and great beasts.

26 There go the ships: there is that leviathan, whom thou hast made to play therein.

27 These wait all upon thee; that thou mayest give them their meat in due season.

28 That thou givest them they gather: thou openest thine hand, they are filled with good.

29 Thou hidest thy face, they are troubled: thou takest away their breath, they die, and return to their dust.

30 Thou sendest forth thy spirit, they are created: and thou renewest the face of the earth.

31 The glory of the LORD shall endure for ever: the LORD shall rejoice in his works.

32 He looketh on the earth, and it trembleth: he toucheth the hills, and they smoke.

33 I will sing unto the LORD as long as I live: I will sing praise to my God while I have my being.

34 My meditation of him shall be sweet: I will be glad in the LORD.

35 Let the sinners be consumed out of the earth, and let the wicked be no more. Bless thou the LORD, O my soul. Praise ye the LORD.

Selection 39
PSALM 107 : 1-22

1 O GIVE thanks unto the LORD, for he is good: for his mercy endureth for ever.

2 Let the redeemed of the LORD say so, whom he hath redeemed from the hand of the enemy;

3 And gathered them out of the lands, from the east, and from the west, from the north, and from the south.

4 They wandered in the wilderness in a solitary way; they found no city to dwell in.

5 Hungry and thirsty, their soul fainted in them.

6 Then they cried unto the LORD in their trouble, and he delivered them out of their distresses.

7 And he led them forth by the right way, that they might go to a city of habitation.

8 Oh that men would praise the LORD for his goodness, and for his wonderful works to the children of men!

9 For he satisfieth the longing soul, and filleth the hungry soul with goodness.

10 Such as sit in darkness and in the shadow of death, being bound in affliction and iron;

11 Because they rebelled against the words of God, and contemned the counsel of the Most High:

12 Therefore he brought down their heart with labor; they fell down, and there was none to help.

13 Then they cried unto the LORD in their trouble, and he saved them out of their distresses.

The Psalter

14 He brought them out of darkness and the shadow of death, and brake their bands in sunder.

15 Oh that men would praise the LORD for his goodness, and for his wonderful works to the children of men!

16 For he hath broken the gates of brass, and cut the bars of iron in sunder.

17 Fools, because of their transgression, and because of their iniquities, are afflicted.

18 Their soul abhorreth all manner of meat; and they draw near unto the gates of death.

19 Then they cry unto the LORD in their trouble, and he saveth them out of their distresses.

20 He sent his word, and healed them, and delivered them from their destructions.

21 Oh that men would praise the LORD for his goodness, and for his wonderful works to the children of men!

22 And let them sacrifice the sacrifices of thanksgiving, and declare his works with rejoicing.

Selection 40

PSALM 107 : 23–43

1 THEY that go down to the sea in ships, that do business in great waters;

2 These see the works of the LORD, and his wonders in the deep.

3 For he commandeth, and raiseth the stormy wind, which lifteth up the waves thereof.

4 They mount up to the heaven, they go down again to the depths: their soul is melted because of trouble.

5 They reel to and fro, and stagger like a drunken man, and are at their wit's end.

6 Then they cry unto the LORD in their trouble, and he bringeth them out of their distresses.

7 He maketh the storm a calm, so that the waves thereof are still.

8 Then are they glad because they be quiet; so he bringeth them unto their desired haven.

9 Oh that men would praise the LORD for his goodness, and for his wonderful works to the children of men!

10 Let them exalt him also in the congregation of the people, and praise him in the assembly of the elders.

11 He turneth rivers into a wilderness, and the watersprings into dry ground;

12 A fruitful land into barrenness, for the wickedness of them that dwell therein.

13 He turneth the wilderness into a standing water, and dry ground into watersprings.

14 And there he maketh the hungry to dwell, that they may prepare a city for habitation;

15 And sow the fields, and plant vineyards, which may yield fruits of increase.

16 He blesseth them also, so that they are multiplied greatly; and suffereth not their cattle to decrease.

17 Again, they are minished and brought low through oppression, affliction, and sorrow.

18 He poureth contempt upon princes, and causeth them to wander in the wilderness, where there is no way.

19 Yet setteth he the poor on high from affliction, and maketh him families like a flock.

20 The righteous shall see it, and rejoice: and all iniquity shall stop her mouth.

21 Whoso is wise, and will observe these things, even they shall understand the loving-kindness of the LORD.

Selection 41

PSALM 110

1 THE LORD said unto my Lord, Sit thou at my right hand, until I make thine enemies thy footstool.

The Psalter

2 The LORD shall send the rod of thy strength out of Zion: rule thou in the midst of thine enemies.

3 Thy people shall be willing in the day of thy power, in the beauties of holiness from the womb of the morning: thou hast the dew of thy youth.

4 The LORD hath sworn, and will not repent, Thou art a priest for ever after the order of Melchizedek.

5 The Lord at thy right hand shall strike through kings in the day of his wrath.

6 He shall judge among the heathen, he shall fill the places with the dead bodies; he shall wound the heads over many countries.

7 He shall drink of the brook in the way: therefore shall he lift up the head.

PSALM 111

8 PRAISE ye the LORD. I will praise the LORD with my whole heart, in the assembly of the upright, and in the congregation.

9 The works of the LORD are great, sought out of all them that have pleasure therein.

10 His work is honorable and glorious: and his righteousness endureth for ever.

11 He hath made his wonderful works to be remembered: the LORD is gracious and full of compassion.

12 He hath given meat unto them that fear him: he will ever be mindful of his covenant.

13 He hath showed his people the power of his works, that he may give them the heritage of the heathen.

14 The works of his hands are verity and judgment; all his commandments are sure.

15 They stand fast for ever and ever, and are done in truth and uprightness.

16 He sent redemption unto his people: he hath commanded his covenant for ever: holy and reverend is his name.

17 The fear of the LORD is the beginning of wisdom: a good understanding have all they that do his commandments: his praise endureth for ever.

PSALM 112

18 PRAISE ye the LORD. Blessed is the man that feareth the LORD, that delighteth greatly in his commandments.

19 His seed shall be mighty upon earth: the generation of the upright shall be blessed.

20 Wealth and riches shall be in his house: and his righteousness endureth for ever.

21 Unto the upright there ariseth light in the darkness: he is gracious, and full of compassion, and righteous.

22 A good man showeth favor, and lendeth: he will guide his affairs with discretion.

23 Surely he shall not be moved for ever: the righteous shall be in everlasting remembrance.

24 He shall not be afraid of evil tidings: his heart is fixed, trusting in the LORD.

25 His heart is established, he shall not be afraid, until he see his desire upon his enemies.

26 He hath dispersed, he hath given to the poor; his righteousness endureth for ever; his horn shall be exalted with honor.

27 The wicked shall see it, and be grieved: he shall gnash with his teeth, and melt away; the desire of the wicked shall perish.

Selection 42

PSALM 113 : 1-6

1 PRAISE ye the LORD. Praise, O ye servants of the LORD, praise the name of the LORD.

The Psalter

2 Blessed be the name of the LORD from this time forth and for evermore.

3 From the rising of the sun unto the going down of the same the LORD'S name is to be praised.

4 The LORD is high above all nations, and his glory above the heavens.

5 Who is like unto the LORD our God, who dwelleth on high,

6 Who humbleth himself to behold the things that are in heaven, and in the earth!

Psalm 115

7 NOT unto us, O LORD, not unto us, but unto thy name give glory, for thy mercy, and for thy truth's sake.

8 Wherefore should the heathen say, Where is now their God?

9 But our God is in the heavens: he hath done whatsoever he hath pleased.

10 Their idols are silver and gold, the work of men's hands.

11 They have mouths, but they speak not: eyes have they, but they see not:

12 They have ears, but they hear not: noses have they, but they smell not:

13 They have hands, but they handle not: feet have they, but they walk not: neither speak they through their throat.

14 They that make them are like unto them: so is every one that trusteth in them.

15 O Israel, trust thou in the LORD: he is their help and their shield.

16 O house of Aaron, trust in the LORD: he is their help and their shield.

17 Ye that fear the LORD, trust in the LORD: he is their help and their shield.

18 The LORD hath been mindful of us: he will bless us; he will bless the house of Israel; he will bless the house of Aaron.

19 He will bless them that fear the LORD, both small and great.

20 The LORD shall increase you more and more, you and your children.

21 Ye are blessed of the LORD which made heaven and earth.

22 The heaven, even the heavens, are the LORD'S: but the earth hath he given to the children of men.

23 The dead praise not the LORD, neither any that go down into silence.

24 But we will bless the LORD from this time forth and for evermore. Praise the LORD.

Selection 43

Psalm 116

1 I LOVE the LORD, because he hath heard my voice and my supplications.

2 Because he hath inclined his ear unto me, therefore will I call upon him as long as I live.

3 The sorrows of death compassed me, and the pains of hell gat hold upon me: I found trouble and sorrow.

4 Then called I upon the name of the LORD; O LORD, I beseech thee, deliver my soul.

5 Gracious is the LORD, and righteous; yea, our God is merciful.

6 The LORD preserveth the simple: I was brought low, and he helped me.

7 Return unto thy rest, O my soul; for the LORD hath dealt bountifully with thee.

8 For thou hast delivered my soul from death, mine eyes from tears, and my feet from falling.

9 I will walk before the LORD in the land of the living.

10 I believed, therefore have I spoken: I was greatly afflicted:

11 I said in my haste, All men are liars.

12 What shall I render unto the LORD for all his benefits toward me?

13 I will take the cup of salvation, and call upon the name of the LORD.

14 I will pay my vows unto the LORD now in the presence of all his people.

15 Precious in the sight of the LORD is the death of his saints.

The Psalter

16 O LORD, truly I am thy servant ; I am thy servant, and the son of thine handmaid : thou hast loosed my bonds.

17 I will offer to thee the sacrifice of thanksgiving, and will call upon the name of the LORD.

18 I will pay my vows unto the LORD now in the presence of all his people,

19 In the courts of the LORD's house, in the midst of thee, O Jerusalem. Praise ye the LORD.

PSALM 117

20 O PRAISE the LORD, all ye nations : praise him, all ye people.

21 For his merciful kindness is great toward us : and the truth of the LORD endureth for ever. Praise ye the LORD.

Selection 44

PSALM 118

1 O GIVE thanks unto the LORD ; for he is good : because his mercy endureth for ever.

2 Let Israel now say, that his mercy endureth for ever.

3 Let the house of Aaron now say, that his mercy endureth for ever.

4 Let them now that fear the LORD say, that his mercy endureth for ever.

5 I called upon the LORD in distress : the LORD answered me, and set me in a large place.

6 The LORD is on my side ; I will not fear : what can man do unto me?

7 The LORD taketh my part with them that help me : therefore shall I see my desire upon them that hate me.

8 It is better to trust in the LORD than to put confidence in man.

9 It is better to trust in the LORD than to put confidence in princes.

10 All nations compassed me about : but in the name of the LORD will I destroy them.

11 They compassed me about ; yea, they compassed me about : but in the name of the LORD I will destroy them.

12 They compassed me about like bees ; they are quenched as the fire of thorns : for in the name of the LORD I will destroy them.

13 Thou hast thrust sore at me that I might fall : but the LORD helped me.

14 The LORD is my strength and song, and is become my salvation.

15 The voice of rejoicing and salvation is in the tabernacles of the righteous : the right hand of the LORD doeth valiantly.

16 The right hand of the LORD is exalted : the right hand of the LORD doeth valiantly.

17 I shall not die, but live, and declare the works of the LORD.

18 The LORD hath chastened me sore : but he hath not given me over unto death.

19 Open to me the gates of righteousness ; I will go into them, and I will praise the LORD.

20 This gate of the LORD, into which the righteous shall enter.

21 I will praise thee : for thou hast heard me, and art become my salvation.

22 The stone which the builders refused is become the head stone of the corner.

23 This is the LORD's doing ; it is marvellous in our eyes.

24 This is the day which the LORD hath made ; we will rejoice and be glad in it.

25 Save now, I beseech thee, O LORD : O LORD, I beseech thee, send now prosperity.

26 Blessed be he that cometh in the name of the LORD : we have blessed you out of the house of the LORD.

27 God is the LORD, which hath showed us light : bind the sacrifice with cords, even unto the horns of the altar.

The Psalter

28 Thou art my God, and I will praise thee: thou art my God, I will exalt thee.

29 O give thanks unto the Lord; for he is good: for his mercy endureth for ever.

Selection 45
Psalm 119: 1–24

1 BLESSED are the undefiled in the way, who walk in the law of the Lord.

2 Blessed are they that keep his testimonies, and that seek him with the whole heart.

3 They also do no iniquity: they walk in his ways.

4 Thou hast commanded us to keep thy precepts diligently.

5 O that my ways were directed to keep thy statutes!

6 Then shall I not be ashamed, when I have respect unto all thy commandments.

7 I will praise thee with uprightness of heart, when I shall have learned thy righteous judgments.

8 I will keep thy statutes: O forsake me not utterly.

9 Wherewithal shall a young man cleanse his way? by taking heed thereto according to thy word.

10 With my whole heart have I sought thee: O let me not wander from thy commandments.

11 Thy word have I hid in mine heart, that I might not sin against thee.

12 Blessed art thou, O Lord: teach me thy statutes.

13 With my lips have I declared all the judgments of thy mouth.

14 I have rejoiced in the way of thy testimonies, as much as in all riches.

15 I will meditate in thy precepts, and have respect unto thy ways.

16 I will delight myself in thy statutes: I will not forget thy word.

17 Deal bountifully with thy servant, that I may live, and keep thy word.

18 Open thou mine eyes, that I may behold wondrous things out of thy law.

19 I am a stranger in the earth: hide not thy commandments from me.

20 My soul breaketh for the longing that it hath unto thy judgments at all times.

21 Thou hast rebuked the proud that are cursed, which do err from thy commandments.

22 Remove from me reproach and contempt; for I have kept thy testimonies.

23 Princes also did sit and speak against me: but thy servant did meditate in thy statutes.

24 Thy testimonies also are my delight, and my counsellors.

Selection 46
Psalm 119: 33–48, 89–96

1 TEACH me, O Lord, the way of thy statutes; and I shall keep it unto the end.

2 Give me understanding, and I shall keep thy law; yea, I shall observe it with my whole heart.

3 Make me to go in the path of thy commandments; for therein do I delight.

4 Incline my heart unto thy testimonies, and not to covetousness.

5 Turn away mine eyes from beholding vanity; and quicken thou me in thy way.

6 Stablish thy word unto thy servant, who is devoted to thy fear.

7 Turn away my reproach which I fear: for thy judgments are good.

8 Behold, I have longed after thy precepts: quicken me in thy righteousness.

9 Let thy mercies come also unto me, O Lord, even thy salvation, according to thy word.

10 So shall I have wherewith to answer him that reproacheth me: for I trust in thy word.

The Psalter

11 And take not the word of truth utterly out of my mouth; for I have hoped in thy judgments.

12 So shall I keep thy law continually for ever and ever.

13 And I will walk at liberty: for I seek thy precepts.

14 I will speak of thy testimonies also before kings, and will not be ashamed.

15 And I will delight myself in thy commandments, which I have loved.

16 My hands also will I lift up unto thy commandments, which I have loved; and I will meditate in thy statutes.

17 For ever, O LORD, thy word is settled in heaven.

18 Thy faithfulness is unto all generations: thou hast established the earth, and it abideth.

19 They continue this day according to thine ordinances: for all are thy servants.

20 Unless thy law had been my delights, I should then have perished in mine affliction.

21 I will never forget thy precepts: for with them thou hast quickened me.

22 I am thine, save me; for I have sought thy precepts.

23 The wicked have waited for me to destroy me: but I will consider thy testimonies.

24 I have seen an end of all perfection: but thy commandment is exceeding broad.

Selection 47
PSALM 119 : 97–120

1 O HOW love I thy law! it is my meditation all the day.

2 Thou through thy commandments hast made me wiser than mine enemies: for they are ever with me.

3 I have more understanding than all my teachers: for thy testimonies are my meditation.

4 I understand more than the ancients, because I keep thy precepts.

5 I have refrained my feet from every evil way, that I might keep thy word.

6 I have not departed from thy judgments: for thou hast taught me.

7 How sweet are thy words unto my taste! yea, sweeter than honey to my mouth.

8 Through thy precepts I get understanding: therefore I hate every false way.

9 Thy word is a lamp unto my feet, and a light unto my path.

10 I have sworn, and I will perform it, that I will keep thy righteous judgments.

11 I am afflicted very much: quicken me, O LORD, according unto thy word.

12 Accept, I beseech thee, the freewill offerings of my mouth, O LORD, and teach me thy judgments.

13 My soul is continually in my hand: yet do I not forget thy law.

14 The wicked have laid a snare for me: yet I erred not from thy precepts.

15 Thy testimonies have I taken as a heritage for ever: for they are the rejoicing of my heart.

16 I have inclined mine heart to perform thy statutes always, even unto the end.

17 I hate vain thoughts: but thy law do I love.

18 Thou art my hiding place and my shield: I hope in thy word.

19 Depart from me, ye evil doers: for I will keep the commandments of my God.

20 Uphold me according unto thy word, that I may live: and let me not be ashamed of my hope.

21 Hold thou me up, and I shall be safe: and I will have respect unto thy statutes continually.

22 Thou hast trodden down all them that err from thy statutes: for their deceit is falsehood.

23 Thou puttest away all the wicked

The Psalter

of the earth like dross: therefore I love thy testimonies.

24 My flesh trembleth for fear of thee; and I am afraid of thy judgments.

Selection 48

Psalm 121

1 I WILL lift up mine eyes unto the hills, from whence cometh my help.

2 My help cometh from the LORD, which made heaven and earth.

3 He will not suffer thy foot to be moved: he that keepeth thee will not slumber.

4 Behold, he that keepeth Israel shall neither slumber nor sleep.

5 The LORD is thy keeper: the LORD is thy shade upon thy right hand.

6 The sun shall not smite thee by day, nor the moon by night.

7 The LORD shall preserve thee from all evil: he shall preserve thy soul.

8 The LORD shall preserve thy going out and thy coming in from this time forth, and even for evermore.

Psalm 122

9 I WAS glad when they said unto me, Let us go into the house of the LORD.

10 Our feet shall stand within thy gates, O Jerusalem.

11 Jerusalem is builded as a city that is compact together:

12 Whither the tribes go up, the tribes of the LORD, unto the testimony of Israel, to give thanks unto the name of the LORD.

13 For there are set thrones of judgment, the thrones of the house of David.

14 Pray for the peace of Jerusalem: they shall prosper that love thee.

15 Peace be within thy walls, and prosperity within thy palaces.

16 For my brethren and companions' sakes, I will now say, Peace be within thee.

17 Because of the house of the LORD our God I will seek thy good.

Psalm 123

18 UNTO thee lift I up mine eyes, O thou that dwellest in the heavens.

19 Behold, as the eyes of servants look unto the hand of their masters, and as the eyes of a maiden unto the hand of her mistress; so our eyes wait upon the LORD our God, until that he have mercy upon us.

20 Have mercy upon us, O LORD, have mercy upon us: for we are exceedingly filled with contempt.

21 Our soul is exceedingly filled with the scorning of those that are at ease, and with the contempt of the proud.

Selection 49

Psalm 124

1 IF it had not been the LORD who was on our side, now may Israel say;

2 If it had not been the LORD who was on our side, when men rose up against us:

3 Then they had swallowed us up quick, when their wrath was kindled against us:

4 Then the waters had overwhelmed us, the stream had gone over our soul:

5 Then the proud waters had gone over our soul.

6 Blessed be the LORD, who hath not given us as a prey to their teeth.

7 Our soul is escaped as a bird out of the snare of the fowlers: the snare is broken, and we are escaped.

8 Our help is in the name of the LORD, who made heaven and earth.

Psalm 125

9 THEY that trust in the LORD shall be as mount Zion, which cannot be removed, but abideth for ever.

10 As the mountains are round about Jerusalem, so the LORD is round about his people from henceforth even for ever.

The Psalter

11 For the rod of the wicked shall not rest upon the lot of the righteous; lest the righteous put forth their hands unto iniquity.

12 Do good, O LORD, unto those that be good, and to them that are upright in their hearts.

13 As for such as turn aside unto their crooked ways, the LORD shall lead them forth with the workers of iniquity: but peace shall be upon Israel.

PSALM 126

14 WHEN the LORD turned again the captivity of Zion, we were like them that dream.

15 Then was our mouth filled with laughter, and our tongue with singing: then said they among the heathen, The LORD hath done great things for them.

16 The LORD hath done great things for us; whereof we are glad.

17 Turn again our captivity, O LORD, as the streams in the south.

18 They that sow in tears shall reap in joy.

19 He that goeth forth and weepeth, bearing precious seed, shall doubtless come again with rejoicing, bringing his sheaves with him.

PSALM 127

20 EXCEPT the LORD build the house, they labor in vain that build it: except the LORD keep the city, the watchman waketh but in vain.

21 It is vain for you to rise up early, to sit up late, to eat the bread of sorrows: for so he giveth his beloved sleep.

22 Lo, children are a heritage of the LORD: and the fruit of the womb is his reward.

23 As arrows are in the hand of a mighty man; so are children of the youth.

24 Happy is the man that hath his quiver full of them: they shall not be ashamed, but they shall speak with the enemies in the gate.

Selection 50
PSALM 130

1 OUT of the depths have I cried unto thee, O LORD.

2 Lord, hear my voice: let thine ears be attentive to the voice of my supplications.

3 If thou, LORD, shouldest mark iniquities, O Lord, who shall stand?

4 But there is forgiveness with thee, that thou mayest be feared.

5 I wait for the LORD, my soul doth wait, and in his word do I hope.

6 My soul waiteth for the Lord more than they that watch for the morning: I say, more than they that watch for the morning.

7 Let Israel hope in the LORD: for with the LORD there is mercy, and with him is plenteous redemption.

8 And he shall redeem Israel from all his iniquities.

PSALM 131

9 LORD, my heart is not haughty, nor mine eyes lofty: neither do I exercise myself in great matters, or in things too high for me.

10 Surely I have behaved and quieted myself, as a child that is weaned of his mother: my soul is even as a weaned child.

11 Let Israel hope in the LORD from henceforth and for ever.

PSALM 132

12 LORD, remember David, and all his afflictions:

13 How he sware unto the LORD, and vowed unto the mighty God of Jacob;

14 Surely I will not come into the tabernacle of my house, nor go up into my bed;

15 I will not give sleep to mine eyes, or slumber to mine eyelids,

16 Until I find out a place for the LORD, a habitation for the mighty God of Jacob.

17 Lo, we heard of it at Ephratah : we found it in the fields of the wood.

18 We will go into his tabernacles: we will worship at his footstool.

19 Arise, O LORD, into thy rest ; thou, and the ark of thy strength.

20 Let thy priests be clothed with righteousness : and let thy saints shout for joy.

21 For thy servant David's sake turn not away the face of thine anointed.

22 The LORD hath sworn in truth unto David ; he will not turn from it ; Of the fruit of thy body will I set upon thy throne.

23 If thy children will keep my covenant and my testimony that I shall teach them, their children shall also sit upon thy throne for evermore.

24 For the LORD hath chosen Zion ; he hath desired it for his habitation.

25 This is my rest for ever : here will I dwell ; for I have desired it.

26 I will abundantly bless her provision : I will satisfy her poor with bread.

27 I will also clothe her priests with salvation : and her saints shall shout aloud for joy.

28 There will I make the horn of David to bud : I have ordained a lamp for mine anointed.

29 His enemies will I clothe with shame : but upon himself shall his crown flourish.

Selection 51

PSALM 133

1 BEHOLD, how good and how pleasant it is for brethren to dwell together in unity !

2 It is like the precious ointment upon the head, that ran down upon the beard, even Aaron's beard : that went down to the skirts of his garments ;

3 As the dew of Hermon, and as the dew that descended upon the mountains of Zion : for there the LORD commanded the blessing, even life for evermore.

PSALM 134

4 BEHOLD, bless ye the LORD, all ye servants of the LORD, which by night stand in the house of the LORD.

5 Lift up your hands in the sanctuary, and bless the LORD.

6 The LORD that made heaven and earth bless thee out of Zion.

PSALM 135

7 PRAISE ye the LORD. Praise ye the name of the LORD ; praise him, O ye servants of the LORD.

8 Ye that stand in the house of the LORD, in the courts of the house of our God,

9 Praise the LORD ; for the LORD is good : sing praises unto his name ; for it is pleasant.

10 For the LORD hath chosen Jacob unto himself, and Israel for his peculiar treasure.

11 For I know that the LORD is great, and that our Lord is above all gods.

12 Whatsoever the LORD pleased, that did he in heaven, and in earth, in the seas, and all deep places.

13 He causeth the vapors to ascend from the ends of the earth ; he maketh lightnings for the rain ; he bringeth the wind out of his treasuries.

14 Who smote the firstborn of Egypt, both of man and beast.

15 Who sent tokens and wonders into the midst of thee, O Egypt, upon Pharaoh, and upon all his servants.

16 Who smote great nations, and slew mighty kings ;

The Psalter

17 Sihon king of the Amorites, and Og king of Bashan, and all the kingdoms of Canaan :

18 And gave their land for a heritage, a heritage unto Israel his people.

19 Thy name, O LORD, endureth for ever ; and thy memorial, O LORD, throughout all generations.

20 For the LORD will judge his people, and he will repent himself concerning his servants.

21 The idols of the heathen are silver and gold, the work of men's hands.

22 They have mouths, but they speak not ; eyes have they, but they see not ;

23 They have ears, but they hear not ; neither is there any breath in their mouths.

24 They that make them are like unto them : so is every one that trusteth in them.

25 Bless the LORD, O house of Israel : bless the LORD, O house of Aaron :

26 Bless the LORD, O house of Levi : ye that fear the LORD, bless the LORD.

27 Blessed be the LORD out of Zion, which dwelleth at Jerusalem. Praise ye the LORD.

Selection 52

PSALM 136 : 1-9, 23-26

1 O GIVE thanks unto the LORD ; for he is good : for his mercy endureth for ever.

2 O give thanks unto the God of gods : for his mercy endureth for ever.

3 O give thanks to the Lord of lords : for his mercy endureth for ever.

4 To him who alone doeth great wonders : for his mercy endureth for ever.

5 To him that by wisdom made the heavens : for his mercy endureth for ever.

6 To him that stretched out the earth above the waters : for his mercy endureth for ever.

7 To him that made great lights : for his mercy endureth for ever :

8 The sun to rule by day : for his mercy endureth for ever :

9 The moon and stars to rule by night : for his mercy endureth for ever.

10 Who remembered us in our low estate : for his mercy endureth for ever :

11 And hath redeemed us from our enemies : for his mercy endureth for ever.

12 Who giveth food to all flesh : for his mercy endureth for ever.

13 O give thanks unto the God of heaven : for his mercy endureth for ever.

PSALM 137 : 1-6

14 BY the rivers of Babylon, there we sat down, yea, we wept, when we remembered Zion.

15 We hanged our harps upon the willows in the midst thereof.

16 For there they that carried us away captive required of us a song ; and they that wasted us required of us mirth, saying, Sing us one of the songs of Zion.

17 How shall we sing the LORD'S song in a strange land ?

18 If I forget thee, O Jerusalem, let my right hand forget her cunning.

19 If I do not remember thee, let my tongue cleave to the roof of my mouth ; if I prefer not Jerusalem above my chief joy.

PSALM 138

20 I WILL praise thee with my whole heart : before the gods will I sing praise unto thee.

21 I will worship toward thy holy temple, and praise thy name for thy lovingkindness and for thy truth : for thou hast magnified thy word above all thy name.

22 In the day when I cried thou answeredst me, and strengthenedst me with strength in my soul.

23 All the kings of the earth shall

praise thee, O LORD, when they hear the words of thy mouth.

24 Yea, they shall sing in the ways of the LORD: for great is the glory of the LORD.

25 Though the LORD be high, yet hath he respect unto the lowly: but the proud he knoweth afar off.

26 Though I walk in the midst of trouble, thou wilt revive me: thou shalt stretch forth thine hand against the wrath of mine enemies, and thy right hand shall save me.

27 The LORD will perfect that which concerneth me: thy mercy, O LORD, endureth for ever: forsake not the works of thine own hands.

Selection 53
PSALM 139 : 1–12, 14–24

1 O LORD, thou hast searched me, and known me.

2 Thou knowest my downsitting and mine uprising; thou understandest my thought afar off.

3 Thou compassest my path and my lying down, and art acquainted with all my ways.

4 For there is not a word in my tongue, but, lo, O LORD, thou knowest it altogether.

5 Thou hast beset me behind and before, and laid thine hand upon me.

6 Such knowledge is too wonderful for me; it is high, I cannot attain unto it.

7 Whither shall I go from thy Spirit? or whither shall I flee from thy presence?

8 If I ascend up into heaven, thou art there: if I make my bed in hell, behold, thou art there.

9 If I take the wings of the morning, and dwell in the uttermost parts of the sea;

10 Even there shall thy hand lead me, and thy right hand shall hold me.

11 If I say, Surely the darkness shall cover me; even the night shall be light about me.

12 Yea, the darkness hideth not from thee; but the night shineth as the day: the darkness and the light are both alike to thee.

13 I will praise thee; for I am fearfully and wonderfully made: marvellous are thy works; and that my soul knoweth right well.

14 My substance was not hid from thee, when I was made in secret, and curiously wrought in the lowest parts of the earth.

15 Thine eyes did see my substance, yet being unperfect; and in thy book all my members were written, which in continuance were fashioned, when as yet there was none of them.

16 How precious also are thy thoughts unto me, O God! how great is the sum of them!

17 If I should count them, they are more in number than the sand: when I awake, I am still with thee.

18 Surely thou wilt slay the wicked, O God: depart from me therefore, ye bloody men.

19 For they speak against thee wickedly, and thine enemies take thy name in vain.

20 Do not I hate them, O LORD, that hate thee? and am not I grieved with those that rise up against thee?

21 I hate them with perfect hatred: I count them mine enemies.

22 Search me, O God, and know my heart: try me, and know my thoughts:

23 And see if there be any wicked way in me, and lead me in the way everlasting.

Selection 54
PSALM 141 : 1–3

1 LORD, I cry unto thee: make haste unto me; give ear unto my voice, when I cry unto thee.

The Psalter

2 Let my prayer be set forth before thee as incense ; and the lifting up of my hands as the evening sacrifice.

3 Set a watch, O LORD, before my mouth ; keep the door of my lips.

PSALM 142

4 I CRIED unto the LORD with my voice ; with my voice unto the LORD did I make my supplication.

5 I poured out my complaint before him ; I showed before him my trouble.

6 When my spirit was overwhelmed within me, then thou knewest my path. In the way wherein I walked have they privily laid a snare for me.

7 I looked on my right hand, and beheld, but there was no man that would know me : refuge failed me ; no man cared for my soul.

8 I cried unto thee, O LORD : I said, Thou art my refuge and my portion in the land of the living.

9 Attend unto my cry ; for I am brought very low : deliver me from my persecutors ; for they are stronger than I.

10 Bring my soul out of prison, that I may praise thy name : the righteous shall compass me about ; for thou shalt deal bountifully with me.

PSALM 143 : 1-11

11 HEAR my prayer, O LORD, give ear to my supplications : in thy faithfulness answer me, and in thy righteousness.

12 And enter not into judgment with thy servant : for in thy sight shall no man living be justified.

13 For the enemy hath persecuted my soul ; he hath smitten my life down to the ground ; he hath made me to dwell in darkness, as those that have been long dead.

14 Therefore is my spirit overwhelmed within me ; my heart within me is desolate.

15 I remember the days of old ; I meditate on all thy works ; I muse on the work of thy hands.

16 I stretch forth my hands unto thee : my soul thirsteth after thee, as a thirsty land.

17 Hear me speedily, O LORD ; my spirit faileth : hide not thy face from me, lest I be like unto them that go down into the pit.

18 Cause me to hear thy loving-kindness in the morning ; for in thee do I trust : cause me to know the way wherein I should walk ; for I lift up my soul unto thee.

19 Deliver me, O LORD, from mine enemies : I flee unto thee to hide me.

20 Teach me to do thy will ; for thou art my God : thy Spirit is good ; lead me into the land of uprightness.

21 Quicken me, O LORD, for thy name's sake : for thy righteousness' sake bring my soul out of trouble.

Selection 55

PSALM 144

1 BLESSED be the LORD my strength, which teacheth my hands to war, and my fingers to fight :

2 My goodness, and my fortress ; my high tower, and my deliverer ; my shield, and he in whom I trust ; who subdueth my people under me.

3 LORD, what is man, that thou takest knowledge of him ! or the son of man, that thou makest account of him !

4 Man is like to vanity : his days are as a shadow that passeth away.

5 Bow thy heavens, O LORD, and come down : touch the mountains, and they shall smoke.

6 Cast forth lightning, and scatter them : shoot out thine arrows, and destroy them.

7 Send thine hand from above ; rid

me, and deliver me out of great waters, from the hand of strange children ;

8 Whose mouth speaketh vanity, and their right hand is a right hand of falsehood.

9 I will sing a new song unto thee, O God : upon a psaltery and an instrument of ten strings will I sing praises unto thee.

10 It is he that giveth salvation unto kings: who delivereth David his servant from the hurtful sword.

11 Rid me, and deliver me from the hand of strange children, whose mouth speaketh vanity, and their right hand is a right hand of falsehood :

12 That our sons may be as plants grown up in their youth ; that our daughters may be as corner stones, polished after the similitude of a palace :

13 That our garners may be full, affording all manner of store ; that our sheep may bring forth thousands and ten thousands in our streets :

14 That our oxen may be strong to labor ; that there be no breaking in, nor going out ; that there be no complaining in our streets.

15 Happy is that people, that is in such a case : yea, happy is that people, whose God is the LORD.

PSALM 146

16 PRAISE ye the LORD. Praise the LORD, O my soul.

17 While I live will I praise the LORD : I will sing praises unto my God while I have any being.

18 Put not your trust in princes, nor in the son of man, in whom there is no help.

19 His breath goeth forth, he returneth to his earth ; in that very day his thoughts perish.

20 Happy is he that hath the God of Jacob for his help, whose hope is in the LORD his God :

21 Which made heaven, and earth, the sea, and all that therein is : which keepeth truth for ever :

22 Which executeth judgment for the oppressed : which giveth food to the hungry. The LORD looseth the prisoners :

23 The LORD openeth the eyes of the blind : the LORD raiseth them that are bowed down : the LORD loveth the righteous :

24 The LORD preserveth the strangers ; he relieveth the fatherless and widow : but the way of the wicked he turneth upside down.

25 The LORD shall reign for ever, even thy God, O Zion, unto all generations. Praise ye the LORD.

Selection 56

PSALM 145

1 I WILL extol thee, my God, O King ; and I will bless thy name for ever and ever.

2 Every day will I bless thee ; and I will praise thy name for ever and ever.

3 Great is the LORD, and greatly to be praised ; and his greatness is unsearchable.

4 One generation shall praise thy works to another, and shall declare thy mighty acts.

5 I will speak of the glorious honor of thy majesty, and of thy wondrous works.

6 And men shall speak of the might of thy terrible acts : and I will declare thy greatness.

7 They shall abundantly utter the memory of thy great goodness, and shall sing of thy righteousness.

8 The LORD is gracious, and full of compassion ; slow to anger, and of great mercy.

9 The LORD is good to all : and his tender mercies are over all his works.

The Psalter

10 All thy works shall praise thee, O LORD; and thy saints shall bless thee.

11 They shall speak of the glory of thy kingdom, and talk of thy power;

12 To make known to the sons of men his mighty acts, and the glorious majesty of his kingdom.

13 Thy kingdom is an everlasting kingdom, and thy dominion endureth throughout all generations.

14 The LORD upholdeth all that fall, and raiseth up all those that be bowed down.

15 The eyes of all wait upon thee; and thou givest them their meat in due season.

16 Thou openest thine hand, and satisfiest the desire of every living thing.

17 The LORD is righteous in all his ways, and holy in all his works.

18 The LORD is nigh unto all them that call upon him, to all that call upon him in truth.

19 He will fulfil the desire of them that fear him : he also will hear their cry, and will save them.

20 The LORD preserveth all them that love him : but all the wicked will he destroy.

21 My mouth shall speak the praise of the LORD : and let all flesh bless his holy name for ever and ever.

Selection 57

PSALM 147

1 PRAISE ye the LORD: for it is good to sing praises unto our God; for it is pleasant; and praise is comely.

2 The LORD doth build up Jerusalem : he gathereth together the outcasts of Israel.

3 He healeth the broken in heart, and bindeth up their wounds.

4 He telleth the number of the stars ; he calleth them all by their names.

5 Great is our Lord, and of great power : his understanding is infinite.

6 The LORD lifteth up the meek : he casteth the wicked down to the ground.

7 Sing unto the LORD with thanksgiving ; sing praise upon the harp unto our God :

8 Who covereth the heaven with clouds, who prepareth rain for the earth, who maketh grass to grow upon the mountains.

9 He giveth to the beast his food, and to the young ravens which cry.

10 He delighteth not in the strength of the horse : he taketh not pleasure in the legs of a man.

11 The LORD taketh pleasure in them that fear him, in those that hope in his mercy.

12 Praise the LORD, O Jerusalem ; praise thy God, O Zion.

13 For he hath strengthened the bars of thy gates ; he hath blessed thy children within thee.

14 He maketh peace in thy borders, and filleth thee with the finest of the wheat.

15 He sendeth forth his commandment upon earth : his word runneth very swiftly.

16 He giveth snow like wool : he scattereth the hoar frost like ashes.

17 He casteth forth his ice like morsels : who can stand before his cold ?

18 He sendeth out his word, and melteth them : he causeth his wind to blow, and the waters flow.

19 He showeth his word unto Jacob, his statutes and his judgments unto Israel.

20 He hath not dealt so with any nation : and as for his judgments, they have not known them. Praise ye the LORD.

The Psalter

Selection 58

Psalm 148

1 PRAISE ye the Lord. Praise ye the Lord from the heavens: praise him in the heights.

2 Praise ye him, all his angels: praise ye him, all his hosts.

3 Praise ye him, sun and moon: praise him, all ye stars of light.

4 Praise him, ye heavens of heavens, and ye waters that be above the heavens.

5 Let them praise the name of the Lord: for he commanded, and they were created.

6 He hath also stablished them for ever and ever: he hath made a decree which shall not pass.

7 Praise the Lord from the earth, ye dragons, and all deeps:

8 Fire, and hail; snow, and vapor; stormy wind fulfilling his word:

9 Mountains, and all hills; fruitful trees, and all cedars:

10 Beasts, and all cattle; creeping things, and flying fowl:

11 Kings of the earth, and all people; princes, and all judges of the earth:

12 Both young men, and maidens; old men, and children:

13 Let them praise the name of the Lord: for his name alone is excellent; his glory is above the earth and heaven.

14 He also exalteth the horn of his people, the praise of all his saints; even of the children of Israel, a people near unto him. Praise ye the Lord.

Psalm 149

15 PRAISE ye the Lord. Sing unto the Lord a new song, and his praise in the congregation of saints.

16 Let Israel rejoice in him that made him: let the children of Zion be joyful in their King.

17 Let them praise his name in the dance: let them sing praises unto him with the timbrel and harp.

18 For the Lord taketh pleasure in his people: he will beautify the meek with salvation.

19 Let the saints be joyful in glory: let them sing aloud upon their beds.

20 Let the high praises of God be in their mouth, and a twoedged sword in their hand;

21 To execute vengeance upon the heathen, and punishments upon the people;

22 To bind their kings with chains, and their nobles with fetters of iron;

23 To execute upon them the judgment written: this honor have all his saints. Praise ye the Lord.

Psalm 150

24 PRAISE ye the Lord. Praise God in his sanctuary: praise him in the firmament of his power.

25 Praise him for his mighty acts: praise him according to his excellent greatness.

26 Praise him with the sound of the trumpet: praise him with the psaltery and harp.

27 Praise him with the timbrel and dance: praise him with stringed instruments and organs.

28 Praise him upon the loud cymbals: praise him upon the high sounding cymbals.

29 Let everything that hath breath praise the Lord. Praise ye the Lord.

The Psalter

1   William Russell (1777-1813)

2   Sir Joseph Barnby (1838-1896)

3   Gregorian: arr. by Tallis

4   Sir George A. Macfarren, 1850

5   Hart

Glory be to the *Fa*ther | and · to the | Son ‖ *and* | to the | Holy | Ghost;
As it was in the beginning * is *now*, and | ever | shall be ‖ *world* without |
end · = | A · = | men.

www.ingramcontent.com/pod-product-compliance
Lightning Source LLC
Chambersburg PA
CBHW030300240426
43673CB00040B/1015